HOW USURY CAME TO RULE THE WORLD

How Usury Came to Rule the World

THE ASCENDANCY OF USURY OVER
JUDAEO-CHRISTIAN AND MUSLIM COMMERCE

Ammar Abdulhamid Fairdous

Copyright © Ammar Fairdous, 2023 CE/1445 AH

How Usury Came to Rule the World
The Ascendancy of Usury over Judaeo-Christian and Muslim Commerce

Published by:	Diwan Press Ltd.
	311 Allerton Road
	Bradford
	BD15 7HA
	UK
Website:	www.diwanpress.com
E-mail:	info@diwanpress.com

All rights reserved. No part of this publication may be reproduced, stored in any retrieval system or transmitted in any form or by any means, electronic, mechanical, photocopying, recording or otherwise without the prior permission of the publishers.

Author:	Ammar Fairdous
Edited by:	Uthman Ibrahim-Morrison
Cover graphic from:	Death and the Usurer, Basel,
	http://www.dodedans.com/Exhibit/Basel/Xlarge/basel-26.jpg

A catalogue record of this book is available from the British Library.

ISBN-13:	978-1-914397-06-6	Casebound
	978-1-914397-07-3	Paperback
	978-1-914397-08-0	ebook

بسم الله الرحمن الرحيم
وصلى الله على سيدنا محمد
وآله وصحبه وسلم

USURY – A SYNOPSIS

The practice of lending money for profit, any profit, minimal as it may be, was considered to be a deadly sin in Abrahamic religions. In Judaism, the practice was seen *inter alia* as equivalent to robbery, shedding of blood and even rejecting God. A hostile attitude towards the practice was also adopted in Christianity for at least three quarters of its history. There was a time when Christians who asked more than they had given were under pain of refusal of confession, of absolution and of Christian burial; not to mention the invalidation of wills and excommunication. Likewise, the practice attracts severe punishments in the Quran – the Muslim holy book. Those believers involved are threatened with *"war from Allah and his Messenger"* in this life, and hellfire in the afterlife. The question is, however, how these strict anti-usury attitudes developed into the more relaxed financing practices of today. This thesis proposes that there have been three principal methods by which the adherents of the Abrahamic religions, throughout their respective histories, have sidestepped scriptural prohibitions against usury. The first is by reinterpreting the concept of usury itself. The second method is by exemption, i.e. by excluding the counter-party from the scope of scriptural prohibition. The third method is by the concealment of usury in classical commercial contracts. Curiously enough, none of these methods were exclusive to any one religion, although, for theological reasons, some of them became more popular among the followers of one religion than others.

Acknowledgements

First and foremost, I should thank Allah for enabling me to come through, in one piece, all of the trials and tribulations involved in completing this thesis. I also thank Him for entrusting me to the loving care and attention of the most dutiful and deserving of parents, without whom I couldn't imagine what my fate may have been. I regard it as a mark of His generosity and favour that they succeeded, by way of wise parenting, to instil within me the ambition, the discipline and the determination of character that would eventually carry me not only to enter the challenge, but right through to the finish line. I also found a constant source of moral inspiration in the words of Moses: *"My Lord, because of Your blessing upon me, I will never be a supporter of evildoers"* (Qur'an: 28:17).

In more worldly terms, my next major debt of gratitude goes to Uthman Ibrahim-Morrison of the Muslim Faculty of Advanced Studies for his invaluable encouragement and guidance and for acting, to all intents and purposes, as my own private and personal thesis supervisor, which includes his meticulous attention throughout to the editorial integrity of the final text, not to mention his myriad thoughtful comments and suggestions. I would like to express here my sincere gratitude to him for his unstinting support of my PhD studies, his patience, motivation and useful knowledge. His confidence in me helped to sustain me throughout, but especially at those times when there appeared to be very little light, if any at all, at the end of the tunnel. I could not have asked for a better advisor and mentor for the duration of this long and demanding academic journey.

I would also like to acknowledge my debt to the organisers of the International Seminar of Islamic Economy held in Indonesia in June 2014, for allowing me the opportunity, under the auspices of the Muslim Faculty of Advanced Studies (MFAS), to share some of the relevant findings of my thesis. Subsequently to this, and most thankfully, I was further invited by MFAS to participate in the delivery of their key Module on The Question Concerning Economics held in Norwich in October 2014.

These acknowledgements would not be complete without thanking My wife Entesar and daughters Asma, Rahaf and Abrar who were always on hand to provide me with the best possible home environment, to assuage my lowest moods, to endure my constant distractedness and frequent anxieties, and not least of all, for always being there to remind me to eat and drink regularly! I must of course, express my thanks in general to the Ihsan Mosque community in Norwich for many inspiring conversations and their active engagement with the pressing issue of usury in the global economy and the implications of its Qur'anic prohibitions, which led me to embark on this thesis in the first place.

Notes

Footnotes, which are numbered i, ii, iii etc. and restart on every page, contain explanatory material. Endnotes, which are numbered 1, 2, 3 etc. are placed at the end of the book, and contain references to books and articles consulted and cited.

Contents

USURY – A SYNOPSIS	vii
ACKNOWLEDGEMENTS	ix
NOTES	vi
INTRODUCTION	1
USURY IN PRE-ABRAHAMIC CIVILISATIONS	7
Usury in Mesopotamia	8
Usury in Hinduism and Buddhism	12
Usury in Ancient Greece	13
Usury in Ancient Rome	17
USURY IN ABRAHAMIC RELIGIONS	22
Usury in Judaism	23
Jews and Usury	23
The Jewish Law – *Halakha*	28
The Concept of Usury in Judaism	31
Usury: Definition and Interpretation	31
Usury in the Old Testament Sources	33
Usury in the Rabbinical Sources	39
Usury in Christianity	42
The Devil's Work	42
The New Testament Sources	43
Cleansing of the Temple	43

The Parable of the Talents	47
Love Your Enemies	49
The Fathers of the Church	52
Early Ecclesiastical Legislation	62
Introduction to the Medieval Period	65
The Scholastic Interpretation	68
Extrinsic Titles	74
The Five Per Cent Contract and the Jesuits	81
The Reformers' Approach	85
Calvinism – a Counter theory	89
The Church of England	96
Trade is One Thing, Religion is Another	107
USURY IN ISLAM	119
Riba: Interest, Usury or Both	119
Islamic law – The *Shari'a*	123
Riba in Islamic Law	130
Riba in the Qur'an	131
Riba in the *Sunnah*	138
Riba in the Fiqh literature	139
Dissenting Views	145
Reasons for the Prohibition of *Riba*	153

EVADING THE TAINT OF USURY 157

REINTERPRETING THE CONCEPT OF USURY 163

EXCLUSION OF THE 'OTHER' 186

   Treatment of Gentiles in Rabbinical Tradition 187

   St. Ambrose's Justification of Usury as a Weapon 194

   The Hanafi Doctrine of the Abode of War 208

THE CONCEALMENT 224

   'Avaq Ribbit 225

The Position of the Early Poskim	822
Relaxing the Biblical Injunctions	230
The Heter *Iska*	233
Fraudem Usurarum	241
The Medieval Campaign Against Usury	241
Contracts in Fraudem Usurarum	249
Bay' al-'inah	262
The Dual 'Inah Contract	263
The Tripartite 'Inah Contract (al-Tawarruq)	268
The Maliki Form of 'Inah Contract (**Murabahah**)	271
CONCLUSION	278
BIBLIOGRAPHY	280
NOTES	296

"The subject of usury has been discussed ... through thousands of years and by countless learned men. After the Hebrew prophets and law givers, Caesar and Cato and later Justinian in Rome, and the Greek philosophers, debated on it; prelates, kings and great judges of great courts have studied and expounded it; parliaments, congresses, legislatures have turned it inside up and outside down; discourses on it in such bodies, in the pulpit, from the bench, have been innumerable in number, infinite in extent."

      Metcalf LS and others, *The Forum* (Forum
         Publishing Company 1918)

Introduction

In recent decades Islamic jurists have taken the Islamic banking and finance (IBF) industry to task on the grounds that the contractual forms offered by Islamic banks present a *de jure* distinction that lacks a de facto difference from their conventional counterparts.[i] This is well-attested in many of the Islamic banking financial instruments which are in essence simple classical contracts that have been restructured into complex contractual devices in order to achieve similar ends to explicitly interest-based transactions.[1]

Islamic banks, with the help of their *Shari'a* boards, have devised a number of financially engineered and carefully structured arrangements through which the risk of failure is borne entirely by the customer, whilst the Islamic bank, as is the case with conventional ones, receives a fixed rate of return at the end of the contractual period.[2] Furthermore, this rate of return is very often based on a benchmark interest rate such as LIBOR.[3] Nonetheless, the practice has not been without its critics, who often assert that IBF is merely a semiotic cloaking device intended to disguise the charging of interest (i.e. the substitution of 'profit rate' or 'mark-

---

i   One of the main reasons for this is probably the very nature of a wide range of financial transactions, e.g. consumer, government and personal finance, which the Islamic profit/loss sharing paradigm is not designed for and thus, not readily amenable to. For further information, see M.K. Lewis, 'In what ways does Islamic banking differ from conventional finance' 4 Journal of Islamic Economics, Banking and Finance (JIEBF)

up rate' for 'interest rate').[4] The proponents of Islamic banking, on the other hand, reject this view, alleging that these restructured transactions are fully "*Shari'a* compliant" since the contractual form, rather than the commercial substance, is what counts in Islamic law vis-a-vis commercial transactions.[5]

Interestingly, however, the argument with regard to what constitutes interest is not confined to the Muslim world. Both Talmudic and Canon law in their respective histories imposed severe restrictions on charging interest, which both Jewish and Christian lenders long sought to circumvent.[6]

Historically, the practice of charging interest was vigorously condemned throughout the Middle Ages, even though this prohibition was effectively circumvented.[7] The ban prompted a myriad of contractual innovations, which were devised to serve as a means of concealing the usurious practices of the merchants involved.[8] Interest bearing loans were recast into various versions of what were regarded as classical contractual forms, in which the operational risk was allocated to the borrower. In the course of time, the merchants developed more complicated and sophisticated contractual devices, which continued to violate the spirit, but not the letter, of the law against usury. As De Roover noted: "If it has not been for the usury doctrine, why would merchants have adopted a cumbersome procedure when simpler methods were available."[9] Among these transactions were the *contractum trinius* (triple contract), the *retrovenditio* (resale contract), the *census* (annuity); whilst specifically amongst Jewish traders there were the *heter iska*, (equity partnership), *mohatra* (revocable sales) and others instruments.

Curiously enough, some of these mediaeval interest-masking transactions are identical, or very similar, to certain financial instruments that are to be found in the Islamic banker's toolbox today, but of course, bearing Arabic and Islamic names. It would appear that the jurists of Islamic banks are following the lead of the mediaeval formalistic approach to the laws pertaining to usury.

The central thrust of this thesis is an examination of the development and applications of usury law within the Abrahamic religions, i.e. Judaism, Christianity and Islam.[i] It hopes to throw useful light on the relationship between laws on lending and credit on the one hand, and actual commercial practices as developed over time, on the other.

To begin with, it is generally agreed that the foundation of law, irrespective of its subject, leans either on the good it produces or the evil it prevents. The purport of all legislation is to benefit society at large and to restrain whatever is prejudicial to it. However, it is a fact of life that mankind will never cease to differ in their judgments as to what constitutes good and evil. More often than not, the essence of the dispute is ideological rather than cognitive. This is readily noticeable in the diversity of jurisprudential approaches to the issue of usury. To the question as to the causes that give rise to interest, a consensual knowledge-based answer can be provided. But whether interest, *per se*, is good, just, and useful or not, remains largely a matter of divided opinion.[ii]

---

i In its most general sense, 'Abrahamic religion' is a monotheistic religion that includes Abraham ﷺ (Hebrew: Avraham אַבְרָהָם ; Arabic: Ibrahim إبراهيم) as a part of its history. It is held by Muslims that Islam is an Abrahamic faith and shares a common ground with Christianity and Judaism: *"Say: Verily, my Lord hath guided me to a Way that is straight, – a religion of right, – the Path (trod) by Abraham the true in faith, and he (certainly) joined not gods with God"* (Qur'an 6:161). *"The same religion has He established for you as that which he enjoined on Noah – The which We have sent by inspiration to thee – And that which We enjoined on Abraham, Moses and Jesus: Namely, that ye should remain steadfast in Religion, and make no divisions therein: To those who worship other things than God, hard is the (way) to which thou callest them. God chooses to Himself those whom He pleases, and guides to Himself those who turn (to Him)."* (Qur'an 42:13).

ii In his *Capital and Interest*, Bohm-Bawerk offered a good example in this context: "Suppose, for instance, that by the soundest of reasoning it was shown to be probable that the abolition of interest would be immediately

The answer to such a question is highly likely to be coloured by one's outlook upon the world, or upon the relationship of man to the world and to community in all its aspects, i.e. one's ideology. Law, on the other hand, can be seen as a practical reflection of such ideology.[10] In reality, however, the relationship between law and ideology is somewhat intricate and contentious. This is attributable to the diversity of definitions of 'ideology' and the various forms in which law might be intertwined with them.[11]

The term 'ideology' is used in a number of senses in the arena of social science.[12] As a concept, the term was originally coined by the French philosopher, Destutt de Tracy (1754-1836). He used the term to label a new scientific discipline that systematically studies the formation of ideas on the basis of feelings – the science of ideas.[13] This conception has since changed and ideology has come to refer not to a science of ideas, but to the ideas themselves, or rather, ideas that are political in character. Thus, an ideology exists to serve and reflect some form of political standpoint. It is a rigid organised system of ideas and values that aims to motivate people to act in certain ways, and therefore, it may involve a process of philosophical justification to provide a rationale for adopted social and political actions.[14] In this context, ideology could be defined as "A consistent integrated pattern of thoughts and beliefs explaining man's attitude towards life and his existence in society, and advocating a conduct and action pattern responsive to and commensurate with such thoughts and beliefs."[15]

---

followed by a decline in the material welfare of the race, that argument will have no weight with the man who measures by a standard of his own, and counts material welfare a thing of no great importance—perhaps for the reason that earthly life is but a short moment in comparison with eternity, and because the material wealth that interest ministers to will rather hinder than help man in attaining his eternal destiny." See. E. von Böhm-Bawerk, *Capital and Interest: A critical history of economical theory* (Macmillan and Co. 1890), p. 21

Law, on the other hand, could be seen as the product of a dominant ideology. Law is ideological in that it conveys and reflects a certain set of attitudes, values and theories about aspects of society.[16] From another angle, law is a legal expression of the citizens' political principles and beliefs, whether tending toward liberalism, socialism, feminism or other political outlooks. While an ideology defines values and ends, law embodies the means and procedures by which these values and attitudes are put into effect.[17] However, it is not necessarily the case that law will reflect one particular ideology since any number of ideologies may be contesting within society for legal primacy. Therefore, law could be seen as a mirror reflecting the prevailing ideologies of its place and time.[18]

This intimate relationship between law and ideology has made it essential to study the ideological dimension of law, or what is referred to as: 'legal ideology', 'legal theory' or 'jurisprudence'. In order to understand the law, it is of paramount importance to consider not only the historical or geographical context but also the ideological context in which a given law has been proposed, developed and applied:

> "You will not mistake my meaning or suppose that I depreciate one of the great humane studies if I say that we cannot learn law by learning law. If it is to be anything more than just a technique it is to be so much more than itself: a part of history, a part of economics and sociology, a part of ethics and a philosophy of life."[19]

On this basis, the main purpose of the second chapter is to shed some light on the nature of the ideology behind laws pertaining to usury in pre-Abrahamic civilisations. The subject of the third chapter will be the development of such laws in Abrahamic religions. But, in order to keep this thesis within manageable limits, I have restricted myself to the usury teachings within the Sunni branch of Islam, and within the Catholic and Protestant branches of Christianity. It is generally recognised that these branches represent the overwhelming majorities within their respective spheres. The fourth chapter examines, compares and contrasts the methods that have been used by the adherents of Abrahamic religions for the sake of evading the scriptural prohibitions on usury. The fifth and final chapter will be the conclusion.

Usury In Pre-Abrahamic Civilisations

In tracing the history of laws pertaining to usury, one cannot fail to observe the universal opprobrium and antipathy that the practice has incurred. Through the ages, it has consistently been censured by the prophets, philosophers, priests and poets of almost every nation as one of the greatest evils against society.

The Hebrew prophet Ezekiel placed usury alongside rape, murder, robbery and idol worship, as crimes that would receive the punishment of God – "He has done all these abominable things: he shall surely die; and his blood shall be upon himself."[20] The Roman Senator Cato reports that it was less disgraceful to have your father be considered a thief than a usurer.[i] Dante, reflecting similar attitudes, placed usurers in the lowest extreme of the seventh circle of hell (a destination shared by the denizens of Sodom).[21] Perhaps, a considerable part of the social ostracism and excommunication that Jews experienced in the mediaeval period was due to their activities as money-lenders.[22] The character of Shylock, the archetypal Jewish usurer, in Shakespeare's *The Merchant of Venice* embodies to some extent the common social attitudes towards Jews as usurers and money-lenders at that time.[23] According to the Muslim holy book, the Qur'an, those involved in the practice are threatened with war from Allah and his Messenger in this life, and hellfire in the afterlife.[24]

---

i   Cato said: "In preference to farming one might seek gain by commerce on the seas, were it not so perilous, and in money-lending, if it were honourable ... How much worse the money-lender was considered by our forefathers than the thief ..." See, *On Agriculture*, I, 1

The condemnations here are not directed towards excessive interest rates, as assumed by the modern understanding of the concept of usury, but any and all interest, regardless of the rate. Neither was there any conceptual distinction drawn between a 'productive' loan and a 'consumer' loan.[i]

The concept of lending money for a profit has been regarded with disfavour for much of human history, and as a result, has always been subject to strict legal regulation. This legislation tended to fall into two categories. On the one hand, it could be restrictive in character, often taking the form of a prohibition on the charging of interest above a certain maximum rate, under penalty of forfeiture or punishment. Whereas, on the other hand, the legislation might take no account whatever of any distinction between moderate or excessive interest rates, as both were considered equally illegal. However, seldom, in the known history of man has any civilisation of note allowed interest to be taken completely without constraint.[25]

Usury in Mesopotamia

The phenomenon of lending at interest is as old as the recorded history of human society itself.[ii] Documented contracts from the Sumerian civilisation circa 3000 BCE reveal systematic use of credit.[26]

At the time, the Sumerians created what was probably the oldest high civilisation in history in Mesopotamia (ancient Greek for

---

i Throughout this thesis, usury is used in its old fashion meaning for any increase of a loan, great or small, whether authorised or forbidden by the civil state.

ii The idea of interest was present in prehistoric times, and probably existed and originated during the beginnings of agriculture, about 8000 and 5000 BCE. In the Middle East, dates, olives, figs, nuts or seeds of grain lent to the farmers were expected to be returned with interest – an additional amount over the amount lent. See, S. Homer and R.E. Sylla, *A History of Interest Rates* (Rutgers Univ Pr 1996), p. 18; and Smita Roy, 'Historical Evolution of Interest and it's Analysis in Economic Literature' SSRN eLibrary, p. 5

land between the rivers, referring to the Tigris and Euphrates).[27] Living in large cities such as Ur, Kish and Lagash, the Sumerians pioneered irrigated farming, architecture and commerce.[i] They traded as far afield as Egypt and India, exporting their textile products in exchange for other goods and necessities. The business of lending was also a very profitable one, as can be observed from the great number of entrepreneurs who involved themselves in it.[28] Perhaps, cuneiform writing was primarily invented with the purpose of facilitating the rising credit and trading activities. Most of the surviving Sumerian writings today are in the form of temple accounts (records of supplies and goods exchanged) and commercial transactions, amongst which some of the earliest recordings of interest-bearing loans are detailed.[29]

The main creditors were private citizens, royal treasuries and temples, while their general customers were farmers and traders.[30] The contracting parties enjoyed a high degree of autonomy in setting the rate of interest, but the most common cases were loans of silver at annual rates of 12-30% and loans of barley at 20-50%.[31] A prominent feature of these credit arrangements is the fact that the charging of interest was routinely practised and socially accepted.[ii] However, the widespread failure to repay such loans led to the excessive incidence of debt-bondage to wealthy landowners, prompting the reigning monarch to adopt a more restrictive approach to the regulation of lending practices.[32]

---

i   Sumerian civilisation is credited with developing the world's first wheeled vehicles, the first ox-drawn ploughs, the first city-states, and the first system of writing. See, S.C. Easton, *A Brief History of the Western World* (Barnes & Noble 1962), p. 15-17

ii The Sumerian word for interest was '*mas*', a term also used to refer a lamb. It was commonly accepted in the agricultural system of Sumer to the landlords to tax the herd expended of the tenant of his field. The tax was paid in the form of a small number of lambs. Likewise, the interest was seen as a 'grazing fee' to be paid when the advance of silver or barley was returned. Van De Mieroop, op. cit., p. 25

The Sumerian penalties for debtors defaulting were severe. Creditors were entitled by forfeiture to seize not only the physical but also the "human" assets of the debtor.[33] Bankrupt paterfamiliases were obliged to deliver their wives, servants, children or even themselves into forced servitude to pay their creditors. In the course of time, large portions of the Sumerian population who were not already languishing in prisons were sold into debt slavery to live miserable lives alongside prisoners of war.[34] The social consequences of usury, therefore, urged many Sumerian and Babylonian kings to intervene.

The trend started with Urukagina, King of Lagash in about 2350 BCE, who introduced many legal reforms, including provisions relating to the release of persons imprisoned for debt.[35] This practice was followed by subsequent rulers,[i] and commercial matters came to constitute a considerable proportion of many of the legal codes devised during the era. Most notable is the code of Eshcnunna, about 1700 BCE, in which interest rate ceilings of 33.3% for grain and 20% for silver were imposed.[36] The same rates are mentioned in the famous code of the Babylonian King Hammurabi in about 1750 BCE.

The Hammurabi code, like the Sumerian ones, consists of a set of amendments and additions to the prevailing *Lex mercatoria* (i.e. unwritten common law), rather than a complete reiteration of the entirety of the law.[37] The code, which is relatively well preserved, contains 280 laws regulating many aspects of human life covering both public and private matters. Some of the earliest surviving written usury laws can be found in the following extracts:

> "[§ L] If a merchant has given corn on loan, he may take 100 sila of corn as interest on 1 gur; if he has given silver on

---

i Most notable is King Ammisaduqa of Babylon (1646-1626 BCE.) who stated that: "if ... a citizen ... placed his own person, his wife or his children in debt servitude for silver... he is released, his freedom is in effect." Quoted in Van de Mierop, op. cit., p. 25

loan he may take ⅙ shekel 6 grains as interest on 1 shekel of silver. [§ M] If a man who has raised a loan has no silver to repay it but has corn, [the merchant] may then take corn for his interest (at a rate) in accordance with the ordinances of the king; but, if the merchant has increased his interest above [100 sila of corn] on 1 gur [or] over ⅙ shekel 6 grains [on 1 shekel of silver] and has taken (it), he forfeits whatever he has given (on loan)."[38]

Similarly, the Babylonians used both grain and ingots of silver as a medium of exchange with legal maximum interest rates being 33⅓% per annum for loans of grain and 20% per annum for loans of silver. The law was applicable to the whole of Babylonian society and remained intact for many centuries until the Persian conquest of 539 BCE.[i]

The economic role played by Babylonian shrines is noteworthy. The temples were not only religious houses, schools and courts, but they were also centres of financial and monetary transactions similar to the national banks of today.[39] In fact, it is the Babylonian temple of *Samas*, the sun-god, which is believed to be the first bank in the world.[40] Like many other shrines, the income of the *Samas* temple was based primarily on the tithes paid by ordinary individuals as well as royal families. The abundant surplus of wealth led the temple to engage in various commercial activities, a major part of which consisted of providing interest-bearing productive loans for the public.[41] Consumer loans for the poor, on the other hand, were alleged to be interest free although interest was to accrue if the loan was not returned in time.[42]

It seems that the levying of interest was a matter of course in the ancient Near Eastern civilisations. Although some legal codes

---

i After losing her independence, the centre of economic progress and activity shifted to Rome and Greece, which will be considered later in this chapter. Homer, p. 30

initiated a tradition of interest rate regulation, as mentioned above, not one contained a single law prohibiting the practice entirely; nor is there any known recorded expression of negative attitudes towards interest *per se*. As noted by Saggs, "Feeling against usury ... was entirely absent from the Sumero-Babylonian world where payment of interest upon a loan is regarded as a normal and respectable phenomenon."[43] It is in the ancient Indian religious manuscripts where, most probably, the earliest sentiments of contempt for interest are expressed.

Usury in Hinduism and Buddhism

Unlike the Mesopotamians, the concept of taking interest has a tinge of something socially and religiously reprehensible in the ancient Orient.[44] Several texts from the Vedas and Sutras of Hinduism and the Jatakas of Buddhism express ethical admonitions against usury.

In early Indian society, it was not possible to draw a precise line between usury and interest. The term '*Kusida*', which refers to both the practices of evil persons and the persons themselves, was used several times in the Vedic texts (2000-1400 BCE)[i] to refer to any lending at interest, regardless of the rate.[45] Along with expressions of disdain for the practice, more detailed references to the payment of interest are to be found, as well, in the later Sutra texts (700-100 BCE).

Lending money for profit was so socially abhorrent at that time, that many legislators like Vasistha, a well-known Hindu law maker, imposed a legal ban on usury for the highest two of the four Indian classical castes, namely, the Brahmans (Vedic priests) and the Kshatriyasa (warriors). This unwholesome activity was, however, assigned as a legitimate occupation to the lower castes; the Vaisya

---

i   The Vedas are the oldest scriptures of Hinduism and the most ancient religious texts in any Indo-European language. The authority of the Vedas as stating the essential truths of Hinduism is still accepted to some extent by all Hindus.

(cattle herders, agriculturists and merchants) and Shudra (labourers, artisans).[46] He states, "If Brahmana murder and usury are weighed in a balance, the murderer of a Brahmana rises to the top while the usurer trembles."[47] In Buddhism, the Jatakas (600-400 BCE) [i] refer to the giving and taking of interest in a deprecating manner, claiming that "hypocritical ascetics are accused of practising it."[48]

Yet, later in mediaeval India even Brahmans and Kshatriyasa were allowed to practise lending at interest.[49] Moreover, virtually all of the legal texts introduced by Hindu lawgivers, such as Brhaspat, Baudhayana and Kautilya, implied a clear distinction between the concepts of interest and usury.[50] The latter has been diluted to refer only to interest charged above the prevailing socially and legally accepted rate (*dharmya vrddi*). Ironically, the approved legal rates were considered as interest rather than usury, albeit in some cases it rose as high as 240%.

By this time, the rate of *dharmya vrddi* showed a tendency towards gradual increase. In Narada texts, interest on grain loans can be restricted to 'friendly' rates of less than 5%. Baudhayana set 10 per cent as a maximum rate, while Brhaspat raised it to 25 per cent per annum. Later, the idea of different rates of interest for different types of loans appears. Kautilya prescribes 15% per annum as legal interest, but 60% for commercial transactions, and 120% for traders who traverse forests, and 240% for those trading by sea.[51] This precedent was followed by subsequent lawgivers.

A similar pattern of classification of interest rate according to the risk and form of credit could be observed in both ancient Greek and Roman civilisations.

Usury in Ancient Greece

In ancient Greece, lending money for profit was commonplace. The practice was never prohibited, though it had never been

---

i   Jatakas are ancient folktales of India organised into verses about the Buddha and included in his biography.

universally approved either.⁵² During the archaic period (8th to 6th centuries BCE), Greece came to prominence as a centre of economic progress and activity. By the time of the great expansion of trade, spurred by improved navigation and the invention of coined money, the subsistence agricultural economy was left under a great deal of pressure.⁵³ Humble farmers were suffering from fluctuating prices, inflation and competition from cheap slave labour to the extent that one poor harvest was enough to leave them prey to inescapable interest-bearing loans.⁵⁴ The consequence of a failure to service these debts was slavery, according to the Athenian constitution established by Draco.

By 594 BCE, in a manner similar to the Sumerian debt crises, the bulk of the Athenian population became gradually indebted to the rich to such an extent that they were practically slaves.⁵⁵ Others had already lost their property and been sold into slavery to service their debts. Since usury was pervasive mainly among the tenants in the countryside around Athens, revolt was inevitable. To overcome the crisis, Solon, the father of Athenian law, introduced many constitutional reforms.⁵⁶ Notable amongst them was *Seisachtheia*, the relief of burdens. Land debts were cancelled, enslaved debtors were freed and the law of debt slavery was no longer applicable. Notwithstanding, Solon did not outlaw the practice of interest nor restrict its rates. In fact, the legal pronouncement, "money is to be placed out (*to argurion slasimon*) at whatever rate the lender (*ho daneizon*) may want" is attributed to him.⁵⁷ Perhaps, it was this 'deregulation' that enabled creditors to accept his removal of their power to enslave debtors, according to some historians.⁵⁸

During the following centuries, however, banking grew rapidly in Athens.⁵⁹ Its functions were performed, in tandem with temples,ⁱ by the 'trapezites', who maintained the confidentiality of the wealthy

---

i Most notable are the shrine of Delphi and Delos. The later was described as the greatest bank of the Greek world. See, Hommer, op. cit., p. 38

traders who borrowed from them.[i] At this period productive loans had become popular among most of the citizens since the lender could legitimately claim a share in the productivity of his loan, especially where the transaction involved undertaking a risk.[60] Many orators claimed that such loans at reasonable interest rates benefited trade and fostered wealth. The term '*tokos*', which in Greek also means offspring, was commonly used as an euphemism for usury. Nevertheless, several strains of opposition did exist.

Greek philosophers condemned the concept of interest as an unnatural and unjust mode of acquiring money. Aristotle (384-322 BCE) saw money only as a tool for facilitating the transfer of goods and services, not as something that should by itself grow at interest.[61] He compared money to a barren hen, which laid no eggs; "a piece of money cannot beget another piece of money."[62] The purpose of economic activity, he contended, is to satisfy human physical requirements, such as food and clothing. In so doing, money should be produced through normal ways; whether naturally, through agriculture or extracting materials from the earth, or artificially, through transforming natural materials, or through commercial production via transporting things from one place to another or storing them for a certain period of time.[63] Of itself, usury, on the other hand, produces nothing that helps to meet these needs. Hence, Aristotle conceives usury as a practice contrary to nature. He stated:

> "The most hated sort, and with the greatest reason, is usury, which makes a gain out of money itself, and not from the natural use of it. For money was intended to be used

---

[i] Writes Sidney Homer, "the bankers, the *trabzitai*, changed money, received deposits, made loans to individuals and states, made foreign remittances, collected revenues, issued letters of credit and money orders, honoured cheques and kept complete books." Ibid. Also, see J. Mokyr, *The Oxford Encyclopedia of Economic History* (Oxford University Press 2003), p. 325-327

in exchange, but not to increase at interest. And this term usury (*tokos*, i.e., offspring, produce), which means the birth of money from money, is applied to the breeding of money because the offspring resembles the parent. Wherefore of all modes of money-making this is the most unnatural."

Money was also sterile in the eyes of Plato (427-347 BCE). But, he was more concerned with the social consequences of usury rather than the very nature of it *per se*. Through usury, money-lenders did not only multiply their capital, but also the number of paupers. According to Plato, this resulted in widening the gap between the rich and poor, which in turn led to turmoil amongst the citizenry and therefore, on these premises, the practice should be prohibited by the law.[64] He went further, in that he exhorts the debtor not to repay either the principal or interest on his debt. In his *Leges*, Plato writes: "No one shall [...] lend at interest, since it is permissible for the borrower to refuse entirely to pay back either interest or principal."

However, the writings of both Aristotle and Plato had scant effect on the business of money-lending at that time, though it later inspired the Church's opposition to usury for centuries. The rate of interest generally followed an upward trajectory. The ordinary rate paid on monthly basis, amounted to 12% per annum. Mortgages and commercial loans were offered at 16% and 18%, while maritime loans had rates of 20%, 40%, 60% and even 100% depending on who the borrower was, the destination of the ships and the political and economic conditions.[65]

Although it was philosophically condemned, the ancient Greeks in general had no prohibition against taking interest and no statutes restricting the rate of interest. The Athenian credit market, therefore, stands as one of the earliest examples of a *laissez-faire* approach to usury in which market forces alone set the rates of interest without state intervention. Unsurprisingly, however, this deregulation gave free rein to avaricious lenders and loan sharks, who exploited the weak bargaining position of needy debtors. In some cases, interest rates on consumer loans were as high as 25% per day (over 9000% per year).[66] These loans were probably intended to function as short-term finance, but compounding over the course of time, left borrowers in irrecoverable situations.

Despite this, the Athenian approach inspired many economists and policy makers in modern times. In England, the philosopher Jeremy Bentham, advocated vehemently the *laissez-faire* theory in his *Letters in Defence of Usury*, and for 46 years, from 1854 to 1900, English market lending operated without any interest law of any form.[i]

Usury in Ancient Rome

The attitude of the laws of ancient Rome toward interest[ii] tended to vacillate. The Romans experimented between the *laissez-faire* approach to usury and the other extreme of forbidding any interest, before they later took a middle course of allowing profit-making loans but at regulated rates.

Unlike the Greeks, the Romans were a nation of citizen-farmers and soldiers. The early Republic, founded around 509 BCE, was governed by the rich patrician class while the status of poor plebeians was threatened by the increasing burden of non-regulated interest-bearing agrarian loans.[67] In 494 BCE, the story seems to repeat itself. A civil revolt, known as the first secession, occurred primarily as a result of a widespread debt crisis. It is said that the revolution was sparked when an ex-veteran shares his pathetic story

---

i   Further discussion will be provided in the following chapter in the context of considering the practice of interest in the modern times.

ii The modern term 'interest' is in fact derived from the Roman law expression for an indemnification for loss due to the delay in the interval (*interesse*) before repayment. See, E.R.A. Seligman and A.S. Johnson, *Encyclopaedia of the Social Sciences*, Vol. 9 (The Macmillan company 1932), p. 131

in a public forum, elaborating on how his creditor imprisoned and tortured him, after a series of calamities that left him prey to high interest loans.[68] To service his debt, he was forced to sell his substantial property, his personal belongings, and finally he was consigned to a lifetime of servitude. His story was similar to many other debt slaves (*nexi*), who crowded the streets of Rome.

The law of *Twelve Tables*[i] was partly a response to the debt crisis of the first secession.[69] Contrary to Athenian practice, the *Tables* ignored the debt bondage while imposing a maximum legal rate of 8 ⅓% per annum, with a penalty of fourfold damages for violation.[70] Prompted by plenty of serious debt crises,[71] the legal rate was gradually reduced in many subsequent *leges* until entirely abolished in 342 BCE by a law extorted by the plebeians: the famous *Lex Genucia*.[72] Later, the practice of debt bondage too was abrogated, by the *Lex Poetelia* of 325 BCE.

It is interesting to note that it was the Romans who enacted the earliest legal prohibitions of interest, despite the fact that they were, in effect, inoperative. The law led to the invention of elaborate ways of evading the prohibition, among them was the use of intermediaries.[73] Ironically enough, it was during this period of prohibition, in particular between 318-310 BCE, that the first bankers' shops appeared on the scene.[74] The professional bankers (*argentarii*) installed their '*trabezai*' (lit. 'tables') in the Forum and started doing business, probably through foreign agents, since the law forbade interest dealing amongst compatriots.[ii] The usury restrictions, therefore, were later extended to include citizens of allied states (*socii*) and provincials, as provided in the *Lex Sempronia* (194 BCE), even though it was rarely enforced.[iii]

---

i The Twelve Tables, drawn up in 451-450 BC, is considered the first major codification of existing Roman laws and customs.

ii They continued operating until the end of the Principate in CE 284, when their profession disappeared. Ibid.

iii In fact, the efficiency of both the interest prohibition and interest ceiling

However, the illegality of taking interest was revoked during the period of *Lex Uniciaria* (88 BCE).⁷⁵ With reference to partly annulled debt, the new law re-established the maximum legal interest rate at 12% per year,ⁱ an official rate that remained in operation for several centuries until the promulgation of the code of Justinian (533 CE). Otherwise, the latter was more detailed and sophisticated, introducing different rates of interest for different loans according to the status of the creditor as well as the loan's riskiness.⁷⁶ Argentarii were allowed to charge the highest interest rates of 8% while ordinary citizens were limited to charging 6%. Interestingly, distinguished personages, e.g. senators, were restricted to charging 4% rates of interest per annum. The interest rate for agricultural loans was capped at 4%, which was a half of the legal rate permitted for maritime loans due to the high risk entailed. The Justinian code generally prevailed throughout the rest of Byzantine history, though interest prohibition was sporadically revived.

In parallel with the class struggle and debt crisis, the philosophical condemnations of interest contributed to a great deal of new legislation. Similarly, to their Greek counterparts, the Roman philosophers denounced the practice but without bringing much by way of new argumentations to the dispute. Cicero (234-149 BCE), whose *De Officiis* casts a long shadow over the scholastic traditions, vilified usury as being odious to mankind. The practice, he contends, was utterly abhorrent not only to the poor debtors but also for many of the wealthy whose agricultural yields were being entirely 'swallowed' by the creditors.⁷⁷ He states that "those means of

---

were to some extent questionable. The maximum legal rate was practically ignored during troubled time through primarily "under the counter" deals which the needy borrower were enforced to accept it. See, Cornell, op. cit., p. 366; Ackerman, op. cit., p. 70

i The main purpose of the law was to help the wealthy landlord who suffered from confiscation of their properties during the social war. See, ibid.

livelihood are rejected as undesirable which incur people's ill-will, as those of tax-gatherers and usurers."[78]

Furthermore, Cicero cites that when Cato the Elder (234-149 BCE) was questioned respecting the nature of usury, he replied, "What about murder? The borrower asks you for medicine and you give him poison; bread and you offer him a sword; liberty and you condemn him to slavery."[79] Yet, ironically, Plutarch, a Greek historian, asserts that Cato himself participated surreptitiously in maritime loans through the agency of his "freedmen".[80]

Statements critical of lending at interest also appear in the writings of Seneca (4 BCE – 65 CE). Influenced by Aristotle's approach, he inveighed against interest on account of the fact that money is sterile. Moreover, he considered usury to be morally wrong because it involves the selling of time, an idea that became the cornerstone of Aquinas's analysis of prohibition. Like Cato, Seneca also perceives usury as tantamount to homicide.[81] Nevertheless, in his *Epistles*, he reproached the debtor who repays a loan without adding interest, and considered his action an act of ingratitude.[82]

It seems that in Rome, as in Greece, these philosophical invectives against usury were reflected in the public opinion of the time, not only because of the social evils associated with the practice but also because of the existence of the intolerable burden of debt incurred across society.[i] These interest loans, attesting the theory of Plato, were the most frequent causes of sedition and discord among Romans, leaving the citizenry in a great deal of disharmony and social unrest. As Cicero notes,

---

i Petronius, a Roman author contemporary of Seneca, said:
   "Dirty usury and the handling of money has caught the people in a double whirlpool and destroyed them… There is no house that is safe and no man that is not mortgaged. In despair they resort to violence; and bloodshed restores the goods squandered by luxury." As quoted in, T.F. Divine, *Interest: An Historical & Analytical Study in Economics & Modern Ethics* (Marquette University Press 1959), p. 22

the dispute among debtors and creditors served as one of the prime instigators of the Social War.[83] Therefore, the law in this respect seems to have been grounded rather on practical reasons of state: "In almost all the social disturbances of the Greco-Roman cultural world, land distribution and the cancellation of debt were primary demands."[84]

It would appear that the old civilisations of Mesopotamia, as well as those of Greece and Rome, had found it necessary to enact usury laws. The ancient policy makers, quietly approaching the subject matter in the dry light of reason, made several attempts to assuage the harmful social side effects of usury upon society. Among these attempts were formal debt cancellations, alleviation of the severe default penalties and the development of sophisticated lending regulations. On the other hand, the response of the Abrahamic religions to the problem of usury, at least in their heyday, is one of less tolerance. In the former, various rafts of lending regulations were introduced to serve as a 'palliative' to the ill effects of usurious practices, while in the latter the cause of the corruption is simply removed by banning the entire practice.[85] Islam may appear as the only religion in the Abrahamic stable that maintains a prohibition upon usury at present, yet this distinctiveness was not always the case. Both Judaism and Christianity have a long and varied history of opposition to the practice.

Usury in Abrahamic Religions

Since economic activity is an integral part of human life, economic precepts have constituted a considerable proportion of Divine guidance down the ages, a method that continues to apply in the revealed books of Judaism, Christianity and Islam. These books abound in precepts dealing with both economic activities and ethics in a fashion that provides an ideological framework within which adherents can orientate themselves morally. It is generally recognised that the religious thematisation of justice, mercy and righteousness has an impact on adherents' attitudes and their behaviours in economic as well as social and ritual spheres. Gradually, these religiously derived attitudes constitute the central elements of societal values that shape the rules, principles and institutions governing such societies.[86]

This section, therefore, investigates the teachings on usury, as well as its theological interpretations in the scriptures of the three Abrahamic religions, in order to consider the relevance they may have in the development of lending and credit laws in the pre-modern and modern worlds, with an eye toward how these attitudes developed into the more relaxed financing practices of today.

Judaism, as the oldest of the three Abrahamic monotheistic religions, is the natural starting point for this investigation.

Usury in Judaism

Jews and Usury

Cicero warned his son that the two occupations that must be avoided as bringing public odium upon their undertakers are tax-collecting and money-lending.[87] Generally speaking, the 'sons' of Israel seem to have ignored the dangers.[i] Over centuries, Jews have been involved in money-lending and money-changing in Europe, North Africa and the Middle East. Exaggeratedly or otherwise, they have historically been held notorious as usurers across the ancient and mediaeval world, and the accusing finger has periodically pushed its way into modern centuries, albeit, more often than not, at the instigation of irrational anti-Semitic hatred or groundless 'conspiracy theories'. These incidences of anti-Semitism are of tangential relevance only and have no major bearing on the technical concerns central to this research. However, there can be little doubt that they have combined with other historical factors (as we will see below) in such a way that over time the terms 'Jew' and 'usury' have sometimes become synonymous.

Since a very early date the usurious practices of Jews appear to have invited opprobrium, albeit this fact has sometimes been disputed.[88] A papyrus from Egypt (dated 41 BCE) shows Heracleids, a young man, being advised to be careful with money-lenders and not to fall prey especially into the hands of the Jews.[89] They were also infamous in the Muslim world of Babylonia (750-1258 CE). The Qur'anic prohibition of usury seems to be echoed in public opinion; the practice was left to minorities, primarily Jews.[90] Ibn Taghribirdi, an Egyptian historian, writes that in 908 CE Muqtadir Billah, the Abbasid Caliph, created a register

---

i   Besides widespread involvement in money-lending activities during much of their history, they were also notorious as tax collectors in early mediaeval Western Europe. For further details, see M. Tamari, *With all your possessions: Jewish ethics and economic life* (Free Press 1987), p. 167-168

of Jewish bankers.[91] Muqtadir himself used to borrow 30,000 dinars per month from two Jewish bankers to fund the infantry in Baghdad, the Capital of the Empire.[92] Yet, during the ninth to the thirteenth century, many Jews voluntarily migrated from the Muslim Middle East to Christian Europe as specialists in many skilled urban occupations, most notably money-lending.

High mediaeval Europe seems to have been a fertile ground for Jewish money-lenders. At the time, the Catholic Church had strictly enforced a ban on Christian usury, whilst acknowledging the right of Jews to engage in the practice.[93] This attitude was derived from the scholastic principle rooted in the Old Testament, that anything that accrued to the capital was usury. But, the Exception of St Ambrose, which authorised usury 'between enemies' and included later in the *Decretum Gratiani* (1140 CE),[94] seems to give free rein to the usurious practices of the Jews.[95] Furthermore, some scholars contend that the Church turned a blind eye toward Jewish usurers in order to enable the papacy to continue raising funds for the "greater good" of crusading success, without directly exposing Christians to contamination.[96] At any rate, the ban left Jews in an advantageous position with respect to the entire credit market across Europe.

Consequently, Jewish money-lenders began to appear on the mediaeval European scene. By the tenth century, lending money for profit had become for the Jews their primary occupation in England. It was also a very important one in France, and was significant, amongst others, in Germany and Italy.[97] By the thirteenth century, almost all Jews in France, Germany, and Italy were involved in the business of lending money.[98] In Poland, they were referred to as "a group whose main business is money-lending against pledges" as well as "protected money-lenders" in a first charter of privileges granted to them in the mid-thirteenth century.[99] A very similar one was issued by Duke Frederick II for Jews in Austria in the same period.[100] In Spain, by the fifteenth century, they were not only money-lenders but also served as financial advisors to the political elite, such as Rabbi Yitschak Aberbanel, who served in the court of the Catholic Monarchs, Ferdinand and Isabella.[101] Likewise, many German emperors were to call on Jewish money-lenders, while in France, it was said they "belonged to the barons".[102] Jews everywhere in Europe appeared to be engaged in money-lending as their main occupation, financing not only individuals but also popes, kings and the secular nobility.[103]

It is not surprising, therefore, that in the course of centuries the term "usury" was automatically associated with Jews and Jewish business practices, often in a pejorative sense.[104] Sometimes even Christian usurers were referred to as "baptised Jews".[105] This stigma has probably been reinforced by the practices of some extortionate Jewish money-lenders. As borne out in the tone of canon 67 of the fourth Lateran Council:

> "... to protect the Christians against cruel oppression by the Jews, we ordain in this decree that if in the future under any pretext Jews extort from Christians oppressive and immoderate interest, the partnership of the Christians shall be denied them till they have made satisfaction for their excesses."[106]

The popular cultural image of the Jew as usurer has become immortalised in much European literature, most notably Shakespeare's character, Shylock. However, by the end of the sixteenth century, the exclusively Jewish figure of the usurer had become increasingly rare, since the disgrace associated with the 'profession' was lessening in Europe; charging interest had begun to be lawfully and commercially commonplace between Christians.

Yet, by the mid-fifteenth century rich Jewish money-lenders and financial dealers had migrated to the Ottoman dominions and settled in.¹⁰⁷ Thus, an entirely new page in the Jewish involvement in usury had already commenced. Prior to the nineteenth century, lending money for profit was technically forbidden by the Ottoman rulers due to the Islamic anti-usury laws.¹⁰⁸ However, Jews and Christians, as *dhimmis*,¹⁰⁹ seemed to be excluded; the business of usury, therefore, was almost entirely left in their hands for more than two centuries.¹¹⁰ Just as was the case with their mediaeval European ancestors, money-lending became the dominant economic activity for most Jews under Ottoman dispensation. They were infamous as money-lenders and bankers in many Arabic-speaking lands. Sir John Bowring in his report, addressed to the secretary of state for foreign affairs, states:

> "The principal money-lenders and traffickers in specie, throughout the East, are the Jews ... They form a numerous body throughout all Syria; they are some of the richest merchants and bankers at Aleppo, Damascus, Beirut, Antioch, Hama, and all the principle towns of Palestine. It must not be forgotten, that the right of the Jews to lend on heavy interest (usury) to strangers is specifically recognised by the Mosaic Law, and it cannot be wondered at that they should avail themselves of it, but it is a main cause of the opprobrium to which they are subjected."¹¹¹

Many of the cases cited in the *Responsa* literatureⁱ as well as Turkish archives (dated from the 16th to 18th centuries) attest that Jewish creditors operated on a large scale in non-Arabic-speaking lands as well. They were not only "selling" interest loans to "Muslims in villages", as told by one *Responsum*,¹¹² but also financing merchants, prominent personages, and sometimes local governors.¹¹³ In one case from 18th century Rhodes, some Jews,

---

i   Legal decisions given by Torah scholars often as a response to a question addressed to them.

who had lost hope of obtaining repayment for the loan they had made to a high Turkish official, demanded the unpaid loans to be deducted from their tax assessment. The Rabbi refused their request, with the justification that:

> "for most of our living today comes from lending money to non-Jews ... and here in Rhodes it is customary to take into account for tax assessment all credits and loans, and most of what is written down in the tax assessment register is of this type."[114]

It would appear that lending money to non-Jews was, indeed, one of the main sources of livelihood for Jews in Rhodes as well as many other Ottoman territories at that time.

Against this background, the question may arise as to why Jews, in general, tended to be so intensely involved in financial activities during much of their history. There appears to be little consensus in response to this question. The reasons for this apparent proclivity have been, and still remain a matter of controversy.

Some contend that political and economic factors forced the Jews into money-lending as almost their sole source of sustenance, particularly in mediaeval Europe. Blamed for the crucifixion of Christ, the Jewish people, indeed, experienced a high level of hostility that sometimes resulted in expulsion or even persecution. More often than not, they were disallowed to own land in societies where farming was the main source of sustenance for the great majority. Therefore, it is argued, the resident Jews had to be either merchants or money-lenders.[115] Jews might have inclined to be the latter given that the monarchs and gentry were in need of their services, thereby, obtaining in return the security and the livelihood they could not get otherwise. Sometimes, in circumstances where there were no resident Jews in a city, such as 14th century Florence, they "...were imported to conduct a business forbidden to Christians."[116]

Nevertheless, the argument above would fail to account for the dominance of financial activities in the economic life of Jews in the Muslim world under which the hostility that Jews encountered in European societies was relatively absent. In this context, Tamari, an ex-Chief economist at the Bank of Israel who also taught economics at Bar Ilan University, states:

> "Primarily the argument has been that it was a hostile society which forced the Jew into money-lending and banking ... The major flaw in this argument seems to be the existence of Jewish bankers and money-lenders in the Moslem world, where the economic basis of Jewish life was not as restricted as in Christian Europe... there was very little religious incentive for economic discrimination against Jews... expulsion, relegation to a special economic status, or existence on the periphery of economic world were never major features of the Moslem world as they were of Christian Europe."[117]

Another important factor that often seems to be overlooked is the position of the *Torah* and other Jewish writings on lending money for profit. As seen previously, while both Canon and Islamic law exclude, to some extent, the mediaeval Christians and Muslims from taking interest, the Jewish law appears not to act in the same way for Jews. Dealing in usury seems to be opposed by very few real obstacles. Questions as to how such dealings were justified, and whether or not lending money for profit is permissible under Jewish law can only add to the controversies noted above.

The Jewish Law – *Halakha*

Since this section will be dealing primarily with Jewish law, a brief introduction to the nature and sources of Jewish law would be appropriate.

Jewish laws are known as *Halakha*, though a literal translation does not yield 'law'.[118] The term is derived from the Hebrew root *halokh*, which means 'to go'. It implies the path or the way in which a Jew should conduct himself in order to comply with God's will. In the Hebrew Bible, the good life is often visualised as a way along which adherents are 'to go'.[i] *Halakha*, however, has come to refer to the legal side of Judaism, as opposed to *Aggadah*, which denotes the homiletic materials of rabbinic literature.[119] In its broad sense, *Halakha* is the entire body of Jewish law, both civil and ritual, but in its narrow sense, it may stand for a single law or decision in a given context.[120]

As a legal system, *Halakha* originates in different sources. It would be useful, therefore, to address in some detail these sources in order to understand their functions, and how they relate to each other.

The first and primary source of Jewish law is the written Torah – the five books of Moses – the Pentateuch. The Orthodox view is that the Torah is of Divine origin and was received by Moses ﷺ on Mount Sinai.[121] From a legal point of view, the Torah contains 613 positive and negative commandments (*taryag mitzvoth*), some of which are binding on the Jews at the individual level, others at the collective level.[122] These commandments are the foundation from which the entire body of Jewish law is derived.[123] All other sources, including the rest of the Hebrew Bible: the Prophetic books and the holy writings, serve as a sort of commentary, expansion or elucidation of the laws introduced therein.

The second major source is the Oral Torah (*Torah she-be-'al peh*), which is believed to have been orally transmitted to Moses at Mount Sinai in conjunction with the written Torah. After that it was transmitted by word of mouth through long centuries before

---

i   For example, "and shalt show them the way wherein they are to go and the work that they must do." Ex. 18:20

being codified and written down in the *Mishnah* (by 200 CE).¹²⁴ The purport of the *Mishnah* (lit. to study) was to maintain the authority of those traditions, rules and interpretations, which had accumulated in the course of time around the Jewish system of life.¹²⁵ Therefore, it would rather serve as a sort of *Lex mercatoria*ⁱ to the written code of law (the Torah). Danby states that:

> "This is but an assertion that side by side with a written code there exists a living tradition with power to interpret the written code, to add to it, and even at times to modify it or ignore it as might be needful in changed circumstances, and to do so authoritatively. Inevitably the inference follows that the living tradition (the Oral Law) is more important than the Written law, since 'the tradition of the elders', besides claiming an authority and continuity equal to that of the Written Law, claims also to be its authentic and living interpretation and its essential complement."¹²⁶

The *Mishnah* and its commentary, the *Gemara*, both the Babylonian (400 CE) and the Palestinian (500 CE), constitute the whole body of the Talmud, or what is traditionally referred to as *Shas*, the "six orders" of the Oral Law of Judaism.¹²⁷ Because the Talmudic texts were difficult in language and thought alike, further rabbinical commentaries have been produced, of which the most notable are Rashi's commentary (1040-1105), Maimonides' *Mishnah* Torah (1170-1180), Ben Asher's *Turim* (1269-1343) and Karo's *Shulchan Aruch* (1488-1575). The latter is considered to be the most widely accepted compilation of Jewish law.

The final major source of *Halakha* is the *Responsa*, which are the legal opinions that are issued by rabbis, scholars or heads of academies in response to questions addressed to them.¹²⁸ The response literature extends for a period of over a thousand years,

---

i   *Lex mercatoria* used in this context to refer to unwritten common law, i.e. customary societal or communal norms.

and deals with myriad practical, as well as theoretical, questions affecting the ritual, economic and social life of Jews.[129] Legally speaking, *Responsa* literature has generated a substantial body of legal precedent; past decisions which a Jewish judge will rely upon in his rulings, though not bound to do so.[130]

All of these three sources, along with legislation and custom, comprise the main body of *Halakha*. The whole legal structure of Judaism has been visualized as an upside-down Pyramid with the Torah at the base and from which rise the Prophets, Scriptures, *Mishnah*, *Gemara*, *Responsa*, legislation and custom as interpretations.[131] Hence, it will be important, in trying to move toward a Judaic understanding of usury, to address in some detail the concept of usury in both the Written Law – Torah, Prophets and Scriptures as well as the Oral Law, i.e. the rabbinical commentaries.

The Concept of Usury in Judaism

The Hebraic decree on usury exerted a deep and lasting influence on the life and thought of the Western World.[132] The teachings on usury in the Hebrew Bible, which was to become the Christian Old Testament, have aroused interdenominational disputations and theoretical controversies, which cast a long shadow on the social as well as economic structure of many European lands prior to the Renaissance and beyond. Jews and Christians alike may receive these teachings as of Divine origin, yet they embraced and developed, in the course of time, very different conceptions of usury.

Usury: Definition and Interpretation

In the modern sense, the term 'usury' has come to be used to refer to a rate of interest that is above the legal or socially acceptable rate (i.e. excessive interest). In the Jewish law, however, any charge for the use of money, minimal as it may be, constitutes 'usury'. Therefore, it is important from the beginning to note that there is no conceptual distinction drawn in *Halakha* between various rates of interest, since all interest (of any kind, in any amount) is seen as prohibited.

> "The biblical law, in all dealings among Israelites, forbids all 'increase' of the debt by reason of lapse of time or forbearance, be the rate of interest high or low, while it does not impose any limit in dealings between Israelites and Gentiles. Hence in discussing Jewish law the words 'interest' and 'usury' may be used conterminously."[133]

In the language of the Torah (Hebrew), there are two terms employed to denote 'interest', *neshekh* and *tarbit*.[134] The term *neshekh* literally means 'bite', as in a 'snakebite'. According to more than one commentator, the term is used because the victim of snakebite would feel slightly uncomfortable at the initial stage, but later the venom spreads throughout the entire body till it reaches the vitals. So too, with interest, which at first might be bearable, but with time it accumulates to become a tremendous sum, leaving the lender in an irrecoverable situation.[135] It is interesting to note in this analogy the Jewish social attitude toward interest. This also might be more evident in the rabbinical literature in which, for example, a Jewish man is allowed to lend to his wife or his son at interest "only to let them know the taste of usury."[136] Yet, the term *tarbit*, which also designates 'interest' in the Bible, has a different denotation the literal meaning of which is 'increase'. It could be seen that, etymologically, interest is called *tarbit* from the point view of the creditor, and *neshekh* from that of the debtor.[137]

Nonetheless, various interpretations have been made by Talmudic scholars as to the exact connotations of the two terms. For example, the *Mishnah* regards *neshekh* as 'interest' obtained in a currency transaction, whereas *tarbit* refers to an 'increase' derived from the lending of produce;[138] Maimonides suggests that *neshekh* refers to compound interest, while *tarbit* to the fixed rate of interest;[139] and 'The Jewish Publication Society' renders *neshekh* as 'advanced interest' and *tarbit* as 'accrued interest' which is added at the time of payment.[140] Perhaps, the most authoritative view in the Talmud is that of Rave (a fourth century Babylonian sage) who sees no real distinction between these two terms, *neshekh* and *tarbit*. Furthermore, he maintained that the Torah used two synonyms in the prohibition in order to make a Jew liable for two transgressions from making the same single interest-bearing loan.[141]

Whatever the case may be, it is quite obvious that from a *halakhic* point of view the biblical prohibitions of *tarbit* and *neshekh* are not exclusive to illegal or exorbitant interest, i.e. 'usury', in the contemporary usage of the term, but rather, applicable to all interest-bearing transactions irrespective of the interest rate. Since this understanding appears to be derived mainly from biblical as well as rabbinical sources, it would be useful to consider in further detail the circumstances, context and nature of the interest prohibitions in these sources.

Usury in the Old Testament Sources

The criticism of usury in Jewish law is well established in the Torah, which includes three statements of the law prohibiting interest:[i]

> "If thou lend money to any of my people that is poor by thee, thou shalt not be to him as an usurer, neither shalt thou lay upon him usury." Exodus 22:25

> "And if thy brother be waxen poor, and fallen in decay with thee; ... Take thou no usury of him, or increase: but fear thy

---

i   Please note that quotes from the English Bible in this thesis are according to the traditional Authorized King James version (from the year 1611) unless indicated otherwise.

God; that thy brother may live with thee. Thou shalt not give him thy money upon usury, nor lend him thy victuals for increase." Leviticus 25:35-37

"Thou shalt not lend upon usury to thy brother; usury of money, usury of victuals, usury of anything that is lent upon usury: Unto a stranger thou mayest lend upon usury; but unto thy brother thou shalt not lend upon usury: that the Lord thy God may bless thee in all that thou settest thine hand to in the land whither thou goest to possess it." Deuteronomy 23:20-21

Lending money for profit is spoken of with disapproval in the Book of 'Prophets' as well. Ezekiel, Psalms and Proverbs all contain verses that describe taking interest as a practice that a 'just man' would not engage in, but only a 'wicked man' might do so.[142]

It is self-evident that these Judaic teachings on usury did not develop in a vacuum. They emerged out of a specific ideological, as well as historical and economic context. Their purpose, therefore, is not only to promote general moral ideals, but to produce a code for a specific living community. Addressing the social and economic aspect of that society would inevitably contribute to a thorough understanding of the interest prohibitions, their purport, applications and interpretations.

The Historical and Economic Context

Judaism was born in the primitive agricultural society of the ancient Near East. In these societies, lending money for profit was considered socially and legally acceptable. Only Israel had a law against loans at interest. This outstanding contrast brings with it different theories as to the historical, as well as economic and social context in which these laws had come into effect.

Legally speaking, the Pentateuchal laws prohibiting interest-taking are referred to in different ancient Hebrew legal codes, the 'Code of the Covenant' (Ex 20:22-23:33), the 'Law of Holiness' (Lev 17-26), and the 'Deuteronomic Code' (Deut 12-26). Yet, each of these codes appears to illustrate different economic and social standards.[143]

The Code of the Covenant is generally agreed to be the earliest; it dates from the eighth, ninth or tenth century BCE.[144] Some scholars have focused their attention on the Mosaic age of the Code, implying that it had developed in the wilderness to which the Jews, who were pastoralists, had escaped from their bondage in Egypt, and were on the verge of entering the Land of Canaan (the earlier indigenous name of Palestine).[145] Notwithstanding, the directions about slaves, cattle, fields, vineyards and houses in the code cannot apply to a non-settled or to a partially settled population. Therefore, it is likely that the code begins its development during the years subsequent to the conquest of Canaan.[146] At the time, Israelites had not yet undergone the complete transformation from a pastoral to an agricultural mode of life. This would be evident in the Code itself, which presupposes a Jewish economy that is pastoral in character.[147] Neither kings, horses, nor any other aspect of urban life features in the Code. In contrast, cattle are repeatedly mentioned; the ox alone is referred to more than twenty-three times. Moreover, Stein noticed that:

> "Only six out of eighty-six verses deal with agriculture. It seems, therefore, that agriculture played only a secondary role in the society for which the Book of Covenant was destined. ... its legislation ... can best be understood as belonging to a group of half sedentary people who were on the point of settling permanently but who, for the time being, were assured of their livelihood by their pastoral mode of life."[148]

On this basis, it has been argued that Israel's laws were tailored only for a semi-nomadic community that presumably lived mostly by cattle rearing.[149] In such a community, of course, loans are very often provided to the poor for consumption only, rather than for productive purposes.[150] Unlike its neighbours, there was no need to develop a commercial system of loans at interest in Israel at the time. But, "If Jewish law had been drawn up during the more sophisticated times of the kingdom, interest would not have been forbidden."[151] The purport of the interest prohibition, therefore, was most likely for the protection of God's people, the poor, by promoting the "kinship morality of a tribal society," since relatives could not be allowed to oppress or take interest from their own needy kin.[152]

Nevertheless, the interest prohibitions were also referred to in the Law of Holiness (Lev. 25:35-38) as well as the Deuteronomic Code (Deut. 23:20-21), despite the fact that these codes would reflect, to some extent, high economic and political standards. The origins of these codes are ascribed to the period following the reigns of David and his son Solomon.[153] At the time, the Jewish community in Palestine was no longer organised as fragmented pastoral tribes but as one political nation. Economically, after they had settled the land, Israelites engaged heavily in agricultural activity, and by terracing and watering they were able to produce not only for subsistence but for markets in larger towns.[154] However, they were not completely excluded from the conduct of trade and commerce. The treaties that were concluded with Israel's neighbours protected the caravan routes and thus increased both foreign and domestic trade.[155] Although political troubles arose after Solomon's death, this economic development seems to have continued without serious disruption during the following centuries.[156]

It is apparent from this context that these codes were formed during a period of political and economic life that was much more advanced than that of the Code of Covenant. Despite this evolution, each of them contained laws prohibiting interest. It would appear, therefore, that the interest prohibition in the Code of Covenant was not meant to be restricted in its application, i.e. confined to one specific context. In fact, the interest prohibitions in the other codes were more detailed and emphatic.

The Nature of the Prohibition

A close reading of the three versions of the law against interest shows some critical differences in legal formulation as well as implementation.

Influenced by Albrecht Alt, scholars tended to categorise the biblical laws by form into two types; casuistic and apodictic.[157] Casuistic law, or case law, is characterized by its impersonal style; it often consists of *protasis* and *apodosis*, (e.g. if he/they ... then ...). This form of law was common to other Near Eastern legal codes, but what is unique in apodictic biblical law (e.g. you shall/shall not ...) is the formulation of the command in the *second person*. According to Alt, the casuistic law has its origins in Canaanite law codes (by way of Mesopotamia), while the apodictic law is the product of a genuine Israelite legal system. But, it might be difficult to apply his classification to the law against interest. Although the formulations in Exodus and Leviticus begin in a casuistic fashion, "if thou lend money..." and "if thy brother be waxen poor...", their import is apodictic in character. They do not define a penalty or remedy. Moreover, both provide the command in the second person "thou shall not ..." In dealing with this problematic combination, some have suggested that it may provide evidence that the 'Book of the Covenant' as a mere law-code has been transformed partly into a 'covenant-code'.[158] However, the formulations in Deuteronomy are apodictic throughout. It begins with, "you shall not lend upon usury" and includes no conditional clauses.

From another angle, Rabbi Ishmael, in his *Mekhilta on Exodus* (c. 2nd cent.), contended that every 'if' in the Torah stands for a non-obligatory act.[159] But this, he argued, does not apply to, *inter alia*, usury law in Exodus, since lending money to the poor was reintroduced in a positive command in another scriptural verse, "Thou shalt surely lend to him" (Deut. 15.8). He thought, therefore, that it was obligatory for Jews, rather than discretionary, to lend freely, demanding no interest of one's brother in need.

Substantially, however, the three statements of interest prohibition express different aspects of the biblical law against interest. The provision in Exodus prohibits in general terms the lending of money at interest to the "poor by thee". Leviticus includes in the prohibition lending both money and food at interest, but to a brother who "be waxen poor". Apparently, these laws are merely concerned with loans to the needy and destitute. Hypothetically, if they were the only anti-interest laws appearing in the Bible, one could simply conclude that the prohibitions were directed at consumer and not commercial loans. But this is not the case. The Deuteronomic law introduced an absolute prohibition that differs from the two preceding ones, in that it includes not only money and food but also, "anything that is lent upon usury", without making reference to the economic status of the borrower. Albeit, the law mentions twice the prohibition against lending at interest to a 'brother', "Thou shalt not lend upon usury to thy brother" (Deut. 23:20) and "…but unto thy brother thou shalt not lend upon usury" (Deut. 23:21). Both instances ignore the condition of the brother in question. The law, therefore, seems to apply to all members of the Jewish community, whether they are rich or poor.

Further, the laws in Exodus and Leviticus indicate that the prohibition is exclusive to Israelites. The use of the terms "poor by thee" and "thy brother" imply that the usury ban applies only to loans amongst the Hebrew brotherhood. Charging interest to foreigners seems to be condoned. The law in Deuteronomy refers to this fact explicitly, "Unto a stranger thou mayest lend upon usury; but unto thy brother thou shalt not lend upon usury" (Deut. 23:20). This 'Deuteronomic double standard', as termed by Nelson, gives rise to myriad theories, assumptions and interpretations.[160] However, how Jews received these teachings on usury may become more evident in the rabbinical literature and commentaries.

Usury in the Rabbinical Sources

On the basis of the biblical texts, the rabbis had elaborated a most generic doctrine that condemned not only interest, *per se*, but any form of profit that might even resemble interest, "*avaq ribbit*" (lit. the dust of interest). The Talmud draws a clear distinction between biblically and rabbinically prohibited interest.[161] The former, called *ribbit ketzutzah*, is violated only when the interest is explicitly stipulated in a loan transaction.[162] In the latter, however, the interdiction is extended considerably to include various forms of 'increase' that might accrue to the creditor.

The Talmud and other Jewish writings distinguish three main types of these rabbinically prohibited forms of increase; 'the mere dust of increase', 'the semblance of increase' and 'increase payable by some other means than money'.[163] The first of these denotes indirect forms of interest that were often received in the course of business transactions. The *Mishnah*, in the fifth chapter of *Baba Mezia* (BM), enumerates certain types of sales, rent agreements and work contracts that might ultimately result in usurious transactions and which are, therefore, forbidden. For example, it says:

> "The creditor may not dwell without charge in the debtor's courtyard or hire it from him at a reduced rate, since that counts as usury."[164]; "If a man sold his field and was given a part of the price and said to the buyer, 'Pay me (the rest of) the price when you will, and then take what is yours,' this is forbidden."[165]

The second kind, the 'semblance of interest', refers to interest paid out of sheer gratitude for a past loan[i] or out of the desire to induce a future one. This is illustrated by *Siphre on Deuteronomy*,

> "The commandment has been formulated to show that there is a type of interest which precedes and a type which follows. How? A man is seeking to borrow from someone and he sends him a present saying, ' ... so that you might lend to me.' That is interest which precedes. A man has borrowed from someone and sends him small coins and a present, saying, ' ... for your inactive money which I have.' That is interest which follows."[166]

The third form of increase – 'increase payable by some other means than money' – includes many disparate cases, known as *ribbid devarim*, in which the lender is treated deferentially or given other favours by the borrower.[167] For example, if A has received a loan from B, he should not greet B in the street unless he was accustomed to doing so before.[168] Greeting him, from a rabbinical point of view, would appear as doing something extra for him in consideration of the loan. Some contemporary rabbis go a step further and state that the borrower should not even say "thank you" to the lender.[169] Others, however, allow a simple "thank you."[170] It would appear, therefore, that in both the *Mishnah* and the Talmud, "all forms of profit – all forms! – constitute nothing other than 'usury' that Scripture condemned."[171]

Whether these measures, mentioned above, are exaggerated or not, it is interesting to note how relentless rabbis were in the detection of usury, being even more unbending than the Pentateuch

---

i   Strangely, this form of increase seems not to be absolutely forbidden to Torah scholars. The Baba Mezia (75a) reads: "Scholars may borrow from each other on interest, Why? Fully knowing that usury is forbidden, they merely present gifts to each other." I.e. because they know interest is prohibited and they consider the extra a gift.

itself. This, however, might be attributable to the gravity of the prohibition against interest in the Oral tradition. The practice was seen as equivalent to robbery,[172] shedding of blood[173] and even denying God.[174] Furthermore, the prohibition has been connected with Israel's covenant with Yahweh. The *Siphra* on Leviticus states: "I, the Lord your God, have brought you out of Egypt on the condition that you accept the commandments on usury. Whoever professes them professes the exodus from Egypt, and vice versa."[175] The practice seems to be so abhorrent to the rabbis, that selling one's daughter into slavery was seen as preferable to borrowing money on interest.[176] The *Sanhedrin*, moreover, has included usurers, alongside gamblers, pigeon-trainers and traders who persist in their transactions during the sabbatical year, as people regarded as unfit to act as witnesses or judges.[177]

It is not only the lender who incurs guilt in usurious transactions but also the borrower, the guarantor, the witnesses and even the scribe who writes the document.[178] Although the lender is the most culpable, all are violating a number of biblical commandments from a Talmudic point of view.[i] However, all these rabbinical laws are limited in their application to transactions between Jews. When transacting with a gentile, a Jew may agree to pay or charge interest without restriction.[179] Likewise, in Deuteronomy 23:19-20, The Talmud put it in explicit terms that, "Money may be borrowed from gentiles on usury and lent to them on usury, and the same applies with a resident alien."[180] Some rabbis even went further and asserted that to demand interest from a non-Israelite is a positive biblical command.[181] This, however, should not be surprising in view of the ideological basis provided for the prohibitions. This will be considered further in the next chapter.

---

i Namely: 'Not to give' (Lev. 5.37); 'and not to take' (Lev. 5.36); 'Thou shalt not be to him as a usurer' (Ex. 22.24); 'Neither shall you lay upon him interest' (Ex. 22.24) and 'nor put a stumbling block before the blind' (Lev. 19.14).

Usury in Christianity

The Devil's Work[i]

The Church adopted a hostile attitude towards usury during the majority of its history. There was a time when Christians who asked more than they had given were under pain of refusal of confession, of absolution and of Christian burial; or the invalidation of wills and excommunication.[182] All interest rates greater than zero were regarded as usurious.[183] Even hoping for anything beyond one's principal was declared sinful.[ii] Taking of interest was equated with the crimes of theft, murder, fornication and heresy; it was considered to be a form of avarice, a moral evil, inherently unjust and a sin against Old and New Testaments alike as well as Natural Law.[184] But, the practice today is no longer regarded with quite such dread.[185] The morality of interest-taking seems to be a foregone conclusion amongst most Christians. They may lend or borrow money at moderate interest with a clear conscience.

This remarkable reversal of attitude raises awkward questions for the Church. Did she err or change its teaching on usury? Is it the only teaching that has been changed due to changing circumstances or have there been others? How could a divine law that is derived by revelation as holy, just and good be subject to such modification?

In responding to such questions, some argued that there was a genuine development, but not a change, in the Christian

---

i In the 13th-century morality tale written by Jacques de Vitry, a French preacher, money-lenders were portrayed as damned people who were doing the devil's work. See T.F. Crane, *The Exampla Or Illustrative Stories from the Sermones Vulgares of Jacques de Vitry* (Burt Franklin 1971)

ii As noted by Hawkes, "Medieval commentators had already condemned "mental usury" as the hope or expectation of usurious profit, and they denounced it as a sin regardless of whether the hope was realised." See, D. Hawkes, *The Culture of Usury in Renaissance England* (Palgrave Macmillan 2010), p. 22

doctrine of usury.[186] Fr. Gary Coulter claims that: "Papal teaching and Church councils never stated that interest in itself and under all circumstances is wrong, only the taking of interest without a just title to it."[187] This is a very familiar sounding argument, one in need of closer examination. However, he then concludes:

> "What changed? Not the church's teaching on usury. At one time, the only cost to the lender was the loan itself, and so the Church taught in that particular time nothing above the principal could be taken on such loans. Today, the title of lost profit is a general fact of life. In economic terms, there is an "opportunity cost" of loaning one's money, which deserves just remuneration."[188]

It is the purpose of this section, therefore, to trace the historical development of the concept of usury and to indicate its successive connotations and their social and ethical significance, from the Biblical sources, through the early Fathers, the Scholastics, the Protestant Reformers and the Jesuits to the current position of Christian economic thinking. This study can be rewarding not only because it would result in a better understanding of the doctrine but also because instructive of the way Christian thinking lives and changes.

THE NEW TESTAMENT SOURCES

Cleansing of the Temple

Usury was customary in the time of Jesus . Ironically, one of the places where the practice flourished was in the Second Temple in Jerusalem. As described in the New Testament, the corridors of the Temple were crowded with money-changers, who were not only dealing with coins of different denominations, brought to the temple as part of the tithes of Jews, but also allowing interest on money deposited with them.[189]

Historically, the period of the Second Temple saw the development of the coinage system, especially in the days of the Maccabean kings, who issued what are considered to be the first Jewish coins.[190] Yet, it was not only the Israelite currency that prevailed in Jerusalem at the time. Coins from different sources were brought to the city, primarily as part of the Jewish obligatory and charitable offerings to the Temple, from both the Land of Israel and the Diaspora. This mixture of coinage contributed to the emergence of money-changing as a permanent part of the Jewish economy. Although three main currencies were used in the Land of Israel at that time: the local Jewish currency, which may have been minted at Caesarea, the official Roman currency and the provincial Greek-standard currency; it was only the provincial one that was acceptable in paying the tithes and offerings for the Temple. It is not surprising, therefore, that money-changers (*shulchani*) installed their tables in the corridors of the Temple.[191]

However, the business of the *shulchani* was not confined to money-changing. They used to accept deposits from private individuals for safety or investment, and lent these sums at interest to various people.[192] Their usurious activities were supposed to be forbidden by the strict prohibition of interest-taking in the Hebrew Bible. Nevertheless, they found ways to sidestep the prohibition, mainly through concealment of the practice in classical commercial contracts. The *Mishnah*, therefore, is replete with passages addressing the interest-masking transactions devised by them as well as by merchants.[193] The term '*shulchani*' in these passages often stands for both a banker and a trader. Hence, the Temple of Solomon, the House of God, which should fulfil the laws of Moses against the taking of interest, became, in effect, the birthplace of Jewish money-lending.[194]

One could read the famous account of Jesus' encounter with the money changers at the Temple in this historical context:

"Then Jesus went into the temple of God and drove out all those who bought and sold in the temple, and overturned the tables of the money changers and the seats of those who sold doves. He said to them, "It is written, 'My house shall be called a house of prayer'; but you have made it a den of thieves."[i]

In justifying his 'righteous indignation' at the Temple, Saint Thomas Aquinas noted that:

"... in obedience to the Law ... innumerable victims were sacrificed, especially on festival days, bulls, rams, goats; the poor offering young pigeons and turtle-doves, that they might not omit all sacrifice. But it would happen that those who came from a distance would have no victim. The Priests therefore contrived a plan for making a gain out of the people, selling to such as had no victim the animals which they had need of for sacrifice, and themselves receiving them back again as soon as sold. But this fraudulent practice was often defeated by the poverty of the visitors ... They therefore appointed bankers who might lend to them under a bond. But because the Law forbade usury, they bethought themselves of another scheme; instead of bankers they appointed '*collybistae*,' a word for which the Latin has no equivalent."[195]

According to Saint Thomas, ancient writers such as Pollux, Suidas, Oriegen and others understand by 'collybists' those who change good coin for bad, to the injury of those who employ them. A different sense of the word has been given, however, by Jerome and Hesychrus who interpret 'collyba' as sweetmeats, thus 'collybists' are those who provide it. Saint Thomas reported that:

---

i   Matthew 21:12; See also Mark 11:15, where the temple cleansing is also depicted at the beginning of Jesus' ministry – whereas in Luke 19: 45 it comes at the end, after Jesus has ridden into Jerusalem on the donkey.

"Sweetmeats and other trifling presents they called 'collyba,' such, for example, as parched pulse, raisins, and apples of divers sorts. As then they could not take usury, they accepted the value in kind, taking things that are bought with money, as if this was not what Ezekiel preached of, saying, 'Ye shall not receive usury nor increase." [Ezek 18:17] This kind of traffic, or cheating rather, the Lord seeing in His Father's house, and moved thereat with spiritual zeal, cast out of the Temple this great multitude of men."[196]

There are, of course, other explanations provided for this famous incident. The cleansing of the Temple by an act of coercive force seems to trouble the Christian conscience.[197] Some even doubt its historicity.[198] But, however, the tale consistently inspires Pope Gregory VII in his meditations on the evils of usury, and those who engaged in this prohibited practice. Further, Bernard of Clairvaux advised the Pope, Eugenious III to ignore the wrangling of jurists, and deal with those who defend the practice as Christ did with the money-lenders in the Temple, stating, "He did not take time to listen; he took out a whip to beat them."[199]

Curiously enough Jesus equates money-changing with robbery in this legendary passage – "it is written, 'My house shall be called a house of prayer'; but you make it a den of thieves." His attitude appears to be derived from the fact that many of the money-changers, besides exchanging coins, were involved indeed in interest-masking transactions as evident not only in the Talmudic literature, discussed earlier, but also in the teachings of Jesus himself, namely in Matt. 25:30 where he used the term 'exchangers' to refer to usurious practitioners.[i] By denouncing this part of their business, Christ appears to share the same rhetoric,

---

i   In Matt. 25:30, Jesus said "Thou oughtest therefore to have put my money to the exchangers, and then at my coming I should have received mine own with usury."

and perhaps the same line of reasoning, with the Greek and Roman philosophers who perceived usury as tantamount to theft.

However, there are three other references to usury in the teachings of Jesus; two are identical and relate to the Parable of the Talents, the third one is found in the Gospel of Luke 6:34-35.

The Parable of the Talents

In the entire New Testament, the term 'usury' occurs only twice. These are found in Matt. 25: 14–30; Luke 19: 12–27 and are synoptic accounts of Jesus' parable of the talents and pounds. Yet, it was mentioned incidentally in these parables to address the excuses of slothful servants, and in both as the unjust and oppressive act of a hard and dishonest man. The purport of the parables appears to be the necessity of faithfulness. Faithful servants were rewarded in the end, whilst the unfaithful were punished.

The parable, as featured in Matthew, tells of a master who, before leaving his home on a journey, had entrusted his possessions to three of his servants. To the first he gave five talents,[i] to the second two talents, and to the third he gave one. The one who had received the five talents set to work at once and traded with them, and gained five more talents. Likewise, the one who had the two talents gained two more talents. But the one who had received the one talent did not invest his master's money; instead he dug a hole in the ground and buried it. After a long time the master of those slaves came and settled accounts with them. Then the one who had received the five talents came forward, bringing five more talents, saying, "Lord, thou deliveredst unto me five talents: behold, I have gained beside them five talents more."[200] His master said to him, "Well done, good and faithful servant; thou hast been faithful over a few things, I will make thee ruler over many

---

i A talent was a weight of 75 pounds and the original text says this was of silver, representing a very large sum of money.

things: enter thou into the joy of thy lord."²⁰¹ And the one with the two talents also came forward, saying, "Lord, thou deliveredst unto me two talents: behold, I have gained two other talents beside them."²⁰² His master said to him, "Well done, good and faithful servant; thou hast been faithful over a few things, I will make thee ruler over many things: enter thou into the joy of thy lord."²⁰³

But, the servant with the one talent brings his talent with an excuse, which is a charge against the character of his master:

> "Lord, I knew thee that thou art an hard man, reaping where thou hast not sown, and gathering where thou hast not strawed: And I was afraid, and went and hid thy talent in the earth: lo, there thou hast that is thine."²⁰⁴

The master in reply revealed the inconsistency of his excuse by assuming that he bore the hard character charged upon him by his slave:

> "Thou wicked and slothful servant, thou knewest that I reap where I sowed not, and gather where I have not strawed: Thou oughtest therefore to have put my money to the exchangers, and then at my coming I should have received mine own with usury."²⁰⁵

Notwithstanding this, some writers inferred from this very part of the interview that the taking of usury has been disregarded in the New Testament. They often quoted only the master saying – "thou oughtest therefore to have put my money to the exchangers, and then at my coming I should have received mine own with usury" – to allege that Jesus affirmed the legitimacy of the practice through the parable of talents.²⁰⁶ However, setting this statement in its context would prove the contrary.²⁰⁷

The conversation may be represented as follows, the unfaithful servant said to his master: 'I know the kind of a man you are.

You are dishonest. You take what does not belong to you. You reap what other people sow, and you grab what others earn. I was afraid of you: Here is all that which you gave me and all that which belongs to you.' Judging him out of his own mouth, the master replies 'look if I am indeed a wicked, austere man who reaps where he does not sow, why did you not put my money out at interest just like the wicked do?' Such a rendering is not only in accord with its context, but also in harmony with the teachings of the Old Testament, where the one who lends on interest is depicted as wicked.[208] Not to mention that it would be incompatible to suggest that Jesus, who cast out the exchangers from the Temple and called them thieves, would berate one of the servants for not putting his money with them so he could receive it later with interest accrued! There are other writers who believe that the parables are not relevant whatsoever.[209] Rev. Patrick Cleary maintains:

> "There is indeed a reference to usury in the parable of the talents, but from the context it is quite evident that Christ has no intention of making a pronouncement on the morality of any economical doctrine; he simply utilises the prevailing practice of the Roman bankers to point a moral on co-operation with divine grace."[210]

Such an understanding, however, is not popular, at least amongst the early Fathers of the Church, as will be seen.

Love Your Enemies

The third reference to usury in the New Testament is found in the text of St. Luke 6:34-35. It reads:

> "And if ye lend to them of whom ye hope to receive, what thanks have ye? For sinners also lend to sinners, to receive as much again. But love ye your enemies, and do good, and lend, hoping for nothing again; and your reward shall be

great, and ye shall be the children of the Highest: for He is kind unto the unthankful and to the evil."

As with the previous ones, this passage has been the subject of considerable controversy. Aquinas, in his *Summa Theologica*, interpreted it as a counsel in respect of the repayment of the loan, but it is a matter of precept as to not to seek profit by lending. On the contrary, Mastrofini, in his treatise on usury, reads the passage as implying neither a precept nor a regulation. He maintains that the word 'do' in "Do good, and lend, hoping for nothing again" does not refer to money or other objects lent at usury. Rather, "[it] merely point[s] to that universal and active benevolence which should mark our relations with others, not worldly rewards, but because of the positive precept of God, who wishes us to respect in all men the work of His hands."[211] Other interpretations have been attempted by modern writers. As Milles points out:

> "An alternative rendering of the final phrase could be 'lend, without hoping to receive any return' – a translation which employs an idiom known to be current from at least the fourth century. In the context of v.34, this could either mean that lending was to be undertaken without any thought of a pecuniary return in the form of interest or it could speak of lending without any thought of recovery of the principal from the inception of the loan. The 'loan' would then effectively become a gift ... Marshall,[212] however, argues that 'receiving the equal amount' cannot refer to the extension of a loan with no thought of repayment because this is indistinguishable from a gift. Rather, he suggests that the phrase refers to receiving offers of loans in return. Some sort of equal treatment through reciprocal loans must then be the meaning of 'receiving a return' in v.35. The contrast is drawn between 'sinners' who lend to each

other in the hope of being able to call on a return favour in the future (cf. Luke 14:12) and the obedient disciple who lends without entertaining such selfish motives."[213]

Yet, it would be insightful to consider that this teaching was made in light of a predominantly agricultural and/or small business society where borrowing itself would take place on a frequent basis more often between friend and friend, kinsman and kinsman, 'sinner' and 'sinner'. Not only coined monies were lent in such communities, but also tools, seed, livestock, help, etc. Lending at interest was regulated, with a maximum rate of 12 percent, under Roman law at the time. But, Jews were subject to the Law of Moses, which banned the entire practice. However, they construed the relevant verses in the 'Old' Testament as permitting the taking of interest from foreigners or enemies. Thus, when Jesus came usury was already forbidden among Jews; so a mere prohibition of the practice would not be strange, and obedience to the law would not demand any special reward. It is clear that Christ's attention was directed toward advancing the already received doctrines of the Jews. He shifted the emphasis in a universalistic fashion from lending to only 'brothers', in Deut. 23:19, to lending to anyone, including enemies, and even if there is no hope of repayment. By doing so Jesus has broken down the barrier between Jew and Gentile and inaugurated a world-wide community in which the brother/foreigner distinction no longer held.

These were the references to usury found in the New Testament. Did Jesus exhibit a distinctly anti-usury attitude when he cast the money-changers from the Temple? Was he displaying the disdain of the Old Testament Prophets through the parables of talents? Did his teaching in Luke include a precept, or a simple counsel against lending at interest? These questions appear to be answered differently throughout the history of the Church. However, the way in which they were addressed, at least by the early Fathers, was not inclined to tolerance.

THE FATHERS OF THE CHURCH

The Fathers of the Church vehemently denounced usury in their writings, homilies and moral sermons.[214] They perceived it as unjust,[i] immoral,[215] evil,[ii] a snare of the devil,[216] a diabolical activity,[217] an injury to Christ[iii] as well as a sign of disobedience that brings down God's wrath.[218] Further, they depicted those involved

---

i   Chrysostom (344 – 407 CE) maintains that nothing comes from injustice which includes usury would be accepted by God. Further, he says: "For those who demand usury I have no promise, neither with soldiers who extort others, turning to their advantage the misfortunes of others. For God will accept nothing from that council." See, John Chrysostom, *Hom. in 1 Cor.* 43, PG 61.374

ii   Cyril of Jerusalem (315-387) admonishes his audience to avoid diabolical actions among which he placed usury. Furthermore, he considered intemperance, avarice and usury as the snares of the devil:
"Shun every diabolical activity, and do not be misled by the apostate Serpent ... give attention neither to prophecies nor observations of the skies, nor omens, nor to the legendary oracles of the Greeks ... knowing neither gluttony nor hedonism, rising superior to all avarice and lending on interest." See, Cyril of Jerusalem, Lecture 4; On the Ten Points of Doctrine, Colossians, PG 33.501. N.B. I

iii   In his *Tractatus in Ps. XIV*, Hilary of Poitiers (315-367) states that,
"Remember that the person from whom you seek interest is the poor needy man for whom Christ himself became poor and needy. Therefore, whether you do good or evil to the poor man, know that you do it to Christ." As translated in Robert P. Maloney, 'The teaching of the fathers on Usury: an historical study on the development of Christian thinking' 27 *Vigiliae Christianae* 241, 247

in the practice as liars,[i] lower than dogs,[ii] prolific wild beasts,[iii] predators,[iv] thieves,[v] murderers,[vi] public enemies, menaces, serpents

i Basil of Caesarea in his *Homilia in Psalms*, described how the money-lenders were deluding people:
"Calling down curses on himself and swearing that he is entirely without money, and is looking around to see if he can find someone who lends money out with interest, he is believed in his lie because of his oaths, and incurs the guilt of perjury as the evil gains of his humanity. But, when he who is seeking the loan makes mention of interest and names his securities, then, pulling down his eyebrows, he smiles and remembers somewhere or other a family friendship, and calling him associate and friend, he says, "We shall see if we have any money at all reserved. There is a deposit of a dear friend who entrusted it to us for a matter of business. He has assigned a heavy interest for it, but we shall certainly remit some and give it at a lower rate of interest." Basil, *Hom. in Ps.* (PG 29:265–68)

ii Since "Dogs, when they have received something, are pacified, but the money-lender, on receiving something, is further provoked. He does not stop railing but demands more." Ibid., (PG 29:269–72)

iii Chrysostom's *Homily 13 on First Corinthians*, equates the rich and usurers with animals gorging themselves constantly:
"but of what kind are those who are rich? [They are] of swine and dogs and wolves, and all other wild beasts. For some of them concern [themselves] perpetually with what is on the table, and condiments and an abundance of wine and perfumes and garments and all the rest of the extravagances. And others about usury and lending money." See, Chrysostom, *Hom. in I Cor.* 13, PG 61.114

iv Gregory of Nyssa, in *Contra usurario*, likens the usurer to "hunters who deplete each populated valley of wildlife, then move on with their nets to the next fertile valley." Gregory of Nyssa, *Usur.* (PG 46:445; J 202)

v In his fourth homily from the *Commentary on Ecclesiastes* Gregory of Nyssa posed a question that "What is the difference between getting someone else's property by seizing it through covert housebreaking or taking possession of the goods of a passer-by by murdering him, and acquiring what is not one's own by extracting interest." See, Gregory of Nyssa, *Hom. 4*, from *Homiliae in Eccl.* (PG 44:615–754),

vi According to John Chrysostom:
"Is it not murder—one might say even worse than murder—to hand a poor man over to famine, and to throw him into prison, and to enslave him not only to famine and tortures, but measureless sufferings? For even if (on the one hand) you do not do these to him, you (on the other hand) are responsible for them being done, even more than the attendants who

in the garden, eager for the downfall of the innocent for their own gain[219] and of course there is no place for such individuals in the Lord's eternal tabernacle.[i] Many other illustrations have also been used by them to demonstrate their absolute condemnation of the practice. Usury had no redeeming features in their eyes.

The taking of interest seems to have been pervasive among their communities.[ii] Those who engaged in the practice were not happy to hear what the theologians had to say. Gregory of Nyssa (335-395 CE) noticed that many of his listeners were "murmuring under their lips" while he was castigating usurers.[220] John Chrysostom (344-407 CE) when he stood up to talk about usury, he stated that he knew that many would have preferred him to remain silent, but that he had to speak.[221] Ambrose (340-397 CE) retorted, "So has sin" to those who objected that usury had been commonly practised.[222] Basil of Caesarea (329-379 CE) commenced his sermon on usury by admitting that although he had run out of time preaching on the Psalm the previous day, he dared not finish it for the sake of his audience because he understood the "great power in the affairs of life" and "probably, it escaped the notice of most of you."[223] The latter statement would suggest his audience considered usury to be a matter of course, and therefore not in need of special treatment or comment. Indeed, taking of moderate interest was a common

---

do them." John Chrysostom, *Hom. in Rom.* 11, PG 60.491.

i Athanasius (c. 295-373 in his commentary on Ps. 14 (15),2-5.28 listed ten special precepts that men must follow if they want to dwell with the Lord in his eternal tabernacle, of which is avoiding usury. See, Athanasius *Expositio in Ps.* XIV2-5 (PG 27,100) as translated in Maloney, 'The teaching of the fathers on Usury: an historical study on the development of Christian thinking' op. cit., p. 246

ii F. Gary Coulter argued, in his book *The Church and Usury*, that "the Generosity of Christians was such that usury must have been unknown" at that time. Notwithstanding, a brief examination of what the fathers said in the subject reveals that they were addressing a problem that was quite relevant in their own era.

practice in the Graeco-Roman world. Its public legality seemed to encourage many, not only men but also women[i] and sometimes, even clergy.[ii] One of the difficult conundrums for the early Fathers was how to deal with a practice that was legally accepted by civil law but morally questioned by divine law.

The Fathers' teaching on usury was based mainly on the Old and New Testaments, but it seems also to have been influenced by classical Graeco-Roman thought, this will emerge more clearly from a detailed examination of what they said. This section, however, will summarise their teachings on the subject through two specific questions: How did they define prohibited usury? And how did they rationalise this prohibition?

The patristic prohibitions against usury distinguish neither between rates of interest nor between the purposes of loans. In his letter to Letoius, Gregory of Nyssa contends that the sacred scripture forbids the taking of any surplus over and above principal, no matter what pretence at legality is made, i.e. no matter what the laws of the empire say, the law of God still forbade it.[224] Reflecting a similar attitude, Augustine, in a letter to Macedonius, complains of the civil law and of judges who order that interest be paid.[225] Ambrose, in his *De officiis*, disapproved both the Roman legal *centesima* (twelve per cent,

---

i According to the Constitutions, women living off of subsistence from the Church were investing what they had been given and were "heaping up to themselves plenty of money and lend at usury." See, *The Apostolic Constitutions* 3.7 (*ANF* 7), p. 428

ii Cyprian reprimands severely those clergy who, neglecting their pastoral duties, engage in the pursuit of temporal gain, even taking usury. *De lapsis*, c. 6, Migne, P.L., t. 4, cols. p. 470-1 as translated in Divine op. cit., p. 28; Also appears form Canon 17 of the First Ecumenical Council of Nicaea in 325 which threatens those clergy who engaged in the practice that once caught *in flagrante delicto*, they will be cast from their grades.

per annum)[i] as well as the illegal *anatocism* (compound interest).[ii] "Whatever exceeds the amount loaned" is usury for him.[226] Jerome also defined the practice as receiving of anything more than the amount loaned, whether of money or of corn or of wine or oil or of anything else.[227] The financial status of both the creditor and the debtor were also immaterial. Augustine says that the usurer may claim that interest-taking is his only livelihood, but the robber, the magician and the pimp could say the same, and their occupations are clearly illicit.[228] Apollonius attacked the Montanist prophets because they were *inter alia* taking interest from the rich and sometimes even from the poor. Gregory, likewise, censured interest-loans to rich and poor alike.[229] Both have been pleaded with by Basil not to borrow at interest, "Are you rich? Do not borrow. Are you poor? Do not borrow. If you are prospering, you have no need of a loan; if you have nothing, you will not repay the loan. Do not give your life over to regret, lest at some time you may esteem as happy the days before the loan."[230]

i In which he says:
"How different is the wickedness of the prince of this world! The usurer or money-lender has a mortgage on one's head, he holds one's signature, he reckons his capital, he exacts his hundredth (*centesimam*) ... The Lord freed the hundredth sheep – that was the hundredth of salvation, this, of death – and the good earth returns fruit a hundred-fold ... Ought they not by that very word by which they designate it hundredth, to recall to memory the Redeemer, who came to save the hundredth sheep, not to destroy it?." See, Ambrose, *DT 42, 45* (PL 14,775-77) translated by ibid., p. 254

ii He noted that:
"The first of the month arrives, the capital brings forth its hundredth; each month comes, interest is born, evil offspring of evil parents. This is the generation of vipers. The hundredth has developed; it is demanded, it is not paid; it is applied to the principal ... And therefore it begins to be no longer interest, but principal that is to say, not a hundredth of interest, but interest on a hundredth" See, Ambrose, *DT 42* (PL 14,775) translated by ibid.

In fact, the only exception to the usury prohibition to appear in the patristic sources is that provided by Ambrose. In addressing the 'Deuteronomic double-standard', Ambrose construed the 'stranger' mentioned in the text – Unto a stranger thou mayest lend upon usury – as an enemy. The Israelites were allowed, he argued, to take interest from the enemies of God's people since they had a right to bear weapons against them in the first place. Hence, he concludes that:

> "Upon him whom you rightly desire to harm, against whom weapons are lawfully carried, upon him usury is legally imposed. On him whom you cannot easily conquer in war, you can quickly take vengeance with the hundredth. From him extract usury whom it would not be a crime to kill. He fights without a weapon who demands usury; without a sword he revenges himself upon an enemy, who is an interest collector from his foe. Therefore, where there is the right of war, there is also the right of usury."[231]

Ambrose taught that, while a man might take interest from an enemy if the warfare is justifiable, he should not take it from a brother in any way; he defined 'brother' as one who has the faith, or is at least a compatriot.[232] A very similar definition is provided by Clement of Alexandria. In his *Stromata*, he says: "the law prohibits a brother from lending with usury; a brother not only in name, born from the same parents, but even one of the same community, and also who is of like mind in the same Word."[233] Confusingly, this implies that one might charge interest from a foreigner, but not from one of the same religious or national identities.

However, turning to the Old Testament texts to address the subject of usury was a method followed, not just by Ambrose but also, by many Fathers. As Robert Maloney remarks, Tertullian, Jerome, Basil, Chrysostom and Clement often cited the Old Testament prohibitions in Ex.22:25; Dt.23:19-20; Lev. 25:35

Ps.15:5 and Ez.18:8 as still binding on Christians.[234] The references to usury in the New Testament, on the other hand, were seen as fulfilling the law rather than destroying it. Tertullian, for example, suggests that the purpose of the law laid down by Ez. 18:8 was to prepare for the Christ's demand to forgo the principal as well.[235] Jerome also argued that the legal sections of the Old Testament (Lev. 25,35 and Dt. 23,20-21) forbade interest only among the brethren, but in the prophets (Ez. 18,8) all interest-taking is prohibited and in the New Testament another step is taken when the Lord says, "Lend to those from whom you can expect nothing in return."[236]

Along with the scriptures, the early Fathers used different rationales for condemning the practice. The evil of usury is considered to inhere in its origin and in its effect. Its origin is greed and avarice in the heart of the usurer, which contradicts Christian love among the brethren, especially love toward the poor. Referring to Luke 6:34, Basil said: "Hear ye rich, how because of your inhumanity we must give this counsel even to the poor."[237] Gregory of Nazianzus, inspired by the parable of the talents, stated: "[o]ne has defiled the earth with usury and interest, both amassing where he had not sowed and reaping where he had not strewed not farming the earth but the want of those in need."[238] Hilary of Poitiers assails the usury problem from a similar viewpoint, asking that:

> "What could be more intolerable than to bestow a benefit on a poor man in such a way that he becomes poorer, or to bring him help only to increase his misery? If you are a Christian, what reward can you expect from God if you do not seek to help men but to harm them? If you are a Christian, why do you scheme to have your idle money bear a return make the need of your brother, for whom Christ died, the source of your enrichment."[239]

Similar scolding questions have been posed by Commodianus as well.[i] Yet, its effects were seen to be disastrous not only to the poor. Basil in his sermon against usury indicated that some borrowed only to maintain a 'lifestyle':

> "He who has received the money is at first bright and cheerful, gladdened by another's prosperity and showing it by the change in his life. His table is lavish, his clothing more costly, his servants are changed in dress to something more brilliant; there are flatterers, boon companions, innumerable dining hall drones. But, as the money slips away, and the advancing time increases the interest due, the nights bring him no rest, the day is not bright, nor is the sun pleasant, but he is disgusted with life, he hates the days which hasten on towards the appointed time, he fears the months, the parents, as it were, of his interest."[240]

Also the lender would experience such torments since he continually fears not being paid and thus his fortunes could soon vanish. As described by Gregory of Nyssa, the usurer would undergo even greater anguish in the case he had lent to merchants given that the risk is greater. He watches the debtor anxiously as the date of repayment approaches. "Fathers do not rejoice as much at the birth of children," Gregory states ironically, "as usurers do at the end of the month."[241]

---

i   He states:
    "Why do you senselessly pretend to be good as you wound others? From what you bestow, another is daily weeping. Do you not believe that the Lord sees those things from heaven? ... if you lend at interest ... you want to give alms that you might expiate evil with that which is also evil. The Almighty absolutely rejects such works as these. Your donation has been wrung from tears ... O wicked one; you deceive yourself, but no one else" 246 Commodianus, *The Instruction*, PL 59.163; *ANF* 4: 64. 216.

Influenced by classical Greek thought,[i] the Fathers also pointed out the evils that usury could bring to society. Gregory of Nyssa maintains that the practice would lead to natural disaster due to "... [It] results from an evil union unknown to nature which has the power to make sterile things bear fruit, even though nature itself has made only animate things."[242] The Aristotelian concept of the sterility of money also appeared in one of the questions of Hilary mentioned above – "If you are a Christian, why do you scheme to have your idle money bear a return."[243] Basil argued that usury must be called *tokos* (i.e., offspring) because of the evils it carries; unlike other offspring, which grow only until they reach maturity, usury never ceases to grow, bringing with it ever-increasing sorrow.[244] Ambrose treats usury in similar fashion.[ii] Like Plato, Lactantius was concerned with the social consequences of usury:

> "Whatever is given to those who are not in need, for the sake of popularity, is thrown away; or it is repaid with interest, and thus it will not be the conferring of a benefit. And although it is pleasing to those to whom it is given, still is not just, because if it is not done, no evil follows. Therefore the only sure and true office of liberality is to support the need and unserviceable. This is that perfect justice which protects human society."[245]

Nevertheless, some objections have been brought forward

---

i As noted by Maloney, "There are ideological similarities between the patristic texts and both the *Politica* [of Aristotle] and the *Leges* [of Plato] but there are no certain explicit or implicit citations." Ibid, p. 256

ii *DT 42 (PL 14,775)*. He is clearly inspired by Cato the Elder's statement mentioned above, which he emulates in style and content, writing that, "Even the poor man is fruitful to you unto gain ... You are merciful men, certainly, who enslave to yourselves him whom you free from another! He pays usury who lacks food. Is there anything more terrible? He asks for bread, you offer him a sword; he begs for liberty, you impose slavery; he prays for freedom, you tighten the knot of the hideous snare." See, *DT 28, 29* (PL 14,769) translated by ibid., p. 253

against these philosophical rationales. Some money-lenders argued that it is not unjust to take interest on loans if borrowers made profits from the use of the money that was lent to them. One of the examples provided is that of a creditor who lends some grain to a debtor, and at harvest time the yield amounts to ten times the original quantity of the principal. Does not the creditor in this case have the justifiable right to ask for one and a half times the quantity of the principal in return? Jerome answers, rather confusingly, that interest-taking is still illicit nevertheless:

> "Let the merciful usurer tell us briefly whether he gave to someone who had possessions or to one who did not. If to someone who had possessions, he should not have given to him at all, but he gave as if to someone who did not have anything. Therefore why does he demand more back as if from someone who had something?"[246]

A similar counter argument is provided by Augustine, who asked the money-lender that from the first place "what did you intend when you did lend on usury? To give money, and receive money; but to give a smaller sum, and to receive a larger."[247]

Other money-lenders have challenged the idea of sterility of money itself through arguing that, "… hares bring forth and at the same time both rear young and become doubly pregnant. So also with money-lenders, the money is lent out and, at the same time, it reproduces from itself and is in a process of growth." Yet, Basil retorted that, "You have not yet received it in your hands and you have been required to pay out the interest for the present month."[248] Further, he warned that for the human world: what is natural in their world is immoral in ours.[249]

> "But what do you require," a money-lender objected, "that I should give another for his use that money which I have not got together, and which is to me useful, and demand

no recompense?" Chrysostom replies: "Far from it: I say not this; yes I earnestly desire that you should have a recompense not however a mean nor small one, but far greater; for in return for your gold, I desire that you should receive heaven for usury."[250]

Many other objections have also been addressed by the Early Fathers. Whether their counter-arguments were convincing or otherwise, it is interesting to see through these examples that their condemnation of interest taking was not confined to loans for consumption as some have argued. It is reflects the fact that they were addressing a problem that was quite common in their own era. From their point of view taking interest regardless of the rate is harmful not just to those who borrow, but also to those who lend as well as to the community at large. In attempting to dissuade Christians from becoming involved in such 'evil' practices, they developed a varied theological and philosophical approach. Whether they succeeded or not, their train of thought had great influence on the future preaching and teaching of the Church. As will be shown below, much of their argumentation became standard especially in the Middle ages. Not to mention that their attitude toward usury is also echoed in examples of the ecclesiastical legislation of their period.

Early Ecclesiastical Legislation

The first instance of a canonical prohibition against usury is found in the 20th canon of the provincial Synods of Elvira (306 CE).[251] Yet, the scope of this canon is subject to question, since its text as found in Ivo and in Gratian merely applies to the clergy, whereas that of Mansi applies to both clergy and laity. The latter runs:

> "Should any cleric be found to have taken usury, let him be degraded and excommunicated. Moreover, if any layman shall be proved a usurer, and shall have promised when

corrected to abstain from the practice, let him be pardoned. If, on the contrary, he persevere in his evil-doing he is to be excommunicated."[252]

Unquestionably, however, the prohibition in the subsequent legislation was directed merely toward usurious clergy. The 12th canon of the Council of Arles, CE 314, in which were represented all of the Western Church, forbids usury to clergy under the pain of being deposed. The 17th canon of the first general Council of Nicaea, CE 325, reiterated this deposition for those clerics who "in lending require their twelve per cent."[253] But, no positive or negative regulation has been made for usurious laity in any of these Synods. This can be ascribed to political reasons. As suggested by Patrick, the influence exercised by Constantine (274-337 CE) is highly likely what left the Fathers of these Councils silent in this respect.[254] The Roman Emperor who presided over both the Council of Arles and the Council of Nicaea declared just a month before the latter took place that the old 'centesima' standard, i.e. interest of 12 per cent per annum, was to be retained. Instead of conflicting with the civil power, the Fathers, therefore, preferred to refrain from any decree concerning the laity. But, at the same time they condemned the practice on grounds applicable not only to clergy but also to laity. For example, the 17th Canon of Nicaea runs, "Since many persons of the ecclesiastical order, being led away to covetousness, and a desire of filthy lucre [*turpe lucrum*], have forgotten the Holy Scripture which says, he gave not his money to usury ..."[255] Add to that the frequent emphasis on clerical usurious practices in these councils, which could be because "what is reprehensible on the part of the laity is much more worthy of condemnation in the clergy" as bishop Gratus stated in the Council of Carthage, CE 245.[256] A disapproval of lay usury is found in Canon 12 of this Council.

Perhaps, the most formal general prohibition of usury enunciated by ecclesiastical authority at this period is the *Papal Encyclical Nec hoc quoque* of Saint Leo the Great, Pope from 440 to 461. In his letter, sent to Bishops of Campania, Pisa and Tuscany, the Pope said that he can no longer pass over in silence this practice of usury either by the clergy or by the laymen who desire to be called Christian and, he decrees, therefore, that: "those who have been convicted be punished sharply, that all occasion of sinning be removed."[257] This epistle forms the cornerstone of later anti-usury legislation. It was included in the *Hadriana*, a collection of canons that was the most influential body of ecclesiastical legislation for Charlemagne's empire.[258] Thus, by 784, at the Council of Aix-la-Chapelle under Charlemagne usury was banned for everyone, laity as well as clergy.[259] This ban is a watermark in that it was the first time that Christian teaching on usury found expression in the secular legislation of the State. Thereafter the Church and State together press the fight against usury.

Consequently, the ban was reinforced in the following capitularies, synods and councils.[260] The Nynweger capitulary of 806 defines usury as "where more is asked than is given." The Paris synod of 829 declared that besides money usury may occur in commodity goods and thus dismissed the argument that the loan of grain could be a source of profit to the borrower, in which the lender is entitled to share. The Synod of Pavia in 850 went so far as to treat interest as robbery and prescribed full restitution to their living victims and a half to their heirs. Similar sanctions were also invoked against usurers in England by the Council of Northumberland, Alfred the Great (849-899), and Edward the Confessor (1003-1066).[261] In the East, King Basilius of Macedonia (830/835-886) issued a law prohibiting usury under heavy penalties as well. However, his law was soon repealed by his son and successor, King Leo the Wise. The latter's justification ran that though usury was definitely forbidden by God and hence should not be permitted by civil law, the grossness and avarice of men turns the prohibition null, and brings about disobedience and false swearing.[262]

The Christian doctrine of usury appears to be derived from a combination of scriptural text, patristic opinion and conciliar decrees at this stage. It was defined in a very general sense as taking more than what was lent, and condemned severely on different ethical and philosophical grounds. Inter alia it was shameful gain (*turp lucrum*) which only those motivated by greed, cupidity and insatiable desire of wealth for its own sake would seek. Yet, the doctrine experienced further development in the following mediaeval centuries.

Introduction to the Medieval Period

Two key factors may have contributed to renewing the attention of the Church to the problem of usury in this period. The first was socio-political in character. The power struggle between Pope Gregory VII (1072-1085) and Henry IV over investiture seems to result in opening up what was probably the golden age of the Church.[263] Its personnel and property were no longer controlled by secular power. On the contrary, it is she now who wields the power of making, or unmaking, princes. The Church began to get the upper hand in governing all aspects of Christian life especially thorough the decrees of the pope, who was "more exalted than all the priests of the whole world and foremost among them."[264] Under such control and influence, the opportunity exists for the Church to zealously apply its integrated ethical system that she had repeatedly claimed to be holy, just, good and valid for, and applicable to every place and time. However, her teaching upon interest seems to become a test-case for this claim. Intellectual arguments justifying the practice were seen probably as a threat to the traditional Christian morality at large.[265] Probably infuriated by the voracity and sheer volume of such arguments St. Bernard of Clairvaux advised Pope Eugenious III to ignore the wrangling of jurists, and deal with lawyers as Christ did with the money-lenders in the Temple. With the passage of time the Church seems to begin to lose patience indeed. By 1312, at the Council of Vienne it was declared that anyone arguing that interest is not a sin "is to be punished as a heretic, and inquisitors are to proceed against him."[266] This should not be surprising, as Tawney noted, because:

> "... the issue at stake was not merely a legal technicality. It was the fate of the whole scheme of mediaeval thought, which had attempted to treat economic affairs as part of a hierarchy of values, embracing all interests and activities, of which the apex was religion."[267]

The economic changes, which accompanied the commercial revival of the eleventh and twelfth centuries, also contributed to making the debate on the subject of interest increasingly vigorous in this period.[268] The growth of towns, the development of the handicraft industries, the increase in the bulk of trade, the establishment of retail markets, fairs, etc., brought about profound changes in the commercial life of Europe.[269] The lending and credit, which is never absent in the agrarian economy, came now to play a great role under these new economic conditions. The growing demand for productive loans as well as the abundant sources of liquid capital to which the borrowers for consumption had now access both resulted in increasing the interest-based loan contracts. "Now almost everywhere," declared the Third Lateran Council, 1179, "has the practice of usury become so notorious that many, giving up other forms of business, traffic in usury as though this were a legitimate occupation."[270] In attempting to curb this widespread profusion of the practice, the Church appears to resort to imposing severe penalties on those involved, threatening them, first, to be deprived of communion, Christian burial, as well as rejecting their offerings and alms.[271] And later, the threats included the excommunication of rulers and magistrates of states or communities which permitted usury, as declared in the Councils of Lyons (1274) and refusal of confession, of absolution, the invalidation of wills of Vienne (1312).[272] Nevertheless, the efficiency of these penalties is questionable since myriad contractual innovations were devised to evade the prohibition at the time. This will be discussed in greater detail below.

However, this ecclesiastical attack on usury occurred in conjunction with an intellectual attack led by a group of pioneering academic scholars who were known as the Scholastics or Schoolmen, the most influential of whom was St. Thomas Aquinas (1225-1274). In view of the economic and political changes, these Scholastics probably realised that the problem of the morality of interest needed a broader approach. In the Patristic age, people might have inclined to accept a theological rule simply because it was a theological rule. Moreover, the Patristic justification for interest prohibition relied primarily on the social consequences of the practice. Under the commercial revival experienced at the time, such justifications were probably not convincing enough, especially since the loans were now being given more for commercial purposes, rather than for purposes of consumption. Furthermore, the early Fathers and Canonists often cited from the Hebrew Bible to prove the wrongness of usury, but at the time of the Scholastics the Mosaic Laws were no longer received as functional for Christian believers. Bearing in mind the uncertainty as to whether Jesus had prohibited interest in Luke 6 or not, confirmation of the ban had to be provided as well as rationalised on different grounds.

Obviously, the Schoolmen faced a harder task than their predecessors, the Church-fathers and the Canonists, in addressing the problem of usury.

THE SCHOLASTIC INTERPRETATION[i]

Nevertheless, the approach of the schoolmen to the subject is unique in that it synthesised biblical injunctions, the terminology of Roman law and Aristotelian principles of justice into a coherent theory of credit and usury. As well described by McCall, the Schoolmen translated the general biblical prohibition (divine law) against usury into the language of the Roman law (man-made law) and justified them in terms of Aristotelian philosophy (natural law).[273]

At one point Roman law had sophisticated rules concerning contracts.[ii] Loan contracts were characterized according to whether ownership of the commodity being loaned was transferred during the period of the loan. In a *commodatum*[274] the use of a commodity, i.e. the usufruct, was transferred to the borrower but the ownership remained with the lender. Two developments on the *commodatum* existed: the *locatio*, where free transfer was replaced with a charge for lending the commodity; and the *foenus* where a premium was charged for the loan. These contracts were considered legitimate because ownership, and the associated possibility of loss, remained with the lender. Therefore, the lender was permitted to impose charges beyond the return of the original commodity, or what modern law would call 'rent'.

---

i   For the sake of brevity, and to avoid the inclusion of a comprehensive description of the scholastic position, which would require a complete survey by author or chronology, the focus of this section will be based on the Scholastic usury doctrine as presented in its most advanced and elaborate form in the writing of St. Thomas Aquinas. For further details see in general, Noonan, *The Scholastic Analysis of Usury*, op. cit.

ii Roman law addresses a considerable number of individual contracts, but with no general theory. These contracts have been classified, in the *Institutes* of both Gaius and Justinian, into four categories, real, verbal, literal and consensual. See, A. Watson, *Roman Law & Comparative Law* (University of Georgia Press 1991); R. Zimmermann, *The Law of Obligations: Roman Foundations of the Civilian Tradition* (Juta 1990); G. Poitras, *The Early History of Financial Economics* (Edward Elgar Publishing, Incorporated 2000)

In a *mutuum*, the ownership of the loaned commodity was transferred during the period of the loan to the borrower. Since he became the 'new' owner, the borrower can use or even consume the commodity so long as the same quality and quantity of the commodity was given back at the maturity date. *Mutuum*, therefore, is most suitable to the lending of fungibles, or things that are calculated by weight, number, or measure such as corn, wine etc. It would not apply to the loan of a commodity with special characteristics, such as a horse or a house. Because the ownership of the commodity in a *mutuum* remained with the borrower during the period of the loan, it was considered illicit to impose any charge over and above the return of the commodity in question.[i]

The scholastic analysis of the nature of usury was worked out within the framework of this classification. In the *Summa Theologica*, St. Thomas Aquinas identifies money as belonging to the category of fungible goods and therefore shall be lent only through the gratuitous contractual form of the *mutuum*.[275]

Influenced by the Aristotelian concept of the sterility of money, Aquinas argued that the principal function of money is to serve as a medium of exchange.[276] Its principal use is its consumption, i.e. one can use the money only by giving it away, or by spending it on something. Money is consumed in its use, and like any other consumed-in-use commodity, its use cannot be separated from its ownership. For example, A cannot lend to B the use of one hundred pounds and at the same time retain the ownership of it; otherwise B will not be able to use it. Therefore, a money loan

---

i In general Roman law preserved the gratuitous contractual form of the *mutuum*. During the period when it permitted the charging of a fee for a loan, viz. charging interest, it was conducted through a separate *stipulatio* in which the borrower promised to pay fees. However, it has been argued that the *mutuum* and *stipulatio* are reflecting different type of legal obligations and therefore it could not be combined in one contract. See, Zimmermann, op. cit., p. 155, 158, 163

shall be transacted, not through *commodatum* but only, through *mutuum*, in which the ownership of the commodity passes to the borrower.

As Roman law admitted, the lending of a fungible commodity necessarily implied the transfer of dominion as well as possession. This means that the contract of *mutuum* is essentially a contract of sale; it achieved a similar end to a sale contract in that both the ownership and the use of the goods passed from one party to the other. It is conceived and dealt with on this basis by Aquinas. Once the contract of *mutuum* had been shown to be nothing other than a sale of fungibles, the principle of justice, or strictly speaking, commutative justice, is held to be applicable. Commutative justice is, also, an Aristotelian principle that requires equality in all transactions of exchange between individuals in society. Aquinas re-introduced the principle as follows:

> "In commutations something is paid to an individual on account of something of his that has been received, as may be seen chiefly in selling and buying, where the notion of commutation is found primarily. Hence it is necessary to equalize thing with thing, so that the one person should pay back to the other just so much as he has become richer out of that which belonged to the other. The result of this will be equality according to the "arithmetical mean" which is gauged according to equal excess in quantity."[i]

Equality in exchange transactions was seen as morally required because this type of transaction was designed for the mutual benefit of both parties.[277] They are exchanging things because

---

i   He then gives an example that:
"… if, at the start, both persons have 5, and one of them receives 1 out of the other's belongings, the one that is receiver, will have 6, and the other will be left with 4: and so there will be justice if both be brought back to the mean, 1 taken from him that has 6, and given to him that has 4, for then both have 5 which is the mean." See, ibid., q. 61, a. 1-2

each will find utility in the thing received in exchange from the other. It would be unjust, therefore, for one party to bear the cost of a mutually beneficial transaction. Now, because human beings have started to use money as a medium of exchange between commodities, they should provide a 'just price' for these goods, i.e. a price that corresponds to the actual value of the goods at the time. As referred to by Aquinas:

> "Now whatever is established for the common advantage should not be more of a burden to one party than to the other, and consequently all contracts between them should observe equality of thing and thing. Again the quality of a thing that comes into human use is measured by the price given for it, for which purpose money was invented, as stated in *Ethic.* v, 5. Therefore if either the price exceeds the quantity of the thing's worth, or, conversely, the thing exceeds the price, there is no longer the equality of justice: and consequently to sell a thing for more than its worth, or to buy it for less than its worth, is in itself unjust and unlawful."[278]

Because the contract of *mutuum* is de facto a contract of exchange of fungible items, it is simple to identify the just price for it – which should be the return of fungibles of the same quality and quantity.[279] To put the same in another way, it would be unjust to sell one kilo of corn in exchange for two kilos of corn of the same quality. Likewise, if the particular fungible sold happened to be money, the estimation of the just price was the return of an amount of money of equal value. Those who argued that something additional might be claimed for the use of the money neglected the fact that the money was incapable of being used apart from its being consumed.[280] To ask for payment for the sale of a thing which not only did not exist, but which was quite incapable of existence, was tantamount to asking something from nothing which is of course violating the equivalence of value demanded by commutative justice. Aquinas says:

> "In those things whose use is their consumption, the use is not other than the thing itself; whence to whomever is conceded the use of such things, is conceded the ownership of those things, and conversely. When, therefore, someone lends money under this agreement that the money be integrally restored to him, and further for the use of the money wishes to have a definite price, it is manifest that he sells separately the use of the money and the very substance of the money. The use of money, however, as it is said, is not other than its substance: whence either he sells that which is not, or he sells the same thing twice, to wit, the money itself, whose use is its consumption and this, is manifestly against the nature of natural justice."[281]

This argument is known as the "consumptibility argument."[282] Different examples were given by Aquinas in order to illustrate the injustice of the practice.[283] From his point of view, charging interest on loans is equivalent to charging for a bottle of wine, and then charging the person again for using the wine to drink it, or charging for a kilo of wheat, and then charging the person again who uses the wheat to consume it. This charging for *usura* (from the Latin noun 'use') is obviously unjust.[284] Likewise, the money-lender who charges for transferring the ownership of a sum of money to the debtor, and gets his price, in the form of the return of the same amount at the maturity date, and who charges moreover for the use of money, by demanding interest. He, by doing so is actually charging for something that does not exist, namely, the use of the money; or he is charging for the same thing twice, the money itself. In both cases, his practice offends against the principle of commutative justice.

Some scholastics, although they arrived at the same deduction as Thomas Aquinas, provided different arguments. Duns Scotus (1266 – 1308) argued that since the borrower becomes the owner of the loaned money during the period of the loan according to the *mutuum* contract, the lender has no right to take any return for the use of this money during this period. Otherwise, the latter will be getting compensation for the use of a property that does not actually belong to him. Furthermore, he said:

> "... even admitting that the money remains the lender's, still money does not naturally produce any fruit like other productive things – there is merely a sort of fruit arising from the industry of the borrower. Hence he who wishes a return for money lent seeks what is really the fruit of labour which has not been handed over in virtue of the contract of *mutuum*."[285]

Apparently, Scotus relies in his argument on the Aristotelian concept of the sterility of money in order to demonstrate the injustice of usury.

The third major argument presented by scholastics is known as 'free time argument'. It was fully developed by William of Auxerre (1160-1229). In dealing with charging a higher price for credit than for cash sales, Auxerre argued that a man who charges interest on a loan has charged, in effect, for the passage of time rather than any changes in value of the commodity bought. By doing so he violates both natural and divine law, Auxerre explained as follows:

> "He [the usurer] acts against the universal natural law, because he sells time, which is common to all creatures. Augustine says ... each creature is compelled to give himself; the sun is compelled to give itself to illuminate; similarly the earth is compelled to give whatever it can, and similarly the water. Nothing, however, so naturally gives itself as time:

willy-nilly things have time. Because, therefore, the usurer sells what necessarily belongs to all creatures generally he injures all creatures, even the stones; whence if men were silent against the usurers, the stones would cry out, if they could; and this is one reason why the Church so pursues the usurers. Whence especially against them God says, 'When I shall take up the time, that is, when time will be so in My hand that a usurer cannot sell it, then I will judge justly."[286]

These and other arguments have been deployed by Schoolmen in attempting to provide rational explanations for the rejection of usury. The ultimate conclusion drawn from these arguments is that usury is by its very nature unjust. This implies that its justification could not be effected by any social good it may achieve; and the existence of social evils would only aggravate its evil character. Put another way, it makes no difference whether money is lent to a well-to-do businessman who intends to invest it in a profitable venture or to a pauper who is jobless and has an ill wife and a number of hungry children. In both cases anything beyond the principal of the loan was seen, *per se*, as being contrary to natural justice.[287] Usury was, therefore:

> "any excess whatsoever above the principle of *mutuum*, or loan, exacted by parties to the loan itself, either according to contract or without previous agreement ... whether the rate was high or low, excessive or moderate ... [and regardless] the purpose of the loan."[288]

Extrinsic Titles

Yet, confining the raison d'être for interest prohibition to the fact that it runs counter to natural justice seems to result in loopholes in the form of what the Church and canon law called extrinsic titles.[i] Based upon the same principle of commutative justice, scholastics argued that under certain extrinsic titles, i.e. conditions, the lender is entitled to demand a payment on *mutuum* beyond the return of the original fungible commodity, i.e. to receive a return over principal. While a number of different types of these titles developed,[ii] three were of particular importance: *poena conventionalis; interesse*, which includes *damnum emergens* and *lucrum cessans*. Most of these titles were again borrowed from Roman law.

Chronologically, the first one widely used was the *poena conventionalis*, or a penalty for late payment.[289] Similar to a forfeiture clause, it is a provision inserted in a loan contract to the effect that a financial penalty is to be paid by the debtor if he fails to return the loan at the designated time. An example of such agreement is given by Robert de Courcon in his *De Usura* "I shall let you have a hundred pounds until a certain date, and if you do not then return the hundred you shall pay me as a penalty two hundred instead."[290] Early writers such as Huguccio (d. 1210) and Bernard of Pavia (d. 1213) allowed this kind of agreement by the justification that the penalty levied for the delay is only for encouraging the debtor to pay on time, and thus protecting the creditor from any dilatory tactics.[iii] The justice of the title was also upheld by Alexander of Hales, Duns Scotus and William of Auxerre. The latter contended that "it is just to punish negligent or fraudulent deferment of due payment."[291]

i They are called *extrinsic titles* because they were based on circumstance outside the loan itself, as will be seen.

ii Cardinal Hostiensis enumerated thirteen situations in which, he argued, charging interest was not immoral. See, De Roover, 'The scholastics, usury, and foreign exchange'.

iii Bernard states: "for this, for fear of the penalty the debtor will pay on the agreed day." See, Barnard of Pavia, V:15:9 quoted in Noonan, *The Scholastic Analysis of Usury*, op. cit., p. 107

Nevertheless, principal plus penalty would in effect be the same as a loan at interest. It is no wonder that it was used largely by merchants and money-lenders so as to evade the sanctions of canon law, very often by means of simulating a short term loan and an early default of the borrower.[292] Effectively, when the creditor knew in advance that the debtor would not be capable of returning the loan at the agreed time, the penalty payment became but a disguised form of usury. Scotus referred to this fact when he said: "A manifest sign that a penalty is not in fraud of usury is this: the merchant prefers to have his money returned to him on the agreed day, than to have it tomorrow with the penalty added."[293]

While *poena conventionalis* is a penalty agreed upon in advance for a delay in debt payment, *interesse* is based upon compensation for any loss suffered by the creditor resulting from such delay. The term – *interesse* – derives its name from the words of the Justinian Code "*id quod interesse*," i.e. the difference between.[294] By Roman law, if a debtor failed to make a payment when due, he could be forced to pay the creditor, in addition to the repayment of the loan, a compensation which is estimated by the difference resulting to the creditor's financial position due to the default of the debtor.[295] [i] Such compensatory payment, or interest, was aimed at ensuring that the lender incurred no damage by virtue of engaging in the transaction. Its justification, therefore, as a form of compensation has also been admitted by the scholastics given that it would be unjust

---

i   To put it another way, the borrower was seen as obliged to indemnify the lender for any loss the latter had incurred by reason of the delay in the payment. The amount of such loss is measured by the difference which there is between his financial position had he received the loan on time and his position with the debtor having failed to pay. Once this difference is proved to have occurred, the lender becomes entitled to charge *interesse*. Etymologically, the term 'interest' is derived from the Latin '*inter*' and '*est*' ('between' and 'is').

to the lender to find himself in a worse position because of his having made a gratuitous loan.[296]

However, the legists of the 12-13th centuries developed two *extrinsic* titles under which interest can be claimed. These titles are *damnum emergens* (damage suffered) and *lucrum cessans* (loss of income).[297] In the former, the compensation is given to the lender when the delay in the repayment causes him to incur actual loss, whereas in the latter it is given when the lender, by parting with his funds, misses an opportunity to make a profit elsewhere, or what modern economists refer to as 'opportunity cost'.

The title *damnum emergens* was never seriously questioned by the Scholastics. It was recognised by Albertus Magnus, Alexander of Hales, St. Raymond, John of Rupella and many others.[298] Thomas Aquinas justified it as follows:

> "A lender may without sin enter an agreement with the borrower for compensation for the loss he incurs of something he ought to have, for this is not to sell the use of money, but to avoid a loss. It may also happen that the borrower avoids a greater loss than the lender incurs, wherefore the borrower may repay the lender with what he has gained."[299]

The example which scholastics frequently used to prove the justice of such claim was the case of a creditor, who himself is forced to borrow money at usury to conduct his business, because his loaned money was not returned on time.[300] However, it is of importance to note that *damnum emergens* entitled the lender to be compensated only if he proved a real loss has been incurred by reason of the delay after the expiration of the loan period.

Lucrum cessans, on the other hand, was only gradually accepted and it took until the fifteenth century before it was universally admitted. The basic problem with this title, and the reason for its rejection by many earlier scholastics such as Scotus, Durandus, Laurentius de Rudolphis and others, is that the lender's claim that he would have gained profit from his loaned money appears to be too hypothetical. To ask compensation for something that did not exist, and might never even have existed, is again equivalent to receiving something for nothing, which violates the principle of commutative justice. As noted by Aquinas:

> "the lender cannot enter an agreement for compensation, through the fact that he makes no profit out of his money: because he must not sell that which he has not yet and may be prevented in many ways from having."[301]

He explained this point in further detail when he was dealing with the problem of restitution:

> "... a man may damnify another by preventing him from obtaining what he was on the way to obtain. A loss of this kind need not be made good in equivalent; because to have a thing virtually is less than to have it actually, and to be on the way to obtain a thing is to have it merely virtually or potentially, and so were he to be indemnified by receiving the thing actually, he would be paid, not the exact value taken from him, but more ... the sower of the seed in the field, has the harvest, not actually but only virtually. In like manner he that has money has the profit not yet actually but only virtually: and both may be hindered in many ways."[302]

However, with the expansion of commerce and continually increasing opportunities of investment in the fourteenth and fifteenth centuries, the title appeared to start gaining recognition among many later scholastics though haltingly and under certain qualifying conditions.[303] For these theologians a claim for *lucrum cessans* might be properly put forward by a lender provided that (a) the compensation demanded be reasonable;[i] (b) the creditor proved that an opportunity for

---

i "Lenders," says Jean Buridan (d. 1358), "must not take by way of *lucrum*

profitable investment had been really lost and (c) the loaned money be first lent gratuitously for at least a short period of time.[304] Or in the words of Ambrose de Vignate, compensation must only be made for "the time and just *interesse* of the lost gain, which must be certain and proximate."[305] Some of these conditions were relaxed later nonetheless. The legist Paul de Castro (d. 1441) agreed that a proof of loss of profit could be dispensed with if the lender was a merchant.[306] Peter of Ancarano (d.1459) and Antoninus of Florence (d.1416) extended this concession to non-merchants if they intended to invest their funds in business.[307]

A commonly shared theme between *poena conventionalis* and *interesse*, including *damnum emergens* and *lucrum cessans*, is that they all involved fault on the part of the debtor and actual delay in his repayment of the loan. The scholastics who give these titles a qualified approval justified them on grounds of compensation for the non-return of the money in the stipulated time.[308] The axiom in common use at the time was that "Interest is only owing where there has been delay."[309] The stress laid on the element of the delay is because the interest charge under these titles was seen as a means to avoid loss sustained by reason of delay but not taking gain, or rewarding for the use of money. Hence, in all these titles the creditor is compensated only when the time for repayment has passed and the debtor still has not paid.

A hypothetical question, however, that may arise is that if the lender is morally entitled to be compensated for the loss he would incur after the expiration of the loan period, with this line of reasoning, why then should he not also be compensated for the loss he would have incurred during the contractual period of the loan? St. Thomas and Scotus responded to the question that in the first case the fault is on the part of the debtor who delayed in his debt payment, but in the

---

cessans more than they would have actually made by commerce or in exchange." Quoted in ibid.

second case it is on the part of the creditor who could simply have kept himself unharmed by not engaging in the loan contract in the first place.[310] As noted by Scotus:

> "If [the lender] does not wish to be injured, let him keep back the money he needs, because no-one forces him to do a merciful deed for his neighbour; but if he prefers to show mercy to the other, he is compelled by the divine law not to vitiate the divine law."[311]

Therefore, to identify interest from the beginning of a loan or during its normal term was considered by at least the early scholastics as removing the foundations of the usury prohibition. However, some later theologians such as Bernardino of Siena and Laurentius of Florence argued that interest from the beginning of a loan may be intrinsically lawful.[312] But then what remains of the usury doctrine? This would not only undermine the very notion of *interesse*, but also throw the doors wide open to usurers and bankers. As noted by Mills:

> "This admission that '*lucrum cessans*' could be charged from the outset of a loan proved to be the genesis of uniform rates of interest and a banking system that gave interest upon deposits. It is clearly inconvenient for the lender to have to calculate the profit that he has forgone on every loan made and so it was eventually admitted that *lucrum cessans* could be declared by the lender as a single percentage interest rate that could be charged to each borrower. Once such an admission is made, the development of a banking system and 'money market' cannot be long delayed. If a lender could definitely receive 5% interest as compensation for profit forgone, a bank could also offer him 5% as compensation for making a deposit with it rather than making the loan. The bank

could then justify charging at least 5% for the loans it gave by referring to the cost it was having to incur to attract the deposit or the profit that it was forgoing by not depositing the money with another bank."[313]

Further discussion of the impact of these titles and others on the development of the financial practices of the time will be provided in the next chapter.

With the development of extrinsic titles, the scholastic condemnation of usury appears to be both more severe and more lenient than that of the early Fathers. It is more severe in that it considers all usury to be unjust irrespective of the rate or the purpose of the loan, whereas it is more lenient in that it allows the charging of "interest" even on loans to the poor so long as a proper *extrinsic* title is involved. On the one hand, the Scholastics depict anything received above the loan principal as intrinsically evil but on the other they approved a range of extrinsic *titles* through which a similar end could be achieved. This paradox seems to cause endless difficulties and specious arguments that did so much to bring, to some extent, scholasticism into disrepute, as will be seen.

THE FIVE PER CENT CONTRACT AND THE JESUITS

Generally speaking there was unanimous agreement among Catholic theologians in accepting the fundamental principles of the Scholastic doctrine of usury, at least until the end of the seventeenth century.[314] Yet they disagreed upon what extrinsic titles conferred a right to demand a return over the principal. The disagreements also included a number of interest-masking transactions that were common at the time; of particular concern is *contractum trinius* (lit. the triple contract).

Notably widespread in German speaking lands, the *contractum trinius* involved the combination of three different contracts: a contract of partnership, a contract of insurance; and a contract of sale of profit. Individually, these contracts were deemed permissible by the Church, but collectively they yielded a fixed rate of return from the outset. The way it worked was as follows: the lender would invest a sum, equal to the amount of financing required, with the merchant on a profit-and-loss sharing basis.[315] The lender, then, would insure his capital invested against a loss by means of purchasing insurance from the merchant himself in return for an assignment of the future probable gain. And, finally, the lender would sell to the merchant his share of the uncertain future gain resulting from the investment in exchange for lesser but certain gain, which often amounted to the rate of five percent of the original capital.[i] The net result of these three concurrent and interrelated agreements is that the merchant bore all the risk of failure, while the lender received a fixed rate of return at the end of the period of contract regardless whether the business failed or succeeded. This is tantamount to lending money at a pre-arranged guaranteed fixed rate of return – usury. The practice, therefore, attracted increasing attention from many Catholic moralist and legists in the fifteenth and sixteenth centuries.[316]

It has been defended by such authorities as Angelus de Clavasio, Gabriel Biel, Conrad Summenhart and his pupil John Eck (d.1543).[317] The latter, in his argument at the University of Ingolstadt outside Augsburg, is said even to have defended the opinion that a rate of five percent could be directly contracted for on a loan to a merchant. His opinion was received jubilantly by merchants and money-lenders. As a response to the complaint of

---

i   For instance, (A) invests £100 in (B) for one year. (A) would then insure himself against any loss of wealth by means of a second contract agreed with (B) at a cost to (A) of £5. Finally, (A) would sell back to (B) the right of any future profits of the investment, for a fee of £10 to be paid by (B). The result of these three simultaneously agreed contracts was an interest payment of £5 on a loan of £100 made by (A) to (B). See, ibid.; McCall, op. cit., p.. 90-92, 113; William James Ashley, *An Introduction to English Economic History and Theory: The End of the Middle Ages* (1906), p. 211

the canonists, however, the bishop forbids any further discussion, and Eck was insulted as a scandal monger.[318] Yet, financed by the Fuggers – the most prominent commercial and banking house in Augsburg – Eck travelled to the university of Bologna (the highest authority in Canon law), and argued in favour of the contract for five hours with the dean of its theological faculty, but no official decision was given.

Eck and those who followed his lead, most notably John Mair (d.1550), argued that each part of the triple contract (the partnership contract, the insurance of the capital invested and the exchange of the unlimited share of profits for a fixed return) is permissible, and thus the combination of them shall be permissible as well.[i] Those who disagreed with him, on the other hand, retorted that such combination contracted away the essential element of partnership, i.e. sharing risk, which makes the whole practice but a loan at interest. On this basis, it was reprobated by the majority of Catholic theologians of the sixteenth century. In 1565, a provincial synod at Milan declared that no contract should be made under the forms of partnership by which the return of the principal should be guaranteed.[319] In the same vein, Pope Sixtus V in Bull *Detestabilis* (1583) outlawed any sort of promise by one of two partners to restore the capital unimpaired.[320]

Nevertheless, the practice continued to grow, and in the following centuries the consensus of moralists and canonists seems to have turned in its favour. It was gaining acceptance by many Jesuit theologians such as Petrus de Navarra, Toletus, Gregory de Valencia and Bonacina, Lopez, Gibalinus and

---

i "A man could enter into partnership with B; he could insure himself with C against the loss of his capital; and he could insure himself with D against fluctuations in the rate of profit. If all this was morally justifiable, why should not A make the three contracts with the same man B?" Ashley, *An Introduction to English Economic History and Theory: The End of the Middle Ages*, op. cit., p. 211

many others.³²¹ The triple contract became better known as "the five per cent contract", so named on account of the yields that it typically produced for the lender. Five per cent was perceived by many to be within the range of a just price that the lender could ask for in return for selling his unlimited future profits under the triple contract. In 1567, Francis Borgia, the Secretary-General of the Jesuits, wrote to Canisius saying that Pope Pius V had been consulted by the Jesuits on the triple contract bringing a five per cent return, and that the Pope gave his opinion, as a private theologian, that it is licit.³²² But this unofficial ruling was counteracted by the official papal pronouncement in the Bull *Cum onus*. Throughout the following years, a number of scruples and difficulties related to the five per cent contract were reported to Rome for judgment but apparently received no answer. For example, in 1571, Menginus, a German Jesuit, wrote to the Jesuit procurator, protesting against the embarrassment caused by the silence on the five per cent contract, alluding to the fact that "other religions concede it, turning the whole populace from us."³²³

However, in 1573, the second Roman commission gave its report, and on receiving it, a congregation of Roman Jesuits declared that a direct loan at five per cent was usury, but a number of alternative contracts and titles to interest were not – among these was the five per cent contract. This resolution was reaffirmed in the Congregation of the Jesuits that took place in Rome in 1581. Henceforth, the Jesuits became wholly committed to the defence of the five per cent contract and advocated its 'justice'.³²⁴

Yet, the acceptance of the five per cent contract as a legitimate way to receive a return beyond the principal would be a landmark in the history of the idea of usury. Providing them with different types of contract behind which usury is regularly concealed, it is the Latin Church now who, instruct the merchants and money-lenders on how to violate the spirit, but not the letter, of the interest prohibitions. In view of the sprinkling of such transactions with holy waters, as well as the approval of the extrinsic titles, one could hardly say that the ban on usury was not effectively undermined at the time.

THE REFORMERS' APPROACH

The attitude of the reformers and Puritans towards interest was initially ambivalent. Martin Luther began by inveighing bitterly against the practice.[325] He described those involved in it as thieves, robbers, murderers as well as "great ogres in the world, who can never charge enough per cent."[326] He threatened them with denial of Christian burial if they died unrepentant.[327] Following the example of many early Fathers, Luther maintained that the references to usury in the Old Testament prohibit all sorts of interest-taking and this prohibition is further confirmed as well as universalised by Christ when he said: "lend, hoping for nothing again."[328] He said: "Where one lends money and demands or takes therefore more or better, that is usury,"[329] which is in his view a great evil, a manifestation of greed and contradictory to Christen love.[330] He also condemned the practice on the basis of the doctrine of the sterility of money, explaining that "Money is an unfruitful commodity which I cannot sell in such a way as to entitle me to a profit."[331] To the objection that the borrower may trade with loaned money and make profit, he replied, "this is merely an accidental profit and on accidentals no rules can be based."[332] As to the question of how the Jews were permitted to lend on interest, Luther curiously enough answered that:

> "It was not and is not permitted them because of their merit or by common law but through the wrath of God over the Gentiles, which he wants to fulfil through the Jews as instruments of wrath ... God chose and received them only out of mercy. Thus if you view the matter properly, it

is not the Jews themselves who are usurers, but God, who persecutes the Gentiles through the usury of the Jews."³³³

This 'wrath of God' seems to have been brought down upon his country at the time. In his open letter to the Christian nobility of the German nation, he noted:

> "The greatest misfortune of the Germans is buying on usury. But for this, many a man would have to leave unbought his silk, velvet, cloth of gold, spices, and all other luxuries. The system has not been in force for more than one hundred years, and has already brought poverty, misery, and destruction on almost all princes, foundations, cities, nobles, and heirs. If it continues for another hundred years Germany will be left without a farthing, and we shall be reduced to eating one another."³³⁴

For this crisis, Luther blamed not only the devil who invented the system but also the Pope who sanctioned it. Together, he argued, they have "done untold evil throughout the world."³³⁵ From his point of view, extrinsic titles as well as a number of widespread 'Canon-compliant' transactions are but "fig-leaves" behind which usury covers its shame. He described them as a "pretty sham and pretence by which a man can oppress others without sin and become rich without labour or trouble"³³⁶ and thus, "Should be utterly condemned and prevented for the future, regardless of the opposition of the Pope and all his infamous laws [to the condemnation], and though he might have erected his pious foundations on them."³³⁷ The validity of many of these titles and contracts was questioned by him in his tracts and sermons, for example, he attacked the compensation paid under the *interesse* titles, arguing that the money-lender simply calculates as interest the loss of which he may possibly have suffered as a result of not having back the loaned money at the maturity date. "But in its efforts to make a certainty of what is uncertain, will not usury soon be the ruin of the world?"³³⁸ To those who alleged that the borrower may, out of sheer gratitude, give the lender 5, 6 or even 10 florins on the hundred, he replied, rather sarcastically: "Even an adulteress and an adulterer are thankful and pleased with each other."³³⁹

Yet, Luther's declarations on usury appear to be tempered in his later works. In a letter written to Count Wolfgang von Gleichen in 1543, Luther stated that, "if the interest applied to church were cut off, how could the ministers and schools be maintained?"³⁴⁰ Further, he recommended that the money given to support the "poor youth prosecuting their studies in Holy Scriptures" be lent out at interest, "because it is to be spent on such a good, useful and necessary work."³⁴¹ Likewise, he allowed elders and poor widows and orphans to engage in the practice but only if they could support themselves in no other way. In a pragmatic way, Luther also declared, in a letter to Gregory Bruck, that "people should be encouraged to endure this wrong [i.e., usury] in a Christian way for a while, and to pay the interest until things are improved."³⁴² Strangely, however, it has been reported that in his *Table Talk* in May of 1540, Luther said: "one must observe a little equity, the value of goods has gone up not a little, and one can enjoy a greater profit now than formally. Accordingly, I'm happy to concede what the law and emperor allow, namely five or six percent [interest]."³⁴³ This comment is similar to his assertion in his *Tract on Trade and Usury* where he declared that if usury can be practised "without violating canon law, which provides for the payment of four, five, or six gulden hundred, it may be tolerated."ⁱ

---

i   Ibid. However, as noted by Munro, it seems that historians are far from unanimous on Luther's views concerning usury, some contending that his views do not differ substantially from those of Calvin, which will be presented below, see R. Bainton, *The Reformation of the Sixteenth Century*, Boston 1952 (revised edn, 1985), pp. 247-250, others suggesting that it is Luther's anti-Semitism which influenced his hostility to usury, see *Martin Luther: Theology and Revolution*, translated C. FOSTER, Jr., New York 1991, pp. 369-371. The contention in N. JONES, *God and the Moneylender*,

However, the views of many contemporary reformers were very traditional. Huldreich Zwingli (1484-1531), the founder of the Reformation in Switzerland, considered usury a serious sin that is to be punished by excommunication. He saw usury as a form of unjust and parasitic profit that was prohibited by the Law of God,[i] "God bids us give our worldly goods to the poor and needy without return ... and then he bids us lend without usury.... For this reason, everyone who as much tolerates a licensed Jew or other usurer, so art thou a thief or robber."[344] The German Swiss reformer Philipp Melanchthon (1497-1560) also stated, in a language reminiscent of the Scotus' argument, that:

> "In making loans, such gain demanded over and above the principal, merely on account of the lending itself, is really and truly usury.... Taking usuries is gaining at another's expense, because the loan has transferred out-right ownership, and in fact the thing is not by nature productive. Therefore the gain is not fair."[345]

Yet, Melanchthon admitted the justification of the extrinsic titles of *damnum emergens* and *lucrum cessans*. With the later scholastics, he taught that interest could be contracted for even before the expiration of the loan period.

> "But of emergent loss and cessant gain before delay on the loan, the laws in fact give no action, unless it be

---

cit., pp. 14-15, that Luther supported interest-bearing loans for support of the church and the poor is not substantiated by Bainton; but, according to Jones, Luther did not accept Old Testament dictums on usury as binding. Jones also contends (p. 15), without documentary evidence, that Luther endorsed the right of secular magistrates to "regulate interest for the good of the community." See John H Munro, *Usury, Calvinism, and Credit in Protestant England: from the Sixteenth Century to the Industrial Revolution* (2011)

i   Apparently, he used a language reminiscent of the early Fathers who depicted usury as a shameful gain.

stipulated in the contract what is to be paid by way of interest.... My answer is: It is licit to make stipulations about interest payable before delay."[346]

In the meanwhile, however, a new Christian theory on usury was being developed, mainly by French reformers. This theory attempts to justify the taking of interest by direct rather than by the indirect methods of Scholastic teaching. It could be seen as an application of Occam's Razor to the roundabout process of the extrinsic titles and triple contract.[347] This new approach was at first more critical than constructive, and was advocated only by a minority but later it became a powerful movement followed by many Protestants as well as some Catholic moralists. Some even argued that it was the birth of the modern interest-based capitalist economy.[348]

Calvinism – a Counter theory

For long centuries whatever was added to the principal was deemed usury in Christian thought. Church Fathers, Councils, Canonists, Popes and Scholastics drew no distinction neither between rates of interest nor between the purposes of loans. All usury was damned and prohibited. The first to make the break with this tradition was highly likely the Protestant leader John Calvin (1509-1564).[i] In a letter to Sachinus in 1545, Calvin expressed that he did not consider usury to be wholly forbidden among Christians unless it be repugnant both to justice and to

---

i   It seems difficult to identify who was the first to depart from the tradition. Rose, Roover and Noonan maintain that it was John Calvin. Divine said that it might be Charles Dumoulin (1500–1566). Munro contends that Calvin's views were influenced by the Catholic jurist Charles du Moulin (1500-1566). They all, however, lived in France in the sixteenth century. See respectively, H. Shields Rose, *The Churches and Usury or, The Morality of Five Per Cent* (Clark 1900), p. 29; De Roover, 'The scholastics, usury, and foreign exchange', op. cit., p. 258; Noonan, *The Scholastic Analysis of Usury*, op. cit., p. 365; Munro, op. cit., p. 261; Divine, op. cit., p. 89

charity.³⁴⁹ These principles, he argued, are not to be violated by charging a rich man for the use of money especially in view of the new conditions and circumstances of economic life, wherein both creditor and debtor may gain by a loan at interest.³⁵⁰ In the case of making a loan to a rich man, Calvin, posed this question: "Why should the lender be cheated of his just due, if the money profits the other man and he be the richer of the two?"³⁵¹ In defence of his views, Calvin challenged the essentials of the traditional doctrine arguing that the prohibitions of usury in the Old Testament were exclusive to the Jews,ⁱ that the passages of the New Testament imply not a universal condemnation but rather require the observance of charity and equity toward the poor, and that the early Fathers' condemnations were applicable only to the special circumstances of the times.ⁱⁱ In answer to the argument of the infertility of money, Calvin said:

"The reasoning of Saint Ambrose and of Chrysostomⁱⁱⁱ

i Calvin said: "Now it is said that today, too, usury should be forbidden on the same grounds as among the Jews, since there is a bond of brotherhood among us. To this I reply, that in the civil state there is some difference; for the situation in which the Lord had placed the Jews, and many other circumstances, made it easy for them to engage in business among themselves without usury. Our relationship is not at all the same." Cited in Harkness, op. cit., p. 206

ii He said: "In the first place, by no testimony of the Scriptures is usury wholly condemned. For the meaning of the saying of Christ, commonly thought to be very clear, i.e., "Lend, hoping for nothing again" (Luke 6:35) has been perverted. As elsewhere in speaking of the sumptuous feasts and ambitious social rivalry of the rich he commands rather that they invite in the blind, the lame and the poor from the streets who cannot make a like return, so here, wishing to curb abuses in lending, he directs us to loan chiefly to those from whom there is no hope of receiving anything ... The words of Christ mean that he commends serving the poor rather than the rich. Thus we do not find all usury forbidden." Cited in ibid.

iii Interestingly, Calvin refers to this argument not as Aristotle's but as St. Ambrose's and St. John Chrysostom's. This would indicate that he recognised that the attitude of the early Fathers was against all usurious

that money does not beget money, is in my judgment too superficial. What does the sea beget? What does the land? I receive income from the rental of a house. Is it because the money grows there? The earth produces things from which money is made, and the use of a house can be bought for money. And is not money more fruitful in trade than in any other form of possession one can mention? Is it lawful to let a farm, requiring a payment in return, and unlawful to receive and profit from the use of money?" And: "How do merchants derive their profit? By their industry, you will say. Certainly if money is shut up in a strong-box, it will be barren – a child can see that. But whoever asks a loan of me does not intend to keep this money idle and gain nothing. The profit is not in the money itself, but in the return that comes from its use. It is necessary then to draw the conclusion that while such subtle distinction appear on the surface to have some weight, they vanish on closer scrutiny, for they have no substance."[352]

Yet Calvin gives no free rein to the practice. He permits interest payments but only under certain restrictions: (1) "that usury never be demanded of poor and needy men"; (2) "that he who lends be not addicted to his gain and profit," while maintaining proper regard for his poorer brethren; (3) "that no condition inserted or put into the covenant of the loan [be] other than is agreeable to Christ's commandment"; (4) "that he who borrows ... may gain as much or more by the money than he who lends"; (5) that we must not "measure equity by the iniquity of the race of mankind, but by God's word alone"; (6) that "covenants drawn up [involving loans] stand rather to the good than to the harm of the commonwealth"; and, finally, (7) "that we exceed not the maximum rate or limit laid down in any country or commonwealth."[353]

---

loans whether for consumption or production purposes.

Thus, as described by the Protestant divine Roger Fenton (1565-1615), Calvin seems to deal with usury "as apothecary does with poison."[354] He attacked a general usury prohibition, but did not approve outright usury permission either. He believed that reasonable usury is necessary for business, but it would be better if all usury were abolished.[355] Furthermore, he condemned those who habitually took usury as a major part of their income, inciting their expulsion from the Church of God and the well-ordered state.[i][356] The fact that Calvin was not enthusiastic about permitting usury appears also in his refusing of the interest titles allowed by scholastics. They are just innovations designed to evade the laws against usury and they deceive not God. Referring to those who pretend not to lend at usury under these titles, Calvin says:

> "They treat usury as if it were compensation of as much loss as the difference caused by the lack of the use of their money. But there is no kind of usury which this specious title may not cloak. For each one has present money, when he loans it, which would have been useful to him if he had bought something, and at each moment matter of profit presents itself. So always will there be a place for compensation, since no creditor gives his money to another without loss."[357]

Bearing in mind that through extrinsic titles "interest" could be charged even on loans to the poor, Calvin appears to be more relentless than the scholastics on this point. But by allowing a direct interest on commercial loans he is obviously more concessional than the Jesuits who approved the triple contract and the like. In practice, however, all of them appear to share the same outcome. For what Calvin justified by its own right, the scholastics would

---

i   In his *Institutes*, Calvin stated that "it is a very rare thing for a man to be honest and at the same time a usurer." Cited in Harkness, op. cit., p. 210; Noonan, *The Scholastic Analysis of Usury*, op. cit., p. 366

concede by the presence of extrinsic titles and Jesuits by the triple contract.

In summary, Calvin's opinion was that 'moderate' usury on business loans and on loans to the rich are legitimate, but that the usury taken from the poor or taken at excessive or illegal rates is uncharitable, unjust and, therefore, illegitimate. His views have been followed especially by Heinrich Bullinger (Zwingli's successor), Peter Baro and Theodore Beza. But the two reformers who notably added to the theory were Charles Du Moulin (Molinaeus) (1500–1566) and Claude Saumaise (Salmasius) (1588–1653).

Like Calvin, Molinaeus interprets the scriptural texts relevant to lending not in terms of a literal reading, but in terms of "justice and charity". He holds that only usury that is taken from the needy is biting and violates charity and is therefore prohibited.[358] In support of this position, Molinaeus undertakes to criticise a number of Scholastic rational arguments especially those emphasising that all usury is injustice and necessarily evil. Molinaeus described the Thomistic argument of the integrity of use and consumption as "puerile" because, he contends, "the use and fruition of money not only consist in the first momentary expenditure or application, but also in the successive use of the wares or goods bought with it."[359] [i] He also questioned the fact that the ownership of the loaned money is transferred to the borrower under *mutuum* contract, but even if this be the case, he argued, one may sell the property of another if there is a debt due him.[360] In respect of the concept of the sterility of money, Molinaeus replied that like money neither land nor anything else can be fruitful without the aid

---

i   i.e. because the use of money consists in not only the immediate spending of the money but also the use of the goods or wares which it enables the borrowers to acquire or to obtain command over, it may be sold independently.

of human effort.[361] Hence, Molinaeus concludes that not all usurious loans are against natural justice. In the case of loans made to other than the needy, Molinaeus asserts that the lender has the right to charge for the utility offered by his money especially if it could result in some profits to the borrower. Moreover, Molinaeus contends that the practice would benefit society at large, as tradesmen and merchants would not be able to evolve in their business without borrowed capital.[362]

Salmasius, on the other hand, took the theory a step further. He eased the restrictions imposed by Calvin and Molinaeus on the practice, arguing that lending at interest is nothing more than selling of the use of money, and therefore should not be treated differently from any other selling-based business. Salmasius said:

> "If it is licit to make money with things bought with money, why is it not licit to make money from money? Everyone makes his living from someone else; why should not the usurer? The seller of bread is not required to ask if he sells it to a poor man or a rich man. Why should the money-lender have to make a distinction?"[363]

Further, he added:

> "The rates he charges are those approved by the State, or if there is no maximum legal limit, they are the rates set by supply and demand. There is no fraud or theft in charging the highest market price for other goods; why is it wrong for the usurers to charge the heaviest usuries he can collect?"[364]

But would not heavy charges hurt the poor? Salmasius replies, that they are beneficial in stimulating the borrowers to repay more quickly nevertheless. Salmasius followed the lead of Calvin and Molinaeus in denying the validity of the scriptural as well as the rational arguments advocating the prohibition of usury. Many of their argumentations have been featured in his writings such as *De Usuries* (1638), *De Mode Usurarum* (1639) and *De Foenere Trapezitico*, (1640). In the latter, however, Salmasius rejected the Roman legal classification of the loan transactions arguing that the lender should be allowed to impose charges beyond the return of the original commodity regardless whether the contract is a *mutuum* or *commodatum*, i.e. whether the loaned commodity were fungible or non-fungible. To the objection that in the former case the use cannot be separated from its consumption, Salmasius answers that if it is impossible to transfer the use of the commodity in question then the whole contract is void and must be condemned. Moreover, he argued that if charging for the use is permitted in case the loaned commodity is durable by reason that the associated possibility of loss remained with the lender then, by the same reason, it should be permitted if the loaned commodity was perishable as well. Taking up more rational arguments, Salmasius replies: To the argument that usury is unnatural since it tends to infinity, that "almost all men seek as much money as they can get, and once you permit them to seek what is "sufficient," rather than what is strictly necessary, there is no limit one can rightly set"; To the argument that usury discourages agriculture, that "if usury increase and farmers diminish, competition between the usurer will drive down the price of money" and to the argument that money is sterile, that also idle house and fields are fruitless without the cooperation of human industry as well.[365]

The new doctrine of Calvin-Molinaeus-Salmasius of the justification of taking 'reasonable' usury, or interest by modern definition, appears to have initiated an era in which usury was not only legalised but also started to be moralised, or to receive at least a religious sanction. The usurious financiers could now point to an authority in support of their practices. Although it is what eventually prevailed across the whole of Christendom, in practice if not in theory, this position, however, has been fiercely contested, not only by Catholics but surprisingly also by many English Protestant Divines, scholars and even parliaments for many a long year.

THE CHURCH OF ENGLAND[366]

The overthrow of the old Roman Catholic approach to usury is commonly portrayed as the work of the Protestant, namely Calvinist, Reformation.[i] What is often overlooked is the fact that most of the early Reformers were, in effect, more hostile to usury than were their Catholic counterparts, and generally more hostile than Calvin himself had been, as will be seen below.[ii] It was not until the middle of the seventeenth century that this hostility began to diminish. The interesting change, which culminated at the time in the new Protestant position on the taking of interest, is obviously one of the crucial events in the modernising of the Western Christian ethic. Certain aspects of this change, therefore, will be considered here. The focus will be on the attitudes of the

---

i   Some even suggested a sort of connection between Protestantism and Capitalism, asserting that it was the 'liberal' attitude of the former toward capital accumulation that gave rise to the latter. See for example, Weber and Kalberg; Tawney and Gore, *Religion and the Rise of Capitalism: An Historical Study (Holland Memorial Lectures, 1922)*

ii Three major studies have emphasised how the early Reformers endorsed and maintained long-held Scholastic views against usury at least until the mid-seventeenth century, these were: N.L. Jones, *God and the Moneylenders: Usury and law in early modern England* (Basil Blackwell Oxford,, United Kingdom 1989) and Tawney, *Historical Introduction to: Thomas Wilson, A Discourse Upon Usury By Way of Dialogue and Orations* op cit., and Kerridge op. cit. In his work, Kerridge states that "the Protestant reformers were all substantially orthodox concerning usury and interest," and that "the Reformation made no real or substantial change to fundamental Christian teachings about usury, or to any of the Christian attitudes to it, remedies for it, or laws against it." Ibid., p. 23. Furthermore, Tawney believes that "if it is true that the Reformation undermined the theoretical supremacy of religion over matters of economic conduct, it did so without design and against the intention of most Reformers " Tawney, op. cit., p. 55

English reformers, as 'Protestant' England was perhaps the leading exponent in all Europe of Calvinist theology during that epoch.[i]

To begin with, usury, or any sort of increase, was frowned upon by both the Church and the State in pre-Reformation England. The ancient Saxon and Norman kings were severe on usurers.[367] Edward the Confessor (1003-1066) regarded usury as "the greatest root of the vices" and if any usurer was convicted in his kingdom, he declared, "he would lose all his possessions and be considered an outlaw."[368][ii] Only the Jews were allowed to take interest, but with certain constraints, as laid down in a couple of clauses of the historic Magna Carta of 1215.[iii] However, the privilege did not last for long. It was repealed and Jews were expelled from the whole

---

i   Historically, England, in 1545 under Henry VIII, was the first of the European countries to establish a "legal" rate of interest. Though this action was soon reversed, interest was again made legal in 1571, and has remained so ever since. See, Jarret C Oeltjen, 'Usury: Utilitarian or Useless' 3 Fla St UL Rev 167, 173

ii Usury was defined as lending money in hope of gain, and a usurer as a person who is involved in such an act or habit. See, Rees, op. cit., sec. 31

iii Which reads as following:
"§10. If anyone who has borrowed from the Jews any sum of money, great or small, dies before the debt has been be paid, the heir shall pay no interest on the debt so long as he remains under age, of whomsoever he may hold. If that debt shall fall into Our hands, We will take only the principal sum named in the bond."
"§11. And if any man dies indebted to the Jews, his wife shall have her dower and shall pay nothing of that debt; if the deceased leaves children under age, they shall have necessaries provided for them in keeping with the estate of the deceased, and the debt shall be paid out of the residue, saving the service due to the deceased's feudal lords. So shall it be done with regard to debts owed persons other than Jews." Translated by A.E.D. Howard, *Magna Carta: Text and Commentary* (University Press of Virginia 1998),
Commenting on these clauses, Swabey interestingly says: "the essence of the charter was to prevent any class or party from exercising monarchy, and it is probable that our forefathers had some idea of the monarchy that usury can introduce." See, Swabey, op. cit., p. 13

country by a famous ordinance issued by Edward I in 1290.[i] In the time of Edward III, in 1341, the English parliament itself passed a law "Against Usurie."[369] It is said that it was the stress and strain that the nation went through, namely the Black Death and other plagues, which made it harder to withstand the usurers.[370] The practice was seen as both unchristian and criminal – a public attitude that continued to hold sway until the Reformation, before it turned gradually from opprobrium to acceptance.

The issue of usury became a focus of great concern in England in the wake of the Reformation. It is manifest in the considerable bulk of writings on lending and borrowing in the sixteenth and seventeenth centuries. It appears that almost "Everyone wrote about usury" at the time.[371] This can be attributable to a number of economic, social as well as political factors. In England, and also across Europe, this was a period of important capitalistic growth.[372] Commerce was on the rise. Wool was the main export, but home manufacture and export of finished cloth was increasing in importance. A new commercial class was growing in size and wealth. Capital was needed on an unprecedented scale to meet the opportunities for investment in new enterprises, especially in industry, trade, mining and farming. The geographical rediscoveries of America and the Far East and the resulting high-risk trading and colonial ventures also played a role in increasing the demand for vast amounts of capital which money-lenders were more than ready to furnish, but of course, not on the basis of profit and risk sharing. Therefore,

---

i   He ordained and decreed that:
    " ... no Jew thenceforth should lend anything at usury to any Christian on lands, rents or other things, but that they should live by their commerce and labour; and the same Jews, afterwards maliciously deliberating among themselves, contriving a worse sort of usury which they called courtesy (*curialitatem*), have depressed our people aforesaid on all sides under colour thereof, the last offence doubling the first; whereby, for their crimes and to the honour of the Crucified we have caused those Jews to go forth from our realm as traitors..."

usury begins to spread mainly among the merchants, and more for reasons of production than for consumption.[373] With the course of time, a financial market, where rates would be determined by economic considerations, began to emerge. The Tudor monarchs, who were notoriously keen to be allied to the commercial class, seem to be tolerant, if not supportive of, the usurious practices of the merchants.[374] As noted by Ackerman:

> "The Tudors and their advisors recognised that foreign trade was an important factor in international politics. In addition, customs and import duties provided an important source of Crown revenue. Adopting a quasi-mercantile approach, the Tudor kings worked hard to foster English trade and win concessions from other nations." [375]

The medieval prohibition on interest came under increasingly heavy attack with these new realities. The implication of taking interest started, therefore, to be extensively and hotly debated, by ordinary laymen as well as by Divines, scholars, jurists and the parliamentary legislature.

In this debate, however, the main stream of English Puritan opinion was, at least in the beginning, much more inclined to the pre-Reformation point of view that prohibited all interest as usury, regardless of the rate or the purpose of the loan. Resorting to persuasive dialectical eloquence, close reasoning and sometimes the same anti-usury scholastic rationales, many eminent reformers put up a stubborn resistance to the legalisation of the practice, fighting valiantly to keep England free of usury.

Standing against the practice in the parliament, for example, the English jurist Edward Coke (1552-1634), appointed Solicitor General in 1592 by Elizabeth I, categorically stated that, by former statutes "all usury is damned and prohibited," and that "usury is not only against the law of God and the laws of the realm, but against the laws of Nature."[376]

Thomas Wilson, a scholar, judge and diplomat,^i also declared that usury was "forbidden in all ages and by almost all laws: by scripture, by Canon law, by the Fathers, by the Councils and by others."³⁷⁷ In his famous *Discourse Upon Usury*, Wilson compared usurers to spiders, cankers, serpents and devils; usury, he maintained, is a felony as grave as murder, adultery and theft.³⁷⁸ "Evil in itself, it cannot be used to promote a good cause."³⁷⁹ It is evil, he explained, because it is against charity, it motivates by covetousness and cupidity; it places the wealth of the world in a few men's hands; it raises the price of wares as the interest that tradesmen had to pay would eventually be passed to consumers in the form of higher prices; it decreases royal revenues and results in the loss of trades and occupations, given that the rich would preferably invest their money in lending rather than in commerce or industry, where their risk would be much greater; it involves selling time, which belongs only to God; it violates the equivalence of value demanded by commutative justice and because, as Aristotle said, money is a barren thing that cannot breed its kind. Hence, like the "biting of an asp" and the "devouring of caterpillars" usury would bring ruin and bankruptcy upon the lender, upon the whole country.³⁸⁰

Robert Bolton (1572-1631), a well-known clergyman and academic, noted as a preacher, also exhorted against the practice. Addressing a number of common casuistries that seemed to have gained popular circulation at the time, he replied, in his debate with M.S. "a man of no great note ... [who] occasioned upon a quarrel hee tooke at a Sermon of Bolton's preached against Usury", to the reasoning that the usury of the rich is justifiable, that "like

---

i As suggested by R. H. Tawney in his introduction to a 1925 edition of *A Discourse*, Wilson was representative of a traditionalist impulse reflecting early Protestant efforts to rebuild community and re-establish a sense of structured equity. Tawney quotes a letter of Wilson's (1572 [1925], p. 15), "The state is unfortunate in which nothing is permitted to anybody, but much more unfortunate in which everything is permitted to all."

reason prove it no sin to rob a rich Man: because in Prov. 22. 22 It is said: Rob not the poore ..."; to the notion that usury can be taken from foreigners according to the Deuteronomic text, that they were the enemies of God's chosen and "Usury was as teeth given them the Jews, and allowed by God to eate them up withall ..." But "The partition wall is now taken away, and both Jew and Gentile, rich and poore are Brethren; and therefore we must exact Usury of none, except we would be worse than Jews"; to the argument that many millions of pounds are put out to Usury in England yearly, that "If one argues that because such and such a custom prevails, it is therefore right, where is the necessary eternal and immutable basis of ethical precept?" to the argument that usury at moderate rate becomes legal, that "Such 'legality' in no way mitigates the Moral offence: do we condone 'moderate' adultery."[381] These and many other arguments were addressed by Bolton. He described them all as "hypocritical trifles of the ungodly conscience."[i]

No less scathing was Thomas Adams (1586-1667/8), a clergyman and preacher of high repute, who was called "the Shakespeare of the Puritans." He warned against the temptation to consider usury as less than a sin.[382] To those who allege that God forbade only excessive 'biting' usury but not 'toothless' moderate usury, on the basis of word-juggling distinctions between *neshek* ("biting" usury, from the Hebrew derivation) and *marbit* and *tarbit* ("increase," the word used in Leviticus XXV, 36, 37), Adams retorted that they, "spinne Usurie into such fine threads of distinction that... they conceive a toothless practice" but leads him also to define the usurer as "one that lives upon his monies ... his wit workes like a Mole, to digge himselfe through the earth into hell."[383]

Among the foremost advertisers of the dangers of usury there were also William Gouge (1575–1653), John Preston (1587–1628)

i   Probably inspired by Shakespeare's play *The Merchant of Venice*, he, compared the usurer's greedy grasp to a cannibal's voracious jaws.

and John Cotton. Among the non-Puritan Calvinists of the English Church were Archbishop James Usher (1581-1656), Dr. Henry Airay (1560-1616), Lancelot Andrews (1555-1626), Robert Sanderson (1587-1663) and many others.

On the other hand, however, men of repute such as William Perkins (1558–1602), Francis Bacon (1561-1626), Dudley North (1581-1666), John Winthrop (1587-1649) William Ames (1576-1633) John Locke (1632–1704) and Thomas Culpepper (1656-1723) stood for legalising interest, putting forth, also, a number of religious, philosophical as well as economic arguments for the practice. Some of their arguments are worthy of note.

In his treatise, *A Godly and Learned Exposition of Christ's Sermon on the Mount*, Perkins maintained that a loan between two rich people must be left to their "own libertie and discretion."[384] If the borrower decided to return the loan with "increase" in "way of thankfulness" or, if the lender wanted to be compensated for damage he incurred by his lending, interest should be allowed by "both the law of nature, and the laws of all countries." In his *The Foundation of Christian Religion Gathered into Six Principles*, Perkins even went a step further by permitting interest to be directly asked for by the creditor as long as the debtor could make an "honest gaine" out of the borrowed money. This, he justified, would be in harmony with the law of nature giving that "Albeit money in it selfe bee not fruitfull, yet it is made very fruitful by the borrower's good use, as ground in which is not fruitful except it be tilled." In the same vein, Ames argued that in itself, "money might be barren," and "yet it may easily bee changed into merchandise, which yield fruit: and the industry of the user being added, it bestowes its power to bring forth fruit."[385]

North and Locke both claimed that taking interest should not be less equitable or lawful than land rent, since owners of both, land and capital, hire them out to those who avail from them.[386]

Bacon, on the other hand, allowed the practice only as a practical matter of necessity. He noted that:

> "Many have made witty invectives against usury ... I say this only, that usury is a *concessum propter duritiem cordis* [a thing allowed by reason of the hardness of men's hearts]; for since there must be borrowing and lending, and men are so hard of heart as they will not lend freely, usury must be permitted."[387] [i]

A similar opinion has been provided by Sir Thomas Culpepper. Putting the blame on the predecessors who ignored the inevitability of taking interest, he stated that:

> "Now, though some have, perhaps, of late discovered, (by what light I know not) the weakness of our Ancestors in this Point; Or rather, in regard some must borrow, and will not lend for God's sake (subsisting, as we do, by Husbandry and Trade) It hath been found necessary still to permit a certain Rate of Usury, more moderate, than unconscionable Creditors, (despising Church Censures) might otherwise exact; Yet, surely, Princes are the more concerned, (both as Christians and Law-makers) to Provide; That, at least, the Rate thereof be such, as may neither spoyl their Subjects Markets abroad, nor make their Husbandry and Manufacture uneasie or unprofitable to them at home."[388]

Culpepper also attempted to lessen the stigma attached to the usurers, claiming that: "Common usurers I defie, as the scandals of the Church, Cankers of the State; Lenders upon

---

[i] Bacon opined that legal interest with a rate limitation is a means of balancing two requirements: (1) "the tooth of usury be grinded that it bite not too much" and that (2) "there be left open a means, to invite moneyed men to lend to the merchants, for the continuing and quickening of trade." He is often quoted as saying that "Usury is the certainest Meanes of Gaine, though one of the worst." See, ibid., p. 69, 411

usury I partly excuse, knowing many of them to be persons truly conscientious."[389]

The lawyer, Winthrop, devised a more sophisticated religious-based theory. In his *A Modell of Christian Charity*, he proposed that God had created some to be rich and some to be poor. To keep the two sorts in immutably different spheres, God had instituted two rules, justice and mercy, which "are all ways distinguished in their Act and in their object, yet may they both concurre in the same Subject in each respect; as sometimes there may be an occasion of shewing Mercy to a rich man in some sudden danger of distresse, and allsoe doeing of meere Justice to a poor man in regard of some perticuler contract etc." Winthrop asked, "What rule Must we observe in lending?" and answered, "Thou must observe whether thy brother hath present or probable, or possible meanes of repayeing thee, if there be none of these, thou must give him according to his necessity, rather than lend him as hee requires; if he hath present meanes of repayeing thee, thou art to looke at him, not as an Act of mercy, but thou arte to walke by the rule of Justice." And "justice," he argued, allowed the charging of interest. If, however, the borrower's "meanes of repayeing thee be onely probable or possible then is hee an object of thy mercy thou must lend him, though there be danger of looseing it."[390]

The arguments for and against interest appear to be echoed, among people in the street, as well as in the Houses of Parliament, resulting in a great deal of what could be described at the time as a 'legislative hysteria'.

As noted earlier, usury was legally banned in pre-Reformation England. The first breach was made by a statute that an increasingly commercial Parliament of Henry VIII passed in 1545.[i] The statute, cunningly titled *"An Act against Usury"*,

---

i The first breach in the whole of Europe was an ordinance that Emperor Charles V (r1519-1556) issued on 4 October 1540, evidently with the support of the Staten Generaal of the Habsburg Netherlands, to make permitted, for the first time in England's history, the charging of a 'rate' of 10 percent for "the payment of a true just and profytt debte, or for the performance of any other true covenantes made or to be made uppon a just and true intent hadd betweene the parties."[i]

Nonetheless the Act was repealed only seven years later. Henry's son, Edward VI abrogated, in a *"Byll Against Usurie"* (1552), his father's policy and outlawed all interest seeing that the "terrible threatninges of Goddes wrathe and vengeaunce that justly hangeth over this Realme for the great and open Usurie therein dailye used and practysed."[391] According to Tawney, this abrogation was the harvest of the urging of such radical reformers as Ponet, Lever, Latimer, Crowley and others.[392]

The practice remained forbidden, of course, throughout the reign of Henry's Catholic daughter Mary, but legalised again under the reign of his daughter Elizabeth, in 1570. Interestingly, it has been suggested that Elizabeth desired not to be put in the role of enforcing a practice that was still seen as a "Vyce" "forbydden by the Lawe of God ... [as] synne and detestable."[393] So she made her statute in a fashion that left the door open for debtors to refuse to repay anything above the principal. Its conclusion reads: ".... this Braunche of this present Statute shall forfayte so muche as shal be reserved by way of Usurie above the Principall for any Money so to be lent or forborne."[394]

Nevertheless, in the reign of James I, the maximum legal rate

---

interest payments legal up to a limit of 12 percent throughout the Low Countries, but only on commercial loans. See, Munro, op. cit., p. 263

i Statute 37 Hen. VIII, c. 9 (1545), in *Statutes of the Realm*, Vol. III (London 1963), p. 996:
"no person or persons... by way or meane of any corrupte bargayne, loone, or schaunge chevisaunce ... shall have receyve accepte or take, in lucre or gaynes, for the forbearinge or givinge daye of paymment of one hole yere of and for his money ... above the some of tenne poundes in the hundred, and so after that rate..."

of interest was reduced from ten to eight percent. The Act of King James, passed in 1623, is remarkable, firstly, because it is the first legal statute in which the term "interest" is used[i] and, secondly, as it reflects how wide the gap between religion and economics had grown, as appears in the last paragraph of the statute, which reads: "No worde in this Law contayned shall be construed or expounded to allow the practise of Usurie in point of Religion or Conscience."[395]

Apparently, the practice had become ubiquitous by this time. In his *A Treatise of Usurie* (1611), Roger Fenton, the chaplain to the Lord High Chancellor of England, and also a member of the committee that produced the King James Bible that same year, deplored the pervasiveness of the practice among Londoners. Usury was, he asserted:

> "so woven and twisted into every trade and commerce, one moving another, by this engine, like wheels in a clocke, that it seemeth the very frame and course of traffick must needes be altered before this can be reformed."[396]

Fenton was among the few who still opposed the practice, but their voices were not heeded. Their moral arguments were likely undermined by the growing availability of profitable and relatively safe financial investments.

Notably, in the following years the focus of debate in Parliament seems to have shifted from the morality of interest, *per se*, to the question of the most beneficial limits with regard to rates, i.e. the subject was now being discussed on purely economic grounds. Some argued, for example, that lower interest

---

i   Obviously the word 'interest' was common at the time. The reader will remember that in *The Merchant of Venice* Shylock remarks of Antonio: "He hates our sacred nation; and he rails, Even there where merchants most do congregate, On me, my bargains, and my well-won thrift. Which he calls interest." See, Shakespeare, op. cit., p. 13

rates would facilitate commerce by furnishing a cheap supply of money, whilst others feared that this would lead to a flight of capital to other countries.[397] But, in both arguments scant attention was paid to religious considerations. Consequently, in the subsequent legalisation the maximum legal rate of interest was gradually reduced until it reached 5 per cent by an Act of Queen Anne in 1731[398] – a rate which remained until 1854, when Parliament finally abolished the usury laws altogether, i.e. the legal maximum rates of interest.

TRADE IS ONE THING, RELIGION IS ANOTHER

Although a few tracts condemning the practice continued to appear, by the close of the eighteenth century taking interest was a matter of course for most English Protestants. It has since, or perhaps from even earlier,[i] come into service as a modern, rational, useful and unavoidable economic convenience. In contrast, the prohibition of interest started to be seen as a work of the "dark Ages of monkish superstitions and civil tyranny," when "commerce was also at its lowest ebb."[399] But, said Sir William Blackstone (1723–1780), in his influential *Commentaries on the Laws of England*, first published by Clarendon Press at Oxford, 1765–1769, "when men's mind began to be more enlarged, when true religion and real liberty revived, commerce grew again into credit; and again introduced with itself its inseparable companion, the doctrine of loans upon interest."[400]

By the time the temper of the English business world could be characterised, by the likes of Tawney, in terms of "impatient rejection of all traditional restrictions on economic enterprise," business practices were becoming completely isolated from

---

i   According to Tawney, Protestant preachers were unceasing in their condemnation of the "soul corrupting" taint of usury, up to the Civil War and Commonwealth-Protectorate era (1642-1660). Tawney, *Historical Introduction to: Thomas Wilson, A Discourse Upon Usury By Way of Dialogue and Orations* op. cit.

religious considerations. The new emerging philosophy was that "trade is one thing and religion is another."[i] Furthermore, welfare and religion were, on occasion, depicted as being diametrically opposed to each other.[ii] A new ethic and ideology were taking hold, arguably in order to accommodate the rapid accumulation of capital in Western Europe at the time. This accumulation of wealth came as a result of the excess of production over consumption.[401] Hard work and thrift were the ideals, and money was respected. The surplus capital was not exhausted in the consumption of luxury

---

i   The expression is attributed to Tawney, *Historical Introduction to: Thomas Wilson, A Discourse Upon Usury By Way of Dialogue and Orations*. However it seems to be excerpted from the following text:
"What meets us in the sixteenth, and still more in the seventeenth century, is the decline of the whole body of ideas of which the attempt to create a Christian casuistry of economic conduct had been the practical expression ... By the beginning of the eighteenth century the view that trade is one thing and religion another, if not explicitly asserted, is tacitly accepted."
As found in *Conference on Christian Politics, Economics and Citizenship* (Conference Office 1924), p. 108

ii John Wesley (1703-1791), who organised a breakaway movement from the Church of England known as Methodism, expressed the following:
"I fear, wherever riches have increased, the essence of religion has decreased in the same proportion. Therefore I do not see how it is possible, in the nature of things, for any revival of true religion to continue long. For religion must necessarily produce both industry and frugality, and these cannot but produce riches. But as riches increase, so will pride, anger, and love of the world in all its branches. How then is it possible that Methodism, that is, a religion of the heart, though it flourishes now as a green bay tree, should continue in this state? For the Methodists in every place grow diligent and frugal; consequently they increase in goods. Hence they proportionately increase in pride, in anger, in the desire of the flesh, the desire of the eyes, and the pride of life. So, although the form of religion remains, the spirit is swiftly vanishing away. Is there no way to prevent this – this continual decay of pure religion? We ought not to prevent people from being diligent and frugal; we must exhort Christians to gain all they can, and to save all they can; that is, in effect, to grow rich." See, J. Wesley and J. Emory, *The Works of the Reverend John Wesley, A. M* (J. Emory and B. Waugh, for the Methodist Episcopal Church, J. Collard, printer 1831), p. 317

goods, or in unproductive expenditures, such as the building of great cathedrals, but rather utilised by the rich in further production. For the poor, on the other hand, who lacked capital, it was imperative to provide them with a new religiously-derived casuistry that would justify the medieval Christian communal ideal's giving way to these new capitalistic values. As pointed out by Ertl:

> "The psychological consideration and attitudes toward work, thrift and accumulation of wealth were assisted by the rethink applied to Christianity, freeing it from the influence of the early Christian Fathers, and using it as vehicle to promote the new capitalist ideology."[402]

One of the main religious doctrines that seems to have been redefined for capitalistic purposes is that of Natural Law. The doctrine which, originally invoked by the medieval Scholastics in order to place a moral restraint upon economic self-interest, as mentioned above, was being re-introduced in a fashion that made economic self-interest, *per se,* morally commendable, and thus something to be encouraged. "Nature," says Tawney, "had come to connote, not divine ordinance, but human appetites, and natural rights were invoked by the individualism of the age as a reason why self-interest should be given free play."[403]

The old notion that Natural Law is derived from the eternal and necessary essence of justice, equity, goodness, and truth was questioned simply because it is not based on observable phenomena.[404] There are no such innate perceptions of moral principle.[405] All knowledge came from outside the mind in the form of received sensations.[406] What could not be perceived was, therefore, non-existent, and inbred inborn morality is no exception. It is the mere will of the human legislator that determines what is moral and what is not, some argued.[407] Others claimed that the source of moral obligations is the 'natural' social inclinations of human beings.[408] Like animals, people are instinctively social, i.e. tending to herd with those of their own species. Their sociability is produced from the instinct of self-love, and not from some sort of inbred moral impulses. "The reason is plain," says Bolingbroke, one of the pioneers of the theory, "we have a natural sociability; that is we are determined by self-love to seek out pleasure and our utility in society."[409] Bolingbroke clarifies that: "When I make sociability the daughter of natural law ... I mean plainly this. Self-love, the original spring of human actions, direct us necessary to sociability."[410] To put it another way, the satisfaction of mutual wants is what motivates people to act in a social manner. They might accept the virtues of justice, benevolence and concern for the public good, but only because their own private happiness is contingent upon the well-being of society at large.

Hence, love thyself, not thine enemy, is to become the golden rule – the origin of all virtue. It has been set forth as a moderate, rational ethic intended to be the best possible way to achieve the common good.[i] Furthermore, it was depicted as a part of the divine plan. Since the law of nature is the law of God, it is God who desired that men live in communities, and therefore, in order to insure such sociability, he provided them with the self-love motive.[411] Or as Alexander Pope, the eighteenth-century British poet, paraphrased it, "The God and nature formed the general frame/ And bade self-love and social be same."[412] Accordingly, any positive law that makes its ultimate purpose the maximisation of self-interest is, in theory, helping people to remain together, and by doing so, fulfilling the will of God. Alluding to this conclusion, Josiah Tucker (1713-1799), a Welsh churchman, known as an

---

i   In the same vein, Robert G, Olson says in his book *The Morality of Self-interest*: "The individual is most likely to contribute to social betterment by rationally pursuing his own base long-range interest" Quoted in R. Shafer-Landau, *Ethical Theory: An Anthology* (Wiley 2012), p. 195

economist and political writer, whom Warburton accused that religion was his trade, and trade his religion, wrote: "National commerce, good morals and good government are but part of one general scheme, in the designs of Providence."⁴¹³

Ironically, however, this political philosophy not only furnishes people in society with the right to judge, *inter alia*, when an economic practice, such as usury, occurred and whether it is good or bad, but furthermore, makes their volatile judgment rather Providential in character. Hence, the Church's teachings vis-à-vis economic morality would no longer be needed, since the pursuit of self-interest coincided with the purposes of God for economic life. As pointed out by Tawney: "Naturally ... such an attitude precluded a critical examination of institutions, and left as the sphere of Christian charity only those parts of life which could be reserved for philanthropy, precisely because they fell outside that larger area of normal human relations, in which the promptings of self-interest provided an all-sufficient motive and rule of conduct. It was, therefore, in the sphere of providing succour for the non-combatants and for the wounded, not in inspiring the main army, that the social work of the Church was conceived to lie."⁴¹⁴

Stemming from this ideological perspective, of so-called 'Ethical Egoism',⁴¹⁵ Adam Smith, the eighteenth-century Scottish philosopher and economist, known as 'the father of modern capitalism', postulated that in economic life each man should seek his private good without any interference, given that "By pursuing his own interest, he frequently promotes that of society more effectively than when he really intends to promote it."⁴¹⁶
ⁱ This positive outcome is guaranteed, according to Smith, by

---

i This idea of self-realisation, or so-called 'Ethical Egoism', has been frequently defended by a considerable number of philosophers, economists and writers down to the twentieth century, for example, Ayn Rand (1905-1982), a Russian-American novelist and philosopher, said that:
"The first right on earth is the right of the ego. Man's first duty is to himself. His moral law is never to place his prime goal with those of other

some sort of "invisible hand" by which we all are led "to promote an end which has no part of his [a human being's] interest." What exactly Smith had in mind when he wrote of an 'invisible hand' is a bone of contention among modern economists. Surprisingly, however, when it comes to usury, Smith seems to lose his belief in the influence of such a 'hand'!

Rather than calling for unfettered financial markets, Smith proposed setting a legal limit on interest rates, suggesting that such a limit not to be "much above the lowest market rate". Justifying his proposition, Smith maintained that: "eight or ten percent ... the greater part of the money which was to be lent would be lent to prodigals and projectors, who alone would be willing to give this high interest."[417] What Smith meant by 'projectors' here, as explained elsewhere in his book, seems to be the "chimerical projectors", "the drawers and re-drawers of circulating bills of exchange, who would employ the money in extravagant undertakings, which ... would never repay the expence which they had really cost."[418] Without caps on interest rates, Smith believes that spendthrift and inventive speculators would outbid "sober people." The result being that, "a great part of the capital of the country would... be ... thrown into those [hands] which were most likely to waste and destroy it."[419] Therefore, according to Smith, in order to safeguard the 'capital of the country' a low interest rate ceiling should be imposed by the state. On the contrary, the utilitarian[i] philosopher and jurist

---

persons. His moral obligation is to do what he wishes, provided his wish does not depend primarily upon other men." See, R. Mayhew and others, *Essays on Ayn Rand's Anthem* (Lexington Books 2005), p. 105

i   Utilitarians seem to share with Ethical Egoists the same ideological foundations. "Nature," says Bentham, "has placed mankind under the governance of two sovereign masters, pain and pleasure. It is for them alone to point out what we ought to do." To put the same in another way, the moral good shall be determined exclusively on the grounds of maximising pleasure and minimising pain, which becomes known as the

Jeremy Bentham (1748-1832) saw no gain, but rather harm, for such state interference in private contracts.

Bentham introduced a landmark shift in attitudes in a series of letters published as his *Defence of Usury* (1787). Adopting the *laissez-faire* attitude of the times,[i] Bentham produced in these letters a number of adept arguments, and counter-arguments, against laws regulating the rates of interest.[420] In Bentham's view, money-lending is a trade like any other, and therefore it would be 'absurd' for the government to intervene and set an artificially low price. Questioning the concept of usury, Bentham said:

> "Why a man, who takes as much as he can get … for the use of a sum of money should be called usurer, should be loaded with an opprobrious name, any more than if he had bought a house with it and made a proportionable profit by the house, is more than I can see."[421]

Bentham also compared fixing interest rates and fixing the prices of horses in order to demonstrate the absurdity of usury laws.[422] For Bentham, there is no such thing as right or wrong interest rates, there is only custom and custom is variable: "… blind custom, has varied, from age to age, in the same country: it varies, from country to country, in the same age."[423] Therefore, the lender should not be deprived of the opportunity of asking for any rate of interest he can get from selling his money. As a free man he should not be "hindered" from "making such bargain."[424] Not to mention that the borrower who pays high interest may still be better off for the borrowing, as for example, on a loan needed

---

'Greatest Happiness Principle'. However, the guiding principle for the utilitarians is the greatest good for the greatest number. See, H.R. West, *An Introduction to Mill's Utilitarian Ethics* (Cambridge University Press 2004), p. 23

i   Thinkers such as Adam Smith, Benjamin Franklin and Thomas Jefferson contributed largely in creating a feeling that freedom from restrictions is the "natural order".

to prevent a great loss, or to take advantage of a great economic opportunity.

In support of his position, Bentham undertook to refute the old as well as the new arguments against giving free rein to the practice. To the Aristotelian argument of the sterility of money, Bentham replied, rather banteringly:

> "As fate would have it, that great philosopher, with all his industry and all his penetration, notwithstanding the great number of pieces of money that had passed through his hands (more perhaps than ever passed through the hands of philosopher before or since), and notwithstanding the enormous pains he had bestowed on the subject of generation, had never been able to discover in any piece of money any organs for generating any other such piece."[425]

To the scholastic argument of just price, Bentham questioned the wisdom of looking only for a justification for the price of interest while ignoring other prices. The practice of exchanging present money for future money at interest is not substantially different from any other exchange-based transaction. So:

> "Why a policy, which, as applied to exchanges in general, would be generally deemed absurd and mischievous, should be deemed necessary in the instance of this particular kind of exchange, mankind are yet to learn."[426]

Turning to Smith's arguments for statutory rate caps, Bentham rebutted that legal limits would necessarily result in precluding the prodigals from borrowing, since for the sake of fulfilling over-indulgent desires, they, besides many other ways, may simply sell, or pledge to sell, their property.[427] In respect of 'bad' projectors (speculators), Bentham conceded that their excesses may be curbed by imposing interest ceilings, yet, however, this, he argued, would also thwart the 'good' projectors, and this would be more adverse to the national economy at large.[428] Bentham explained that new projects are often associated with a high level of risk. What seduces money-lenders to finance such risky projects is the excessive interest rate that they are promised to be paid in return. Imposing low interest rate ceilings would discourage them from participation. By contrast, liberating the loans market would furnish the investors with the funds required to carry out their innovative projects. Rather than fear that the nation's capital would be wasted in the hands of mountebanks, Bentham seems to highlight in this argument, what he believed to be the fundamental role that *laissez faire* money-lending plays in unleashing 'the projecting spirit'.[429]

There were other potential drawbacks that Bentham alleged against the interest rate cap policy. For example, he warned that: (1) fixing interest rates would fix the security required at levels which would lead to the detriment of those who do not have sufficient collateral with which to obtain loans; (2) the usury law would be widely evaded and thus become ineffective; and (3) there are many other cases which are not regulated where men may take high risks for high profits.[430]

For the poor who may fall prey to loan sharks as a result of deregulating usury laws, Bentham betrays little concern. He assumes that they are as competent as the rich with regard to determining their own interests.[431] They may look, of course, for a low rate of interest but their 'willingness' to pay a higher rate was an indication, according to Bentham, of the value of the loan to them. Bentham advocated Locke's line of reasoning, that is the "want of money" alone that should "regulate its price", or the so-called "natural interest rate".[432] Further, he added that the determination of the interest-rate should be left for the lender and borrower because they know more than the legislator "who knows nothing, nor can know anything, of any one of all [the] circumstances, who knows nothing at all about the matter."[433]

Many other arguments were developed by Bentham. What he seems to ignore, nevertheless, is the fact that, unlike the wealthy, the needy often borrow for consumption purposes, which leaves them in a vulnerable bargaining position. In spite of this, Bentham proudly claims: "May I flatter myself with having succeeded at last in my endeavours, to recommend to the same powerful protection, two other highly useful and equally persecuted sets of men, usurers and projectors."[434] His attitude can be understood in view of the greatest happiness principle, which he, as a utilitarian, believed in.[i]

Bentham's polemic provoked criticism in the early nineteenth century.[435] But, it finally succeeded with the abolition of all usury laws in England in 1845.[ii] Most of Europe soon followed this lead: Denmark in 1855, Spain in 1856, Geneva, Holland, Norway, Sardinia and Geneva in 1857, Saxony and Sweden in 1864, Belgium in 1865, and Prussia and the North German Confederation in 1867.[436] However, the economic debate whether to regulate interest rates or not, has continued up until very recent times.[iii]

i   Generally speaking, as already noted above p. 110 fn. i, Utilitarianism shares with Ethical Egoism the same ideological foundations. "Nature," says Bentham, "has placed mankind under the governance of two sovereign masters, pain and pleasure. It is for them alone to point out what we ought to do." In other words, the moral good shall be determined exclusively on the grounds of maximising pleasure and minimising pain. However, the overarching principle for Utilitarians is the greatest good for the greatest number, or the so-called 'Greatest Happiness Principle'. See, H.R. West, *An Introduction to Mill's Utilitarian Ethics* (Cambridge University Press 2004), p. 23

ii For 46 years, there was no usury law of any type in England. Then, in 1900, the English Parliament established the Money-lenders Act which did not define an absolute lawful rate of interest but prohibited unconscionable rates; rates above a set maximum were presumed to be unconscionable. The Consumer Credit Act, 1975 also shows that it is legal to charge any rate of interest as long as it is not proven in court to have been extortionate in the circumstances. See, W.S. Holdsworth, *A History of English Law*, Vol. 8 (2d edn, 1937), p. 112

iii See, for examples, Norman N Bowsher, 'Usury laws: harmful when effective' Federal Reserve Bank of St Louis Review. Curiously enough,

It is curious to observe that, once Protestant opinions toward interest begin to shift, how inexorably they progress from one extreme to the other. The practice that Luther first warned would bring down the wrath of God upon Germany, later found acceptance with Calvin in France, provided that usury was 'moderate' and taken only from the rich, before it was then advocated in England by Bacon as a necessary evil, and further argued by Winthrop that, although it is no act of mercy to take interest, it is an act of justice.

Protestant attitudes toward interest advanced along a radical course. By the beginning of the eighteenth-century, free trade had begun to be considered one thing and religion another. Some even claimed that they were mutually incompatible with each other, but by the end of the century the Protestant philosophers furnished society with a new ethical perspective with a rationale that made the freedom of trade a religious purpose in itself, thus excluding the Church from the need for direct involvement in the economic sphere, by using the very instrument that had hitherto been the customary and exclusive monopoly of the Church – namely, the license to interpret the will of God.

The length of the journey from opprobrium to acceptance also illustrates how vehemently and with how much determination the early reformers opposed the practice. Despite the fact that they were theoretically no longer bound by the Canon Law, the early reformers endorsed and maintained long-held Scholastic views against taking any interest. Their literature is replete with impassioned sermons, erudite treatises and popular pamphlets. It is self-evident that the vigorous tradition of Christian opposition to usury was not readily

---

Most of the United States have laws governing interest charges and, furthermore, there is a federal law which applies to all national banks in the absence of a state law; it prohibits a charge by banks in excess of 7 per cent, per year. See, Rudolph C Blitz and Millard F Long, 'The economics of usury regulation', The Journal of Political Economy 608

abandoned. Indeed, when Henry VIII denied the supremacy of the Pope in 1529, Catholic dogma began to be reviewed but yet not rejected altogether. As noted by Wilson:

> "Therefore I would not have men altogether be enemies to the Canon Law, and to condemn everything therein written, because the Pope was author of them, as though no good law could be made by them. Nay, I will say plainlie, there be some such laws made by the Pope as be right godly, saie others what they list."[437]

English public opinion, at the time, also seems to be in adherence to the original post-Reformation teachings on usury. As detailed above, the attempts of the Tudor monarch to legalise the practice, through their increasingly commercial Parliaments, were not always successful. The Act of King Henry VIII that legalised interest at 10 percent lasted only seven years before it had to be repealed amid a storm of controversy. Even when Queen Elizabeth I tried to revive her father's law, she, deliberately or otherwise, formulates her Acts in a fashion that leaves the door open to different interpretations. The Act of King James I was unequivocal, yet still, he replaced the term 'usury' with the term 'interest' most likely in order to avoid the stigma and the condemnation that was associated with the former. Moreover, he concluded his Act with a noticeably generic and political statement.

Yet, the evolution in practice and thinking that occurred later was not unexpected. With the enlivening of commercial markets and the expansion of the British Empire, as well as the trend toward secularised laws,[438] it is no wonder that the ideas of philosophers such as North, Locke, Bolingbroke, Hobbes, Shaftesbury and Bentham were to be headed especially by the "new men" of the English Renaissance.

Another point worth noting is the fact that change in Christian ethics toward usury is effected by non-Catholics. When the conflict between the new economic need and the older ideal of social justice appeared, the Catholics show a tendency to evade the usury prohibition by adopting and adapting a considerable number of extrinsic titles, as well as interest-masking transactions through which the money-lender could take interest, but only by way of compensation. This Catholic tendency most probably arose from not wishing to confront the theological difficulty of having to admit that the early fathers, popes and canonists misinterpreted the usury prohibitions in the Bible. Or maybe, as some argued, because the Church itself was Europe's greatest creditor which, in order to maintain its position, imposed a variety of complicated financial regulations that individual money-lenders could not comply with – what is known in modern economic terms as 'regulatory capture'.[439] In contrast, the Protestants were able to deal with the issue of usury more candidly. As seen above, while the Catholic jurists in the seventeenth-century were arguing whether or not the triple contract was Canon-compliant, their contemporary Protestant counterparts were questioning the entire idea of usury. Evidently, however, what emerges in the long run, is the dominant point of view that what is prohibited in the Bible, to all practical intents and purposes, is the charging of excessive rates of interest as opposed to more moderate charges.

USURY IN ISLAM

RIBA: INTEREST, USURY OR BOTH

Usury in Islam is called *riba* (lit. excess or addition), and it has been prohibited in unequivocal terms in the Muslim Holy Book – The Qur'an.[i] Whether this prohibition applies to modern bank interest seems to arouse controversy amongst Muslim scholars,

---

i The verse 2:276, part of which reads: *"Allah has permitted trade and He has forbidden riba"*, left no room for debate or dispute among Muslims. Please note that unless otherwise noted, all citations from the Holy Qur'an are from the translation of A. Bewley and A.A. Bewley, *The Noble Qur'an: A New Rendering of Its Meaning in English* (Madinah Press 1999)

dividing them into two main schools of thought: the *Riba*-Interest-Equivalence school and the Non-Equivalence school.[440] For the first school, interest and *riba* are considered to be coterminous and interchangeable with each other and thus, both are forbidden to Muslims. The proponents of the other school, however, claiming that modern interest is different from the Qur'anic concept of *riba*, which they claim refers either to oppressive rates of interest, i.e. usury in the modern sense, or to the interest on consumption loans only. It is no coincidence that some modern Qur'anic commentators in English, e.g. Muhammad Asad, used the term 'usury' for *riba*, while others preferred the term 'interest'.

The implications of this argument are critical. If *riba* is defined as usury (in its modern sense), then as long as interest rates remain at a socially and legally acceptable (i.e. non-usurious) level, all interest transactions conducted in an Islamic society are permissible (*halal*). But if *riba* is defined as interest, then the whole civil and commercial structure of such a society becomes tainted with illegality (*haram*). In order for more light to be shed on these views further discussion will be provided later in this section.

To begin with, interest and usury appear to be synonymous in the literature of the traditional Islamic law. All the classical schools of law (*Madhhabs*) are in agreement that any interest regardless of the rate constitutes *riba*, or rather *riba al-nasi'a* under which is subsumed any positive return that has been fixed in advance.[441] Their consensus has been advocated by the vast majority of the Islamic scholars of modern times; this is well-attested in the verdicts of many international conferences of *fuqaha* (Muslim jurists) held to address the question of *riba*, including the Mu'tamar al-Fiqh al-Islami, which took place in Paris in 1951 and in Cairo in 1965, the Islamic Fiqh Academy of the Organization of the Islamic Conference (OIC) and the Council of the Islamic Jurisprudence Academy (IJA) meetings held in 1985 and 1986 in Cairo and Makkah respectively.[442] The Pakistan Council of

Islamic Ideology concluded in its 1980 report on the elimination of interest from the Pakistan economy that:

> "The term *Riba* encompasses interest in all its manifestations irrespective of whether it relates to loans for consumption purposes or for productive purposes, whether the loans are of a personal nature or of a commercial type, whether the borrower is a government, a private individual or a concern, and whether the rate of interest is low or high."[443]

Likewise, the Federal *Shari'a* Court in Pakistan declared in its famous judgment in 1992 that: *"riba* includes both 'usury' and 'interest' as known in English terminology." This equivalence of *riba* to interest seems to occupy a dominant position in the culture of the Muslim world, paving the way for the development of 'interest-free' Islamic banking. Nevertheless, minority opinions permitting modern forms of interest continue to surface from time to time.

The last few centuries have seen the emergence of a new Islamic thinking on interest that tends to draw a critical distinction between modern day interest and the Qur'anic concept of *riba*. The trend, it is highly likely, was initiated by Ebusuud Efendi, a politically-appointed Grand Mufti under the Ottoman Authorities between 1545-1574 CE, who issued a *fatwa* (legal dictum regarding Islamic Law) authorising the act of interest-taking at the rate of 15 per cent, especially by *awqaf* (pious foundations), as a practical matter of necessity.[444] Although his *fatwa* had been rejected by the majority of scholars around the Arab world at the time, it was sanctioned by the Ottoman Sultan, Suleiman the Magnificent, as evidenced in a circular sent by him to the judges in the Peloponnesus in 1565.[i] Over the following centuries a number of *fatwas* were issued by

---

i   In which he states that, "In our time, the Sultanic decree and the noble *fatwas* of His Excellency the Mufti of the Age are that ten should not be given for more than eleven and a half (15 per cent)." See, ibid.

the Ottomans in the same vein.[445] In the nineteenth century, in India, Sir Sayyid Ahmad Khan (1817-1898), the reformist leader of the Aligarh Movement, also argued that interest is not usury.[446] He differentiated between businesses or non-distress loans, on which, he believed, it was rational to take interest, and distress loans, which should be made free of charge.[447] Such ideas did not take long before they started to appear even in the Arab Muslim world.

Muhammad 'Abduh (1849-1905), the Grand Mufti of Egypt, as narrated by his disciple, Muhammad Rashid Rida (1865-1935), claimed that what are prohibited in Islam are very specific forms of compound interest that were in vogue during the pre-Islamic period (*riba al-jahiliyya*), but not modern simple bank interest.[448] The first increase, both argued, on a termed loan is *Shari'a*-compliant, but if at the maturity date the parties agreed to postpone the payment against a further increase, this would be the prohibited-*riba*.[449] It is probably on the basis of this distinction that a famous *fatwa* was issued in 1903 authorising the deposit of funds in the Egyptian Post Office Savings Bank (*Sunduq at-Tawfir*) where the depositors would accrue a "dividend" of 2.5 per cent.[450] This *fatwa* played a major role in the establishment of Banque Misr, the first Egyptian-owned bank founded in 1920, especially as the Bank's founder, Tal'at Harb, was close to Rida and strongly influenced by his thought.[451]

Over the twentieth century, on very similar grounds, a number of prominent scholars have also alleged that interest is not *riba*, including, but not limited to, Muhammad Abu Zayd, who maintained that exorbitant interest alone is outlawed; Marouf al-Daoualibi who claimed that the Qur'an banned interest only on consumption loans; Abd al-Razzaq Sanhuri who held that what is prohibited is interest on interest, and Mohammad Draz, who was among those who were referred to in the Appeal to the Pakistan Supreme Court against the prohibition of all interest in the country as part of the *Shari'a* law.[452]

This polemic seems to have rebounded in recent years with a high-profile *fatwa*, issued in Dec. 2002, from the most august Azhar Islamic Research Institute (IRI), which authorised the collection of interest on conventional bank deposits (by considering it as a fixed profit rate in investment agency).[453] Unsurprisingly, the *fatwa* has been devastatingly critiqued by numerous scholars across the Arab and Islamic world. As a result, after only one month the Council of the Islamic Jurisprudence Academy (IJA) issued a rebuttal, reiterating many of the arguments that had been made by those scholars who reject the Islamic legitimacy of all forms of bank interest.[454] For them, interest and usury are nothing more than two sides of the same coin – *riba*.

It is clear that the definition of *riba* and its scope have been the subject of a protracted jurisprudential debate in the Arab and Muslim world, especially in recent centuries: What constitutes *riba*? Whether or not interest and *riba* are completely equivalent or convergent? Does the purpose of the interest loan matter? These questions appear to be catalysts for controversy amongst Muslims today, as with the Christians in the Middle Ages. In attempting to address such questions, and to work toward an Islamic understanding of usury, this section will consider in further detail the development of the theories of prohibited-*riba* in Islamic law. By way of preparation, a basic understanding of the sources of Islamic law will prove helpful.

ISLAMIC LAW – THE *SHARI'A*

Islam is very much an action-oriented religion, necessitating an accepted pattern of conduct for Muslims in the ritual as well as social and economic spheres. As much of the discussion of the concept of usury in Islam will centre on legal opinions and decisions in one form or another, this section provides a brief and focused overview of the structure, methodology, and personalities of the *Shari'a* which produce that pattern.

The *Shari'a*, in a broad sense, refers to the totality of commands that Allah has revealed to the Prophet Muhammad ﷺ. Yet, the term is often used, in a narrow sense, to designate only legal rules.[i] In common with other legal systems, the *Shari'a* could be seen as a seamless web, and therefore difficult to embrace comprehensively. To begin to grasp the *Shari'a*, it would be useful to consider in some detail its principal sources and understand the function of, and the relationships between, those sources.

The Qur'an is the first source of Islamic law.[ii] By its own testimony, the Qur'an is the very word of God as revealed in Arabic to the Prophet Muhammad ﷺ through the archangel Gabriel ﷺ.[455] It was revealed piecemeal over a period of twenty-three years both in Makkah and Madina,[iii] according to the needs of time and to provide solutions to the problems that came before the Prophet ﷺ.[456] It contains 114 *suras* (chapters) each of which is traditionally named in reference to a creature, object or event mentioned in the text. In the sense that legal material occupies only a small portion of its text, the Qur'an is neither a legal code nor a constitutional document.[457] The Qur'an describes itself as *huda*, i.e. guidance, not as a code of law.[458] Those verses of the Qur'an that bear an 'explicit' legal content are known academically as *ayat al-ahkam*, that is, the verses

---

i   As with the Hebraic halakha, the term *Shari'a* is derived etymologically from a root meaning 'road to be followed', the Qur'anic verse 45:18 reads, *"Then We placed you on the right road (sharia) of Our Command, so follow it. Do not follow the whims and desires of those who do not know."* See, A.R.I. Doi and A. Clarke, *Shari'ah: Islamic law* (Ta-Ha 2008), p. 22; J. Schacht, *An Introduction to Islamic Law* (Clarendon Press 1982), p. 1; H. Janin and A. Kahlmeyer, *Islamic law: the Shari'a from Muhammad's time to the present* (McFarland & Co. 2007); Mohammad Hashim Kamali, 'Law and society: The interplay of revelation and reason in the *Shari'a*' The Oxford History of Islam 107, 119-120

ii 'Qur'an' literally means 'reading' or 'recitation'. It also calls itself by alternative names, such as *kitab, huda, furqan,* and *dhikr* (book, guide, distinguisher, and remembrance respectively).

iii Both are located nowadays in Saudi Arabia.

that form the bases of Islamic legal rulings.[i] They are concerned with various legal matters, including personal status, commercial and financial transactions, crimes and penalties, justice, equality, citizens' rights and duties, consultation in government affairs as well as many dogmatic and devotional matters.[459]

Many Islamic scholars (*ulama*) have attempted to gather and classify these verses according to their subject, with the purpose of deducing juristic injunctions and rulings from them. While doing so, they have also provided the explanation of verses, research into difficult words, discussion of the geo-historical context as well as the causes of the revelation (*asbab an-nuzul*), if any. The books that were compiled in such manner often bear the title of *Ahkam al-Qur'an* (the legal injunctions of the Qur'an); the most reputable are, *Ahkam al-Qur'an* by Abu Bakr al-Jassas al-Hanafi (d. 990 CE); *Ahkam al-Qur'an li al-Shafi'i* by Imam al-Bayhaqi al-Shafi'i (d. 1066 CE); *Ahkam al-Qur'an* by Imam Ilkiya al-Harrasi al-Shafi'i (d. 111 CE); *Ahkam al-Qur'an* by Qadi Ibn al-'Arabi al-Maliki (d. 1148 CE).

The second source of Islamic law is the *Sunnah*, or Prophetic tradition. The *Sunnah* stands for both the teachings as well as the exemplary conduct of the Prophet ﷺ, including "his sayings, acts and tacit approval (or lack of condemnation) of the conduct of his Companions and some of the customs of Arabian society."[460] The legal authority of the *Sunnah* is derived basically from a number of Qur'anic verses, such as in *sura* 53:2-3, which affirm that the Prophet's words are not his own but revealed by God and *sura* 4:80 and 59:7 which make obedience to him a religious duty

---

i   According to Kamali, less than only one-tenth of the verses of the Qur'an, which are over 6,200, bear an 'explicit' legal content. However, there is disagreement on the number of legal verses that Qur'an contains. Higher estimates are that they are not more than 500 verses. For further information, see Doi and Clarke, op. cit., p. 66; Janin and Kahlmeyer, op. cit., p. 16-17

that is a part of obedience to God Himself. It is generally agreed, therefore, among Muslim scholars that the *Sunnah* is accorded the status of the revelation in declaring what is lawful (*halal*) and what unlawful (*haram*). The following from Kamali is illustrative of the function of and the relation between the Qur'an and the *Sunnah* in Islamic legal tradition:

> "The *Sunnah* relates to the Qur'an in various capacities. It may consist of rules that merely corroborate the Qur'an, it may clarify ambiguous parts of the Qur'an, or it may qualify and specify general rulings of the Qur'an. These three varieties comprise among them the bulk of the *Sunnah*, and the *ulama* are in agreement that they are integral and supplementary to the Qur'an. The *Sunnah* may also consist of rulings on which the Qur'an is silent, in which case the *Sunnah* represents an independent source of *Shari'a*. There are a number of hadiths that fall under this category… [and thus] the *Sunnah* is not only an explanation and supplement to the Qur'an, but it is also an independent source of the *Shari'a*."[461]

Due to this legal significance, written reports (*ahadith*, sing. *hadith*) of the sayings, as well as acts, of the Prophet ﷺ began to be collected during his life and continued after his death.[462] The collections of these *ahadith* continued to increase as they were gathered from the Companions of the Prophet and their successors, nevertheless they were subjected to critical scrutiny and criticism. The compilers of the *ahadith* while carrying out their work, developed a range of highly specialised techniques for the purpose of verifying both the chain of transmission (*isnad*) and the transmitted text (*matn*) of these *ahadith*.[463] One of the notable and well known techniques for *isnad* criticism is 'Asma' al-Rijal (lit. 'the names of the men'), by which an assessment is made of the competency of the *hadith* narrators followed by classification according to the level of reliability and authenticity of the *ahadith* that are reported through them.[464]

A summary of the classification is given briefly in Table1 below.[465] It is important to note that only the *ahadith* that accord with the criteria of the first two categories (*Sahih* and *Hasan*) can be relied upon in matters of religious rulings. It may be acceptable, to some extent, to benefit from *Da'if ahadith* namely in matters of lesser significance, but *Mawdu' ahadith* are, of course, not acceptable under any circumstances.

Criteria	**Classification**
A hadith reported by an uninterrupted chain of narrators each one of whom is pious with a strong memory provided that the report does not contradict a greater number of narrators and does not suffer from a hidden defect.	*Sahih* (authentic)
A hadith with an uninterrupted chain of narrators at any given level, each of whom is pious but of a memory that is not as strong as those individuals in the chain of a *sahih* hadith yet stronger than those in the *da'if* category.	*Hasan* (good)
A hadith which, at any one level, has a reporter who is either not pious or has weak memory.	*Da'if* (weak)

| A hadith reported by someone known to be a liar. | *Mawdu'* (fabricated) |

Table 1

Many large *hadith* collections began to appear successively during the Abbasid Caliphate in the ninth century, the most authentic are known as *al-Kutub al-Sittah* (lit. 'The Six Books') which are, *Sahih Al-Bukhari*, collected by Imam al-Bukhari (d. 870 CE); *Sahih Muslim*, collected by Imam Muslim b. al-Hajjaj (d. 875 CE); *Sunan al-Sughra*, collected by al-Nasa'i (d. 915 CE); *Sunan Abu Dawud*, collected by Abu Dawud (d. 888 CE); *Jami' al-Tirmidhi*, collected by al-Tirmidhi (d. 892 C.E); *Sunan Ibn Majah*, collected by Ibn Majah (d. 887 CE).[466]

The Qur'an and the *Sunnah* serve as textual sources of *Shari'a*, making the latter a text-based law system.[467] Yet, these two sources are generally recognised to have their limits thus resulting in lacunae in the law that need to be addressed.[468] To fill the vacuum, the qualified Islamic jurists (*fuqaha*) expend considerable effort to examine the textual evidences found in the revealed sources so as to arrive at a ruling in *Shari'a* for new cases and issues.[469] Their intellectual exertion in doing so is referred to in Islamic parlance as *ijtihad* (lit. effort). Owing to its renewable nature, *ijtihad* is a vital source of Islamic law. As Kamali indicates:

> "The main difference between *ijtihad* and the revealed sources of the *Shari'a* lies in the fact that *ijtihad* is a continuous process of development whereas Divine Revelation and Prophetic legislation discontinued upon the demise of the Prophet. In this sense, *ijtihad* continues to be the main instrument of interpreting the Divine message and relating it to the changing conditions of the Muslim community in its aspirations to attain justice, salvation and truth."[470]

He also adds that *ijtihad* derives its legal authority from Divine Sources, and therefore its propriety is measured by its consistency with these sources.[471] Further, he asserts that "the essential unity of the *Shari'a* lies in the degree of harmony that is achieved between revelation and reason" and that "*ijtihad* represents the principal instrument of maintaining this harmony."[472] All of the secondary sources of Islamic law such as consensus of opinion (*ijma'*), analogical reasoning (*qiyas*), juristic preference (*istihsan*), and considerations of public interest (*maslahah*) underpin the process of *ijtihad*, each providing a different method by which a ruling based on juristic reasoning can acquire the binding force of law. *Ijma'* and *qiyas* are the most common. Both adopted by the vast majority of the *fuqaha*. *Ijma'* is unanimous consensus achieved among a scholarly community of a particular time on particular religious issues.[473] It manifests not only an agreement upon the authenticity of a given text but also its meaning and implications. Yet, because of its very nature, which demands an absolute and universal consensus, *ijma'* has always been difficult to claim especially in modern times.

Qiyas is another expression of *ijtihad*, by which the jurists may extend a legal ruling (*hukm*) to an analogous case, provided that there is a sufficient nexus between the *ratio legis* (*ilah*) of the precedent (*asl*) and the new case under consideration (*far'*).[474] A popular example of *qiyas* can be found in the Islamic prohibition of alcohol. Wine consumption is prohibited by explicit text in the Qur'an due to the intoxicating effect. Hence, by analogy, if wine made from grapes is forbidden, liquor made from barley, dates, or whatever, must also be forbidden since it causes intoxication as well.[475] Yet, the employment of *qiyas* to achieve a legal injunction for new cases was not given free rein in Islamic law. The *'illah*, upon which the whole process of analogy is premised, must comply with certain requirements in order to ensure harmony between revelation and reason in developing the law; otherwise the divine element of *Shari'a* might be compromised.[476]

It is vital to note that there is no unanimous agreement among Muslim scholars on the legal authority of the methods of *ijtihad*. In fact, the question of what Islamic law comprises would be answered differently by different schools of law:

> "... whereas the Zahiris confined the sources of law to the Qur'an, the *Sunnah*, and consensus, the Hanafis added analogy, juristic preference, and custom, and the Malikis added public interest and the notion of 'blocking the means' (*sadd al-dhari'a*), which ensured the consistency of means and ends with the *Shari'a* by blocking the attempt to use a lawful means toward an unlawful end."[477]

As will be shown below, this lack of unification adds to the complexity of the concept of *riba* in Islam and played a critical role in the development of modern Islamic banking practices.

Riba in Islamic Law

It would appear that Islamic law is composed of different elements not all of equal value since some are regarded as being of divine origin (Qur'an and *Sunnah*) and others the product of human reasoning (*ijtihad*). This 'dual identity' of *Shari'a*, as termed by Kamali, is reflected in its two Arabic designations, *Shari'a* and *fiqh*.[478] Although these terms are sometimes used interchangeably, the term *Shari'a* bears a stronger affinity with the Islamic legal rules derived directly from the revelation, whereas the term *fiqh* (lit. understanding) is used mainly for those produced through the methods of *ijtihad*, mentioned above.[479] Therefore, to address the problem of usury in *Shari'a*, it is crucial to look at the prohibition on *riba* as to be found in the texts of the Qur'an and the *Sunnah* as well as in the *fiqh* literature in which these prohibitions were expounded and elaborated.

Riba in the Qur'an

The Text and Context

The prohibition of *riba* in Islamic law has its roots in four Qur'anic revelations in which the practice is forbidden, discouraged or scorned. These revelations are quoted below in the order in which they appear in the Qur'an, but, chronologically, *sura* 30:39 is the first of these revelations. It appears to have been revealed in the early years of the Prophet's mission in Makkah, probably in the sixth or seventh year before the *Hijra* (that is, CE 615 or 616), based on the internal evidence of the Qur'an.[i]

> "That which you seek to increase by usury (riba) will not be blessed by God; but the alms (zakat) you give for His sake shall be repaid to you many times over." (Sura al-Rum xxx. 39)

This revelation does not prohibit *riba* directly but rather passes some sort of stricture on the practice. It draws a comparison between those who charge *riba*, intending thereby growth and increase, and those who give charity seeking God's pleasure; whereby the former is deprived of the benefit of God's blessings whilst for the latter it is multiplied manifold.[ii]

---

i This assumption is based on the fact that the opening verses of the *sura* refer to the defeat of Romans by Persians in the neighbouring lands, i.e. Syria and Palestine, a battle that occurred historically in the year CE 615 or 616. See, E. Gibbon, *The History of the Decline and Fall of the Roman Empire* (Cosimo, Incorporated 2008); Fazlur Rahman, '*Riba* and interest' 3 Islamic Studies 1, 4

ii Some early commentators, including al-Tabari and al-Fakhr Razi, argued that the term '*riba*' in this verse carries the meaning of a gift, where a man gives a present to another anticipating in return a better one at a later time. Other commentators are of the opinion that the verse refers clearly to the banned *riba*. Contemporary Muslim thinkers tend to agree with the latter interpretation; particularly as it does not contradict the absoluteness of the *ayah* which is that *riba* carries no reward from God. See, Abd-Allah Al-Qurtubi, *Al-Jami 'li-Ahkam Al-Qur'an* (1987), Sura al-Rum, verse 39; S. Qutb, A. Salahi and A.A. Shamis, *In the Shade of the Qur'an* (World

However, this comparatively mild admonition was followed by a categorical prohibition of usury in *sura* 3:130.

"Believers, do not live on usury (riba), doubling your wealth many times over. Have fear of God that you may prosper." (Sura Al Imran iii.130)

This second revelation on the matter, which occurred in Madina around the second year after the Hijra,[i] clearly enjoined Muslims to fear of God and restraint from usury for their own good. Notably, the word used in this verse for taking *riba* is 'devour' which implies that a man who engages in the practice is a glutton, a figure that attracted much lampooning among Arabs at the time.

The third revelation on the subject is in *sura* 4:161, which also occurred in Madina, probably in the fourth year after the Hijra.[ii]

"We forbade the Jews good things which were formerly allowed them, because time after time they have debarred others from the path of God; because they practice usury – although they were forbidden it – and cheat others of their possessions." (Sura al-Nisa iv.161)

It is considering some of the outlawed activities of the Jews, who, although it was prohibited for them, were involved heavily in

---

Assembly of Muslim Youth 1981), Sura al-Rum, verse 39; al-Tabari, *Tafsir al-Tabari* (Dar al-Ma'arit 1972), Sura al-Rum, verse 39.

[i] The position of these verses within the *sura* describing the battle of Uhud led to this conclusion. Furthermore, some commentators argued that this revelation was to prevent Muslims from financing their armoury for the battle through usurious loans as the disbelievers did. See, Justice Muhammed Taqi Usmani, 'The Text of the Historic Judgment on *Riba*, 23 December 1999' 80 The Supreme Court of Pakistan.

[ii] The exact time of revelation of these verses is very difficult to ascertain. Yet, since the three Jewish tribes in Madina the usurious practices of whom these verses relate, had each been banished from the city by the fourth year after Hijra, the verses are probably revealed around that time. Ibid., p. 8

taking usury, a practice that has been placed in juxtaposition with the wrongful appropriation of other people's possessions. It may be noted that unlike *sura* 30:39, in which usury was expressed by the word 'give', in this verse, when usury is related to the actions of Jews, the word 'took' is used instead. This would indicate the tendency of the Jews to act as takers of *riba*, rather than as payers, at least in the Medinan community of the time.

Likewise, the fourth revelation, *sura* 2:274-278, which was revealed only a few months before the death of the Prophet ﷺ, severely censured those who engaged in the practice.[i]

> "*Those who practise riba will not rise from the grave except as someone driven mad by Shaytan's touch. That is because they say, 'Trade is the same as riba.' But Allah has permitted trade and He has forbidden riba. Whoever is given a warning by his Lord and then desists, may keep what he received in the past and his affair is Allah's concern. But all who return to it will be the Companions of the Fire, remaining in it timelessly, for ever. Allah obliterates riba but makes sadaqa grow in value! Allah does not love any persistently ungrateful wrongdoer. Those who believe and do right actions and establish the prayer and pay zakat, will have their reward with their Lord. They will feel no fear and they will know no sorrow. You who believe! have taqwa of Allah and forgo any remaining riba if you are believers. If you do not, know that it means war from Allah and from His Messenger. But if you repent you may have your capital, without wronging and without being wronged.*" (Sura al-Baqara 275-280)

It refutes their most common claim that "*trade is like usury*" with the assertion that Allah made the former (trade) lawful and

---

i   It is generally agreed that these verses are the last revealed in relation to the prohibition of *riba*. See, M.S. Abdul-Rahman, *Tafsir Ibn Kathir Juz': Al-Fatihah 1 to Al-Baqara 141 2nd Edition* (MSA Publication Limited 2009), p. 335

made the latter (usury) unlawful.[i] Furthermore, this revelation imposed a retrospective ban on the practice; the believers were instructed to waive what was still due to them from usury by taking no more than the principal amount due, otherwise war would be declared against them by God and His Apostle in this life, and hellfire would be their destination in the afterlife:

Thus, the Qur'an explicitly and emphatically proscribes *riba*. The phraseology of the relevant verses in which people are urged to shun *riba* and the severity of the admonition left no room for dispute among Muslims in this respect. But, the problem is that there is no delineation of *riba* in these verses, nor an explanation of the transactions that arise from it; this was one of the main reasons that generated impassioned controversy, especially on whether modern bank interest is to be considered *riba* and thus subjected to the Qur'anic prohibition. Considering usury as it was practised among Arabs in the pre-Islamic period (*Riba al-Jahiliyyah*), against which the *riba*-prohibiting verses were directed, would add to the controversies, as well as resulting in a better understanding of the meaning and the scope of the term *riba* as it appears in the Qur'an.

Riba al-Jahiliyyah

It is generally agreed that *riba* was deeply ingrained in the life-texture of the Arabs of the pre-Islamic period, that is, in the seventh century CE. This is apparent in the famous incident recounted by Arab historian Ibn Hisham, in reference to when the powerful merchant tribe of Quraish decided to rebuild the

---

[i] Some commentators attribute this statement to tribe of Thaqif, who equated the sales of camels at a profit with a loan of money at *riba*, arguing that both produced a profit on capital invested and were therefore of no commercial differences; al-Tabari, op. cit., Sura al-Baqara, verse. 278; Abdul-Rahman, op. cit., Sura al-Baqara, verse. 278; Al-Qurtubi, op. cit., Sura al-Baqara, verse. 278

Ka'ba,[i] due to flood damage. They made a pledge not to taint the project with resources gained through harlotry, usury or unjust practices. Because of this pledge, they ran out of funds and were not able to cover the "Hateem area" of the Ka'ba, which remains exposed to this day.[480]

However, a large number of historical reports pertaining to pre-Islamic usurious practices are to be found also in the exegetical literature; examples of which show not only the wide extent of the practice at the time but also its diversity.

Al-Tabari (d. 310 AH) in his *Jami'* maintains that *riba* in the pre-Islamic period referred to doubling and redoubling the principle amount lent. He related on the authority of Mujahid (d. 105 AH) that "In the days of *Jahiliyyah* one man would owe a debt to another. Then he would say to his creditor, [I offer to] you such and such and you give me more time to pay." Through such practices, al-Zamakhshari, in his *al-Kashshaf*, pointed out that even a small debt would often consume all the wealth of a debtor because of repeated increase of the unpaid loan. Al-Tabari also quotes another early authority, Qatadah (d. 117 AH), to explain *riba* in pre-Islamic Arabia:

> "The *riba* of *Jahiliyyah* was a transaction whereby a person would sell something for a payment to be made at a specified future time. Then when the time of payment came and the buyer did not have the necessary amount, the seller would increase [the amount due] and give him more time."

The same explanation has been given by al-Suyuti on the authority of Faryabi (d. 212 AH),

> "They used to purchase a commodity on the basis of deferred payment, then on the date of maturity the sellers used to increase the due amount and increase the time of payment."

---

i   The Ka'ba is a cuboid building in Makkah, Saudi Arabia. It is the most sacred site in Islam.

Ibn al-'Arabi, also presents a similar interpretation of *riba*, that is, *riba al-Jahiliyyah*. Yet, Fakhr al-Din al-Razi (d. 606), in his famous *tafseer*, reports another form of *riba* that was prevalent at the time. He says:

> "... in the days of *Jahiliyyah*, they would advance money on the basis that they will take a specified amount every month and the principal will remain due. Then on the date the debt became due, they demanded the debtor to pay the principal. If payment became impossible (or hard), they would increase the term and the payable amount."

Imam al-Jassas (d. 380), in his *Ahkam al-Qur'an*, reports that "The *riba* which the Arabs knew and practised meant lending money [dirhams and dinars] with a specified maturity at an agreed upon increase over and above the sum borrowed." And if the debtor failed to pay at the maturity, Imam al-Alusi (d.1854) adds, "the creditor would say: offer me more money and I will give you more time."

It was not only lending money at interest that Arabs were accustomed to do. Many reports revealed that they also lent 'food commodities' at interest. On the authority of the son of Zayd b. Aslam (d. 136), al-Tabari related:

> "*Riba* in the pre-Islamic period consisted of doubling and redoubling [of money or commodities] and in the age [of the cattle]. At maturity, the creditor would say to the debtor. 'Will you pay me, or increase [the debt]?' If the debtor had anything, he would pay. Otherwise, the age of the cattle [to be repaid] would be increased ..."

In the same vein, al-Baghawi (d. 510), in his exegesis, quotes a tradition from 'Ata (d. 117) and 'Ikrimah (d. 107), which runs as follows:

"Regarding the word of God: '*O believers fear God and forego what remains of riba*', 'Ata and 'Ikrimah said that it was revealed concerning al-'Abbas ibn 'Abd al-Muttalib and 'Uthman bin 'Affan who bought some dates (not yet harvested). When the time came for harvesting, the owner of the dates said to them: "If the two of you took what is owed to you, I would not have enough for my children. So would you take half and delay the delivery of the remaining half and I will double it for you?" So they acted accordingly and when the agreed time came they asked for the increased amount. This reached the Messenger of God, so he prohibited them. Then God Most High sent down this *ayah*. So they heard and obeyed and took only the capital amount."

In light of these reports, and other similar ones, it can be seen that the usurious practices that were pervasive in the pre-Islamic period were by no means of one form. Arabs seem to be familiar with many types of interest which, in essence, are similar to modern types of interest, such as simple interest as mentioned by Imam al-Jassas, interest-only loans as indicated by Fakhr al-Din al-Razi, compound interest as pointed out by al-Tabari on the authority of Mujahid and Zayd as well as credit sale with late payment penalties as referred to by al-Suyuti and al-Baghawi on the authority of Faryabi, 'Ata and 'Ikrimah. Since these forms were in vogue at the time of revelation, all of them fall within the ambit of the *riba* prohibitions in the Qur'an. It is self-evident that the teachings on usury did not develop in a vacuum. They were addressed to the established usurious practices of those who had lived through the revelation. As is borne out in the tone of the relevant verses themselves, "*... waive what is still due to you from usury*" and "*Do not consume riba.*" Arabs were known to have practised many interest-bearing transactions at the dawn of Islam and when the prohibition was proclaimed, these transactions and similar ones, are leastways the subject of the interest-prohibiting verses.

Yet, the prohibition of taking interest in Islamic law is not only derived from the Qur'an, but also from the *Sunnah*.

Riba in the *Sunnah*

In the *Sunnah* the Qur'anic ban on *riba* was not only upheld but also augmented by additional rules, which resulted in broadening the scope and nature of the *riba* prohibited in Islamic law. The *ahadith* in which these additional rules are mentioned are known by the epithet of the 'six commodities *ahadith*'. They have been reported by a considerable number of Companions but the best known of them are the two that have been related by 'Ubada ibn al-Samit and Abu Sa'id al-Khudri may Allah be pleased with them. Both are presented below along with a brief explanation of their application.

The tradition of 'Ubada ibn al-Samit:

> 'Ubada ibn al-Samit relates that the Messenger of Allah said: "Sell gold for gold, silver for silver, wheat for wheat, barley for barley, dates for dates and salt for salt, like for like, in equal amounts [and] hand to hand. If the genera differ then sell as you wish as long as it is hand to hand."[481]

The tradition of Abu Sa'id al-Khudri:

> Abu Sa'id al-Khudri relates that the Messenger of Allah said: "[Sell] gold for gold, silver for silver, wheat for wheat, barley for barley, dates for dates and salt for salt, like for like, hand to hand. And whosoever increases or demands an increase has engaged in usury. The taker and the giver are, in [the act], equal."[482]

Here, six commodities, also known as *ribawi* commodities, are identified. They include monetary items (gold and silver) and non-monetary fungible items (wheat, barley, dates, salt). According to the *ahadith*, Muslims may sell these commodities as long as two requirements have been met. The first requirement that the item be sold "like for like", demands quantitative equality in the items exchanged. The second requirement that the transaction be "hand to hand" necessitates that the delivery of the items be made in the contractual session. Yet, if the items exchanged do not belong to the same genus, e.g. when gold is exchanged for wheat, only the second requirement must be fulfilled. Failure to observe these requirements in a given transaction makes it a *riba* transaction and thus prohibited in *Shari'a*.

With these rules, it becomes clear that the concept of *riba* in Islamic law includes not only interest-bearing transactions but also a wide range of 'on-the-spot' barter transactions. How Islamic jurists, received, dealt with and derived from these rules can be seen in their literature.

Riba in the *Fiqh* literature[i]

To begin with, the problem of the explanation of *riba* has been a very difficult problem for the Islamic jurists. It is apparent in the problematic statement, attributed to the Caliph 'Umar ؓ in which he says: "the last to be revealed was on *riba* but the Apostle of God expired without explaining it to us. Therefore give up *riba*; and anything doubtful (resembling *riba*)."[483] While some see this statement as a reflection of a general ignorance of the correct interpretation of the verse of *riba* among the Companions themselves, others provide a different point of view.

---

i   A lengthy study of the topic of *riba* in all its details and branches and abundant issues, with which the books of *fiqh* are loaded, is not within the scope of this section. However, in this section it will be important to cover the major topics through which the reader will be able to follow the discussions of the next chapter which elaborate on how the laws of *riba* in *Shari'a* have been evaded on a theoretical level as well as on the practical level.

A well-known Maliki jurist, Ibn Rushd [the Grandfather] (1058 – 1126 CE), concludes that 'Umar did not intend to say that the Prophet ﷺ had not elaborated on the verses of *riba* and their intended meaning, instead he meant that the Prophet did not clarify all transactions in which *riba* is to be found.[484] This would be the case especially as it is known that the Prophet explained in great detail a considerable number of *riba*-bearing transactions, such as gold for gold, silver for silver, 'sale with a loan', 'sale of what you do not have' and suchlike, which amount to an elaboration of what is obscure in the Qur'an. In respect of the cases that are not explained by the Prophet, Ibn Rushd asserts they are to be referred to the general principles pertaining to derivation of the law. So, the Prophet did not pass away before the completion of the religion and the explanation of everything for which the Muslims were in need of an explanation. The Exalted says, "*Today I have completed your religion for you*," which amounts to an elaboration of what is obscure in the Qur'an.[485]

Ibn Rushd's argument is also supported by what is related from 'Umar himself:

> "You say that we do not know about any issue from the issues of *riba* – and no doubt I would prefer to know all these issues ... but there are many issues of *riba* that are not concealed from anyone e.g. purchasing gold for silver on deferred payment basis."[486]

This statement shows clearly that there are types of *riba* which were manifest and well-known to 'Umar, because the *Sunnah* has clarified them, and there are those that were not so. He seems to wish all of them to have been elaborated by the *Sunnah*, so that their prohibition could be derived directly from texts, and not left to *ijtihad*, which often produced different opinions; which is exactly what happened later.[i]

---

i   Whatever the intended meaning of what is related from 'Umar ﷺ, the

Although they agreed that it is *haram*, and that it constitutes a major wrong, Islamic jurists differed indeed in the definition of *riba* and its conditions and classifications. Three main theories can be identified in their *fiqh* literature.

The first is what has been proposed by the early classical jurists[i] of the schools of jurisprudence.[487] These jurists relied mainly upon the six commodities *ahadith*, and other similar *ahadith*, in explaining the situation in which *riba* exists. They classified *riba*, in view of the rules and requirements articulated in these *ahadith*, into two main categories.[488] The first is *riba al-fadl*[489] (the *riba* of surplus), which occurs when a 'surplus' existed in the amount of one countervalue over the other in barter transactions in the *ribawi* commodities made on the spot. The second category is *riba al-nasi'a* or *al-nasa'* (the *riba* of delay) which occurs when a 'delay' happened in taking possession or delivery of one or both countervalues of these specific commodities.[490]

Thus, an exchange in which A delivers one ounce of gold to B in return for two ounces of gold from B, both countervalues delivered at once, amounts to *riba al-fadl*. An exchange in which A delivers one ounce of gold to B now, on condition that B delivers the same amount of gold to A in one month's time amounts to *riba al-nasi'a*. Hence, an interest loan of one ounce of gold now for two ounces of gold to be repaid later is

---

view in itself about the obscurity of *riba* cannot stand since it is self-evident that the teaching of *riba* in the Qur'an did not develop in vacuum; it was directed at least at those usurious practices which were pervasive among Arabs at the time of revelation, i.e. *riba al-Jahiliyyah*, mentioned above.

i   For the sake of research in this thesis, classical Islamic jurists are those who lived between the eight and the fifteenth century A.D. Thus, besides the works of the real classical jurists, the works of jurists who are normally classified as post-classical by many experts of Islamic law, are exceptionally referred to as classical. See for example the classification of C. Chehata, *Études de droit musulman* (Paris, 1971), p. 20-27

subsumed under the prohibited *riba al-nasi'a* because it involves a delay in the settlement of countervalues. It is important to emphasise at this point that it is the element of delay, and not the interest rate *per se*, that makes such loans prohibited in the view of the classical Islamic law.[491]

However, the *ahadith* identified just six specific commodities to which 'riba rules' – equality of offers and immediacy of delivery – are applied. Whether these rules are exclusive to these commodities or they are also applicable to other commodities, such as fiat money made from paper, and if so, what are those commodities? This question raised controversy among the *fuqaha*.

For Zahiris, the answer would be 'No' which should not be surprising as they do not accept *qiyas, per se*, to be a source of law. Most other jurists are of the opinion that these *ribawi* items can be extended by analogy to include other items.[492] They differ, however, in identifying the *'illah* of the prohibition to do so. Hanafis, and most of the Hanbalis, define the *'illah* in the *ribawi* items as being sale by weight or volume, thus any other commodity sold by weight or volume is subject to the *riba* rules. Shafi'is define it as being the function as a medium of exchange for gold and silver, and being an edible commodity for the remainder, to which Malikis add the capacity for being a stable and storable edible commodity. All of them consider 'genus' to be a ratio (reason) in itself. Accordingly, if any homogeneous commodities are exchanged against each other, both the rules of *riba al-fadl* and *riba al-nasi'a* are applied. If any non-homogeneous commodities are exchanged against each other and they share the same *'illah*, only the rule of *riba al-nasi'a* is applied. If any non-homogeneous commodities are exchanged against each other which do not share the same *'illah*, neither the rules of *riba al-fadl* nor the rules of *riba al-nasi'a* are applicable.[i]

---

i The question over the extension of the *ribawi* items by analogy is a germane one. For example, if fiat money made from paper is not one

It is to be noted that classical jurists, and those who followed their lead, often discussed *riba* under the topic of sales and considered the absence of *riba* a condition for the validity of a sale. This is because they perceived, and dealt with, interest loans as being in essence a sale of money now in exchange for money to be received later,[i] and thus, by analogy, subject to the rules of *riba*, or strictly speaking rules of *riba al-nasi'a*, according to their classification.[493] However, a few later classical jurists attempted other types of classifications that remain to some extent disputable.

Ibn Rushd [the Grandson] (1126 – 1198 CE), in his book *Bidayat al-Mujtahid*, has classified *riba* into two different categories. The first is *riba al-duyoun* or *al-qurud* (the usury of loans). The second category is *riba al-buyu'* (the usury of sales) under which he placed *riba al-nasi'a* and *riba al-fadl*.[494] In his view, what has been prohibited in the Qur'an is only the usury of those loans that were pervasive among the Arabs in the time of ignorance, i.e. *riba al-Jahiliyyah*. The usury of sales, on the other hand, is prohibited by the *Sunnah*.[495]

Yet, this distinction between the scope and subject of *riba* prohibitions in the Qur'an and those in the *ahadith* is a matter of controversy among *fuqaha*. The source of their disagreement is the question of whether the meaning of the term *riba* as found in the Qur'an shall be known from its historical context, i.e. the usurious practices of pre-Islamic Arabs, in which case it is

---

of the *ribawi* items, then it will not be prohibited to exchange one hundred pound sterling for two hundred pound sterling at a later date and a loan of fiat money at interest might not be prohibited under this view.

i This can be noticed in a number of their definitions of the term *riba* as well. For example, al-Sarakhsi in his book *al-Mabsut* defined *riba* as "an excess that lacks a counter-value in sale," al-Kasani defined it as "the excess stipulated in sale in the corpus of wealth on the basis of a legal standard…" and al-Subki defines *riba al-nasi'a* as "… a delay in the exchange of the countervalues." All quoted in al-Badawi, op. cit., p. 29.

designated as *'amm* (lit. general), or the term is equivocal and in need of further clarification, in which case it is termed *mujmal* (lit. undetailed).[496] Briefly, Hanafis and the majority of Shafi'is considered *riba* to be *mujmal* in the Qur'an, and therefore it has been illustrated by the six commodities *ahadith* in the *Sunnah*. Directly opposed to them are the Malikis who asserted the general aspect of the prohibition.[497] Bearing in mind the fact that the *Sunnah* stands on equal footing with the Qur'an in declaring what is lawful and unlawful in Islamic law, this argument seems to have borne little fruit.[i] It explains, however, the basis upon which Ibn Rushd built his theory and why his theory is sometimes criticised.[ii]

In modern times, Ibn Rushd's classification appears to be adopted by a number of scholars namely those involved in Islamic banking,[498] others, however, preferred the classical theory of the early jurists.[499] Yet, there is a third theory, which does not seem to have so many proponents.

In his book *I'lam al-muwaqqi'in*, Ibn Qayyim al-Jawziyyah (1292-1350 CE) made another classification where he divided *riba* into open (*jali*) and hidden (*khafi*).[500] Open *riba* has been prohibited because of the great harm and injustice it carries. Hidden *riba*, on the other hand, has been prohibited because it may be used as a route towards open *riba*. Thus, the prohibition of the former is deliberate, while that of the latter is prophylactic. In his view, the *jali* is *riba al-nasi'a*, as it is what was in common usage during the *Jahiliyyah*, whereas the *khafi* is *riba al-fadl*.

On this basis, he argued that the prohibition of *riba al-fadl* is less severe, and therefore, it can be overridden if one were in dire need, or if there were a public interest. To support his argument, he cites

i In other words, whether usury on loans is prohibited by the *Sunnah* or by the Qur'an or by both, they all agreed that it is still prohibited.

ii His theory has been criticised by Nyazee, op. cit.

an example from a *hadith,* which is reported to allow exchange of fresh dates for dry ones in small quantity by estimation. The point of the arguments is that, according to the rule of *riba al-fadl,* exchange of dates should be in exactly equal quantity. But here it is permitted to exchange them by estimation, which is likely to result in a degree of inequality.[501] Influenced by his theory, Waliyullah al-Dihlawi (1703-1762 CE) says, "Remember that *riba* is of two kinds: One is primary.... The other is subject to it. Primary *riba* is only on loans. The other *riba* is called *riba al-fadl* ... and is akin to primary *riba.*"[502]

It can be seen that the interpretation of the concept of *riba* was not an easy task for the *fuqaha*. A wide variety of terminology is found in their literature on *riba* in correspondence with the various methods they used to understand its nature and scope over time. Whether they termed it *riba al-Qur'an, riba al-nasi'a, riba al-duyoun,* or *riba al-jali,* and regardless of their methodological and hermeneutical differences, all classical jurists shared the same conclusion that interest-bearing loans are forbidden. This is the common denominator between their theories of *riba*. Notwithstanding, some modernists tend to interpret *riba* in a fashion that is radically different from the understanding of these *fuqaha* throughout the last fourteen centuries, and is also sharply in conflict with the categorical prohibitions of *riba* laid down in the texts of the Qur'an and the *Sunnah*.

Dissenting Views

As with Christianity and Judaism, from time to time there have been attempts in Islam to justify taking interest. Perhaps, the first of these attempts was made by the Ottoman Grand Mufti Ebusuud Efendi who defended the practice from a practical point of view, arguing that the abolition of interest-taking would result in the collapse of many pious foundations (*awqaf*), a situation that would ultimately harm the Muslim community, and therefore, as a matter of necessity, the act of interest-taking, at the maximum rate of 15 per cent, had to be authorised.⁵⁰³

It is well established, indeed, in Islamic law that extreme necessity can have the effect of exemption from a given prohibition, i.e. necessity knows no law. This principle is derived from several Qur'anic texts.⁵⁰⁴ The questions that need to be asked, however, are what constitutes an extreme enough necessity to permit the *haram*? And did the necessity upon which Ebusuud base his *fatwa*, really meet the necessary criteria in the case of the *awqaf*?

Generally speaking, the concept of bare necessity is defined in Islamic law as: a) a compelling situation in which; b) there is a genuine fear of loss or severe injury to one of the five fundamentals (*al-daruriyat al-khams*); these are preservation of religion, preservation of life, safeguarding the intellect, protection of lineage and safeguarding wealth, of life for the individuals or group in question, and c) committing an illegal act is the only way out of such a situation.⁵⁰⁵ This *haram* act, which is to be allowed out of necessity, d) must also not become established as a norm, but rather as a temporary expedient determined pursuant to the situation. An example of such extreme necessity is when someone who was starving is allowed to eat what is enough to assuage his hunger from a forbidden food, e.g. carrion, and which was the only food available.

It is very difficult to observe these states and conditions of necessity in the case of the *awqaf*. For usurious transactions to be lawful in Islamic law there would need to be a real, pressing necessity, similar to one that would permit the eating of carrion. It is possible to imagine such a situation for the borrower who pays interest, but where is the compelling necessity of the creditor, the *awqaf*, to take interest? Were they not able to invest their funds in trade in lieu of interest-taking practices? Moreover, to whom were they going to lend money at interest? Is it to poor Muslims or rich ones? By doing so, are they not, in effect, helping them to perpetrate a *haram* action from an Islamic point of view?⁵⁰⁶

However, in his *fatwa* Ebusuud has not justified the practice of taking interest in itself, but only as an exception resulting from what he thought a matter of necessity, i.e. he agreed in principle that taking interest is forbidden in Islamic law. It is Rashid Rida who is probably the most famous scholar to claim that interest-taking is lawful *per se*.⁵⁰⁷ Responding to a series of questions posed by subscribers to his monthly magazine, al-Manar (lit. the lighthouse), Rida concluded that what is prohibited in Islamic law is only 'exploitative' or 'exorbitant interest rates' rather than interest *per se*, thereby allowing for a 'fair' return on loanable funds, if needed.⁵⁰⁸ In expressing his view, Rida claims that there was only one form of *riba* practised by pre-Islamic Arabs, which is, according to him, when an increase in debt principal is stipulated at the date of maturity in consideration for an extension of the term after maturity. This practice would result, by repeated increase, in doubling and redoubling the principal sum lent and thus causing substantial injustice.⁵⁰⁹ The prohibition of *riba* in the Qur'an, therefore, belonged only to this peculiar usurious practice. Commenting on the meaning of *riba* in the verse 2:275-8, he says:

> "The particle '*al*' in the term *riba* indicates knowledge and familiarity, which means, 'Do not consume *riba* which was familiar to you and that you used to practise in the pre-Islamic period."⁵¹⁰

Since the simple interest loan of modern banking was not customary at the time of revelation, he argued, it does not fall within the Qur'anic prohibition of *riba*.⁵¹¹ As a result, Rida considered the first simple increase on a termed loan to be lawful but if, at maturity, it is decided to extend the term against further increase, this would be the prohibited *riba al-Jahiliyyah*.⁵¹²

The same line of reasoning was adopted by 'Abd al-Razzaq Sanhuri who suggested it is the compound interest rate that is first and foremost prohibited in the Qur'an.[513] His view has been shared also by the Egyptian scholar of Islamic law, Ibrahim Zaki al-Badawi, before the latter changed his opinion and held that interest of all kinds is *riba* and is prohibited.[514]

A serious weakness with these arguments, however, is that they seem to rely too heavily on the relevant reports related by al-Tabari in his commentary which, on the other hand, overlooked a large number of other reports that demonstrate collectively that Arabs were familiar with, not just one, but many forms of *riba* at the advent of Islam, and some of which are indeed very similar, if not identical, to the interest present in today's commercial transactions, as mentioned above. And even if it is presumed, for the sake of argument, that the *riba*-prohibiting verses were directed exclusively to one form of pre-Islamic *riba*, the prohibition in these verses should also be applied to modern banking interest loans, given the similarity between these two transactions whether in form or in substance.[515]

The pre-Islamic form of *riba* suggested by Rida, consists, in effect, of two separate contracts, the first is when a loan was advanced, or a trade debt was created, for a certain period with no *riba* charged. The second contract concluded at the maturity date, when the creditor would say to the debtor: 'will you pay as agreed or will I add an amount to the original debt?' It is at the beginning of this second contract that interest is stipulated against a delay for the payment, which is the same case with the typical interest loan contracts. Not to mention that in both there is a debtor, a creditor, maturity date and an amount added to the capital in exchange for time and therefore, both should be subjected to the same ruling. Otherwise, one could argue that Roulette, for example, is not prohibited in

Islamic law given that the Qur'anic gambling prohibitions were directed only to the pre-Islamic gambling games enjoyed by the Arabs.

One of the evidences that also refutes these arguments is that in verse 30:39 Muslims are reminded of the wrongdoing of Jews in practising *riba* despite its prohibition in their religion: *"That they took usury, though they were forbidden; and that they devoured men's substances wrongfully."* In interpreting this verse, al-Tabari said, "The order of heaven is one and the same; that the usury which was banned to the Jews is the same usury which is banned to the people of Islam."[516] Now, as detailed above, the concept of usury as found in the Jewish religious writings and as understood and practised by the Jews throughout their history does not take, or at least is not limited to the pre-Islamic form of *riba* as suggested by Rida.

Influenced by Rida's views, however, modernists like Fazlur Rahman, Muhammad Asad, and Said al-Najjar have also argued, but on different grounds, that *riba* in the Qur'an refers only to exorbitant interest rate loans. Some maintained that the concept of *riba* should be defined in light of verse 3:130 which states *"do not consume riba, doubled and redoubled,"* in which, they say, the term *riba* stands for 'usurious' loans, and thus contemporary interest on commercial loans do not fall within this prohibited category. However, such an interpretation is not really consistent with the method followed in the Qur'an. The expression *"doubled and redoubled"* is not to restrict the ban, but rather to highlight some of the greedy usurious practices widespread at the time. This approach is noticeable when, for example, the Qur'an dealt with the problem of prostitution: *"But force not your maids to prostitution when they desire chastity, in order that you may make a gain in the goods of this life."*[517] As the Grand Mufti Mahmud Shaltut noted:

"The purpose here is not to prohibit the act of forcing maids to become prostitutes when they desire to remain chaste, and permit this act when they desire not to stay chaste, but Allah is repudiating and denouncing their actions, which is exactly the same approach taken in the case of al *riba*."[518]

Moreover, defining *riba* as a loan on which excessive (usurious) interest is charged conflicts sharply with the verses in *sura al-Baqara* (2:275-8), which indicate that any increase received over and above the capital is considered to be *riba*:

"You who have iman! Have taqwa of Allah and forgo any remaining riba if you are muminun... But if you make tawba you may have your capital, without wronging and without being wronged."

These verses are generally agreed to be the last *riba*-prohibiting verses, some even argued that they were revealed shortly before the death of the Prophet ﷺ, in which no distinction has been made between simple, compound, fixed or variable interest rates.

Another major argument advanced by modernists is that the Qur'an only bans *riba* on consumption or humanitarian loans, not on loans for commercial purposes since in the early years of Islam borrowing for trade or commercial purposes was not practised.[519] Once again the ban in *sura al-Baqara* does not specify such an exception and none is evident elsewhere in the Qur'an or in the *Sunnah* literature. Moreover, this argument could not stand up before the historical evidences and records, which prove the contrary. As will be discussed in further detail below, commerce and trade was the basic characteristic of the economic life of the Arabs especially in the Hejaz region. Their trade caravans used to travel as far afield as Egypt, Syria, Iraq, Yemen and Ethiopia, exporting their own goods to these countries as well as importing foreign goods to their own cities. Due to the large size of these caravans, e.g. the one led by Abu Sufyan at the time of the battle of Badr, which consisted of one thousand camels and returned with 100% profit, were often funded by a considerable number of contributors. As Jawed Ali noted:

> "What the historians have narrated about the caravans of Makkah reveals that the capital of a caravan never used to be the capital of one individual or a particular family; it rather belonged to the traders of different families and to those individuals who themselves had money or had borrowed it from others and had contributed it to the capital of the caravan, with a hope to earn huge profit."[520]

Thus, commerce and the financing of commerce were both common at the time, and productive loans would not, therefore, have been foreign to pre-Islamic Arabs.

Some modernists tend to interpret *riba* from a 'moral' perspective, arguing that the rationale for the prohibition of *riba* is the injustice that existed, in their view, only when the lender was someone rich who wanted to exploit a weak and poor borrower. Thus, as long as the interest transaction did not entail such cruelty, it would be permissible. This assertion is, however, unsubstantiated. The upholders of this view attempted to support their argument by selectively quoting from the works of early scholars, like al-Razi, Ibn Qayyim and Ibn Taymiyyah, giving them a meaning that was most probably not intended by them, as will be discussed below. Furthermore, modifying a very strict divine law such as *riba* on the basis of a human understanding of its purposes entails a high risk that Muslims may not take.

In spite of their varying arguments, the modernists' view appears not to have many proponents among Muslims today. The consensus prevailing throughout history has been, and continues to be, that *riba,* amongst other things, includes taking interest.[521] This is most likely attributable to two main reasons. The first is the failure to present an alternative consistent persuasive theory of *riba*. As discussed above, the modernists, in order to build their case, took their cue from various verses, reports and works of the earlier scholars. Whilst these materials have been highlighted in their theories, others have been, deliberately or otherwise, overlooked. This selective approach made their arguments, to some extent, easily refutable in contemporary debates on *riba*.

The second reason is the seriousness of the sin of *riba* in Islam. The act was deemed a great crime in the Qur'an. Those involved in the practice were threatened with *"war from Allah and his Messenger"*[522] in this life, and hellfire in the afterlife. The gravity of the action has also been stressed in many crucial statements made by the Prophet ﷺ, some of which are as follows:

> "Avoid the seven destructive sins: associating partners with Allah, sorcery, killing a soul which Allah has forbidden – except through due course of law, devouring interest, devouring the wealth of orphans, fleeing when the armies meet, and slandering chaste, believing and innocent women." (Al-Bukhari and Muslim)

> "The interest adopter, the interest giver, the interest accountant, and the witness to interest dealing, all are cursed and equally, the defaulter." (Muslim, Abu Dawud, Ibn Majah, al-Nasa'i, Ahmad)

> "I came across some people in the night in which I was taken to the heavens. Their stomachs were like houses wherein there were serpents, which could be seen from the front of their stomachs. I asked: O Jibril! Who are these people? He replied, these are those who devoured interest." (Ahmad, Ibn Majah)

"Even when *riba* is much, it always leads to utter poverty."
(Ibn Majah)

As noted by Joseph Schacht, "they (Muslims) were always conscious that a direct breach of the prohibition of *riba* was a deadly sin."[523] In light of these grievous consequences, therefore, no wonder that pious Muslims would be reluctant to adopt a modern view allowing the taking of simple interest; especially as it is rejected by the vast majority of scholars.

REASONS FOR THE PROHIBITION OF *RIBA*

The question that remains is, however, why does the practice incur such severe punishments? That is, what are the reasons (or wisdom) behind these harsh pronouncements?

One of the answers provided is that the prohibition of *riba* is merely a matter of ritual obedience. It is *ta'abbudi* (ritual only) or *ghayr ma'qul al-ma'na* (non-rational): an act of worship similar to prayer and fasting and thus knowing the underlying reason for the obligation is unnecessary.[524] Saadullah says that, "having learnt that interest is banned by the Qur'anic text, the rationale or the wisdom for such a ban is known to God the Almighty."[525] Yet, this answer appears to be provided by a minority. Most scholars are of the opinion that the prohibitions associated with the various doctrines of *riba* are *ma'qul al-ma'na* (rational); they put forward, however, different rational justifications for these prohibitions.

The common and traditional argument often provided is that the reason for this ban is to forestall injustice, as formulated in the Qur'anic statement itself, "... *But if you make tawba you may have your capital, without wronging and without being wronged.*"[526] This, however, leaves another question: how does the practice promote injustice from an Islamic point of view?

Classical scholars offered different answers to this question. Al-Razi propounded that it is the unjustifiable increase of capital for which no compensation is given that constitutes the core of

153

the injustice of imposing interest on loans. He asserts that "The taking of interest implies appropriating another person's property without giving him anything in exchange, because one who lends one dirham for two dirhams gets the extra dirham for nothing."[527] Why not consider it as compensation? Had the capital been retained in the hand of the creditor for the period of the loan, the sum lent may rather have been invested to make a profit. Because, he says, "... such a profit is only hypothetical; it may not materialise whereas taking the interest (increase) is certain. To take the "certain" as a compensation for the "uncertain" involves some harm."[528] Ibn Qayyim drew attention to the injustice suffered by needy debtors whose weak bargaining position might be exploited by rich creditors. In referring to one form of pre-Islamic *riba*, he indicated that although sometimes the debtors were rich persons and businessmen, in most cases they were destitute with no choice but to "pay more for a mere extension of time."[529]

Scholars like Imam al-Ghazali, Ibn Taymiyyah and Muhammad Abdu focused on the injustice caused by the practice not on the micro- but on the macro-economic level. In language very reminiscent of Aristotle's theory, they put forth the main argument that would continually be used against interest in the modem debate. Al-Ghazali says:

> "Allah Almighty has created dirhams and dinars (money) ... so that it may be circulated between hands and act as a fair judge between different commodities and work as a medium to acquire other things ... And whoever effects the transactions of interest on money is, in fact, ... committing injustice, because ... If it is allowed for him to trade in money itself, money will become his ultimate goal and will remain detained with him like hoarded money."[530]

Likewise, Ibn Taymiyyah is against trade in money as it diverts money from doing what it is meant to do, which is, according to him, to serve as "measurement of objects of value."⁵³¹ If this is altered to making money the object of the production of wealth, Abdu adds, "then this will lead to the stripping of wealth from the hands of most people and to concentrating it in the hands of those who limit their works to the exploitation of money by money."⁵³² As a consequence, the rich become richer and the poor become poorer.

Some of these ideas have been further developed by Muslim economists in modern days. Meenai and Ansari assert that trading in money results in an expansion of credit which in turn leads to a discrepancy between real exchanges and cash flows, "the interest-based system of banking creates instability and has a built-in tendency towards inflation as money creation is not linked to productive services."⁵³³ According to Chapra this is what caused, *inter alia*, the recession felt by the 'Asian Tiger' countries in the nineties.⁵³⁴

Another argument forwarded is the adverse effect of the practice on the socio-economic level. It is argued that if interest is prohibited in a society, people would lend to each other with good will, expecting back no more than what they have loaned, while if interest is made permissible the needy will be required to pay back more on loans, thus weakening their feelings of good will and friendliness toward the lender and thus resulting in friction and strife and stripping society of its goodliness. As noted by Sayyed Maudoodi,

> "Interest cuts the roots of human love, brotherhood and fellow-feeling, and undermines the welfare and happiness of human society, and that his enrichment is at the expense of the wellbeing of many other human beings."⁵³⁵

Modern writers on Islamic law also attempted a number of explanations for the proscription of *riba* but they generally revolve around the same arguments mentioned above.⁵³⁶

Of course, it would be difficult to contend which of these explanations is the very raison d'être for the prohibition. Some have argued that taken all together they give the law its final shape[537] while others found none of them to be wholly satisfactory.[538] In the absence of a Qur'anic text clearly stating the reason for the ban, any conclusions drawn on this subject would remain questionable. What is, however, unquestioned by the vast majority of scholars is that the lender has no right under Islamic law to receive any increase over and above the principal. The existence or otherwise of injustice in a loan transaction is irrelevant to the fact that the practice has been emphatically forbidden in the Qur'an as well as in the *Sunnah*. And, a strong sense of the prohibition seems to have persisted in Islamic public opinion down to the present era, as in past ages.[539]

Evading The Taint of Usury

The problem of usury evasion appears in the earliest record of mankind. It is generally believed that it was the ancient Romans who enacted one of the very first secular prohibitions of the practice, as provided in the *Leges Genucia* passed in 413 BCE.[540] The *Lex Genucia* strictly forbade, in principle, the collection of interest. However, it proved rather ineffective. Roman usurers consistently found ways to get around the ban. The amount of legislation indicates that it must have been fairly easy to elude the laws against usury altogether. Many carried on their usurious transactions through the medium of allies, in particular the Latins, as the latter were not subject to the municipal law – in a similar way to Jewish money-lenders who lent to each other through the medium of the gentiles.[541] Some even concealed themselves behind Latin identities – like the mediaeval Christian money-lenders who converted to Judaism in order to take advantage of the Church's exemption at the time that allowed the Jews to take interest.[542] To curb these practices, an ordinance was issued, in 193 BCE, forcing the allies to declare all debts involving Roman citizens. The public declarations unsurprisingly revealed the great size of the interest-bearing loans, which were contracted through the allies, and as a consequence the usury strictures were extended by the Tribune Sempronius, to encompass all the allies and provincials of the Romans, as laid down in the *Leges Sempronia* passed in 194 BCE.[543] The allies, however, seem to have continued to be used by money-lenders but more as a ransom than as a disguise, hence the allies were subsequently barred from any borrowing whatsoever in Rome as stipulated in the *Leges Gabbinia* passed in 139 BCE.[544]

The practice was increasingly prevalent nonetheless. The financiers of the capital devise a considerable number of clever contrivances and colourful shifts, by which their interest-bearing loans were disguised – in the same way that Islamic bankers conduct their business today.[545] The Roman legislator, of course, undertakes to put an end to these innovations, but after a long contest the ingenuity of the usurers seems to prevail over the authority of the legislator; for the latter has never been able to anticipate the multifarious subterfuges of the former.[i] So has it been, and so it remains.

It is self-evident that the problem persists in the modern era. Albeit a certain rate of usury is tolerated, the lenders continued to circumvent the law, especially in times of increased demand for credit. The eminent English Justice, Lord Mansfield (1705-1793), on one occasion asserted that, "when the real truth" (of a bargain) "is a loan of money, the wit of man cannot find a shift to take it out of the statute." [546] However, if Mansfield indicates that once legal evidence shows the transaction in question to be usurious in nature, the law will draw no attention to any pretence or disguise employed, it would be true. But the wit of man does indeed contrive some "shifts," which cannot easily be addressed. The laws of usury were executed with great rigour in England at the time; serving as panel statutes which must be construed strictly.

---

i This is a problem for Law in general. As noted by Professor Samuel W. Buell:
"All law articulated ex ante suffers from the limitations of lawmaker foresight. Theoretical accounts of law often describe this challenge as lawmakers' inability in the face of modernization to fully envision the future in which a law is meant to apply. Continual human advancement guarantees that new behaviours will arise that regulators will lament ex post but could not have specified ex ante." See, Samuel W Buell, 'Good Faith and Law Evasion' 58 UCLA L Rev 611, 612

Nevertheless, they were very frequently and successfully evaded, as evident in a report made by a committee of the House of Commons on the usury laws in 1818, which reads:

> "It is the opinion of this committee that the laws regulating or restarting the rate of interest have been extensively evaded, and have failed of the effect of imposing a maximum on such rate; and that of late years, from the constant excess of the market rate of interest above the legal, they have added to the expense incurred by borrowers on real security, and that such borrowers have been compelled to resort to the mode of granting annuities on lives, a mode which has been made a cover for obtaining a higher rate of interest than the rate limited by law."[547]

So, where the Roman Praetor failed, the English parliament also failed! Even nowadays creditors are resorting to diverse methods so as to sidestep restrictive rates mandated by the laws of most countries.[548] It seems that throughout history, secular usury laws, whether they amounted to outright prohibition or setting limits, were either disregarded, or cleverly evaded by tricks and cunningly devised contrivances. Based on this observation, it has been argued that the law of usury shall "belong less to economic history than to the history of ideas," since apparently it neither stopped usurers nor impeded economic advance.[549] Such arguments will be discussed later. But the question here is whether or not the Divine prohibitions of the practice had been any more successful?

Logically, the Divine law cannot be effectively circumvented. Belief in the sole Supreme Being, i.e. God, who is understood to be Perfect, Omnipotent and Omniscient, should leave the believer with no other avenue than to act obediently. It would be inconsistent with his belief if he sought deliberately to circumvent his God's commands and prohibitions; for it implies that his God is neither Perfect, Omnipotent nor Omniscient, or that he himself is superior in means and methods to his own God. Both cases stand in fundamental contradiction to the concept of God *per se*, as conceived within the Abrahamic traditions. Those who promote interest-masking transactions, whether they are Jews, Christians or Muslims, seem to be keenly aware of this fact. They neither claim that they are deluding God, nor introducing their subterfuges as a bid to defy or deceive Him, as this would be tantamount to blasphemy. On the contrary, they often support their 'legal fictions' with convenient theological interpretations of the scriptural prohibitions, maintaining that they are observing them, rather than nullifying them. This is demonstrated by the reality that both Jewish and Islamic banks today employ boards of religious scholars with the sole aim of certifying, and 'rubber-stamping', their financial products as being "*Shari'a*-compliant" or "*Halakha*-compliant." It is perfectly reminiscent of their early Catholic counterparts. For example, the German Scholastic theologian John Eck (1486-1543) was partly financed by the Fugger banking and mercantile family of Augsburg to undertake a mission to obtain a general theological sanction for one of the most popular interest masking transactions of the time, i.e., the triple contract.[550] Obtaining a favourable theological opinion or religious scholarly support appears always to be imperative for these transactions to gain acceptance amongst pious believers. Such a requirement, on the other hand, may not be needed for eluding man-made usury legislation. Practically, however, both divine and secular laws against usury were, and still are, commonly evaded. The fashions used may differ but they all serve the same purpose.

The concern of this chapter is to examine, compare and contrast the methods that have been used particularly for the circumvention of the Abrahamic scriptural prohibitions of usury. As shown previously, the practice of lending money for profit, any profit at all, minimal as it may be, was considered to be a deadly sin in the Abrahamic religions. In Judaism, the practice was seen *inter alia* as equivalent to robbery, shedding of blood and even rejecting God. It was abhorred to the extent that selling one's daughter into slavery was preferable to borrowing money at interest. Because of the severity of the Torah's prohibitions of the practice, Jewish authorities had elaborated a comprehensive doctrine that denounced not only interest *per se*, *ribbit*, but any form of profit that might even resemble interest, *"avaq ribbit"* (lit. the dust of interest). Numerous Talmudic extensions of the ban were designated to address any payment or transaction that entailed even a hint of increase or unearned profit that might accrue to the creditor. This included, for example, mark-ups on credit sales, future sales, fixed rates of return in partnership agreements, any gift intended to influence the giving of a loan, any gift or service given in gratitude for a loan, and any praise, compliment, or offers of blessing upon the lender while the loan remains outstanding. These latter were regarded as "verbal usury." All these were seen by rabbis as prohibited manifestations of *"avaq ribbit."* Curiously enough, a similar doctrine can also be found in the Islamic tradition.

Usury, or *riba*, invites severe punishments in the Qur'an – the Muslim holy book. Those involved were threatened with *"war from Allah and his Messenger"* in this life, and hellfire in the afterlife. Likewise, a considerable number of Prophetic hadiths condemn the practice, of particular interest is that narrated by al-Nasa'i in his *Sunan*, which reads:

> "The Messenger of Allah ﷺ said: There will come a time when there will be no one left who does not consume *riba*, and whoever does not consume it will nevertheless be affected by its dust."[551][552]

The "dust" of *riba*, here, may refer to the ubiquitous presence of the practice in every corner of society. There are other hadiths that prophesy that the prohibition of *riba* will continue to be evaded on an increasing scale as time progressed. For example, Ibn Qayyim in his book *I'lam al-muwaqqi'in* narrated that Allah's Messenger ﷺ says: "A time is certainly coming to mankind when they would legalise *riba* under the name of *bay'* (lit. sale)."[553] It was warned that if such evasions spread, it would invite disgrace from God. The Companion Ibn 'Umar ﷺ said: "I heard the Prophet of Allah ﷺ say: 'When you [*inter alia*] enter into the *'inah* transaction (an interest-masking transaction) ... Allah will make disgrace prevail over you, and will not withdraw it until you return to your original religion.'"[554]

Likewise, Christianity expressed a great deal of hostility toward the practice for at least three quarters of its history. Christian usurers were, for long years, under pain of refusal of confession, absolution and Christian burial, or the invalidation of wills and excommunication. At the time any interest rate that was greater than zero was considered to be usurious; moreover, hoping for anything beyond one's principal was declared sinful, it was regarded as 'mental usury'.

In spite of the injunctions, exhortations and stern warnings, however, historical evidence shows that the prohibitions of interest were not universally obeyed even during periods of revelation. No religion succeeded any better, notwithstanding the attitude of Orientalist scholars, who tend to classify this as one of the characteristics of 'the Oriental mind'. Attempts to evade the prohibitions of interest are as various in form as they are many in number and are to be found in the Islamic, Jewish and Christian traditions alike. It is suggested here that there are three principal methods whereby these attempts were and continue to be made. The first method is by reinterpreting the concept of usury itself. The second method is by exemption, i.e. by excluding the counterparty from the scope of scriptural prohibition. The third method is by concealment. Interestingly, none of these methods were exclusive to any one religion, although, for theological reasons, some of them became more popular among the followers of one religion than the others. Further discussion will be provided below.

Reinterpreting the Concept of Usury

The Abrahamic scriptural prohibitions of usury have been understood throughout most of their history to refer to the practice of charging financial interest in excess of the principal amount of a loan. However, in more recent times, this understanding has been challenged. Many intellectual efforts have been made to re-interpret the concept of usury as found in the sacred scriptures so as to give sanction to certain rates, or types of interest. Some of these efforts succeeded in persuading the adherents of one religion to become involved in the practice; others failed to do so. This section, therefore, will investigate the reasons for the successes and failures of such efforts. But, before plunging into such complicated currents, we may be well advised at this stage to mark our line of advance by indicating, in terms of jurisprudence, the causes we consider most likely to have given rise to these diverse ventures.

It is generally recognised that one of the essential differences between divine law and human, or man-made, law is that the former is immutable, whilst the latter is prone to frequent change.[i] Human law is often produced for a peculiar time and place.[555] It is generated within society in order to address society's needs. It derives its motivation from the diverse desires, demands and aspirations as expressed by civil society as a whole. As explained by the philosopher Baruch Spinoza (1623-1677), human law is created for the sake of controlling behaviour as a means to achieve

---

i   According to the source from which the law is derived, three main kinds of law can be distinguished: Divine law, which is revealed from God, natural law, which is derived from 'known principles of nature' and human law, which is made by human beings. It is on the basis of these distinctions, that the concepts of Divine law and human law are used here.

specific political ends.⁵⁵⁶ When these ends, or purposes change, man-made laws should, in theory, be modified accordingly.ⁱ By contrast, divine law is considered to be eternal, immutable and valid for, and applicable to, every place and time. It is divine, because it comes from the Divine, or as put by the likes of Brague, "…because it emanates from a god who is master of history."⁵⁵⁷ If this God is good, moral, rational, perfect and infinite, as conceived in the Abrahamic religions, then His resolutions are also supposed to be the same. But here is the rub. Since, once a particular practice, such as usury, is decreed forbidden, this prohibition cannot be dispensed with nor abrogated. Otherwise, it will lead to fundamental inconsistencies. How could one have gone to Hell yesterday, for what today is now to be considered righteous behaviour? How could one have done with curses yesterday that which is deemed praiseworthy for doing today? How is it that a high moral standard once deemed essential and imperative, can later be declared unnecessary? Unlike man-made law, the divine law therefore, is unchangeable.

This very aspect of the divine law seems to result in a great deal of theological and practical difficulty. For the ideals of the divine law seemed not always able to keep pace with the ever-changing demands of society and commerce. This is quite noticeable in

---

i   The authority of a man-made law, therefore, is not contingent upon its rationality, morality or goodness, but rather upon the acceptance of the law among those who avail from using it – that perhaps is what renders human law more variable, dispensable and abrogable with the course of time. Explaining this point further, the Dutch philosopher and Renaissance humanist, Erasmus of Rotterdam (1466-1536) stated:
"… as to human laws; there are sometimes unjust, foolish, and hurtful laws made, and therefore either abrogated by Authority of Superiors, or by the universal neglect of the people … a human law cease of itself, when the causes for which it was made cease; as for instance, suppose a constitution should enjoin all persons yearly to contribute something towards building a church, the requirement of the law ceases when the church is built. Add to this, that a human law is no law, unless it be approved by the consent of those who are to use it."

the problem concerning usury. The practice is categorically prohibited in the revealed laws. Under no circumstances, for the reasons explored above, can this prohibition be repealed. The best that could be done, and has indeed been done, is to advance new 'pragmatic' interpretations of these laws, in such a way as to allow their applicability to vary between subjects or according to circumstances. Nevertheless, in order to be accepted without calling into question the truth of God's words, such interpretations could not deviate blatantly from the literal meaning of the revealed laws. This appeared to be one of the reasons why Calvin's theory of usury was more successful in comparison with similar theories developed within other traditions, as we will see below.[i]

It is commonly agreed that Calvin was the first who broke with the traditional interpretation of the Deuteronomic Law. Rejecting the previous teachings of the Latin Church, Calvin maintained that the brother/foreigner distinction featured in the Deuteronomic verses demonstrates that usury, *per se,* is neither morally evil nor inherently unjust, as perceived by the early fathers and scholastics, given that God himself had made the Jews exempt from its implications. In other words, the prohibition against usury was not intended in the first place to be a universal spiritual law in light of the fact that it was not applicable to their dealings with Gentiles. The raison d'être for the prohibition of interest amongst the Israelites, Calvin concluded, was only to promote their 'political union'. "Our union," he says, "is entirely different." "Therefore I do not feel that usuries were forbidden to us simply, except in so far as they are opposed to equity or charity."[558] Calvin opines that because 'the wall of partition' between Jews and Gentiles has been broken down in the New

---

i These theories have been fully covered above, see section: Dissenting Views. Certain parts of these theories, however, will be highlighted here in order to illustrate how the scriptural prohibitions have been evaded through reinterpreting the concept of usury.

Testament, Jews and Christians are now free to take usury from each other, rather than both being forbidden to do so, but only in so far as it does not run counter to fairness and charity.[559] These virtues, he argued, will not be infringed when a 'moderate' rate of usury is taken from a 'rich man' who has used the money loaned for 'commercial purposes'.[i] Moreover, the parameters of what is considered moderate, as opposed to exorbitant, are to be identified, according to Calvin, based on one's discretion, i.e. the believer's conscience is his guide.[560]

Deliberately or otherwise, by doing so, Calvin has, in effect, passed the practice of usury from being an offence against public justice or morality, as the traditional interpretation indicated, to be a matter of private conscience, or individual intention, of which it is only God who can "judge the secrets of the lender's heart."[561]

The circumstances under which Calvin came up with this 'liberal' interpretation can be identified in his own statements.[ii] Calvin states, in his commentary on Ezekiel: 18:

> "But we must always hold that the tendency of usury is to oppress one's brother, and hence it is to be wished that the very names of usury and interest were buried and blotted out from the memory of men. But since men cannot otherwise

---

i In his commentary on the 'four last books of Moses', Calvin says: "But those who think differently, may object, that we must abide by God's judgement, when He generally prohibits all usury to His people. I reply, that the question is only as to the poor, and consequently, if we have to do with the rich, that usury is freely permitted." See, J. Calvin and C.W. Bindham, *Commentaries on the Four Last Books of Moses: Arranged in the Form of a Harmony* (Calvin Translation Society 1854), p. 131

ii It is generally agreed that Calvin was the first theologian who propounded the modern distinction between interest and usury in such a way as to make the one appear legitimate and the other not. See, H.S. Rose, *The Churches and Usury: or, The Morality of Five Per Cent* (F. Palmer 1910), p. 29; von Böhm-Bawerk, op. cit., p. 36

transact their business, we must always observe what is lawful, and how far it must go."⁵⁶²

Likewise, Calvin says, in his commentary on Deuteronomy 23:19:

"The law of Moses is political, and does not obligate us beyond what equity and the reason of humanity suggest. Surely, it should be desirable if usuries were driven from the whole world, indeed that the word be unknown. But since that is impossible, we must make concession to the common utility." ⁵⁶³

Thus, it was the necessity of 'public welfare' that motivated Calvin to develop his innovative interpretation. Whilst living in Geneva, which was a busy commercial centre, he probably recognised the increasing need for commercial loans, and thus interest-bearing loans, for the flourishing industrial and trade enterprises. This crucial demand for funding was to some extent being met at the time either by Jewish lenders who asked for hefty interest payments in return, or by Christian lenders who used a number of medieval cloaking devices, behind which an excessive interest rate is often incurred as well. Making interest permissible, but with limitations, would curb the monopoly of the former, as well as giving the latter the opportunity to work in broad day-light, thus reducing the cost of providing interest loans, which would reflect positively on commerce and trade, since nothing is of greater service to commerce and trade, as is often claimed, than money being available on loan at low prices, by which, industry, skill and talent are supplied with the capital required to carry out the business of production. Hence, it has been argued that the financial and commercial world was eager and ready for a new theological interpretation that relaxed the ancient prohibitions of usury.⁵⁶⁴ It was under such economic pressure, and apparently for pragmatic reasons, that Calvin had constructed his theory.

Unsurprisingly, however, his ideas were immediately taken up in many European countries such as the Netherlands, Germany and England.[565] Sheltering under his name, financiers started openly and shamelessly dealing in usurious contracts. Seeking to attack the Church's long-standing prohibition of usury, they also began to refer to Calvin as an eminent authority favouring the legalisation of the practice, as well as using his arguments in their controversies.[i] From his time onward the opinion that gradually grew amongst Protestant moralists is that the Latin Church had misinterpreted the scriptures pertaining to usury. As noted by one historian, by 1650, almost all Protestant denominations had come to agree with Calvin's position, that a reasonable rate of interest was not sinful, provided that lenders are in good conscience, and do not exploit the poor.[566] In the next few centuries, furthermore, Calvin's line of thinking was to become the decisive formula for the new spirit of capitalism,[ii] and was being adopted by almost everyone who pleaded for 'economic freedom'. Benjamin Nelson says in *The Idea of Usury*:

---

i Despite the fact that Calvin, in postulating his theory, lays down a number of conditions for the validity of taking interest, these conditions (as detailed in the previous chapter) were neglected, whereas his arguments for the practice were highlighted. As pointed out by Tawney:
"Calvin's indulgence to moderate interest, like Adam Smith's individualism, was remembered when the qualifications surrounding it were forgotten; and the practical effect of his teaching was to weaken the whole body of opposition to usury by enabling the critics of the traditional doctrine to argue that religion itself spoke with an uncertain voice." See, Tawney and Gore, *Religion and the Rise of Capitalism: An Historical Study (Holland Memorial Lectures, 1922)*, p. 120

ii As McGrath points out: "the lending of money at interest was essential to the emergence of modern capitalism." See, A.E. McGrath, *Reformation Thought: An Introduction* (Wiley 2012), p. 260

"Calvin on Deuteronomy became a Gospel of the modem era. Everyone from the sixteenth to the nineteenth century who advocated a more liberal usury law turned to Calvin for support. Even those who would not or could not mention his name were compelled to speak his words. If today we do not appeal to his teachings, it is because we have learned his lessons too well. Religious or even ethical vocabulary is no longer needed to justify the moral and economic postulates which he helped to establish."[567]

This popular success of Calvin's theory of usury appears to be unparalleled. It has no match, neither in Judaism and Islam nor within Christianity itself. It may be surprising to many readers to find that the position that has remained pervasive amongst Catholic theologians down to the present day, is that lending money for profit, whatever profit, be it great or small, amounts to biblically prohibited usury. There was, of course, some Catholic dissenting views, but although such views were generally based on similar Calvinistic arguments, they failed to obtain such a wide and formal acceptance.[568]

Coincident with the reverberations of Calvin's casuistry throughout Protestant countries, during the sixteen and seventeen century, Catholic moralists and legists were embroiled in long and sharp juridical contentions regarding many interest-masking transactions that were in vogue at the time, such as the triple contract, the personal annuity and the foreign exchange contract.[569] The heated disputes among the Schoolmen also encompassed a number of extrinsic titles through which an excess above the principal of the loan was to be permitted as long as it took the form of a compensation.[570] For example, there was a disagreement upon the validity of the title of lost profit, or *lucrum cessans*, and whether or not the lender is required to prove that owing to the loan he had lost the chance of a potentially profitable investment, or whether this was something to be rightly presumed, and thus could be, just like usurious loans, contracted for in advance.[571] Moreover, some argued that in the case of *damnum emergens*, the creditor is entitled to seek compensation for any loss resulting from parting with his money, even if there was no *mora*, or delay, viz. even if the debtor returned the loan at the designated time. Others refused to drop the element of *mora*.[572]

These age-long controversies were often produced from the new economic realities and conditions experienced in Catholic countries. Like Calvin's Geneva, the commercial cities in Italy, Belgium, France and Germany were in growing need of credit facilities. Therefore, the problem of usury was commonly raised in theological circles. With the course of time, three distinct trends of opinion began to emerge, and each of them continued to gain proponents, in varying proportions, to the present today.[573] The first manifests a rigorous and intransigent attitude toward the new innovations as well as calling for a re-imposition of the original strict qualifications required for using the extrinsic titles. On the contrary, the second trend shows a great deal of tolerance towards such innovations and titles. While both of these trends preserved the traditional Scholastic principles of *mutuum* and fungibility in their arguments, the third trend of opinion represents an actual divergence from, and break with, such fundamentals. It was pioneered by a small number of writers who started challenging certain aspects of the conventional doctrine, and adding modifications, or concessions, of their own. It is not usury, Georges Pirot proposed, for example, in his *Apologie pour les Casuiste*, 1657, to take more than the sum loaned since present money is of greater value than future money. The evilness of the practice, Ludwig Engel (d. 1694) asserted, is observable in the case of extracting usury from the poor, not rich. Le Correur distinguished between the *mutuum consumptionis* (consumption loan) and the *mutuum productionis* (production loan). And both Luke Collet (d. 1765) and

Pichler (d. 1779) contended that moderate usury is licit, whereas 'biting', or excessive, usury is not.[574] Apart from Pirot's proposition, these arguments appeared to borrow heavily from Calvin's theory of usury. However, they marked the beginning of a Catholic intellectual movement, which was to grow and gather momentum in the forthcoming period.

Towards the middle of the eighteenth century, the problem of usury became acute in practice, especially in Italy as the City of Verona floated a public loan at four per cent.[i] [575] This resulted in a raging controversy between the two opposing trends, the rigorists, led by theologians such as Daniello Concina (1687-1756) and Petrus Ballerini (1698-1769), and the followers of Calvin's lead, headed by a personal friend of Pope Benedict XIV, Scipio Maffei (1675-1755). The latter, in his famous *Dell' impiego del danaro, libri tre*, which he dedicated to the Pope, defended the legitimacy of the Veronese loan, using the same lines of defence used by Calvinists, that moderate usury is not in itself inherently evil, nor is it contrary to justice, though it could, under certain conditions, offend against charity. The rigorists, on the other hand, vigorously attacked not only the Veronese loan but also a considerable number of widespread interest-masking transactions and practices, despite the fact that many of them were approved by well-known authorities. Since the dispute caused grave doubts about the nature of usury, attention turned towards the Holy See for clarification.

i As early as the twelfth century, several Italian cities such as Venice, Genoa and Florence, took recourse to a system of public debt, also known as *motes profane*, to meet extraordinary emergencies. These loans often took the form of compulsory loans extracted from the citizens to meet emergencies, upon which, to ease discontent, an annual percentage was paid. In the fourteenth and fifteenth centuries, this system gave rise to controversy in which the legality of the system was defended by such authorities as St. Antonino of Florence and St. Bernardine of Siena on the grounds of *lucrum cessans*.

As a response, Pope Benedict XIV appointed a commission of cardinals, theologians, monks, clergy and some mendicants in order to study and report on the subject.[576] The conclusions of the commission were included in the encyclical letter *Vix Pervienit* of November 1, 1745, promulgated in Rome and sent to all Italian Archbishops, Bishops, and priests, with the warning that anyone who dared write or preach to the contrary would be subjected to the penalties imposed by the sacred canons on those who violate Apostolic mandates.[577]

Nevertheless, the encyclical, as the Pope himself emphasised, not once but twice, enclosed neither a formal decision upon the moral character of those interest masking transactions and titles about which theologians were divided in their views, nor a verdict on the legitimacy of the Veronese loan which had precipitated the current controversies. For the latter, the Pope apologised that sufficient evidence for passing judgement was not before him for submission to the commission he had appointed. But could he not have asked for such evidence!? However, the scope of the *Vix Pervienit* was rather limited to a reaffirmation of the traditional Scholastic doctrine of essential gratuity of the *mutuum* and the validity of the original extrinsic titles, as well as condemning the contrary opinions that had begun to spread in Italy, which the Pope depicted as an 'evil' that needed to be remedied before spreading further and shaking those cities of Italy so far not affected.[578]

The *Vix Pervienit* consists of five chief articles, upon which there was, as claimed, consensus among the members of the commission along with the Pope himself. The first defines usury as anything beyond one's principal in the contract of *mutuum*. Although no explicit reference to a specific person or thesis was made, the second article maintains that the sin of usury cannot be countenanced by arguing that the rate of usury is not great or excessive; or that the borrower is rich; or that the money borrowed is not left idle, but is spent usefully, either to increase one's fortune, to purchase new estates, or to engage in business transactions. Notwithstanding, the third article conceded that through some extrinsic titles a compensation in addition to the return of the principal could be justifiably demanded. There are, besides, a number of 'just' non-*mutuum* contracts through which one can fruitfully employ one's money. By using such titles and contracts, the fourth article avers, public welfare and commerce will not be hampered by the prohibition of usury. The fifth article just exhorts that one should not stop aiding one's neighbour by providing him with a simple, interest-free loan contract in order to comply with Christ's teaching: "Do not refuse to lend to him who asks you."[579]

Interestingly, in the conclusion of the letter, the Pope advised his flocks to avoid both those who are so severe as to conceive usury wherever profit was made with money, and others who are so lax as to perceive it nowhere. He proscribed that if someone would like to put his money into the hands of another with the purpose of profit, that if it were a contract of loan, he should assure himself that a proper 'extrinsic title' for a profit existed. In case there were different opinions about the usuriousness of any particular extrinsic title or contract, the opposite opinions, the Pope urged, should be fully respected as long as they were endorsed by renowned clerics.

The *Vix Pervienit*, including both the main body and the papal additions, deserves special attention as it reflects what seems to be the general tendency of the Catholic theologians from the Reformation to the present day. By adhering to the Scholastic teachings that prohibit any profit for the lending of money, regardless of the rate, or the purpose of the loan, this tendency could be seen as conservative in character. Viewed from another angle, however, it appears to be liberal and pragmatic, for it allows a considerable number of extrinsic titles and contracts, as well as deliberately remaining silent on others as seen above in the case of

Pope Benedict XIV, through which such scholastically prohibited profit is able to pass under the guise of compensation; or other classical contracts such as partnership, investment, insurance, annual rent, foreign exchange contracts and the like.

In subsequent centuries, however, the number of Catholic writers questioning the Scholastic analysis of usury increased but they did not bring much by way of new argumentations to the dispute. Men of repute such as Ferdinando Galiani (1728-1787), De Luzerne (1738-1821), Marco Mastrofini (1763–1845), Antonio Ballerini (1805-1881) and Antoine Chevrier (1826-1879) all made attempts to modify the old theory of usury.[580] Their modifications were ignored nonetheless. The essential tenets of the traditional doctrine were reiterated in the most recent canonical pronouncement on usury, the Canon 1543 of the *Codex Juris Canonici* of 1917. It reads as follows:

> "If a fungible thing is given someone, and later something of the same kind and amount is to be returned, no profit can be taken on the ground of this contract; but in lending a fungible thing it is not itself illicit to contract for payment of the profit allocated by law ... [provided that] a just and adequate title be present."[581]

The Canon leaves the last phrase unexplained in a fashion reminiscent of the *Vix Pervienit* in which Pope Benedict XIV explicitly excluded from his decision the extrinsic titles about which theologians and canonists lack agreement. In order to understand the large extent to which such titles contributed to the effective nullification of the prohibitions against usury, one needs look no further than the *interesse* titles, particularly the *lucrum cessans*.

The *lucrum cessans* was rejected by the early Scholastics for being too hypothetical.[582] As asserted by Aquinas himself: "the lender cannot enter an agreement for compensation, through the fact that he makes no profit out of his money: because he must not sell that which he has not yet and may be prevented in many ways from having."⁵⁸³ However, by the fourteenth century, the title begins to be admitted by a small number of theologians. The number increased in the fifteenth century as many distinguished authorities came to the defence of the title. The new general attitude is said to have resulted from the need to justify the imposition of government loans in Italy, the so-called *motes profane*.[i] Nevertheless, for approving the *lucrum cessans* as a form of compensation in practice, the theologians and canonists insisted on the fulfilment of three conditions: (1) a proof of loss of investment opportunity to be provided by the creditor;⁵⁸⁴ (2) there is a delay on the part of the debtor in repaying the loan on the agreed date;[ii] and (3) the compensation demanded be reasonable, i.e. equal to the return that would have been generated had the creditor chosen to invest in an alternative venture.[iii] These conditions were expected to prevent

---

i   Amongst those who approved the title were two saints of capitalistic Tuscany; St. Bernardine of Siena (1380-1444) and St. Antonino of Florence (1389-1459). Both are renowned for their knowledge and competence in theology and canon law. The former explained, in his argument for the fairness of claims for compensation for possible loss of profit:
"it is to be said that money was truly worth more to its owner than itself because of industry with which he would have used it ... and therefore the receiver of the money not only deprives the owner of his money, but also of all the use and fruit of exercising his industry in it and through it."
To put it another way, St. Bernardine opines that the merchant's enforced idleness, by reason of parting with his money, entitles him to ask for compensation. See, Noonan, *The Scholastic Analysis of Usury*, op. cit., p. 126-32

ii Ambrosius de Vignate explains that compensation must only be made for 'the time and just *interesse* of the lost gain, which must be certain and proximate.' As quoted in O'Brien, *An Essay on Mediæval Economic Teaching*, op. cit., p. 103

iii "Lenders," says Buridan, "must not take by way of *lucrum cessans* more than they would have actually made by commerce or in exchange." As quoted in ibid., p. 103

the usurers from misusing the title.ⁱ They were gradually relaxed, nonetheless.

The first condition was modified by the legist Paul de Castro (d. 1441), so as not to be applicable to merchants.⁵⁸⁵ St. Antoninus of Florence (d. 1459) extended this concession to non-merchants provided that they intended to invest their funds in business.⁵⁸⁶ Such intention, furthermore, was later found to be unnecessary because, as Fr. Merkelbach (1871-1942) maintained, if a non-merchant had desired to invest in business, he could have done so.⁵⁸⁷ The second condition was also dispensed with by many theologians in the sixteenth and seventeenth centuries.⁵⁸⁸ Later, by the nineteenth century, it was being argued that it was the supply and demand for money that should determine whether a given claim for compensation was reasonable or not.⁵⁸⁹ And, eventually, in the present era, the whole institution of interest is condoned by the vast majority of the Catholic theologians on the ground that:

> "Nowadays a loan of money (by *mutuum*) raises a presumption of loss of probably profitable investment to the lender, for which compensation in the shape of interest may, rightly be demanded; and this, even where there is no risk of losing the principal and no damage or expense incurred by the lender owing to the loan, ... and even: when the civil law is silent on the matter."⁵⁹⁰

This appears to be the current position of the Catholic Church on the problem of usury.⁵⁹¹ Whilst repudiating the Calvinistic reinterpretation of the concept of usury, by which the practice of lending money for moderate usury was normalised, the Catholic Church authorises her followers to take the same amount of usury, not as a 'profit' for lending money but, as a remuneration for the 'loss' of a chance to make a profit elsewhere, or what modern

---

i   In the absence of these conditions, Joannes Andreae asserted, "The way is open to usury." See, Noonan, *The Scholastic Analysis of Usury*, op. cit., p. 120

economists refer to as 'opportunity cost'. In view of this, it is not unsafe to conclude that both the Protestants and Catholics have today, in effect, arrived at the same practical outcome. For what the former justified by its own right, the latter conceded by the presence of a modified and relaxed variant of the *lucrum cessans* title. Different theoretical paths have been trodden, but one conclusion has been reached; that is, certain payments beyond the principal can be legitimately asked for at the beginning of a loan contract and regardless of whether the debtor returned the money loaned on time or not.

However, this may pose an intriguing question: Why were Catholic theologians of modern times generally so tenacious in retaining the old Scholastic analysis of usury? Why did they not take the same shortcut that Calvin had taken in his approach to the matter, especially as they converge with him upon the same destination, as we have seen?

To this question, once examined against the prevailing politics of religious rivalry and competition generated by the advent of the Protestant Reformation, I am quite prepared to propose here that the answer appears to lie in circumstances arising from the fundamental character of Catholic dogma and its application in practice. In order to maintain its claim to being the sole genuine Church of Jesus Christ, holy and apostolic, the Catholic Church pretends to the attributes of being both indefectible and infallible.[592] These qualities, *inter alia*, are claimed as prerogatives, or gifts, that Jesus Christ conferred upon 'His Church' in order that it should remain to the end of time the institution of salvation. Being indefectible "affirms that the Church is essentially unchangeable in her teaching, her constitutions, and her liturgy."[593] The Catholic Church often prides herself on being continuous with the ancient, pre-modern époque of the divine dispensation; unlike her rivals, namely the Anglican Church and the Episcopalians, who had interrupted any such continuity by introducing radical changes into the principles established during that earliest era. Through her claim to infallibility, the Catholic Church also wanted to ensure that her teaching on subjects of both faith and morals were free from error. It is important to note that the scope of this 'infallibility' was believed to include, not only the divine revelation but also, "any teaching, even historical facts, principles of philosophy, or norms of the natural law that are in any way connected with divine revelation."[594] The traditional view is that through the guidance of the Holy Spirit, in union with the Pope and Bishops, reliable protection is provided from the dangerous possibility of misleading the people of God. Hence, they teach only what they have received. Moreover, they preserve the entire repository of faith; hearing, guarding, explaining, and transmitting everything received from Christ and the Apostles without distortion or corruption.[595]

By making her teachings unchangeable and faultless, the Catholic Church has, in effect, placed herself in an awkward 'theological predicament' for she is now compelled, in principle, to adhere to her original Holy Spirit-guided interpretations, explanations and justifications, especially those related to faith or moral doctrines.[i] In my view, this dilemma is brought into particularly high relief by the problem of usury. It is a historical fact that Council after Council and Pope after Pope had denounced the practice along with the early Fathers who perceived it as

---

i As pointed out by Cardinal Newman, these teachings may be developed but not in a way contradicting, or reversing, previous ones. As clarified in The First Vatican Council, convoked by Pope Pius IX on 29 June 1868, which says there is a possibility of development of doctrine only if "that meaning of the sacred dogmas is ever to be maintained which has once been declared by Holy mother Church, and there must never be any abandonment of this sense under the pretext or in the name of a more profound understanding." See, respectively, J.H. Newman, *An Essay on the Development of Christian Doctrine* (J. Toovey 1846), p. 86; 'First Vatican Council' (1869-1870), https://www.ewtn.com/catholicism/library/first-vatican-council-1505 accessed 23/10/2023

morally evil, the Schoolmen who depicted it as inherently unjust and the Canonists who frequently imposed severe penalties upon those who dared to ask more in return than they had actually given as credit. Such a long heritage of intellectual and active opposition to usury may not have been regarded by Calvin and his followers as binding, but by no means could it be so easily abandoned or simply ignored on the part of the Catholic Church. This is because if she introduced a new relaxed interpretation of the prohibition that contradicted, or that had the effect of abrogating, its previous strict condemnation of usury, this would amount to the Catholic Church providing her 'enemies' with the much sought-after proof that her teaching is neither infallible nor indefectible, as claimed. This, if confirmed, would undermine a number of the foundations upon which the entirety of Catholic dogma is established. Moreover, it would suggest that it was not only her opponents who were guilty of making radical changes to the received doctrines of the pre-Reformation Christian legacy, but that she herself had also done so.

On this basis, I find it reasonably safe to assume that it was and still remains crucial for the Catholic Church to maintain her previous anti-usury teachings fully intact. In reality, however, in the wake of the Reformation, the Catholic Church began to relent in its application of these teachings, as is evident from her approval of a wide range of interest-masking contracts and titles. The justification for this relaxation is argued on the grounds of the need to maintain popular influence,[i] credibility with politicians and scholars,[ii] and mortgaged 'investments'.[596] However, what

---

[i] For example, in 1571, Menginus, a German Jesuit, wrote to the Jesuit procurator, protesting against the embarrassment caused by the silence on the interest-masking triple contract, alluding to the fact that "other religions concede it, turning the whole populace from us." See Noonan above, section: The Five Per Cent Contract and the Jesuits.

[ii] As seen in the Italian case of forced government loans mentioned above.

about Muslims and Jews? Do they follow Calvin's lead or the Catholic approach to the problem of usury?

Like their Catholic counterparts in the sixteenth and seventeenth centuries, contemporary Islamic scholars and writers appeared to be divided into three main streams of thought on the question of usury. The first seeks to exclude modern bank interest from the Qur'anic prohibitions on *'riba'* by developing new interpretations for these prohibitions, which are on the whole, not very different from the interpretations developed first by Calvinists and later by some Catholics in response to the anti-usury passages in the Bible.[i] Yet, this train of thought seems to constitute a minority in view of the verdicts of virtually all the International Conferences of *fuqaha* (Muslim jurists) which continue to insist that the term *'riba'* as featured in the Qur'anic prohibitions stands for interest in all its manifestations regardless of whether it relates to loans for consumption purposes or for productive purposes, whether the loans are of a personal nature or of a commercial type, whether the borrower is a government, a private individual or a company and whether the rate of interest is moderate or excessive.

Whilst this is the view that is held by the majority of Muslim jurists, there is no such consensus upon the standing of the interest-masking financial instruments offered by Islamic banks today. The second stream of thought, which tends to include members of *Shari'a* boards who are appointed and paid by Islamic banks, eagerly defends the compatibility of these financial instruments with the norms of the *Shari'a*. Directly opposed to them are the followers of the third stream of thought who denounce them as deceptions devised in order to circumvent the textual ban on *riba*, but they deceive not almighty God!

Contemporary disputes between the proponents of these diverse positions continue to engage the participants in robust

---

i For examples of these new interpretations for the Qur'anic textual ban on *riba*, please see Noonan above, section: *Riba*: Interest, Usury or Both?

and energetic fashion. The concept of *riba* is still indeed, a lively issue among Muslims, not only amongst the scholarly class, but even at a popular cultural level. For example, the problem of *riba* was touched upon in a controversial episode of the most celebrated, yet controversial, Saudi satirical TV series, 'Tash Ma Tash', or 'No Big Deal', which has been run exclusively during the month of Ramadan for 18 seasons so far, and gained wide popularity especially across Arabian Gulf countries. The episode, as demonstrated by its title: "Zaid is the Brother of Ubaid" (an Arabic saying used to convey a lack of meaningful distinction between two things; as in the English expression, "six of one, half a dozen of the other"), attacked the Islamic banks, depicting them as using deceptive devices to disguise the charging of interest at a rate that is even higher than that set by the conventional banks.[597] The episode also derided the members of *Shari'a* boards who 'rubber-stamp' such devices as being "*Shari'a*-compliant" in return for irresistibly tempting high fees and 'kickbacks' from the owners of Islamic banks, as a result of which, they usually succumb to the influence of this pressure upon them.

Notwithstanding this, the opinion that is favoured by the end of the episode is that the Qur'anic prohibitions on *riba* are not applicable to modern banking interest, given that the currencies in circulation nowadays consist of paper or base metals, whereas the currencies used in the era of the Prophet ﷺ, and mentioned in his *ahadith*, consisted of gold and silver. The episode concluded that a loan of printed fiat money at interest is not *haram*, for paper was neither used as money at the dawn of Islam, nor was it included among the items mentioned in the 'six commodities *ahadith*' to which the *riba* prohibition is applied. The episode ascribed this opinion to the Islamic writer, Hamza Al-Salem. In fact, this was the position first adopted by the Zahari school of thought.[598] Moreover, this attitude is reminiscent of the position of Calvin who severely censured, on one hand, the interest-masking titles and contracts that were popular in his time, chiding those who approved them as treating God, "like a child,"[599] yet, on the other hand, he advanced a new interpretation that legitimised the stipulation of direct simple interest at the outset of a loan contract.

Although it has raised a storm of controversy across the region, the message that the episode sought to convey, appears not to have found a very receptive audience among Muslims in light of the fact that the Islamic banking industry has continued to grow at a double-digit pace since that time, whether in Saudi Arabia, or even in the rest of the Arabic and Islamic world. This is well attested in the latest World Islamic Banking Competitiveness report, issued by Ernst and Young (E&Y), which shows that the assets of Islamic banks increased between 2010 and 2014 at an annual average rate of 20% in Saudi Arabia; 22% in Qatar; 29% in Indonesia; 25% in Turkey and 27% in Pakistan. Some of these rates are two to three times faster than the rate at which conventional banks grew in the same countries over the same period.[600]

The situation within the Jewish context reflects a similar trend. The dominant interpretation held by the rabbinical authorities perceives the charging or receiving of interest in any form as prohibited, but only between Israelites, according to both the Torah and the Talmud.[601] Nevertheless, in practice this prohibition has also been circumvented throughout Jewish history by multifarious interest-masking transactions. Some of these transactions are formally approved under the 'blessing' of contemporary Rabbis. The most famous among them is the *heter iska,* which is a complicated mechanism that restructures a loan into a partnership investment with a pre-determined rate of expected profit in order to mimic the essentials of the interest-bearing loan.[602] As noted by Tamari, an ex-Chief economist at the Bank of Israel, all Israeli banks and financial institutions in Palestine, as well as many in the United States and United

Kingdom, operate at present under the *heter iska*.⁶⁰³ By way of reassurance to their clientele that they are not in breach of the laws of the Torah against taking interest, some of these banks and institutions display on their walls a rabbinical document, known as *Heter Iska Clali*, certifying that their banking operations are consistent with *Halachic* requirements, whilst others employ boards of rabbinical advisors to endorse their lending products and facilities as *Halakha*-compliant – just as their counterparts in the Islamic Banks do.[i]

This shows that a significant proportion of both Islamic and Jewish scholars adopted the Catholic approach to the problem of usury; that is, to maintain the purport of the scriptural prohibitions theoretically unimpaired, whilst in practice supplying the means to sidestep them by giving approval to a considerable number of interest-masking contractual devices. In addition to this, I would further propose that the reason they preferred not to follow Calvin's lead may primarily be attributable to the relatively detailed and rigorous nature of the usury prohibitions contained in the sources of Jewish and Islamic law, as compared with the relatively generalised and informal character of the New Testament scriptures.

As we have seen in the preceding chapter, the practice of charging interest was prohibited in unequivocal terms in the Qur'an. In the *Sunnah*, the prohibition was not only upheld but also augmented by additional rules. Likewise, the injunctions against usury in both the Written and Oral Torah are explicit and forthright. By contrast, the New Testament is full of ambiguities. Usury as such, receives explicit mention only in the parables of the talents and pounds (Matt. 25:14-30; Luke 19:12-27). Moreover,

---

i   The most prominent example is a bank in Baltimore known as the Bank Vaad Hakashrus. For further information see, D. Klein, 'The Islamic and Jewish Laws of Usury: A Bridge to Commercial Growth and Peace in the Middle East', 23 Denver Journal of International Law & Policy 535, 555

it was only mentioned there incidentally to meet the excuses of worthless servants. The reference to usury in Luke 6:35, "lend, hoping for nothing in return," is also not categorical for it can be read as a simple counsel against lending at interest or even as a recommendation for how Christians should generally deal with others, as suggested by some. Therefore, it should not be surprising that the early fathers and canonists often cited from the Hebrew Bible, instead of the Gospel, in order to reinforce the unlawfulness of the practice. But, since the time of the Scholastics, the relevance of the Mosaic Laws to the lives of Christian believers had become a question of some doubt, in spite of the fact that Jesus himself reiterated that He did not come to abolish, but to fulfil the Law of Moses (Matthew 5:17-20).[i]

In short, the fact that the practice of usury was not more explicitly addressed in the New Testament allowed more room for reinterpretation and speculation. In my view, this single circumstance is significant enough to justify, albeit somewhat speculatively in the absence of any explicit evidence of admission to this on Calvin's part, my own willingness to assert here with reasonable confidence that this factor is most likely what enabled Calvin to set himself on a course to discover and express the will of God as it related to the prohibition of usury, and to allow himself to add 'qualifications' of his own to the prohibition. Islamic and Jewish scholars were not able to do the same, for the 'will of God' in this matter had already been clearly articulated in great detail in their scriptures, whether in the revealed Torah and Qur'an or in the Talmud and the *Sunnah*, which are also believed to be of divine origin.

i As noted by Goldingay: "It is a matter of scholarly debate whether Jesus' teaching should be seen as an exposition of the law, or a penetration to its implicit inner principles, or a radicalizing of it, or a replacement of it for the new age, or an independent revelation of God's will which does not relate very directly to the law's concerns." See, J. Goldingay, *Approaches to Old Testament Interpretation* (Clements Publishing 2002), p. 47

Another possible reason I would consider for why Calvin's lead was not followed, is the seriousness of the sin of usury in the sources of Islamic and Jewish law. The act is deemed a great crime in these sources. It incurs severe punishments whether in this life or in the afterlife. Its grievous consequences must have played a role in rendering Jewish and Islamic scholars reluctant to adopt a modern Calvinistic approach, permitting the taking of simple interest directly. We have seen above how because of the strictness of the Torah's prohibition of usury, the Rabbis took it upon themselves, as a precaution, to ban any payment or transaction which contained even a hint of increase or unearned profit that might accrue to the creditor, including, for example, mark-ups on credit sales, future sales, fixed rates of return in partnership agreements and the like. Similarly, a considerable number of 'on-the-spot' barter transactions were prohibited in the *Sunnah* simply, as explained by Ibn Qayyim, because of their hypothetical potential as being a little too open to exploitation for comfort as a means for perpetrating the sin of usury.

In view of the harsher spiritual sanctions threatened on those who were involved in the practice, furthermore, modifying the rigours of the divine prohibition against usury on the basis of a human understanding of its purpose would be seen as too risky an option, one that pious Muslims and Jews would rather avoid, even if an Islamic *fatwa* or a Jewish *responsum* were to have been issued in its favour.

In the case of the New Testament, on the other hand, once again there is no single explicit sanction declared against those who charge interest. The practice was indeed deemed a deadly sin in the Canon law and therefore attracting heavy penalties, but for the Reformers, the Canon law is no longer binding. Neither were the teachings of the early, or later, Church Fathers or Scholastics considered by them to be theologically infallible or indefectible.

To sum up, it could be seen that the provisions against usury in Islamic and Jewish law as well as in the Canon law are more precise and comprehensive. This makes it more difficult (although not impossible, as a number of attempts have already been made) to modify these provisions. In comparison, the relevant scriptural prohibitions featured in the New Testament appear more generic and less daunting. To invoke a new understanding of what God really intends by them is not therefore so challenging for Calvin. The popular success of his opinion among Protestants, if not all Christians today, indicates that although the divine law is immutable in itself, the ways in which divine law may be apprehended and becomes effective can be modified from time to time. In defence of gay rights, for example, the US President Barak Obama said in an interview that, "when attitudes shift, the laws followed."[604] This might be true for human law; for divine law, however, it seems that when popular attitudes shift, what follows is not the divine law, but the interpretation of divine law. This 'following' can be seen not only in the issue of usury but also in many other historical and contemporary instances such as matrimonial law, slavery law and religious freedom, regarding which the Catholic Church has relaxed and altered her original teachings over time. Even nowadays there are a number of Islamic scholars and writers who attempt to reinterpret, for example, the Qur'anic prohibition against wine consumption so as to make it *halal* (permissible), or at least *makruh* (disapproved), as opposed to being outright *haram* (prohibited). This is an interesting phenomenon that would certainly be a fruitful area for continued observation.

Exclusion of the 'Other'

"Hell is other people." This oft-repeated quote from the pen of Jean-Paul Sartre (1905-1980), has become one of the most well-known, yet most misunderstood popular sayings. It implies that one is defined by one's inter-personal relationships. People see themselves through the eyes of others. If relations with others are negative or destructive, they become a source of despair.⁶⁰⁵ Ironically speaking, however, 'others' can be heaven, rather than hell, when interest is accrued. It is suggested here that one of the methods used to circumvent the scriptural prohibitions of usury is by excluding 'the Other', i.e. making them exempt from the divine law. As seen above, a similar method was attempted by the ancient Romans. Yet, 'the Other' here is depicted, deliberately or otherwise, not only as a foreigner, but sometimes as a Gentile or an enemy from whom, therefore, usury could be justifiably and morally extracted. The examination of this question offered here will inevitably also shed useful light on the relations between one's 'brother' and the 'other', or to use Nelson's famous formula, between "tribal brotherhood" and "universal otherhood", as appeared in the Abrahamic traditions.

Treatment of Gentiles in Rabbinical Tradition

The three Pentateuchal laws on usury have aroused endless intellectual and emotional controversy in Judaism, more so, perhaps, than any other laws in the Torah, as well as in Christianity and Islam.[i] They contributed whether directly or indirectly to the rise as well as to the fall, or rather, to the expulsion and complete destruction, of many Jewish communities both in the Christian West and the Muslim East during the Middle Ages or even later.⁶⁰⁶ Early Jewish writings, i.e. the Oral Torah, including the Midrashim, *Mishnah*, Gemera, Baraitha and Tosefta, developed on the bases of these laws a considerable number of rules regulating all aspects of intra-Jewish and Jewish-Gentile loan transactions, allowing on the whole the taking of interest from Gentiles. While this permission has been taken for granted by the vast majority of

---

i   Please note that the text and context of these laws have been considered above. The focus here is on how these laws have been received by Jewish rabbis and *halakhists*.

Jewish authorities throughout their history, the justifications and the explanations provided are many and varied, and sometimes seem to be affected by the non-Jewish environment in which they were produced.

The most famous and comprehensive of the Pentateuchal laws on interest is that featured in Deuteronomy 23:20-21, which reads:

> "Thou shalt not lend upon usury to thy brother; usury of money, usury of victuals, usury of anything that is lent upon usury: Unto a stranger thou mayest lend upon usury; but unto thy brother thou shalt not lend upon usury: that the Lord thy God may bless thee in all that thou settest thine hand to in the land whither thou goest to possess it."

Adopting a literal approach, the Jewish *halakhists* receive these particular verses as giving free rein to engage in usurious transactions with the 'Others', but not with the 'Brothers'.[607] The *Mishnah Baba Mezia* states in explicit terms that, "Money may be borrowed from gentiles on usury and lent to them on usury, and the same applies to a resident alien." [608] Furthermore, the Midrash *Sifre*, followed by a minority of eminent medieval Jewish scholars such as Maimonides (1135-1204),[609] Gersonides (1288-1344), construes: "unto a stranger thou mayest lend upon usury", as a positive injunction.[610] Most of the Jewish commentators, however, interpret the verse as granting permission to take interest from Gentiles but not as an obligation to do so. The Gemera *Makkoth*, in contrast, exhorts that one should not take interest, "not even interest from a heathen."[611] The passage, nevertheless, standing as it does at the end of a tractate, is more homiletic than *halakhic* in nature. Some restrictions on money-lending to Gentiles can be found in other Jewish writings, but interestingly almost none of them are based on grounds of morality or the universal validity of the law.

To highlight a few, the rabbi Rav Hiya (180-230) prohibits lending to Gentiles, unless one is compelled to do so in order to earn a minimal livelihood, because, as explained by Ravina I (375-425), it will lead to general intercourse with them, and therefore should be limited so as to prevent Jews from "exposure to a secular lifestyle."[612] Rabbi Ishmael, in his composition *Mekhilita* (believed to be redacted in the late 3rd century or 4th century), proposes that albeit it is not biblically obligatory, interest-free loans shall be given to Gentiles for "the sake of peace."[613] Several medieval rabbis called likewise for not taking interest from non-Jews, namely Christians, but they introduced different justifications. Rabbi Menachem Meiri (1249-1310) and Albo (1380-1440) contend that interest is to be taken only from an idolater, and Christians are not idolaters. They are Edomites, and the Edomites are our brothers, added rabbi Abravanel (1437-1508).[614] In fact, we are worshipping the same God, avers Jacob Ben Elijah, a thirteenth-century *halakhist*.[615] [i] The credibility of many of these views has been questioned.[616] It has been argued that they were aimed to disarm life-endangering resentment directed at the Jews at the time. In any case, obviously they were not the prevailing ones. The point here, however, is to illustrate that the motive for these exemptions is pragmatic rather than ethical. This can be attributable to the fact that the Talmudists, in general, feel no qualms regarding the practice of taking interest, *per se*.

Unlike the Muslim jurists, the early Christian Fathers and Scholastics, it is not considered to be a moral evil or inherently unjust. As Tamari noted, "The mainstream of *halakhic* authorities saw nothing intrinsically wrong with money earning interest."[617] The purport of the Mosaic injunctions against the practice are held to be to keep it within the framework of righteousness. The preponderant view among rabbis is that the forbidding of taking

---

i   Nowadays a number of Jewish authorities have called likewise for the prohibition of interest-bearing arrangements with Muslims because they worship the same God. See, Klein, 542

interest in the Torah is because the practice vitiates kindness (*hesed*) but not *din* or *sedek* (justice). Explaining the ideological basis for the prohibition, Raba, a Babylonian Amora of the 4th century, declares that:

> "The prohibition of usury could not be derived from the prohibition of overreaching (*'ona'ah*); for in overreaching the victimized party knows neither that he is being deceived nor the extent of the deception, whereas in usury the victimized party is aware both of the fact that he is being deprived of his money (the interest) and of the amount of which he is being deprived. Moreover, the prohibition of usury could also not be derived from the prohibition of stealing, for in theft and robbery the victim loses his money against his wishes, whereas in usury the victim has acceded to his loss. Hence, we may conclude, the ordinary rules of law and justice would not forbid the taking of interest, for it is a product of an obligation undertaken by the borrower with his full knowledge and consent. The obligation is as justified as any obligation to pay for a purchase made regardless of any lack of perfect correlation between money paid and value received; or alternatively, the obligation is as justified as any obligation to pay for "merchandise" (the money) hired for use. If nevertheless the Torah does forbid the taking of interest, it is not on the ground that interest-taking violates *din*, it violates *hesed*."[618]

In the same vein, the author of the Sefer Hachinukh in his commentary on the verse "you shall not take interest from him," asserts that: "According to the normal morality of the world one should be entitled to charge for the use of one's money. However, since the whole purpose of the *mitzvoth* is to purify the Jew, [God] instructed us to give up that which is acceptable by normal moral standards."[619] Many Jewish commentators assured likewise the norm and legitimacy of the practice. For example, Don Isaac ben Judah Abravanel (1437-1508), a famous Portuguese Jewish scholar and philosopher, in his commentary on the Deuteronomy text, contends that:

> "There is nothing unworthy about interest ... because it is proper that people should make profit out of their money, wine and corn, and if someone wants money from someone else, why should the borrower not give the lender a certain amount of interest? ... It is an ordinary business transaction and correct ... Interest-free loans should only be given to the brother, i.e. the co-religionist, to whom we owe special kindness and consideration."[620]

These statements are worth mentioning, for they introduced what appeared to be the first theological rationale underpinning financial behaviours within capitalism. In his best-known and most controversial work: *The Protestant Ethic and the Spirit of Capitalism*, Max Weber relates the rise of a capitalist economy to the Puritans, namely Calvinists. They, he suggests, played a conspicuous part in the history of capitalistic development.[621] However, this research believes that the credit should be given to the Jewish authorities since they were in effect the forerunners, as could be seen in the aforementioned statements and the like, of many of the relevant Calvinistic ethical peculiarities. Not to mention that the striking similarities between the rationales provided, first, by Jewish rabbis in favour of the practice and those given, later, by Protestant and Calvinist divines,[622] could arguably have resulted from a sort of 'cultural osmosis'. The remarkable contribution made by the latter in this matter may lie in their adaptation to the former line of reasoning in a fashion that normalised charging interest not only to 'Others', but even to Brothers.

The question that remains is that if taking interest is a legitimate practice that is prohibited among Jews for violating kindness, as claimed, then why not demonstrate such kindness to non-Jews? Different answers have been offered in response to this question. Probably, the most radical one is that given by Gersonides. He alleged that "It is a commandment to lend money to an alien on interest if he needs it ... because one should not benefit an idolater...and one should cause him such damage as is possible ..."[623] Such extreme sentiments may be caused by the hostility that Jews were experiencing at that time, which often culminated in forced expulsions such as The Great Exile of 1306. There are other rabbis, like Maimonides, who explains that if a Jew provides interest-free loans to a Gentile, the Gentile may simply re-lend the money for profit to another Jew; therefore Jews are required to lend to Gentiles at interest.[624] The most widely consulted, Shulchan Aruch (lit. Set Table), composed by Rabbi Yosef Karo (1488-1575), offers the justification that Jews are bound by a mutual agreement, set out in the Torah, to join in a fraternity whose members offer interest free loans to each other, whereas non-Jews who are not a member in this fraternity should not enjoy the advantages of its membership.[625] Inspired probably by this argument, Rabbi Baruch Epstein, in his *Torah Temimah* (a twentieth-century commentary), vindicates that position:

> "Our refraining from taking interest from one another is similar to the regulations of many trade and other associations in which the members provide each other with special benefits. Such benefits are not available to outsiders. Yet there is nothing to prevent others from establishing similar associations and providing the same help."[626]

The view of the minority, on the other hand, is that interest-taking violates the rules, not of *hesed* but, rather, of *din* or *sedek* (justice).[627] Therefore, they hyperbolically refer to usurious money-lenders as "murderers" or "robbers" in their writings.

Furthermore, Rabbi Nahman ben Jacob, the Babylonian Amora of the 4th century, cursed orphans who used to lend their money on interest.[628] This disagreement between rabbis as to whether the laws of usury represent the legislation of *hesed* or the legislation of *din* is overarching, for those who adopt the first view declare that interest once paid cannot be reclaimed, whilst the proponents of the other view argued that even if the creditor is not obliged by the courts to return usury which he has received, he is obliged to do so "by the laws of heaven".

Nevertheless, it would appear that the view of the minority is more consistent with the seriousness of the sin of usury and its grievous consequences as indicated in both the Torah and the Talmud. If the reason for the prohibition is only to be 'kind' in dealing with fellow Jews, as argued by the majority, why then does it incur such sever punishments, as mentioned previously? However, it is important to note that the subject of this juridical dispute concerns the use of usurious transactions in intra-Jewish business dealings. In respect of Jew-Gentile transactions, the overwhelming majority of authorities allow the taking (or giving) of interest, as clearly attested above.

Taking full advantage of this permission, Jews, generally speaking, became energetically engaged in usurious activities during much of their history. They were not always forced to do so, neither in all places nor at all times.[629] The fact that they were infamous for being money-lenders among many nations can be ascribed at least partly to the way they comprehended, developed and applied the Biblical teachings pertaining to usury. At the time that mediaeval Christians were shackled by these teachings, Jews believed that their religion granted them a free hand to become involved in the practice.[630] In a like manner, when Muslims were deprived from doing the same, especially in 17th and 18th centuries, Jewish, as well as Christian, money-lenders stepped in to seize the financial opportunities.[631]

By adopting a theological interpretation that permitted taking interest from Gentiles, Jews were able to sidestep the scriptural prohibitions against the activity. Their lead, however, has not been followed by Muslims and Christians, presumably for two main reasons. The first is ideological in character. Christian scholars have rejected the Jewish discrimination between 'brother' and 'foreigner'. They preach that Jesus ﷺ has abrogated the barrier between Jew and Gentile and inaugurated a worldwide community in which this distinction is no longer relevant or suitable. Similarly, the Islamic scholars have condemned the Jewish attitude in this respect. The Qur'anic verse 3:74, reads: "... *That is because they [the Jews] say: 'We are under no obligation where the gentiles are concerned.' They tell a lie against Allah and they know it.*" Therefore, it would be difficult for Christians and Muslims to come up with an interpretation that allowed taking usury from 'others'. Such an interpretation may be in harmony with the Jewish dogma setting them apart as the 'chosen people', who accepted God when others denied Him,[632] but it clearly contradicts fundamental Christian and Islamic doctrines. The second reason may relate to a demographic factor, namely that Jews were usually the minority within the Islamic and Christian communities they had settled in, thus the rabbinical allowance of the practice was of great benefit for them. Had they been in the majority, they would not have had so much to gain from the permission to take interest from a small minority of 'others'.

For these reasons the Jewish method was not fully open to imitation by Muslims and Christians, but very similar methods were attempted, nonetheless.

St. Ambrose's Justification of Usury as a Weapon

Whereas the 'Deuteronomic double standard', as it is termed by Nelson,[633] presents little difficulties to Jewish commentators, it causes a great deal of theological and ethical troubles to their Christian counterparts. On theological grounds, the discrimination between 'brother' and 'foreigner' could not be upheld by the Latin Church, for Jesus Christ ☧, as she evangelised, was ransomed for all of mankind. On ethical grounds, taking interest was depicted by the Early Fathers as a moral evil, and by the Scholastics as being opposed to natural justice, so how is it possible that God, or strictly speaking the God of the Old Testament, suffers such an act of evil and injustice to be practised against anyone at all? In order to offer an answer to this so-called 'Deuteronomic dilemma', myriad Christian theories, assumptions and interpretations have been provided throughout the ages. Some of them, especially early ones, emphasise the immorality of the practice, while ascribing the divine allowance given to the Israelites to take interest form 'foreigners' to reasons specifically related to the time and their culture. Others, on the contrary, argued for the morality of the practice, but curiously enough, attributed in this case the prohibition imposed upon the Israelites against taking interest from their 'brothers' also to reasons specifically related to the time and their culture![i]

However, the focus in this section will be on the particular explanation offered by the bishop of Milan, St. Ambrose (340-397). He was one of the very early Christian scholars and theologians who attempted to account for the Deuteronomic discrimination. His opinions were popular and gained wide acceptance, but more importantly they were employed by the medieval Church so as to

i   Summarising the history of this line of argument, Nelson states:
"Modern exegetes friendly to expanding capitalism cherished the isolated Deuteronomic exception as heaven-sent proof of their contention that their medieval predecessors had exceeded the Lord's mandate in proclaiming a universal prohibition of usury. Beginning with Calvin... they showed how it was possible to escape both horns of the Deuteronomic dilemma: they sloughed off the discrimination against aliens by appealing to Christian brotherhood, and sloughed off the prohibition of usury, the inevitable corollary of the Hebrew and medieval exhortations to brotherhood, by triumphantly citing the Deuteronomic exception." See, ibid p.xxiv

enable Christians, first to take interest from Muslims, but later to give interest to Jews – an outcome that most probably was not that intended by Ambrose himself.

Similarly to many Fathers of the Church, Ambrose spoke vigorously in opposition to usury. In his work *De Tobia*, which was dedicated entirely to the problem of usury, Ambrose excoriated any type of interest charge, whether of money, food, clothing or anything else.[634] His view is that whatever is added to the principal is usury, and "if someone takes usury," he said, "he commits violent robbery, and he shall not live."[635] Advising the borrower, he warned that "You are poor: consider the difficulty of paying. Wealth is diminished by interest, poverty is not lightened by interest; for never is evil corrected by evil nor is a wound healed by a wound, but is made worse by an ulcer."[636] Turning to the lender, he asked apprehensively, "Is there anything more terrible? He [the borrower] asks for bread, you offer him a sword; he begs for liberty, you impose slavery; he prays for freedom, you tighten the knot of the hideous snare."[637] Ambrose also criticised the Roman legal interest rate, which is one per cent per month, known as the *centesima* or hundredth, referring to which, Ambrose stated, rather sarcastically: "Ought they not by that very word by which they designate it hundredth, to recall to memory the Redeemer, who came to save the hundredth sheep, not to destroy it?"[638]

Many of these expressions have already been used, or shared, by other Fathers. Yet the fuller treatment of Ambrose for the Deuteronomic exception is what seems to be unprecedented. Ambrose proposed to justify the Deuteronomic discrimination against aliens by an appeal to *"Bilabial antiquities."*[639] He argued for setting the Deuteronomic text in its historical context and interpreted it in view of the 'legitimate war' of the 'Chosen People' against the tribes inheriting Canaan. In his commentary on Deuteronomy, Ambrose asserted that, "The Law forbids you under any circumstances to exact usury from your brother," who is, according to Ambrose, "your sharer in nature, co-heir in grace, every people, which, first, is in the faith, then under the Roman law."[640] Respecting the 'foreigner', i.e. the stranger, Ambrose asked: "Who is the stranger but Amelech [the original inhabitants of the Canaan] – but an enemy? Take usury from him whose life you may take without sin. The waging of war implies the right of taking usury."[641] Explaining this point further, he said:

> "Upon him whom you rightly desire to harm, against whom weapons are lawfully carried, upon him usury is legally imposed. On him whom you cannot easily conquer in war, you can quickly take vengeance with the hundredth. From him extract usury whom it would not be a crime to kill. He fights without a weapon who demands usury; without a sword he revenges himself upon an enemy, who is an interest collector from his foe. Therefore, where there is the right of war, there is also the right of usury."[642]

Ambrose acknowledges that Deuteronomy allows interest taking in the case of the foreigner. However, unlike other fathers, he does not vindicate here that the allowance has already been abolished in the New Testaments, nor does he, like the Jewish commentators, conclude that its application is absolute. Taking a different course, he maintained that it is lawful, even desirable, to exact interest from a foreigner, but only if he were an enemy, and hence Israelites were permitted to take interest from their enemies, the original inhabitants of Canaan, who illegally withheld the land which the Lord had promised to Israel. Relating the permission to the conquest of the Promised Land, which according to the Bible would occur gradually over time,[i] Ambrose implied that usury was left to the Israelites, who

---

i Exodus 23 :29-30 reads: "I will not drive them out before you in a single year, that the land may not become desolate, and the beasts of the field become too numerous for you. I will drive them out before you little by

were unable at the time to defeat the Canaanites, as one of the most effective means to the achievement of that goal. It is, as described by him, an instrument of aggression, vengeance and extermination, by which the notorious foe of God's people will be gradually conquered. Thus, just like an act of killing, usury is inherently evil of itself, but under certain circumstances, such as an authorised war, it can be justified.

Ambrose aimed by this explanation to address the problem of taking interest form foreigners. In doing so, however, he arrives at a possible on-going exception to the interest prohibition. The conquest of Canaan was of course completed, nevertheless if usury was equipped as a financial weapon to be used against the enemies of God's people, then why not this weapon be used by Christians against the enemies of Jesus Christ as well? Such line of reasoning appears to help the medieval Church in finding its way out of the financial predicament that it confronted at the time.

The commercial revival of the eleventh and twelfth centuries,[643] the royal need of funds[644] and the crusades,[645] all of these factors contributed to an increasing demand for credit facilities. Notwithstanding, the Church was far from legitimating usury and was not ready to remove the stigma attached to it. On the contrary, it was during this epoch that her campaign against the practice reached its peak.[646] Thus, "Times were not yet ripe for a divorce between economic thought and moral theology."[647] This resulted in widening the gap between the business ethics preached by the Church, which prohibits Christians from lending money for profit, and the economic necessity of money being available for loan. To bridge the gap, the Church seems to take recourse to the Ambrose defence of the Deuteronomic proviso. His interpretation was given enhanced publicity and authority by its inclusion in the *Decretum Gratiani*, a famous collection of

---

little, until you become fruitful and take possession of the land."

the Church's Canon law compiled at the beginning of the 12th century. It has been incorporated therein as authorising usury 'between enemies'. Using his terminology, commentators on the *Decretum* explained how the practice can become a useful economic weapon in reclaiming the 'Christian rightful heritage' from the modern Canaanites, i.e. Muslims.[648] Even more explicit was Rolandus Baldinelli, who became Pope Alexander III in 1159. He declares that laymen may exact usury from heretics, infidels, and anyone who openly attacks the Church, justifying that it is not to be exacted in order to make gain but to bring such persons in the true fold.[649] Furthermore, Rufinus claimed that through the affliction of usury, Saracens (Muslims opposing the Crusaders) as well as other enemies, who might be too strong to be defeated in battle, will be recalled to 'the unity of the Church', and, if not, they would be compelled to subjection to the Church, or at least not to disturb it.[650] In the time of Pope Innocent III, Bernard of Pavia (d. 1213) likewise supported taxing Saracens with usury. Furthermore, Huguccio (fl. 1188) and Johannes Teutonicus (fl. 1216) authorised taking usury from any enemy, whether he is pagan, Saracen, Jew, heretic, or even Christian as long as there was a right to wage war against him.[651]

Interestingly, however, what starts as a permission to charge the new Canaanites with usury, for the Muslims turned out to be an open route to the payment of interest to God's 'chosen people', the Jews!

Taking their cue from the pontifical adoption of the 'Exception of St Ambrose', the Jews of Europe continued to exact usury from their Christian debtors. Even so, no direct retaliation was taken against them. The Latin Church, strangely enough, maintained a very lengthy silence on the matter of their usurious practices. As noted by Poliakov, the first ecclesiastical provisions relating to Jewish usurers do not appear until late in the twelfth century.[652] When they appeared, nevertheless, they were, at first, concerned with the protection of the Crusaders' patrimonies, and hence absolved them, along with the clergy and nobility, from any outstanding usurious debts, as declared in the Council of Paris, 1188.[653] Then, by the beginning of the thirteenth century, the Church intervenes but this time in order to, as laid down in canon 67 of the Council of Lateran IV, 1215, "protect the Christians against cruel oppression by the Jews." Rather than imposing an outright ban that prevented Jews from lending at interest, the canon merely includes a general warning edict, "if in the future under any pretext Jews extort from Christians oppressive and immoderate interest, the partnership of the Christians shall be denied them till they have made satisfaction for their excesses."[654][i] It is interesting to note in the language of this canon that at this early time, and even before the advent of the Protestants and Calvinists, the 'Catholic' Church, although not expressly stated herein, distinguished between lending at 'moderate' and 'immoderate' rates of interest, denoting that the former might be tolerated from the Jewish community.

Bearing in mind that Christians were under threat at the time of denial of confession, absolution and Christian burial, or the invalidation of wills and excommunication, for any involvement in interest, regardless of the rate,[655] Jews appear to have been given *carte blanche* to dominate the lucrative financial market. No wonder they hardly engaged in any other profession, as pointed out by a number of contemporary *responsa* (Jewish legal dicta).[ii]

---

i   Likewise, a synod at Breslau in 1226 referred to 'burdensome and immoderate usury', threatening Jewish lenders who demand such a thing by excommunication. Parkes, op. cit., p. 305

ii   For example, Rabbi Menachem Meiri, who lived in Provence in the thirteenth century, gives the following summary of this situation: "In our days," he said, "nobody cares to refrain from business dealings with, and interest bearing loans to Gentiles ... Not a Goan, not a rabbi, not a scholar, not a pupil, not a Hasidh, not one who pretends to be a Hasidh." Cited, with many other examples, in Stein, 'Interest taken by Jews from

Their success seems to invoke envy among Christian usurers, tempting some of them to go so far as to disguise their faith and pretend to be Jews, in which guise they were often protected by collusive local princes who falsely say about them, "These are our Jews."[656] Others, including whole churches and individual clergy, placed their funds at the disposal of the Jewish usurers, and collected the profit thereon.[657] However, the financial privilege thus accorded the Jews came at a high price. They were, more often than not, expelled from European countries sometimes to destinations unknown.[i] It is probable that this lack of security is what led some Jewish usurers to demand the high rates of interest indicated in the aforementioned canon.

The reason for which the Latin Church tolerated the usurious activities of the Jews, some argued, was to generate funds for the greater good of crusading success.[658] Nevertheless, the toleration continued even after the end of the main crusades. For example, Pope Clement VI (1291-1352), on hearing about a pious Dauphin who had expelled the Lombards from Dauphine in obedience to the canons, writes to the Governor, who was the Archbishop of Lyons, that the Dauphin should have put up with what the Pope himself was tolerating, and that it was a pity to expel either Jews or Lombards, when it was possible to make profit out of them.[659] The Pope's position in this case seems to cause an argument between a cleric and a knight of the same period, yet the most that the former could say in defence of the Pope is that one must draw a distinction between 'toleration' and 'approval'. It should be, therefore, fairly obvious that there

---

Gentiles', op. cit., p. 144, 148; See also the above section: Jews & Usury

i Numerous cases of violence toward medieval Jewish usurers were recorded. The motivation for at least one act of anti-Jewish violence was revealed when immediately following the massacre of the Jews at York, England in 1990, the conspirators went directly to the place where the records of debt were kept and destroyed them. See, Nelson, op. cit.; Shatzmiller, op. cit., p. 46-51

was indeed a *de facto* papal acceptance, if not *de jure*, for Jewish usurious activities. This can be further demonstrated by the reality that no court decisions can be found against Christians who took interest from Jews, nor against Jews who charged interest from Christians, despite the fact that the Church continually imposed severe punishments on those involved in the practice at the time.[660]

The Church's stance on this issue appears to give the impression to the public that the Jew might make his profit from usury without violating Biblical teachings.[661] This becomes evident in the declaration that Emperor Frederick II made in his *Liber Augustalis* of 1231. Unlike Christians, the Emperor declared, Jews can openly engage in the practice, because, he contended: "it cannot be maintained that usury is illicit for them. The divine law does not prohibit it. They are not under the law established by the most blessed Fathers."[662] One may ask here, which one of the early Fathers is he referring to? Since almost all of them asserted that Jesus ﷺ had already abrogated the Deuteronomic barrier between Jew and Gentile, and moreover urged that in the New Testament the believer is commanded to lend, not only to brothers but to anyone, including enemies, even without hope of repayment.[663] Needless to say, although St. Ambrose allowed the practice in the time of war, which he justified on the ground that it could be used as a special weapon against a militarily superior enemy, the benefit of this logic was not, of course, intended to be used by 'weak' enemies against believers, as suggested here. Frustratingly, however, no explicit clarification was ever issued by the Church that might have dispelled such a notion.[i]

---

i   Interestingly, the Parisian exegete Peter the Chanter (d.1197) noted that some princes were exacting usury from their subjects through Jewish intermediaries. See, Courson, *Summa* (lefevre, ed.), op. cit., p. 41. Translated in John W. Baldwin, *Masters, Princes and Merchants: the social views of Peter the Chanter & his circle* (Princeton University Press 1970), p. 298

In general, therefore, it seems that the Church deliberately condoned usurious activity on the part of the Jews. She may not have given official sanction to the Jews to pursue their usury, but she did not ban it either. This provides support for the belief that the Church recognised the economic need for credit transactions involving profit, but was reluctant to extend the facility to Christians. Poliakov noted that, "In the following centuries, scholastic authors most frequently agreed that it was simply a question of toleration in the case of the Jews, 'to avoid a greater evil'."[664] Jewish usurers were found to be the optimal means to satisfy this need without exposing Christians to the ills of usurious practices. It might be the case especially that the sin of usury was occasionally classed with homicide, sacrilege, perjury, homosexual offences, incest and parricide, and, like them, could not be remitted even by a priest in the confessional.[665] It is not surprising, therefore, that the Church was prepared to impose the harshest penalties upon those among her own flock who worked in that profession, while in the meantime she expressed, and sometimes encouraged a great deal of toleration to be shown, as seen above by Pope Clement VI, toward members of alien confessions who indulged in this evil, in order to maintain the flow of much needed funds.

This appeared to be, by the likes of Parkes, "an admirably simple method of evading the canons," that is, "to lay the mortal sin on the shoulders of someone else."[666] The common misconception that the Jew could lawfully make his profit from usury according to Deuteronomy, or that Father St. Ambrose authorised Jews to take usury from Christians as they are enemies, both probably helped the Church in choosing the Jewish shoulders to bear this heavy sin without much opposition either among Christians and certainly not on the part of Jews.

So, it could be seen that the Jews and medieval Christians share in practical, if not in theoretical terms, the same conclusion: that one could receive interest from (or give interest to) the 'Others' but not the 'Brothers'.

At this juncture in the overall treatise, it is clear that there is one further outstanding question that remains to be properly examined: Could the Muslims be following in the footsteps of their Jewish and medieval Christian predecessors by taking similar advantage of the available minorities (Jewish and Christian) existing in their countries so as to evade the strict Qur'anic prohibitions against interest bearing transactions?

According to Islamic jurisprudence, this question must undoubtedly be answered in the negative. The reason for this is related to the legal standards of treatment extended to non-Muslim subjects who permanently reside under Muslim jurisdiction. They are referred to in formal Muslim terminology as *ahl al-dhimmah* (the people of *dhimmah*), or *dhimmis* (the beneficiaries of *dhimmah*).[i]

The literal meaning of the term *dhimmah* as defined in *Taj al-Lughah*, one of the earliest Arabic lexicons, is sanctity (*hurmah*), surety (*damman*), or assurance of safety or protection (*aman*).[667] Laying special stress upon the covenantal aspects of the term, other classical Arabic glossaries such as *Taj al-'Arus* and *Lisan al-'Arab*, define *dhimmah* as signifying both the agreement (*'ahd*) and the sanctity (*hurmah*) of the agreement.[668] The author of the *Lisan al-'Arab* added that, "the people of *dhimmah* are so-called as such because they enter into 'a covenant of protection' with Muslims." [669] To put it another way, the people of *dhimmah* are the people with whom a covenant of protection has been formally ratified.

The first such covenant of protection conferred in Muslim history, also known as *'aqd al-dhimmah* (lit. *dhimmah* contract), is believed to be that which the Prophet Muhammad ﷺ concluded

---

i They are also known as *al-mu'ahadun*, lit. the contractees.

with the Christian community of Najran (a city located in the present-day south of Saudi Arabia).⁶⁷⁰ ⁱ By the provisions of this covenant, which came into effect in 10 AH (632 CE), the Christians of Najran were assured of complete religious freedom; their judicial and legal autonomy; the protection of their property; exemption from military service; and the guarantee that no army, Muslim or non-Muslim, should set foot on their land.⁶⁷¹ In return, besides acknowledging the sovereignty of the Muslims, they are obligated to pay the *jizyah* (poll-tax).⁶⁷² For those amongst them who willingly convert to Islam, they will be exonerated from paying the *jizyah*; but instead, like all other Muslims, they acquire the obligation to pay *zakat* (commonly translated as poor-tax).ⁱⁱ

The covenant also included an interesting clause that required the Christians of Najran not to engage in any usurious activities, not even amongst themselves. The reason for this condition may be ascribed to the fact that the pact was agreed upon in the same year that the last set of Qur'anic anti-*riba* verses, contained in *sura* 2:247-8, were revealed. The severity of the prohibition against *riba* was declared in these verses, leaving the believers with only two options: either to forgo any remaining *riba* or war would be waged against them by God and his Apostle. Acting accordingly, the Prophet Muhammad ﷺ announced in the same year, in his 'Farewell Sermon' given

---

i   By the fifth century, Najran was an important economic and agricultural centre, in which Christianity was so strongly established that it had its own bishop and had become a place of pilgrimage for Arab Christians. See, J. Kaltner, *Introducing the Qur'an: For Today's Reader* (Fortress Press), p. 145

ii As narrated by Muhammad ibn Ishaq (85-150 AD), the Apostle ﷺ used to send his companion Ali bin Abi Talib to the people of Najran in order to collect *jizyah* from the Christians and *zakat* from the Muslims. See, A. Guillaume, *The Life of Muhammad: A Translation of Ishaq's Sirat Rasul Allah* (Oxford University Press 1955), p. 649

on the occasion of his last pilgrimage to Makkah, that all pre-Islamic *riba*, including the debts due to his uncle, al-'Abbas, were thenceforth cancelled.[i] Thus, the practice was no longer permissible amongst Muslims.[673] For non-Muslims who wished to enter into a peace treaty with him, it is no wonder therefore, that the Prophet ﷺ stipulated that they should first abjure any dealings in *riba*. This was the case not only with the Christians of Najran but also with the Zoroastrians of Hajar (an ancient city in Eastern Arabia) to whom the Prophet ﷺ also sent a letter in the same year, in which he warned that war would be declared against them unless they renounced all outstanding claims due to them from *riba*.[674]

Similar covenants of protection were granted by the Prophet Muhammad ﷺ to other non-Muslim communities dwelling in the Arabian peninsula.[ii] The sanctity of these covenants has been further accentuated in a considerable number of *ahadith* in which the Prophet ﷺ firmly warned his Companions against mistreating *dhimmis*. For instance, he said:

> "If anyone wrongs a [*dhimmi*], detracts from his rights, burdens him with more work than he is able to do, or takes

---

i The Prophet ﷺ stated: "Usury is forbidden but you will be entitled to recover your principal. Do not wrong and you shall not be wronged. Allah [the God] had decreed that there should be no usury and I am making a beginning by remitting the amount of interest which 'Abbas b. Abd al-Muttalib has to receive. Verily it is remitted in its entirety." As quoted in Muhammad Samiullah, 'Prohibition of *Riba* (Interest) & Insurance in the Light of Islam' 21 Islamic Studies 53

ii Muslim historians noted a number of these treaties. For example, al-Baladhuri (278-279 AH/892 CE) in his book, *Futuh al-Buldan*, reported several pacts made by the Prophet Muhammad ﷺ with the non-Muslim people of Tabalah, Jarash, Ayla, Adhruh, Maqna, al-Jarbah, Yemen and Oman, by which they were likewise given protection of their lives, rights, property and beliefs in return for paying *jizyah*. For further information see, Abu al-'Abbas Ahmad Ibn Yahya Al-Baladhuri, *Futuh al-buldan* (Dar wa Maktaba al-Hilal 1988)

something from him without his consent, I will plead for him [the *dhimmi*] on the Day of Resurrection."⁶⁷⁵

Likewise, in another *hadith*, he stated:

"Whoever killed a person having a treaty with the Muslims, shall not smell the smell of Paradise ..."⁶⁷⁶

The Prophetic approach to dealing with religious minorities, as appeared in his actions and sayings, formed the basis of the legal position for Muslims vis-à-vis the people of *dhimmah*;⁶⁷⁷ their lives and properties are considered to be inviolable (*ma'sum*) on equal par with the lives and properties of Muslims.ⁱ Applying this principle to the question of usury, the Muslim jurists (*fuqaha*) of the four schools of Islamic jurisprudence (*madhhabs*) are agreed by consensus (*ijma'*) that it is prohibited for a Muslim to either pay *riba* to or charge *riba* to a *dhimmi* who resides under Muslim jurisdiction.⁶⁷⁸ The prohibition is justified by the fact that the wealth of *dhimmis* is protected by the *'aqd al-dhimmah* so that it cannot be acquired or gained from them by means of invalid or unjust transactions such as *riba*.ⁱⁱ The same holds true for dealings

---

i As evident in a tradition from the Companion of the Prophet Muhammad ﷺ 'Ali b. Abi Talib (d. 40 AH/ 661 CE) in which he said: "They [non-Muslims] pay the *jizyah* so that their lives are [protected] like our lives, and their property is [protected] like our property." As translated in A. Abdullahi, 'Religious minorities under Islamic law and the limits of cultural relativism' Human Rights Quarterly 1, 324, 328-9. For further information, see, Zayn al-Din ibn Ibrahim Ibn Nujaym, *al-Bahr al-raiq: sharh Kanz al-daqa'iq* (Dar al-Kutub al-'Ilmiyya 1997), Vol. 5, 127

ii Furthermore, some of the *fuqaha* called for forcibly preventing *dhimmis* from dealing in *riba* even between themselves. Imam Abu Bakr al-Sarakhsi (d. 1096 CE) in his book, *al-Mabsut*, asserted that using coercion in this case should not be seen as a repudiation of the covenant of protection for three main reasons. The first is that *riba* has already been prohibited in the religions of the people of *dhimmah*, namely Jews and Christians, as mentioned in the Qur'an (4:161). Thus, by preventing them from the practice, the Muslims are not in effect impugning their legal or religious autonomy. The second reason is that as their possessions are

between the Muslim and the *musta'min* (the one who seeks *aman*, or safety).⁶⁷⁹ The difference between the *dhimmi* and the *musta'min* in Islamic law is that the former is permanently settled under Muslim jurisdiction, whilst the latter stays only temporarily and often just for business purposes.⁶⁸⁰

Yet, the unanimity among the *fuqaha* on this issue is limited to *riba*-based transactions that take place in the territory over which the law of Islam prevails. Such territory is often referred to in Islamic political terminology as *dar al-Islam* (lit. the Abode of Islam), in contrast with *dar al-harb* (lit. the Abode of War) or *dar al-kufr* (the Abode of Disbelief), which is deemed to be any territory that is not under Muslim governance. The *fuqaha* are divided in their opinions upon the prohibition of dealings in *riba* in non-Muslim lands. This will be discussed in greater detail in the following section.

The Hanafi Doctrine of the Abode of War

Although it has no textual support, neither in the Qur'an nor in the authentic *Sunnah*, some of the early classical Muslim jurists divided the world into two zones: the abode of Islam (*dar al-Islam*) and the abode of war (*dar al-harb*). The abode of Islam consists of territories where the sovereign power lies with Muslims, the rules of *Shari'a* are applied and Islamic rituals are performed. The people of this abode are Muslims and *dhimmis*. On the other hand, the abode of war comprises all other territories that are not subject to Muslim sovereignty and in which, as a result, the religious rules of Islam are not implemented.⁶⁸¹ Its people are belligerents (*harbis*). This division of the world has been upheld

---

inviolable, the Muslim authority is entitled to intervene to bar them from the consumption of one another's property by dishonest means, i.e. *riba*. The third reason is that the Prophet himself ﷺ rendered the pact of the Christians of Najran, as well as the treaty of the Zoroastrians of Hajar, contingent upon ceasing their dealings in *riba*. See, Muhammad Ibn Ahmad al-Sarakhsi, *al-Mabsut* (Dar al-Kutub al-'Ilmiya 1993), Vol. 14, 58.

primarily by the *fuqaha* of the Hanafi school of jurisprudence. Furthermore, according to the founder of the school, Imam Abu Hanifah Nu'man bin Thabit (699-767 CE), *dar al-Islam* itself may lose its *de jure* status and become *dar al-harb* when three conditions are met: (i) the ascendancy of the rule of polytheism; (ii) the union with *dar al-harb*; and (iii) the non-existence of any Muslims who are safeguarded in living according to their belief or *dhimmis* who were once awarded a covenant of protection by a Muslim polity.[682] Notwithstanding, some Hanafi jurists opine that the ascendancy of the rule of polytheism in *dar al-Islam* is sufficient to turn it into *dar al-harb*.[683] Others maintained that any territory where Muslims have the potential capability of applying Islamic law is deemed *dar al-Islam* even if they do not comprehensively apply it there.[684]

Falling as it does into the midst of today's persistent and often heated debates regarding the tolerance or otherwise of the Muslim faith, this polarising division of the world has been seized upon as a positive proof by notable orientalist scholars, in support of their contention that the logic of Islamic law does not recognise the valid permanence of any non-Islamic polity.[685] The Muslim view of the world, they claim, is that all human beings must either accept Islam or submit to Muslim governance. Therefore, it is a religious duty of Muslims to declare war against non-Muslim dominions everywhere until the final and inevitable triumph of Islam over unbelief is realised.[686]

In response, Muslim scholars and writers maintain that this bipartite conception of the world was not based on provisions laid down in the textual sources, i.e. Qur'an and Hadith.[687] It was merely a contingent thesis evinced by some of the *fuqaha* in the course of applying their minds to the various implications and consequences of war between Muslims and others.[688] The hypothetical scenario is not dissimilar to those posited by contemporary jurists of international law, namely that war splits the international community into two parties: belligerents and non-belligerents, whilst any remaining members of the international community may be considered neutrals.

It has also been said that the real purport of the division of the world as expounded by the Hanafi jurists is to address the legal issues pertaining to the territorial jurisdiction of Islamic law.[689] Unlike the Malikis and the generality of the Shafi'is and Hanbalis, Hanafi jurists are of the view that the Islamic legal system shall take into account the territorial limits.[690] This is what is commonly referred to in Public International Law as the 'territorial principle'. From the perspective of Imam Abu Hanifah and his well-known disciple, Muhammad b. al-Hasan al-Shaybani (d. 805 CE), Muslim courts have no jurisdiction to try a case if the cause of the action arises beyond the geographical boundaries of *dar al-Islam*, given that these courts cannot exercise effective jurisdiction over a territory that is not under the effective government by the Islamic ruler (*Imam*) of *dar al-Islam*.[691] [i] Accordingly, if a Muslim violates an Islamic rule, or if he violates the rights of a non-Muslim in *dar al-harb*, he shall not be held liable in Islamic courts although he will be held liable for his violation in the court of God hereafter.[ii]

---

i In order to support the principle of territorial jurisdiction, Hanafi jurists have also referred to a number of Qur'anic verses and hadiths. For examples, see, Muhammad Mushtaq Ahmad, 'The notions of *dar al-harb* and *dar al-Islam* in Islamic jurisprudence with special reference to the Hanafi school' 47 Islamic Studies 5

ii As noted by Imam al-Sarakhsi (d.1096), one of the greatest and best-known Hanafi jurists: "If a Muslim enters *dar al-harb* ... and lends money to or borrows money from the inhabitants of that territory, or usurps their property or his property is usurped [by them] there, his case will not be heard [in the courts of *dar al-Islam*], because the wrong was committed outside Muslim jurisdiction. For the Muslim who usurped their property after guaranteeing them not to do that, we hold this opinion because he violated his promise, not the promise of the Muslim ruler. However, he will be counselled by way of *fatwa* to return the property though he will not be compelled to do so by the court. As for the inhabitants of that land who usurped the property of the Muslim, we hold this opinion

Similarly, if a non-Muslim violates the rights of a Muslim in *dar al-harb*, he shall not be liable for his violations in Islamic courts even if he is subsequently captured by the Muslims or he otherwise enters into Muslim territory.

The only case to which the territorial principle appears not to be applicable in Hanafi jurisprudence is when a citizen of *dar al-Islam* perpetrates a crime against another of its citizens in *dar al-harb*. This was argued on the ground that although the aggressor and the victim were physically outside the borders of *dar al-Islam* when the crime was perpetrated, they were both legally under the jurisdiction of the courts of *dar al-Islam*.[i] Curiously enough, however, under Hanafi jurisprudence, the person who embraces Islam in *dar al-harb* but does not migrate to *dar al-Islam* shall not be recognised as a citizen of *dar al-Islam* by the Islamic courts.[ii] The same applies in the case of a citizen of *dar al-Islam* who is

---

because they violated their promise at a place where they were not under the Muslim jurisdiction." See, al-Sarakhsi, op. cit., Vol. 10, p. 104. As translated in Muhammad Ashraf, *The Muslim Conduct of State* (1945), op. cit., p. 104

In another place in his book, Imam al-Sarakhsi stated: "If a Muslim soldier commits *zina* [adultery] in *dar al-harb*, the ... punishment cannot be awarded to him because the cause of action arose outside the jurisdiction of the Islamic state." Ibid., p. 20

i Burhan al-Din 'Ali b. Abi Bakr al-Marghinani, *al-Hidayah fi Sharh Bidayat al-Mubtadi* (Dar Ihya' al-Turath al-'Arabi), vo.2, 396. Also, Imam al-Sarakhsi pointed out this justification in his dealing with the case of a Muslim who goes to *dar al-harb* temporarily and leaves behind him a wife in *dar al-Islam*: whether their wedlock is terminated. He asserted that, "because a Muslim is legally a resident of *dar al-Islam* even if he is physically present in *dar al-harb* and physical separation between the two territories cannot terminate the wedlock unless legal separation is also there." Ibid., Vol. 10, p. 69. As translated in Ahmad, op. cit., p. 21

ii As noted by Imam Zayn al-Din ibn Nujaym (d.1563 CE), "According to Abu Hanafah, the position of a person who embraces Islam in *dar al-harb* and does not migrate [to *dar al-Islam*] is like that of a *harbi* in the sense that his property is not protected [by the law of the land in *dar al-Islam*]" Ibn Nujaym, op. cit., Vol. 5, p. 147. As translated in Ahmad, op. cit., p. 12

taken as captive in *dar al-Harb*, since, owing to his captivity, he falls beyond the jurisdiction of *dar al-Islam*.[692] Thus, if a citizen of *dar al-Islam* is charged with the murder of a Muslim inhabitant of *dar al-harb*, the courts of *dar al-Islam* will not hear the case. Likewise, if two citizens of *dar al-Islam* are imprisoned in *dar al-harb* and one of them kills the other during the period of imprisonment.[693]

Briefly, from the Hanafi outlook, Muslims who actually or constructively remain beyond the jurisdiction of Muslim governance are, legally speaking, *ghayr ma'sum* (violable), that is, they are not ensured legal protection of their rights by the Muslim government. Furthermore, anyone who violates their rights, whether they be Muslim or non-Muslim, will therefore not be held liable in the courts of Muslim jurisdiction. Of course, this does not exempt the violator from punishment in the afterlife.

Hence, in view of these legal details, it should be fairly obvious that the Hanafi doctrine of the bipartite division of the world is not necessarily predicated upon a relationship of hostility between the Muslim and the non-Muslim polities. Rather, it represented an affirmation of the principle of territorial jurisdiction evinced by Hanafi jurists. The territory over which the Muslim courts are able to exercise effective jurisdiction was called *dar al-Islam*, whereas the rest of the world that lay beyond the legal competence of the Muslim courts, was the so-called *dar al-harb*.[694] Whether the rest of the world has peaceful or hostile relations with *dar al-Islam* will, from the legal perspective, make no difference as the Muslim courts will possess no competency whatsoever to exercise jurisdiction from the point of view of Hanafi jurists. Their motive was to rationalise in legal terms the consequences of an act committed in a dominion under the hegemony of Muslims where Islamic law is consequently implemented, as opposed to that committed under the hegemony of non-Muslims where their own law is applied. It is for this reason that they limited the division of the world into only two dominions.

However, the majority of the *fuqaha* did not subscribe to the idea of territoriality and proposed other theories as to the division of the world. The leading formulation among them is that propounded by Imam Yahya ibn Sharif al-Nawawi (d. 1277 CE(.[695]

In his *Minhaj*, under *Kitab al-Jihad and al-Jizyah*, Imam al-Nawawi divided the world into *dar al-Islam* (the abode of Islam) and *dar al-kufr* (the abode of disbelief). Depending on the actual attitude of its inhabitants toward Islam and Muslims, Imam al-Nawawi distinguished between three types of *dar al-kufr*. The first is a non-Muslim territory that has concluded a peace treaty with an Islamic polity. This was referred to as *dar al-sulh* or *dar al-'ahd* (the term *sulh* means 'peace' or 'composition', whereas *'ahd* only means 'agreement'). The second type is the territory of truce (*dar al-hudnah*) that is a non-Muslim territory whose residents have entered into a temporary truce from warfare. The third type of *dar al-kufr* is the territory of war (*dar al-harb*). This encompasses all non-Muslim territories that have no non-aggression or truce treaty with *dar al-Islam* and thus it is in a state of war with *dar al-Islam*. According to Imam al-Nawawi, the offensive *jihad* is only associated with this type of territory within the category of *dar al-kufr*.[696]

A good knowledge of these distinctions between the Hanafi concept of world division, that is *dar al-Islam* and *dar al-harb*, and al-Nawawi's concept, that is *dar al-Islam* and *dar al-kufr*, will prove helpful for a fuller understanding of the controversy amongst the *fuqaha* with regard to the prohibition of dealings in *riba* in non-Muslim lands.

The opinion of the vast majority of the Muslim jurists, including Imam Malik (d. 795 CE), al-Shafi'i (d. 820 CE), Ahmad ibn Hanbal (d. 855 CE), as well as some prominent Hanafi jurists such as Ya'qub ibn Ibrahim al-Ansari (d.798 CE), better known as

Abu Yusuf, is that the prohibition of *riba* is universal in nature. Its operation is not subject to location.[697]

Their evidences for this position are more straightforward and sound.[698] These include: firstly, the generality of the scriptural prohibitions of *riba*, which do not specify the prohibition to certain territories rather than to others, nor to certain groups of people rather than to others.[699] Secondly, by extrapolation, the prohibitions in Islamic law have never been a matter limited to the Muslims in Muslim lands, such that when they depart these lands, they are allowed to violate Allah's prohibitions.[700] For instance, by consensus, drinking wine in a non-Muslim land is as prohibited as it is in a Muslim land. Similarly, adultery and prostitution in a non-Muslim land is as impermissible as it is in a Muslim land. The case of *riba* should not be any different on this score. Especially, as the Prophet ﷺ said, "Fear Allah wherever you may be!"[701] Thirdly, just as for Muslims, the prohibition of *riba* is also applied to non-Muslims, namely Christians and Jews, as borne out in the tone of the Qur'anic verses: "*because they [the Jews] practise usury – although they were forbidden it – and cheat others of their possessions.*"[702] Fourthly, prohibiting *riba* in dealings between Muslims, whilst permitting it in dealings between Muslims and non-Muslims, is similar to the behaviour of the Jews, who prohibit *riba* in dealings between themselves, but permit it in their dealings with the Gentiles. This attitude is strongly censured in the Qur'an, as mentioned in verse 3:74, "*... That is because they [the Jews] say: 'We are under no obligation where the gentiles are concerned.' They tell a lie against Allah and they know it.*"[703]

In spite of this, on the other hand, the position of Imam Abu Hanifah and his companion Muhammad ibn al-Hasan and that of Sufyan al-Thawri (d. 778 CE), Ibrahim al-Nakha'i (d. 715 CE), being also one of the narrations from Ahmad bin Hanbal and preferred by Ibn Taymiyyah, appears to permit the dealing in *riba*, along with other Islamically invalid transactions such as selling prohibited commodities like pork or wine, between Muslims and non-Muslims in *dar al-harb*.[704] [i] This is because, as justified by al-Kasani in his *Bada'i al-Sana'i*, one of the major reference works of Hanafi jurisprudence:

> "The wealth of the *harbi* is not protected ... Nevertheless, the Muslim with an agreement of security [given by the *harbis*] is forbidden from seizing it without the approval of the *harbi* due to the treachery and betrayal entailed. But, if the *harbi* gives his wealth by his choice and approval [through *riba*-based contract], then this obstacle is removed, so the taking of his wealth [in this case] becomes a seizing of un-owned, permissible property. Such seizing is legally valid and ensures legal possession, like seizing firewood or hashish. By this it becomes clear that the [*riba*-based] contract here does not justify the possession [of the *harbi's* wealth], but rather it fulfils a condition for possession [of his wealth], i.e. the approval [of the *harbi*], for the *harbi's* possession does not cease without his approval ... but once the *harbi's* possession ceases [by his approval], the possession is established for the Muslim by taking or seizing, not by the contract, so *riba* does not occur here, for *riba* is the name given to a surplus gained through a contract."[705]

To put it another way, the Hanafis argued that the *riba* contract that the Muslim makes with the *harbi* is not the means by which he acquires possession of *riba* increase. What gains him such possession is, in effect, the *harbi's* approval for his money to be taken; by virtue of his approval, the Muslim is released from

---

i   It is important to stress here that what the Hanafis mean by *dar al-harb* is whatever is not *dar al-Islam*, for the categorisation in their view, as detailed above, is twofold, not three-fold. Hence *dar al-harb* for them encompasses what others term *dar al-'ahd* and *dar al-hudnah*.

the bond of the agreement of security awarded to him when he entered into *dar al-harb*, thus returning the wealth of the *harbi* in question to its original state of lawfulness for the Muslim. Hence, the Muslim's taking of the *riba* increase in this case is equivalent to his taking over communal properties such as pastures, which is permissible and does not require a contract, valid or otherwise, in order to be done. In short, the Hanafis look at the *riba* contract in *dar al-harb* as nothing but a means by which a *harbi* is persuaded to part with his wealth willingly, and thereby the question of dishonesty in obtaining his wealth is avoided.

Furthermore, according to Hanafi jurisprudence, the ruling on someone who embraces Islam in *dar al-harb* but does not migrate to *dar al-Islam* is like that of a *harbi* in that his property has no Islamic jurisdictional protection. Therefore, dealing in *riba* with him is permissible. This point has been explicitly asserted in a number of trusted works of the *madhhab* such as *Bada'i' al-Sana'i'* of al-Kasani,[706] *al-Durr al-Mukhtar* of al-Haskafi[707] and the *Hashiyah* of Ibn Abidin. The author of the latter averred that: "This is because the wealth of such a person is not protected; were he to migrate to us, then return to them, there would be no *riba* [permissible], by consensus."[708] This argument is related to the territorial principle, which has been considered in some detail above.

Hanafi jurists also put forth a number of textual evidences for supporting their view.[709] The mainstay of which is the report of Makhool (d. 730) from the Prophet ﷺ that he stated: "There is no *riba* between a Muslim and a *harbi*, in *dar al-harb*."[710] Their second evidence is that narrated in the *Muwatta* of Imam Malik, that the Prophet ﷺ said: "A house or land that has been divided up in the *Jahiliyyah* is according to the division of the *Jahiliyyah*. A house or land which has not been divided up before the coming of Islam is divided according to Islam."[711] Based upon this hadith, the Hanafis argued, any estate allocation in *Jahiliyyah* is maintained, even if it stands in contradiction with the Islamic provisions of inheritance, hence, by analogy, the same should hold true for *riba*-based transactions that take place in *dar al-harb*.[712] Another textual evidence cited by the Hanafis is that Imam al-Tirmidhi narrated in his *Jami'*:

> "When [the following] verses were revealed: '... *The Romans have been defeated in the nearest land, and they, after their defeat, will be victorious in ... [a few] years* (30:1-4).' – on the day that these *Ayat* [i.e. verses] were revealed, the Persians had defeated the Romans, and the Muslims had wanted the Romans to be victorious over them, because they were the people of the Book. So Allah said about that: '*And on that day, the believers will rejoice – with the help of Allah. He helps whom He wills, and He is the Almighty, the Most Merciful* (30:4 & 5).' The Quraysh wanted the Persians to be victorious since they were not people of the Book, nor did they believe in the Resurrection. So when Allah revealed these verses, Abu Bakr al-Siddiq ﷺ went out, proclaiming throughout Makkah [the verses] ... Some of the Quraysh said: 'Then this is [a bet] between us and you. Your companion [the Prophet] claims that the Romans will defeat the Persians in [a few] years, so why have a bet on that between us and you?' Abu Bakr said: 'Yes.' So Abu Bakr and the idolaters made a bet."[713]

The Hanafi jurists argued that despite the fact that gambling is prohibited in *Shari'a*, this hadith shows that Abu Bakr al-Siddiq ﷺ had a bet with the polytheists in the city of Makkah, and that this was with the knowledge and approval of the Prophet ﷺ, as reported in another narration.[714] Since Makkah was at that time *dar al-harb*, this hadith denoted that Islamically invalid transactions are allowed between Muslims and non-Muslims in *dar al-harb*.[715]

These are in general the evidences of the Hanafi jurists for their position, most of which have been controverted and refuted by the *fuqaha* of other schools, nonetheless. As for their citing of the hadith of Makhool, the *fuqaha* retorted that it is an inauthentic (*da'if*) hadith, due to its being *mursal*, i.e. there is a narrator missing between Makhool and the Prophet ﷺ, so that there is no proof in it. However, for the sake of argument, even assuming its authenticity, it is possible that its meaning is forbiddance, similar to the saying of Allah almighty, "*The Hajj [pilgrimage] takes place during certain well-known months, If anyone undertakes the obligation of Hajj in them, there is no sexual intercourse, no wrongdoing, nor any quarrelling during Hajj.*"[716] With the existence of this possibility, the hadith should not be used as a proof in evidence, pursuant to the agreed-upon doctrinal maxim that when an evidence bears several possibilities as to its meanings, using it as evidence for one particular possibility is invalidated.[717]

As for their appealing to the hadith related to the inheritance divided in the pre-Islamic era, the *fuqaha* replied that it is also possible that the meaning of this hadith is that any contracts concluded amongst the polytheists before Islam are not revoked or reviewed. The possibility of this meaning is evident in the hadith of Ibn 'Abbas ﷺ, "Every division allocated in *Jahiliyyah* is as it was divided; every allocation reached by Islam is upon the allocation of Islam."[718] So, there is no solid proof in that hadith either.

As for their calling as witness the bet that Abu Bakr al-Siddiq had with the polytheists in Makkah, the *fuqaha* answered that this was before the prohibition of gambling was revealed, as explicitly mentioned in another narration of that event.[719] In addition, the Prophet ﷺ may have permitted the wager of Abu Bakr as an exception only, since it was for the sake of demonstrating the authenticity of Islam. This might be the case, especially as the Prophet ﷺ did not allow wealth to be gained in this way, as it is narrated that when Abu Bakr won the bet and took the stakes, he brought it to the Prophet ﷺ who ordered him to give it away in alms. Had the gain been *halal*, the Prophet ﷺ would not have ordered him to give it all away.[720]

Yet, this old doctrinal dispute between the Hanafis, on the one hand, and the rest of the *fuqaha*, including the Malikis, Hanbalis and Shafi'is, on the other hand, is not obsolete in the slightest. It has been frequently invoked in modern times. The financial needs of the Muslim minorities living in Western countries prompt a number of Islamic scholars to issue *fatwas* permitting the taking of interest-based loans, particularly to buy houses for residence outside Muslim lands. These *fatwas* are very often underpinned by reference to the Hanafi position on this matter. The effect of this is to promote their general popularity and authority as there is a common notion among Muslims that all Islamic legal opinions, as long as they are confirmed as being ascribed to any one of the four *madhhabs*, may be accepted and relied upon as legitimate foundations upon which to produce tenable legal positions and conclusions, regardless of how these may have been constructed.

An example of this is the *fatwa* that was furnished in the concluding declaration of the fourth session of the European Council for Ifta' and Research, convened in Dublin in 1420 AH (1999 CE). It reads:

> "... the Committee views, in the light of the evidences, principles and considerations of the *Shari'a*, that there is no harm in turning to this method of an interest-based loan to buy a house needed by a Muslim for him and his family to live in, with the conditions that he does not have another house which suffices him, that the house being bought is his main residence, and that he does not have enough spare wealth to buy the house by other means."[721]

The *fatwa*, as stated by the Council itself, has relied upon two main premises. The first is the principle of necessity, or, strictly speaking, the principle of need, which is treated as necessity in allowing that which should otherwise be forbidden. The Council argued that it is at least a need, if not a necessity, for the Muslim individual and the Muslim family to own a home. This need, if it were not fulfilled, would leave the Muslims in hardship even though they are able to survive. Yet, Allah has lifted hardship from this *Ummah* (i.e. Islamic nation) by the texts of the Qur'an, as in the saying of the Exalted in Surat al-Hajj, *"He has not placed upon you any hardship in the religion,"* and in Surat al-Ma'idah, *"Allah does not wish to place hardship upon you."* The rented home is not considered by the Council a viable alternative for, as argued, (i) it places a heavy burden upon the Muslim, and (ii) it does not provide him with the feeling of security because "when he gets old or his income reduces or dries up, he becomes vulnerable to being thrown out onto the street." But, would this not be the case with a mortgage also?!

The second premise provided is simply that, "this is the position of Abu Hanifah and his companion Muhammad b. al-Hasan al-Shaybani ... [that is] the permissibility of dealing in *riba* and other Islamically invalid contracts between Muslims and others in *dar al-harb.*" The Council asserted emphatically that, "they have evidences for this position." Those evidences were not specified therein, however.

A serious weakness with these premises is that they are in essence inconsistent with each other. According to the first premise, the interest-based mortgage is fundamentally prohibited but can be allowed, in the absence of alternatives, as a practical matter of necessity, or, as argued, in the case of pressing need. In contrast, according to the second premise, i.e. the Hanafi position, the transaction is fundamentally permitted irrespective of whether the situation is one of ease or one of being under constraint or pressure. Now, if the Hanafi position is what was genuinely relied upon in issuing the *fatwa*, as claimed, it should have included an absolute permission for the interest-based transactions, along with a permission for the engagement in other invalid contracts, such as gambling, in *dar al-harb*. Since this was not the case, the Council's reference to the Hanafi position appears to be simply for the purpose of gaining additional credibility for its *fatwa*.

Furthermore, from another angle, the Hanafi position applies only to *dar al-harb*, and the ruling does not extend to encompass *dar al-Islam*, whereas the principle of necessity, or of need, which is treated like necessity, is doctrinally applicable to both *dar al-harb* and *dar al-Islam*. Generally speaking, the need for a Muslim to own his home in the latter may be, in effect, more pressing nowadays, due to the deficiency of social welfare systems there. Thus, the Council's permission should not have been extended to mortgages for the purchase of homes in non-Muslim lands only. In actual fact, it should not have included mortgages, *per se*, as there are other needs which for some people may be just as pressing as buying a home, such as the need for future-secured investment, life insurance, or the farmer who needs to buy seeds, or the trader who needs to buy stock, thus these likewise, should be treated as cases of necessity that would permit participation in interest bearing loans. Otherwise, the result is that the application of the law remains open to conspicuous inconsistencies.[722] Needless to say, this permission, if widely adopted, would result in undermining any effort to provide a real Islamic alternative that would help to free Muslims from *riba* and thus protect their religious conscience.

There are other fatal flaws in these premises.[723] Besides the fact that the vast majority of both the early and contemporary *fuqaha* held a contrary view, account must also be taken of the widespread availability of so-called '*Shari'a*-Compliant' banking facilities even in Western Countries; all of these factors seem to contribute towards making this *fatwa*, and its like,[i] less popular among Muslims at present.

---

i   A similar *fatwa* has been included in the concluding declaration of the first Fiqh Conference of the League of *Shari'a* Scholars, convened in Detroit, Michigan, USA in 1999 CE.

By way of bringing our examination of this final question to a satisfactory close, it is my view that the existence of such *fatwas*, as well as the Hanafi position allowing dealings in *riba* in non-Muslim lands, may support the impression that, like the Jews and medieval Christians, the Muslims also found an ideological way to justify receiving interest from (or giving interest to) 'Others' but not 'Brothers'. However, there are three substantial distinctions that must also be taken into account in order to grasp the initial impression within the proper perspective.

The first is that the demarcation line between 'Brother' and 'Other' was one of faith for the Jewish *halakhists* and the medieval Christian Church, whereas for Hanafi jurists it was one of geographical boundaries. This is evidenced by the fact that Hanafi jurists permitted the taking of interest even from a Muslim inhabitant of a non-Muslim land; at the same time, they prohibited the taking of interest from a non-Muslim inhabitant of Muslim territory. Moreover, if a non-Muslim inhabitant of Muslim territory enters a non-Muslim land, Hanafi jurists prohibited the taking of interest from him there as well.[724]

The second distinction is that whilst the medieval Christian Church regarded the Jews and Muslims who lived amongst them as 'enemies', from whom therefore usury could be justifiably extracted, Muslim jurists, on the other hand, labelled Jews and Christians residing in their own midst as '*dhimmis*' whose lives and properties are as inviolable as that of Muslims, so that their wealth could not be taken by immoral means such as usury. This is the opinion of all the Muslim jurists, including Hanafis. Yet, by permitting the taking of interest from non-Muslims in non-Muslim lands, the Hanafi position indeed appeared to share some practical, but not ideological, outcomes with the Jewish attitude toward gentiles.

The third distinction is the fact that the Hanafi position remains confined to them, as the preponderance of the rest of the *fuqaha* maintain that the prohibition of *riba* is universal in scope. By contrast, the permissibility of charging interest to adherents of other faiths was the position adopted by the Church in the Middle Ages, and was included in its Canon law. It remains the prevailing view among Jewish rabbis in modern times.

Finally, in respect of the European Council's *fatwa*, and the like, it also differs in that it permits the practice only as a matter of pragmatic necessity, or in the case of pressing need, whereas the permission given by the Jewish and Christian scholars was, as detailed above, general and unrestricted.

However, the two previous methods of evading the prohibition of usury suffer from critical deficits. Reinterpreting the concept of usury so as to exclude certain rates, or types of, interest from the scope of the prohibition may have indeed produced the desired result for the Protestants. But, obviously, it did not work likewise neither for the Catholics nor for the Jews and Muslims. This can be attributed *inter alia* to the very nature of the prohibition of usury in Islamic and Jewish law as well as in the Canon law which are more precise and comprehensive in comparison with the prohibition of usury in the New Testament which is relatively generic and less daunting and thus allowing more room for reinterpretation and speculation, as demonstrated above. Portraying the 'others' as gentiles, enemies or *harbis* so as to justify extracting usury from them also has its limitations, particularly when the majority happen to be 'brothers' with whom dealing in interest is absolutely not permitted.

Yet, by the concealment of usury through multifarious mechanisms and techniques, the third method used to evade its prohibition, appears to have overcome these shortcomings since it can be used with both 'others' and 'brothers', and with or without the existence of new 'pragmatic' interpretations for the scriptural injunctions. No wonder, therefore, that it was, and still is, the method most commonly used by capital financiers in general from the days of the ancient Romans to the present day.

The Concealment

Throughout history, Jewish, Christian and Muslim usurers cunningly devised myriad clever contrivances and colourful moves for the purpose of skirting their respective prohibitions against usury.[i] The fact that the prohibitions are applied mainly to loan contracts appears to open up the possibility of evading the ban, in practice, by disguising interest-bearing loans under the form of other 'legitimate' and 'lawful' contracts. Hence, it was the wont of money-lenders, brokers and merchants to cloak their usurious activities in the garb of standard commercial transactions. These included, but were not limited to: sale of goods, lending stock, renting property, exchanging currency or even the formation of partnership contracts. These transactions were very often restructured craftily into more complex contractual devices in order to have them achieve similar ends to usurious contracts, whereby the lender would contrive to receive a fixed rate of return without incurring any operational risk.

Such interest-masking contractual devices were frequent and pervasive, especially when the prohibition of usury was at its zenith in the Middle Ages. They were known amongst the Jews as *'avaq ribbit'*. The Muslims called them *'bay' al-'inah'*. Protestants in England labelled them 'false chevisances'. Catholics branded them as *'fraudem usurarum'*. The existence of these names shows that they had become common and regular transactions at the time. By employing them, the usurers, in many cases, succeeded first, in avoiding being prosecuted since the prohibition of usury was for a long period of time not only a religious sin but also a legal offence in medieval Europe; second, in assuring that their

---

i   Some of which are still be employed at present so as to sidestep the usury rates mandated by most countries.

dues were legitimately enforceable even within those jurisdictions where dealing in usury was legally prohibited; and third, in persuading even devout believers to acquiesce in the practice.

Notwithstanding, the religious authorities did not turn a blind eye to such sharp practices, at least not in the beginning. They responded by tightening the relevant provisions. Many of the financial innovations of the usurers were closely scrutinised. Any which were found to result in a 'guaranteed' and 'risk-free' profit for one party were declared to be usurious regardless of the form taken. The usurers responded to this by redoubling their determination in the pursuit of illicit profits by inventing even more complex innovations which included a counterfeit risk and a simulation of uncertainty. Thus, each time one of their subterfuges and legal fictions was detected, the usurers simply invented another. In this way, therefore, the religious authorities, were kept "in almost perpetual motion to meet and repel their manifold and multiform modes of evasion."[725]

Interestingly, however, at a certain point, but only after a lengthy game of 'cat-and-mouse' between them, the religious authorities seem to have decided not only to stop fighting the usurers, but rather to fall in with them, either by ratifying their already existing financial instruments, or by helping them in the creation of new ones. This held true for Jewish, Christian and Muslim religious authorities alike. Therefore, this section, besides providing many examples of the interest-masking transactions used throughout their history, will also consider the shifts in attitude that occurred towards them within the Abrahamic religions.

'Avaq Ribbit

Jewish religious authorities appear to be particularly scrupulous concerning usury; more so than their Muslim and Christian counterparts. The Pentateuch prohibits *ribbis* (interest) mainly when arrangements for the payments were agreed upon at the time that the loan was provided. In Jewish law, this is called *Ribbis Ketzuzah* (lit. pre-arranged usury).[i] Yet, the Talmudic jurists extended the prohibition so as to apply to virtually any sort of benefit that might accrue to the lender. For example, they prohibited the borrower from: offering a gift to the lender before, during or after the loan was paid up;[ii] providing free services to the lender, including religious-related services such as tutoring him or his child in the study of the Torah;[726] selling goods to, or purchasing goods from, the lender at special prices;[727] or even giving the lender charitable donations if he was in need.[728] The lender is similarly banned from borrowing utensils, or using articles that belong to the borrower, during the period of the loan.[729] He is also forbidden from offering a loan on the condition that the borrower will patronise his business, refer other customers to his business, or giving him employment in his business.[730] "Lend to me today and I'll lend to you tomorrow" type agreements between the lender and borrower, are outlawed as well.[731]

Furthermore, the Rabbinical prohibition of *ribbis*, known as *Ribbis D'Rabbanan*, extends even to non-financial benefits. If the borrower had not been in the habit of greeting the lender before

---

i   There are two other cases of Ribbis Ketzuzah. The first is when the term of an interest-free loan is agreed to be extended in exchange for interest payment. The second case is when the depositor agrees to allow the depositary to use the fund in exchange for interest payment. See, Reisman, op. cit., p. 50-53

ii Schuchan Arukh, Yoreh De'ah (Y.D.), 160: 6. For English translation, see: Solomon ben Joseph Ganzfried and others, *Kitzur shulchan aruch : the code of Jewish law* (Mesorah Publications 2008). Please note that the a large body of commentaries have appeared on the Schuchan Arukh, the two major glosses of which is first the 'Hagahot' by Moses Isserles, better known as 'the Rema' and second the 'Sifthei Kohen' (abbreviated as Shach) by Shabbatai ha-Kohen. Both will be referred to in this section. However, since no English translations are found for them, this section will rely heavily upon the references made to them, and similar resources, in Reisman's book, *The Laws of Ribbis*, considered 'the finest English-language guide ever written on the topic'.

the loan was given, he shall not begin to do so afterwards. Even if he had been accustomed to greet him previously, he shall not begin to greet him in a warmer or more elaborate manner.[732] Otherwise, the borrower will be perpetrating the prohibited *Ribbis Devarim* (lit. verbal usury). Praising, complimenting or offering blessings to the lender whilst the loan is outstanding are also considered *Ribbis Devarim*.[733] Moreover, according to some rabbis, the rule of *Ribbis Devarim* prohibits the borrower from even thanking the lender for the loan. Others disagree and rule that a simple 'thank-you' is permitted.[734] [i]

These indirect forms of interest, and many others, are commonly referred to in *Halakha* as '*avaq ribbit*' (lit. the dust of interest). They all were, and still are, proscribed by the vast majority of *halakhists*. *Prima facie*, this would make them appear to have been utterly assiduous and uncompromising in the detection of usury. But, the fact is, that they were not.

Since the Amoraic period,[ii] rabbis in general have played an increasingly active role in creating, rather than blocking, loopholes in anti-usury *halakhic* rules. The intellectual effort that they made in this direction over the centuries is striking. It culminated in modern times with the so-called *heter iska*, which is an interest-

---

i The possible ideological reasons for this militancy in the prohibition of *ribbit* was considered above in the section: Usury in Judaism

ii Rabbinical periods are often divided into seven eras: (1) the Zugot (lit. pairs) refers to the time preceding the Tannaim (-200 – 0 BCE) in which the spiritual leadership of the Jews was in the hands of five successive generations of *zugoth* of religious teachers; (2) the Tannaim (lit. the repeaters) are the sages of the Mishnah (0 – 200 CE); (3) the Amoraim (lit. the sayers) are the sages of the Gemara (200 – 500 CE); (4) the Savoraim (lit. the reasoners) are the classical Perisan rabbis (500 – 650 CE); (5) the Geonim (lit. the prides or geniuses) are the rabbis of Sura and Pumbeditha, in Babylonia (650 – 1038 CE); (6) the Rishonim (lit. the firsts) are rabbis of the early medieval period (1000 – 1500 CE) preceding the Shulchan Aruch; (7) the Acharonim (lit. the lasts) are rabbis from roughly 1500 to the present.

masking contractual device that has been introduced, designed and developed fully by rabbis themselves. Although it appears nowhere in the Talmud, the *heter iska* has been in use now for generations. Almost all Israeli banks established in Palestine, and worldwide, use the *heter iska* in their financial operations. The Israeli Government also uses the *heter iska* to permit the purchase of its bonds. Private individuals have also been furnished with *pro forma heter iska* templates in which the creditor and the debtor need only 'fill the blanks' with the agreed details, i.e. the amount of money that will be received by the former, the additional payments that will be made to the latter, in addition to the principal, and the due date.[735] Further information on the *heter iska*, as well as other rabbinicallly-devised and sanctioned legal fictions, will be provided below. It is interesting to note how the rabbis, who in the beginning extended the prohibition on *ribbit* so as to cover, and invalidate even the most tenuously susceptible behaviours surrounding the actual loans themselves at which, strictly speaking, the Pentateuchal prohibitions were properly aimed, ended up "seeking ways and means to validate transactions clearly or conceivably falling within that prohibition."[736]

The Position of the Early Poskim[i]

For the sake of avoiding even the slightest hint of interest, the early *poskim* of the Oral Torah, namely the Tannaim (CA. 700-200 C.E), subsumed under the *ribbit* prohibition, not only interest-bearing transactions but also, a variety of other transactions in the form of sales, leases, mortgages and investments which were considered to be *ribbis* (usurious) because they failed to observe the principle of equivalence between the amount given by the creditor and the amount repaid by the debtor. This failure renders them tainted with 'the dust of interest', and thus prohibited.

i   Poskem is plural of Posek which stands for the rabbis who decide matters in Jewish religious law, i.e. the decisor.

Therefore, the Tannaim prohibited the borrowing of produce: a person may not borrow goods and commit himself to return even the same amount of goods at a later time because it is possible that the value of the goods will increase by the time of payment.[i][ii] For the same reason, the Tannaim also prohibited paying in advance for goods (with some exceptions for farmers and manufacturers).[737] Credit sales in which the price is increased in return for delay in payment were prohibited as well.[738] If the lender took a pledge from the borrower as security for his loan, the Tannaim prohibited him from using it for himself, for if he were to use it, his benefit would amount to *ribbit*.[iii] The Tannaim also prohibited what they referred to as the 'iron flock' investment.[739] They used the name to label any arrangements whereby the investor is protected from any future loss. It was as if he had invested in sheep made of iron that could not die.[iv] Alternatively, the Tannaim legitimised the half-profit investments whereby any profits, or losses, are shared equally with the working partner.

Theoretically, the Tannaim have also propounded various rationales for why one cannot charge others for the use of one's money (through an interest-loan contract), in the same way one

---

i BM 5:9. This prohibition is known as *seah be seah* (a *seah* is a measure of volume; this term refers to the trading of merchandise – 'a measure for a measure'.)

ii From the point view of the Tanna Hillel (1st century), the only way to be certain of avoiding usury when produce is lent is for the product to be assessed in value at the time of the loan. Then, when the time for repayment came, the debt could be repaid with goods equal in value to the goods borrowed. He stated that, "A woman may not lend a loaf of bread to her neighbour unless she determines its value in money, lest wheat should rise in price and they be found partakers in usury." BM 5:9

iii Only in the case of a poor debtor, was the creditor allowed to hire out the pledge and to use the income for reducing the debt. BM 6:7

iv Such investments were considered to be tantamount to interest loan contracts, for in both cases the financial provider receives a fixed return without bearing any risks.

charges for the use of other kinds of property, such as a house or field (through a rent contract).[740] In responding to such questions, the Tannaim highlighted three distinctions between a rental and a loan. The first is that, in the case of rental, the actual hired item must be returned, whereas, in the case of a loan, a return of the equivalent amount is sufficient. Consequently, the second distinction is that, in the former case, the lessor bears the cost of depreciation, as long as the lessee has used the hired item properly, whilst, in the latter case, the lender always receives the full value of the loan.[741] In addition, the third distinction between a rental and a loan is that, in the case of rental, the lessee is responsible for the theft or loss of the item but not for certain unavoidable accidents. However, in the case of loan, the borrower is responsible even for unavoidable accidents.[742]

An interesting illustration of these distinctions is the Tannaims' acceptance of a rental contract on money that was only to be used for display purposes. Under such transactions, the borrower undertook to return the very coins that were initially lent, their having been used for visual effect only. Therefore, the borrower bears neither the depreciation cost (if any), nor the *force majeure* risk. Both are borne completely by the lender, and therefore he, the lender, is entitled to ask for compensation, in the form of rental charges.[743] Finally, the *Tannaim* put it in explicit terms that, "The use of a subterfuge (*ha'aramah*) to avoid the interest prohibition is not allowed."[744]

Relaxing the Biblical Injunctions

Beginning in the Amoraic period,[745] however, the elaborate Tannaitic legal structure that was constructed to prevent sales, investments, mortgages, leases, and loans of produce from resulting in usury was gradually dismantled. It is said that the change in economic conditions urged the *poskim* to loosen the strict Talmudic injunctions against the practice.[746]

Many Amoraim, and the generality of Geonim, permitted the

loans of produce if the borrower possessed a lesser amount of the goods in question.^i They even permitted it if the borrower had not any of the goods at all, as long as they have a set market price and they are readily available to him on the open market.[747] Moreover, in case none of these conditions apply, the Acharonim[748] suggested that the lender may simply give the borrower a small amount of the goods as an outright gift or sell it to him, "and it is as if he had some and it is allowed."[749]

Similarly, paying in advance was allowed, provided that the price of the goods is to be set according to the market price at the time of payment. This will make the transaction non-usurious, as argued by some Geonim, even if the price of the purchased goods were to have appreciated by the time of delivery, since the buyer could have bought the goods with his money on the open market from the outset, and it would have been his own goods that had appreciated.[750] ^ii Several rabbinical 'solutions' were suggested for eluding the prohibition against profiting in return for accepting delayed payment on sales, as well. One was 'verbal' in character. The Geonim suggested that rather than the seller saying to the buyer: "Pay me later at an increased price," he may say to him: "Pay me immediately at a reduced price." For this stratagem to work, the salesmen, obviously, need first, to include the cost of credit in their 'regular' prices, and then, offer discounts to those who pay from the outset.[751] Another solution,

---

i For example, if the borrower had only one *shesah* of wheat, he could borrow many *kors* of wheat against it. The justification provided is that each *sheah* of wheat borrowed could serve as 'standby' for the next one. See, B. BM 75a

ii Additionally, in one *responsum*, a Rishonim allowed the buyer to stipulate that he would have the option of choosing whether to receive the merchandise itself or its monetary equivalent at the delivery time. R. Issac ben Sheshet Perfet, *She'elot u-teshuvot rivash*, #306, as quoted in Gamoran, *Jewish Law in Transition: How Economic Forces Overcame the Prohibition Against Lending on Interest*, 58

suggested by some Rishonim, is that the salesmen simply make no mention of a lower price for prompt payment, and just sell on credit for a higher price.[752] Legal fictions were also devised to circumvent the prohibition of using the mortgage throughout the period of the loan. As shown in a *Geonimic responsum*, some money-lenders took recourse to writing two separate contracts.[753] The first was a simple sale of the mortgage to the lender. The second contract, which was dated several days later in order to appear independent of the first one, stated that the buyer, out of his own free will, agreed that if the seller should return the money within a specified time frame, then he, the buyer, would resell the land to the seller. Others developed a contractual device called 'Mortgage with Deduction'. Under this device, the creditor would deduct a fixed, pre-agreed sum from the debt each year to offset the benefit that he derived from the usufruct of the mortgage. However, the sum deducted was very often a pittance and did not reflect the real value of the usufruct of the mortgage. Therefore, the legality of this transaction has been a bone of contention amongst the rabbis for centuries. Nevertheless, in modern times, it appears that they have reached a near consensus on its permissibility.[754]

Various other attempts to sidestep the usury prohibition were also made through the course of the years. For example, as noted by Hillel, the Tannaim had declared that were it not for the danger of people getting in the habit of usury, members of a family would be allowed to borrow from each other at interest, considering the additional payments as gifts.[755] Based on this principle, however, many *Amoraim* allowed themselves to borrow from each other at interest, under the justification that they were like part of the same family! Samuel (third century) claimed that since the rabbis knew well that usury was forbidden there was no risk of misleading them, and any additional payment was merely a gift. Samuel himself, as reported, made the following proposal to

Abbuha b. Ahi: "Lend me 100 peppercorns for 120."[756] Similarly, his colleague, Rav, said that he was used to borrow and lend at interest with Raba Bar Chana.[757]

In the same vein, some *Poskim* permitted a person who is seeking a loan to give money in the form of a gift, or wages, to a third party to influence the lender to offer an interest-free loan to him.[758] An example of this mechanism is featured in the *Gemara*. Certain wax merchants used to give balls of wax to Abba Mar in order that he influence his father, Rav Papa (4th century) to lend them money. Rav Papa defended this practice by saying that there is no prohibition against accepting such a 'gift' if you are not the lender.[759]

Some went a step further; to permit a Jew to send his friend to take a loan at interest from another Jew for him, or to give his money at interest to another Jew, arguing that interest is prohibited only as between lender and borrower, but not as between their respective agents.[760] Others permitted this expedient as long as the intermediaries were to be gentiles; because dealings in interest with gentiles are allowed in *Halakha*.[761]

The Heter Iska

Let us now focus on the *heter iska*, for by using it no other legal fictions or subterfuges really seem to be necessary. To begin with, *heter iska* was based on a partnership arrangement known as "*iska*", featured in the *Mishnah, Bava Metzia* 104b.[762] As a substitute for the prohibited 'iron flock' investment, the early Mishnahists proposed an arrangement that enabled investors to enter into profitable business partnerships, but without violating the prohibition on usury. In this arrangement, the investing partner furnishes the funds needed for a business venture, whilst the managing partner uses the funds to run the business.

Yet, the *Gemara* saw this arrangement as '*palga milveh u'palga pikadom*', i.e. half-loan and half-deposit.[763] It was so-called because, as explicated by the *Savoraim*,[764] the half of the funds provided by the investing partner served as a loan to the managing partner, and the other half as a deposit given to him in order to be used to generate profits. This division was found to be crucial, for if the entire sum invested were a loan, then, the investor would not be entitled to profit except by way of taking interest, and if it were all a deposit, then the investor would be totally liable in case of loss. The same applied to the managing partner's part, if it were entirely a loan, the managing partner would be fully responsible for a loss, and if it were a deposit, he would be entitled to none of the profit. Thus, by addressing this arrangement as a half-loan and half-deposit, both the investor and the managing partner could legally share both the profits and any liabilities.

However, identifying half of the business funds as a loan to the managing partner implies that if the business venture turned sour, this half still has to be fully repaid to the investing partner. Indeed, this fact has been affirmed by almost all the *Poskim*.[765] Therefore, albeit that it appears as a 'silent/active' partnership agreement, the *iska* is in essence more similar to a '50-50' partnership agreement, in which both parties contribute the same amount of capital, and thus all profits, and losses, are shared equally.

Yet, the fact that the managing partner in reality does all the work required for the business venture would result in a *ribbis* problem. His labour would amount to doing something 'extra' for the investing partner in consideration of the loan given to him (the half-loan part of the business funds), and this would be construed as interest. Hence, the *Mishnah* had stipulated that the managing partner must be paid for the time and effort that he expends on behalf of the investing partner's portion of the business funds.[766]

How much the managing partner should be paid for his labour was a matter of rabbinical dispute. Amongst the *Tannaim*, R. Simeon required that the managing partner be fully paid for his labour. R. Judah believed that the payment needed to be only symbolic, whilst R. Meir opined that he should be paid lower wages than an idle worker would accept for such a job.[767] The Amora R. Rav (third century) proposed that, in lieu of receiving a separate payment for wages, the managing partner could get two-thirds of the profit, leaving only one third to the investing partner.[768] Nonetheless, the viewpoint that appears to prevail in the *Geonimic period* [769] was that of R. Meir.[770] It has also been endorsed by many eminent *Rishonim*, such as R. Alfas and Maimonides.[771]

The first medieval *Poskim* who clearly relaxed the requirement for the managing partner's pay was probably R. Abraham David, better known as Rabad (12th century). He asserted that if the investing partner desired "to stipulate to pay him a dinar for his labour, he could do so, even though his labour was worth more than that." "Whatever he contracted with him, ... whether much or little," was acceptable.[772] This minor change was followed by a major one, which was also made by Rabad; both together give the *heter iska* its final shape.

The Heter Iska of Rabad

Living in twelfth-century Provence at the height of the so-called commercial revolution of the Middle Ages, Rabad probably recognised, as had Calvin in Geneva, the vital need for commercial loans. He himself was a very rich man. The source of his wealth was not reported, but obviously, as shown in his writing and *responsa*, he was well acquainted with the commercial activities as well as with the needs of merchants. Amongst these needs was of course the need for capital. Although it was fully endorsed by rabbis, Jewish lenders appeared reluctant to furnish merchants with the capital needed through the medium of the *iska,* for perhaps three main reasons. The first was that they had to reimburse the managing partner, i.e. the trader, for his labour. The second reason was that they risked losing the deposit portion of the business funds.⁷⁷³ Needless to say, medieval trade was indeed a high-risk undertaking. The carriage of goods by sea was prone to the hazards of shipwreck and piracy, and by land there were always bandits and robbers.⁷⁷⁴ Even if the goods arrived at their final destination unscathed, there was also the possibility that a shipment of competing merchandise might arrive simultaneously, or even in advance, which would cause the price of the merchant's goods to plummet. The third reason could be the concession that was given by the Church to the Jewish lenders at the time, which may have tempted them to prefer lending to a Christian at interest rather than lending to a fellow Jew through a risky complicated device such as the *Iska*.

Within this economic context, and probably in order to maintain the flow of much needed funds for the Jewish traders, Rabad constructed his new *Iska* formulation that, besides downplaying the importance of the payment due to the managing partner by making even a minimum payment sufficient, to also making the managing partner liable, not only for the loan portion, but for the deposit portion of the *Iska* as well.

Rabad required the identification of the managing partner in the *Iska* agreement as a *shomer*, or paid bailee, for the deposit half of the business funds. Then, the investing partner may stipulate, as a depositor, that the managing partner, as a guardian, must practise his business in a certain, but impossible, way. Otherwise, if he, the managing partner, departed from this practice, he would be totally responsible for any losses incurred. Giving an example of such a crippling condition, Rabad says, "The investor should say to the recipient [the managing partner] ... Lend it [the deposit] only with good pledges of silver and gold and always put the money under the ground in order to guard it from fire and thieves ... and guard the money and the pledges with exceptional guarding." ⁷⁷⁵ Thereby, Rabad concluded:

"... the investor will be able to take his profit without transgressing the usury ban and without worry. ...And after the investor makes these stipulations ... [the managing partner] may lend in any way he wishes, ... for he knows that the investor stipulated with him in order to place all of the liability on him should he deviate [from the stipulations]."[776]

What Rabad was proposing is obviously an *Iska* contract, which both parties knew to be just a fiction. His technique, in effect, gives the investing party the opportunity to profit while being relieved of all liability for his investment by stipulating conditions for the care of the stake that could never be fulfilled by the managing partner. Thus, making the whole transaction nothing but a profitable, risk-free investment for the former, leaving the latter fully responsible for the money he has received in the manner of a borrower, who bears all of the risks for his interest-based loan. Despite that, Rabad's legal stratagem, later known as *Heter Iska*, was accepted by the major rabbinical authorities in his time. It was also included in many of the rabbinical writings in the following century, i.e. the thirteenth century.

The Heter Iska of Isserlien

In the fourteenth century, which was also an era of heavy trade and commerce, another formulation of the *Iska* was developed by R. Israel Isserlien. In responding to a question about whether there is a legitimate way by which the investor could profit without risking his principal, Isserlien said that there is one indeed, "but I am afraid lest by these rules and by seeking strategies to allow business dealings with interest, the words of the Torah will become a laughingstock."[777]

Nevertheless, his concern did not prevent him from proceeding to reveal such strategies! In his answer, Isserlien first referred to Rabad's formulation of the *Iska*, asserting that it is not forbidden, "even though everyone knows that it is not at all the intention of the investor or of the recipient [the managing party] that the stipulation be fulfilled, that is, that he will lend only on silver and gold and will bury it in the ground."[778] Then, he propounded another formula that is to stipulate in the *Iska* agreement that the managing partner, besides accepting liability for gross negligence:

> "... also accepts upon himself that he is not to be believed even with an oath on the Torah, and even with witnesses, and even if there are a hundred who testify that he was not greatly negligent. Only if the Rabbi and the cantor and similar people who are residents of the city and are familiar with the business dealings in the city will testify, will they be believed if they testify with proof and complete knowledge."[779]

By adding these statements in the *Iska* agreement, the investing partner's principal will be, as Isserlien himself maintained, secured "as he always wishes."

> "For if it is lost, ... [the investor] may claim that it was lost intentionally, and ... [the managing partner] will be able to uphold his claim only with the testimony of the Rabbi and the cantor. And it is almost entirely certain that they will not know all [of the details regarding] the liability" [780]

Despite this, Isserlien says, " ... it is permitted to stipulate as has been said ... even though surely neither of them believe that the condition will be fulfilled, and they make these stipulations only in order to take interest in a legal way."[781]

The Heter Iska of Maharam

In the sixteenth and seventeenth centuries, a different type of *Iska* contract was introduced mainly amongst Jewish money-lenders in Poland. The rabbi of Lodomeria, R. Isaiah Menahem, better known as Maharam, appears to combine the formula of Rabad with that of Isserlien in order to produce a new formula, which not only protected the investor's principal from any loss, but also assured him a specific amount of profit. Maharam suggested dividing the investment into two time periods. In the first, the whole business fund would be considered a deposit given to the managing partner, who will be considered a paid bailee, as described in the *Heter Iska* of Rabad. Thus, all of the profit (and liability) will accrue to the investing partner. In the second period, the entire business fund becomes a loan with all of the profits (or losses) accruing to the managing partner. Yet, Maharam proposed that the second period commence only after the managing partner has provided a fixed and agreed-upon amount of profit to the investing partner. And, in case the managing partner claimed that he was unable to realise any profits, or if he claimed any loss, he should not be believed unless supported by the testimony of reliable witnesses, such as those described in the *Heter Iska* of Isserlien.[782]

However, Maharam's formulation of the *Heter Iska* seemed to fail in obtaining a wide acceptance amongst his peers. Many objected that guaranteeing a fixed amount of profit in such manner would amount to nothing short of a loan at interest. After a long dispute, therefore, a new revised form of Maharam's *Heter Iska* was agreed upon, in which the requirement for two qualified witnesses to confirm the business losses is to be applied only to the principal but not to the profit. For the latter, however, the revised form included a phrase whereby the managing partner who did not profit had to give a 'stern oath' stating that he spoke the truth. Most Jews avoided taking such oaths, fearing that they might somehow, inadvertently, swear falsely. As the author of the *Kistur shulhan arukh* put it: "Ordinarily, the recipient [i.e. the managing partner] does not want to take an oath and will give the investor what they have established between the two of them, and this is the *heter iska* that is practised in our day."[783]

Consequently, by using this revised form of Maharam's *Heter Iska*, the investing partner would certainly get back his principal along with, in all likelihood, the sum agreed upon in advance as his profit.

The Modern Heter Iska

The form of *Heter Iska* that is widely used nowadays seems to be a composite of the previously mentioned formulations.[784] It takes from Rabad's formula the element that one *dinar* (which becomes one dollar) should be adequate to pay the managing partner for his labour; from Isserlien's formula comes the suggestion that the principal could be safeguarded by including a clause that required the testimony of two qualified witnesses who are acceptable to the Orthodox Jewish court of law (*Beis Din*), in order to verify any claim of loss; and from the revised formula of Maharam, it takes the feature that a specific amount of anticipated profits could be assured through demanding the managing partner to attest his possible claim of not being able to realise the profit under solemn oath in the presence of a *Beis Din*, while holding a Torah scroll – a type of oath that an Orthodox Jew would traditionally avoid making, as mentioned above.[i] The outcome is a *Heter Iska* that works like "a magic incantation"[ii] to dispel the prohibition of *ribbis* since it shares with the interest-loan contracts the same result, i.e. the provider of financial capital will receive a fixed rate of return without bearing any risks.

---

i   Curiously enough, some contemporary *poskim* have even proposed that if the investing partner is afraid that the managing partner may actually take such an oath, he, the investing partner, may add conditions to the *heter iska* which serve to dissuade him from doing so, such as requiring that the oath be made at the time of the Torah reading in the synagogue, in the presence of the entire congregation.

ii R. Moses Feinstein admonishes that *heter iska* must not be understood as "a magic incantation or luck charm" to allow loans on interest, but, obviously, it becomes just like one. R. Moses Feinstein, *Igrot moshe*, 2:62, as translated in Reisman, op. cit., p. 378

So, this is how the *Iska* agreement, which was introduced twenty hundred years ago as an alternative to the prohibited iron-flock investment, turned into a modern version of the same thing, thereby reducing the rigorous anti-usury Talmudic injunctions to "a laughingstock."[785] Ironically enough indeed, modern rabbis, whilst continuing to exhort observant Jews not to greet the creditor in a warmer or more elaborate manner, as this amounts to the prohibited 'verbal' usury, they themselves provide them with different forms of *Heter Iska* through which 'tangible' usury can be taken instead.

Moreover, because it would be too cumbersome and time-consuming to draft a *Heter Iska* every time a loan is issued, Jewish-owned banks and financial institutions are provided with a rabbinical document, known as *Heter Iska Clali*, testifying that all the loans, or interest payments, given through them will be made in accordance with the rules of the *Heter Iska*. Yet, some of them resort to appointing boards of rabbinical advisors to help in the formulation of the *Heter Iska* that can be used for specific needs, such as where monthly interest payments are required. Thus, through the medium of the *Heter Iska*, a pious Jew today can receive interest from (or give interest to) his co-religionist, establish a fixed rate for periodic interest payments, and do so without violating the letter of the anti-usury *Halachic* rules. Similarly, he could walk into an Israeli bank to take an interest bearing loan or to deposit his money and receive regular interest payments, and still be acting within the framework of Jewish law, thanks to the legal fictions and stratagems which are produced, developed and sanctioned by the religious authorities themselves.

FRAUDEM USURARUM

The Medieval Campaign Against Usury

Perhaps, the most severe religious sanctions ever imposed upon usurers were the ones imposed by the Medieval Church. Yet, this was not always a particularly effective deterrent, as will be discussed later in this section. At the time the practice of usury seemed to have become quite ubiquitous. Pope Alexander III lamented in the Third Lateran Council (1179) that, "in almost every place that practice of usury has reached a stage that many, even abounding other occupations, practise this art."[786] The Parisian exegete Peter the Chanter (d.1197) also complained that unlike the ancient cities where even a single usurer might have been hard to find, nowadays they are everywhere practising their crimes in the open.[787] Similarly, the English cardinal Robert of Courson (1160-1219) complained that the epidemic of usury is so pervasive that merchants, money-changers, burghers and even prelates possessed neither "hide nor hair" that was immune from contagion.[788] In view of the letter that Pope Innocent III sent to the Bishop of Arras in 1208, these declarations appear to be more than the voice of mere religious hysteria or moral panic. In this letter he urged caution in enforcing the decrees of the Lateran Council, because usurers are so numerous that if all were punished many of the churches would have to be closed. Alternatively, the bishop was advised to select only a few of the worst offenders, in order to make an example of them for others.[789] It is unlikely that the Pope was indulging in exaggeration under such circumstances.

The prevalence of usurers can be ascribed mainly to the commercial revolution that commenced in the eleventh century, and which resulted in increasing the demand for commercial funds, thus tempting large numbers of people to become involved in interest-based money-lending activities.[790] The support the usurers received from the contemporary kings and princes may have also contributed to this result, as argued by Chanter.[791] Nevertheless, whilst commerce was revived at the turn of the millennium, the Investiture Controversy (1075-1122) brought unprecedented religious as well as political power to the Church.[i] By drawing on this power for the sake of eradicating the scourge of usury, what is best described as a full-scale clerical campaign against usury was waged.

The campaign began with the Second Lateran Council, convened at the beginning of the twelfth century, and reached its pinnacle in the thirteenth and fourteenth centuries, as evident in the relevant decrees of the Councils of Paris (1212), Lyon (1274), Mainz (1310), and Vienna (1311). However, three different types of weapon appeared to be deployed during the course of the campaign.

The first was intellectual in character. Borrowing from the philosophical works of Aristotle, namely his concepts of 'the sterility of money' and 'the just price', the scholastics (theologians) provided a number of arguments and rational justifications for the rejection of usury,[ii] the ultimate conclusion to be drawn from which was that usury is intrinsically unjust as well as unnatural, and thus in contradiction with the will of God; a line of thinking that was heavily relied upon in convincing the laity of the inherent evils of usury. It was incorporated into the *Concordia Discordantium Canonum,* commonly known as Gratian's Decretum, the earliest collection of the Canon law compiled as a legal textbook between 1130 and 1140. The scholastics found further ammunition in the writings of the early Church Fathers, especially that of St. Ambrose, which reads: "if someone takes usury, he commits violent robbery (*rapina*), and he shall not live."[792] The assumption that usury is theft runs throughout their literature. Gratian quoted the line verbatim. Peter Lombard (d. 1116), in his *Sentences,* expounding on the Seventh Commandment, states, "Here also usury is

---

i   For further information, see above section: Introduction to Medieval Period.

ii These arguments have been fully addressed above in section: The Scholastic Interpretation

prohibited, which is contained under robbery."⁷⁹³ Raymond of Penafort (d. 1275) justifies why he has chosen to discuss usury after he addressed robbery in his penitential tradition: "because usury differs little, or not at all, from robbery."⁷⁹⁴ Usury was considered tantamount to robbery for, as explicated by Thomas of Chobham (d. 1233) in his *Summa Confessorum*, even though a debtor may claim that he pays usury willingly, he does not do so with an absolute will (*voluntate absoluta*) but only with a comparative will (*voluntate comparativa*) for he would rather pay something to the creditor than be without the loan. Explaining this point further, William of Auxerre (d. 1231), in the *Summa Aurea*, says:

> "According to his absolute will the owner of the money does not want the usurer to receive it, but according to his comparative will he wants him to receive it and to have it, because the usurer will not grant him the loan for nothing. Therefore, the usurer takes what belongs to another against the owner's will, when this expression, "against the will," is understood in the sense of removing his absolute and separate will, and thus it is evident that usury is theft."⁷⁹⁵

Similar explanations were given by many other influential scholastics like Roland of Cremona (d. 1259), Peter of Tarentasie (d. 1174), Thomas Aquinas (d. 1274) and, his student, Giles of Lessines (d. 1304). An additional and even more powerful reason for asserting that usury is theft was furnished by the canon lawyers. Influenced by the Roman law, many of them, including Paucaplalea (d.1148), Huguccio (d. 1210) and Hostiensis (d. 1271), defined usury as gain owed or exacted by agreement from a *mutuum* contract.⁷⁹⁶ Technically, the *mutuum* is a contract pertaining to the loan of an article in return for a promise to repay an exact replica later on. The contract is *ipso facto* applicable only to a class of goods classed as *fungibles*, viz. goods that can readily be estimated and replaced according to amount (such as money), weight (such as gold and silver) and measure (for example, grain and wine). Roman law provided that when lending such goods the ownership is to be passed to the borrower. The term *mutuum* itself literally means: what had been mine [*meum*] becomes thine [*tuum*]. This view is perfectly sensible for, firstly, by the very nature of the contract, the lender would never regain dominion over the specific article, and, secondly, because a fungible good is one that is consumed by its use, the borrower will not be able to use it unless he owned it. However, because of the transfer of ownership to the borrower, the canon lawyers argued, any payments above principal would be a receipt for the use of something that the lender does not own.[797] Even if the principal has produced great profits for the borrower, by exacting an additional amount, the lender is, in effect, robbing the borrower of the fruits of his own industry through the use of capital that had become his own property. Thus, the usurer takes what belongs to another, which implies that usury is actually a theft, and should therefore be banned.

Moral sermons and *exempla* were the second weapon used during the course of the campaign. With colourful and impassioned expressions, mendicant friars, namely the Franciscans and the Dominicans, who by virtue of their direct connection with the beliefs, behaviour and attitude of everyday life, had probably more impact on common practices and opinions than canonists and theologians, contrived a considerable number of stories about the dreadful fates awaiting usurers in and after death, and, by their unabated, virulent preaching, persuaded many of the faithful that, in the scale of values, usurers are, "linked with the worst evildoers, the worst occupations, the worst sins, and the worst vices."[798] Usurers were depicted in their homilies and public pamphlets as fitting only to associate with Jews, bandits, prostitutes, simoniacs (i.e. barratores) and heretics, yet were worse than all of them. "They are worse than the Jews," Jacques de

Vitry (d. 1240) castigated, "for the Jews do not lend at usury to their brothers."[799] St. Bernard of Clairvaux (d. 1153) called them "baptized Jews."[800] They were also labelled as robbers of time, which is a divine possession, and a common possession. Thomas of Chobham admonished that: "The usurer sells nothing to the borrower that belongs to him. He sells only time, which belongs to God."[801] Similar statements were made by St. Anselm of Canterbury (d. 1109) and Peter Lombard (d. 1160). An *exemplum* of rubric 304 in the *Tabula Exemplorum* added that usurers are beings damned in advance as they sell time which is the common good of all creatures, and they sell light and repose, the light of day and repose of night.[802] Usurers were regarded as worse than prostitutes as well. Peter the Chanter scornfully noted that like prostitutes in the brothel, public usurers are to be located in distinctive quarters in the town, were exclusively licensed to ply their traffic manifestly and notoriously, and were accessible to all.[803] Still, with prostitutes there were mitigating circumstances; for, as Thomas of Chobham remarked, albeit their work is shameful, at least they work, unlike the usurer who, as Thomas contended elsewhere in his *Summa*, "wants to make a profit without doing any work, even while he is sleeping, which goes against the precepts of the lord, who said, 'by the sweat of your face shall you get bread to eat.' [Gen. 3:19]"[804] So that the most 'ignominious' profits are what the usurers acquire from lending at interest, both Peter and Thomas affirmed. Equating usury with heresy, Robert of Courson maintained that just as the faithful are bound to work for the conversion of the heretics, so they should redeem the former, first by attempting to convert them, and finally, if other means fail, by public accusation.[805] Jacques de Vitry indicted them for simony, warning that: "Our usurers have become the intimate friends ... not only of lay princes but also prelates, to whom they render services and to whom they lend money, so that their sons can be elevated to ecclesiastical benefices."⁸⁰⁶ So did Peter the Cantor.ⁱ This militant rhetoric created a social stigma against usurers as a result of which both Christian and Jewish money-lenders were occasionally persecuted and expelled from towns at the behest of the populace.⁸⁰⁷ However, if while living, the ordeal of the usurer was intense, death will by no means bring peace to him. Myriad *exempla* were narrated about the tragedies that lay ahead for usurers. On the deathbed he will be surrounded by a diabolic cohort of evil beasts waiting for him.⁸⁰⁸ During his dying, the devils will put silver pieces in his mouth so he can neither confess nor express his last wishes before a cloud of crows will come to take possession of his soul. He will be pursued to the grave by hellhounds amidst a thousand torments.⁸⁰⁹ Leeches, flies, spiders and toads inhabit his tomb. The latter will pluck silver pieces from his purse and stick them in the heart of the cadaver.⁸¹⁰ By night, demons will come after him to snatch his interred corpse. And, when the Judgment Day comes, "all the saints and all the angels of paradise then cry out against him, saying, to hell, to hell, to hell.' Also, the heavens with their stars cry out, saying, 'to the fire, to the fire, to the fire.' The planets also clamour, 'to the depths, to the depths, to the depths."⁸¹¹ Yet, the depths of hell here stands for, as clarified by several *exempla*, the bitterness of purgatory, which is a place set aside from hell in which the souls of sinners are severely punished for the expiation of their sins before going to heaven.⁸¹² However, in Dante Alighieri's *Divine Comedy* (1265-1321), there are no usurers in purgatory: they are all in hell, at the bottom of the seventh circle, "punished in the burning sands."⁸¹³

The third, and probably the strongest, weapon in the campaign's armoury were the sanctions. Those who insisted on lending money

---

i   He said: "The detestable usurers are now the bosom companions of princes and prelates, who surrender to the blandishments of the money bags and promote their sons to the highest posts in Church and state." As translated in Baldwin, op. cit., p. 298

for profit came to have harsh social and spiritual penalties inflicted on them.[814] The penalties included stigmatization of their names, i.e. to be held in infamy, which entails that they are ineligible for the reception of dignities and honours and their testimonies banned in court;[815] excommunication, first from the sacraments and later, if they remain obdurate, from all intercourse with the community of the faithful;[816] refusal of burial in Christian ground, so as to emphasise the loss of salvation;[817][818] prohibition of their offerings and oblations, thus excluding them from the essential practice of public beneficence;[819] invalidation of wills and the confiscation of their properties after death.[820] These penalties were promulgated, renewed and recalled by multitudes of general and local councils as well as papal decrees. Furthermore, they were directed not only against those who actually take usury, but also against their wives and children who might share with them in its fruits;[i] against their heirs who oppose restitution of ill-gotten gain;[821] against their servants who fail to disown them;[822] against landlords who lend or grant them places for carrying out their traffic;[823] against their victims who do not, within a month, denounce them;[824] against notaries who help them in drawing up their usurious contracts, and the witnesses of such contracts;[825] against 'magistrates, rulers, consuls, judges and similar officials' who enact, or enforce usury laws that either hold debtors to payment of usury or deny them the right to recover usury already paid;[826] against princes and public powers who protect usurers;[827] and against those who argue that the taking of usury is not sinful.[828] Special penalties also existed

---

i Interestingly, the can. 6 of the Council of Paris, 1212, states that it is better for the wife of a usurer, and his children, to beg rather than accept any support from him, for he gives what is not his. Furthermore, if she could not dissuade him from doing this evil, she is bound to seek a separation. However, the Council of Mainz, 1310, allowed her to live with him rather than become public beggars or starve provided that she denounce him to the bishop. Otherwise, the sacraments are to be refused from her as well as her children as ordained by canon 141 of the Council of Trier, 1310.

for clerics guilty of the crime of usury or who neglected to apply the canons against usury (e.g. giving absolution to unrepentant usurers).[829] Whole groups, *collegia*, *universitates* and *communitates* may be punished.

Moreover, convinced by this campaign against usury, many of the secular rulers also enforced a ban on usury, making the practice not only a religious sin but also a legal offence. As noted by Helmholz, usury trials appear regularly in the records of both civil and religious courts throughout medieval Europe.[830] In many places, such as in England, convicted usurers suffered the penalty of losing all of their possessions and being sentenced as outlaws.[831]

Nevertheless, neither the terrible punishments of the afterlife forewarned by the friars, nor the drastic temporal sanctions imposed by Popes, councils and secular rulers, appeared to succeed in curbing the widespread extent of the practice. The sin of usury was probably one that many Christians found difficult to resist, especially in view of the increasing demands for credit. Some lenders just flouted the bans and continued to conduct their illicit traffic publicly, even in notorious quarters and under distinctive nomenclatures such as the Cahorsins and the Lombards – itinerant bankers. They were called 'manifest usurers',[832] against whom the whole wrath of the Church, along with her anti-usury canons, were directed. Other lenders pretended to be Jewish so that they could charge interest and at the same time not be charged with a crime.[833] However, the majority of the lenders resorted to evade the ban, and escape the penalties, mainly through hiding their demand for interest under seemingly legitimate non-*mutuum* formulas. Therefore, they were labelled as "occult usurers." Canonically, if discovered, they were only forced to pay restitutions, not necessarily to their individual victims, but to the generality of the poor, that is preferably to the charitable institutions of the Church. The interest-masking contractual devices developed by the occult usurers were described as '*fraudem usurarum*' (i.e. fraudulent lending practices). They were not in the slightest condoned or tolerated by the Churchmen, not in the beginning at least.[834]

Contracts in Fraudem Usurarum

The early medieval Christian theologians and canonists appeared very attentive to the various guises and concealments behind which usury could be taken, since they prohibited not only usurious loan contracts but also a considerable number of other commercial contracts that may have been, and were, used as a means of receiving more than what had been given. Some of these transactions will be considered here.

The Mortgage

Some of the earliest covert forms of usury were the mortgages (lit. dead pledges). The term had been used to identify an arrangement by which the borrower provides an income-producing *gage* to be held as security by the lender until the debt is paid. The revenues of the *gage* are agreed to be fully enjoyed by the lender during the period of the loan. As the borrower will not benefit whatsoever from the *gage*, whilst the loan is outstanding, it becomes for him a 'mortal *gage*'. But, for the lender, the *gage* obviously would provide him with something over and above the amount of money loaned. Therefore, the arrangement was considered by the canonists *fraudem usurarum*, and thus prohibited.[835] Otherwise, Pope Alexander III, in the Council of Tours (1163), suggested that when the *gage* has been given for a loan the revenues are to be applied to reduce the principal of the loan after the normal expenses of the *gagee* had been deducted. As opposed to the mortgage, this approved arrangement was entitled a *vifgage* (lit. living pledge).[836]

Conditional Sale

Unsurprisingly, the *vifgage* was not adopted by the moneylenders. Instead, they sought to circumvent the prohibition of the mortgage by turning the whole transaction into a conditional sale. As lamented by Pope Alexander III in several letters, (which were later inserted in the Decrees), the public usurers now, rather than granting the loan on security, buy the *gage* in question for the amount of the loan with the stipulation to sell it back to the borrower after a certain time, thus profiting from the revenues while the *gage* was in their possession. Pope Alexander concluded that this is usury.[837] Pope Innocent III held likewise.[838]

Retrovenditio (Selling Back)

Under the pretence of sale, several other attempts were also made to conduct usury. As noted by the canonist Joannes Andreae (d. 1345), some usurers sell a commodity on credit to the one who is seeking a loan; then immediately repurchase the good at a lower cash price. This type of transaction became known as *retrovenditio* (lit. selling back). The net result of which is that the borrower will be left with ready cash, along with a debt for the larger amount of credit.[839] Other usurers, as pointed out by the canonist Henry of Hesse (1397), buy from the borrower his house for one year, and then rent it to him for a fixed sum. At the end of the year, the house will be sold back to the borrower for the original purchase price. Obviously, the interest was already taken from the rent.[840] Both of these contracts were also judged to be in *fraudem usurarum*.

Double Contracts

Another deceptive method of obtaining usury was by combining two contracts in one. For instance, A lends B ten pounds and a poor horse worth five pounds for six months and demands twenty pounds in return. Such practices were labelled usurious fraud.[841] The same was applied to selling on credit for a higher price than that for cash. Since it was perceived by theologians and canonists as a double contract: the first is a sale contract in which A buys from B the goods at the current price, and the second is a loan contract in which B agrees to lend A the price of the goods for a certain time at a rate of usury represented by the difference between the current price and the credit price. Both Pope Alexander III and Pope Urban III outlawed this practice.[842] In addition, the Council of Paris, which convened in 1212, also declared that all who sell goods on credit and increase the price on account of the delay in payment incur both the penalties and the guilt of usurers. Similar decrees were issued by a number of general and local councils.[843]

Amongst other contracts examined by the canonists in discussing fraudulent methods of eluding the anti-usury laws are loans recompensed by intangible services, and the practice of lending goods when they were cheap to be returned when they were valued more dearly.[844] But, even while these stringent anti-usury measures were taken, the cleverness of those who were called upon to draw up and defend such interest-masking contracts were able to nullify even the most strenuous efforts made to put a stop to them.

The Church campaign against usury appeared to be met with a veritable financial revolution, led by capital-wealthy lenders, who, in the course of time, developed more sophisticated financial instruments designed in such a way as to make them exempt from the penalties of Canon Law, i.e. to make them Canon-compliant. Some of these took the form of complex legal fictions that had features implicit in interest-bearing loans, and others of which were based upon exploiting the loopholes found within the Scholastic theory of usury, by means of so-called *extrinsic titles*. Examples of the most commonly used will be provided below.

Legal Fictions

Safe Partnership Contracts

Whether it takes the form of *societas* in which two (or more) persons combined their money (or skills) for trading purposes, sharing *pro rata* in any profits or losses, or it takes the form of *commenda* where one person puts his capital at the disposal of another to trade with on condition of receiving a share in any profits made, partnership contracts were considered legitimate by scholastics.[845] The permissibility of profiting from such contracts was justified on the ground that, unlike the *mutuum* contracts, the ownership of the capital provided remained with the investing partner, thus leaving him fully liable to the risk of loss if something untoward occurred. As Aquinas explained:

> "He who commits his money to a merchant or craftsman by means of some kind of partnership does not transfer the ownership of his money to him but it remains his; so that at his risk the merchant trades or the craftsman works with it; and therefore he can illicitly seek part of the profit then coming from his own property." (*Summa Theologica*, II-II:9:78:2)

Thus, the incidence of the risk serves as a proof for the retention of ownership by which the investing party is entitled to gain. The importance of the element of risk was, therefore, insisted upon in strong terms by many theologians and canonists. For example, Rebert of Courson said, "Any merchant making a contract with another for trading must, if he wishes to be a participant of the profit, show himself a participant of the danger and expenses which attend all buying and selling."[846] Paul de Castro (d. 1444) stated, "A partnership when the gain is shared, but not the loss, is not to be permitted."[847] "The legitimacy," Brants asserted, "of the contract of *commenda* always rested upon the same principle; capital could not be productive except for him who worked it himself, or who caused it to be worked on his own responsibility. This latter condition was realised in *commenda*."[848]

Foenus Nauticum (Sea Loans)

Nonetheless, the money-lenders developed usury-evasive types of partnership whereby the burden of the risk of loss was unequally born by the parties. The most famous of these are the *foenus nauticum* (i.e. sea loans). In this arrangement, the investing partner lent money, or goods, to seafaring merchants with the understanding that if the ship were lost at sea, the merchant need not repay the amount invested. But, if the voyage were successful, the merchant must return the sum loaned along with an agreed percentage of the expected profits irrespective of the actual outcome of the business, whether the merchant gains or loses with his wares.[849][850] Theoretically, the contract was recognised as half-loan (during the on-land period) and half-partnership (when at sea). Effectively, however, it enables the investing partner to gain a return in excess of the principal by assuming only the risk for the voyage, which is negligible compared with the business risk that is left to be fully incurred by the borrower. Hence, it should come as no surprise that sea loans were popular amongst lenders in the eleventh and twelfth centuries. This was supposed to have been prohibited by Pope Gregory IX's *decretal Naviganti* of 1227-1234, which condemned sea loans as usurious for, as explained by Cardinal Goffredus of Trani (fl. 1245), they do not reflect a true partnership, where all risk of loss is borne in common.[851] Nonetheless, a small number of canonists including Hostiensis and Albercius still argued for the practice.[852]

Contractum Trinius (Triple Contract)

A usury-evasive type of partnership can also be found in the so-called *contractum trinius*. The lender was designated as the investing partner in a business venture. The working partner, in separate contracts, guaranteed full repayment of the investment even if the venture failed, and stipulated a fixed share of profits for the investor. This will provide the 'borrower' with a large amount of capital whilst it gave the 'creditor' a guaranteed return.⁸⁵³

Commenda (Silent Partnership Agreement)

Since receiving interest on a deposit was considered usury, many medieval bankers and their clients tended to resort to another usury-evasive partnership agreement whereby the latter will supply the former with a certain amount of money in order to be employed in lawful trade, and profits accruing therefrom were to be shared equally between them. However, the business funds supplied by the client were in reality the deposit whereas the profit provided by the bank was the interest. Since the interest rates are *ipso facto* not mentioned in such contracts, the working partner (the bank) was empowered to give variable returns to the investing partner (the depositor), from year to year, sometimes more, if the year had been good for the bank, or less, in case it had been poor. The mechanism is comparable to modern income bonds on which interest is paid only when earned. Many of the deposits with the famous Medici bank are reported to have been made on this basis.⁸⁵⁴ Most of the depositors were Italian nobles, businessmen and even clerics. An interest rate of 10 per cent. was often paid.⁸⁵⁵

Depositum Confessatum

Amongst the subterfuges also used to conceal interest-paying loans was the *Depositum Confessatum*. Inherited and adapted from the Roman law, the *depositum* is not dissimilar to the modern deposit account. It is a contract made in good faith by which one person (the depositor) entrusts to another (the depositary) a movable good to be guarded, protected and returned at any given moment the depositor may ask for it.⁸⁵⁶ However, according to Roman law, if the good deposited was non-fungible (e.g. a horse or heirloom), the depositary would be expected to return the very same item to the depositor, strictly in the same condition in which it had been left with him. But, if the deposited item was fungible (e.g. money, corn or oil), the depositor would be required to return not necessarily the original item, but its equivalent. The latter case is known as *'depositum irregulare'*. It entitles the depositary to utilise the item deposited as long as an exact equivalent is safely and securely held, and kept available for the depositor. In the event of failure on the part of the depositary to fulfil this obligation, i.e. being neither able to return the deposit nor an exact equivalent on demand, not only was he held to be guilty of theft by misappropriation, but he was also obliged to pay compensation to the depositor for any delay in repayment, as laid down in the *Corpus Juris Civilis* (Digest, 16, 3, 25, 1).

Taking the cue from this legislation, many mediaeval bankers and their clients expressly declared that they had taken part in a *depositum* irregulare contract whilst they had actually concluded an interest-bearing loan contract. The method of concealment to which this declaration belonged was called *'depositum confessatum'*.[857] It was nothing but a simulated deposit to which, at the end of the agreed-upon term, the banker 'confessed' could not be returned, and would thus pay a 'penalty' in the form of 'interest' to compensate for the presumed 'delay'. Interestingly, this method of circumventing the usury law is thought to have played a role in the subsequent emergence of fractional-reserve banking and fiat paper money. For example, as pointed out by de Soto:

> "Bankers who had used the *depositum confessatum* to disguise loans and deposits and to justify the illegal payment of interest, eventually realised that the doctrine which held that deposits always concealed loans could also be extremely profitable to them, because they could employ it to defend even the misappropriation of money which had actually been placed into demand deposits and had not been loaned."[858]

As a response, and in order to put an end to the pretence of the *depositum confessatum*, some canonists concluded that all deposits, even real ones made with the essential aim of safeguarding the goods in question, were usurious in nature, and thus prohibited.[859]

Cambium per Litteras

Another artifice used by the bankers to avoid the accusation of usury, was to conceal the loan in an exchange transaction (*cambium per litteras*) or bill of exchange. As described by Roover, the typical medieval bill of exchange involved four persons and two payments. On one side of the contract are the lender (known as a deliverer, normally a banker) and his agent (payee) who resides in another city. On the other side are the borrower (known as a taker) and his correspondent (payer). The deliverer gives the taker a certain amount of money in the local currency in return for a bill, which is an order to give the payee an agreed-upon sum in a foreign currency. This is called 'the exchange payment'. The deliverer then sends the bill to the payee who in turn takes it to the payer and receives the amount written in the bill. This is called the 're-exchange payment.'[860] Most bills were payable at *usance* (the period allowed for the movement of bills between cities). In the fourteenth century, the *usance* between Bruges and Barcelona was thirty days after sight. Between Bruges and most Italian centres, including Florence, Genoa, and Venice, the *usance* was two months after date.

Since a designated time separated the exchange and re-exchange payment, this arrangement could also perform as extended credit. In fact, the lenders operated with it on this basis. They made their profit by disguising interest in the exchange rate, i.e. by asking the borrowers, who are seeking a given sum in local currency, to promise much more than the equivalent in foreign currency payable abroad at a future agreed-upon date.⁸⁶¹ The practice was defended on the basis that the lender still bears the risk of loss because of the fluctuations in exchange rates.⁸⁶² In reality, however, these fluctuations were often governed by the supply and demand for foreign balances, which could be predicted with great accuracy by 'international' bankers at the time. Moreover, the 'taker,' 'payer' and the 'payee' were in many cases the same individual or financial institution which means that money itself was moving only between two accounts on paper, rather than between locations.⁸⁶³ Because of the involvement of time and credit, some canonists were reluctant to approve of the bill of exchange. The majority, however, accepted the practice.⁸⁶⁴

Legal Exceptions

Merchant bankers also misused a number of *extrinsic titles* so as to achieve the same cash-flow effect as interest. These titles were in essence 'legal exceptions' to the usury prohibition that permitted the lender to receive some payment beyond the principle on account of reasons external to the loan contract itself. The scholastics introduced them mainly as variations necessary for the better fulfilment of the requirement for commutative justice. In practice, however, their main contribution was to undermine the whole prohibition of usury. For by permitting these legal exceptions, the scholastics, deliberately or otherwise, provided "escape-hatches within the framework of the doctrine of usury."⁸⁶⁵ Three of these have already been discussed in great detail in a previous chapter. Two more will now receive a brief examination below.

Gratis Dans

Unlike the Jewish *poskim*, Christian theologians permitted the lender to receive something in excess of the capital in the form of *gratis dans* (i.e. gift). Pope Innocent III, in a letter of 1206, maintained that it is not to be considered usury what the borrower may gift to the lender provided that there was no exaction, nor express or tacit agreement that a gift would be offered.[866] In order to be licitly accepted, Bernard of Pavia explained, the gift must be wholly gratuitous and offered without compulsion or constraints.[867] It should be given spontaneously by the borrower merely as an indication of appreciation for the kindness and generosity of the lender. Yet, the latter was exhorted not to lend money in hope or expectation of receiving a gift, otherwise he would be committing usury, or strictly speaking 'mental usury', regardless of whether or not his hope was realised.[868] In the case that this was the intention of the lender, Pope Innocent III declared, he is then obliged to make restitution. But who can know what is in the heart of the lender, apart from the lender himself? Without his confession, it was almost impossible to convict him in a court of law. No wonder, then, that the title was thoroughly exploited by money-lenders!

Many Italian bankers, including the Bardi and Peruzzi, lent indeed large sums of money to both political and merchant princes and in return were reimbursed for their efforts by *discreziones* (discretionary gifts).[869] The bankers also used to accept 'time deposits' (deposits made for a certain period), returning them with a discretionary financial gratuity at the maturity date. The 'gifts' usually ranged from 7 to 10 per cent on the loan. But, as there was no contract the banker was not obliged to pay anything. However, consistent failure to pay the *discreziones* would result in his depositors going elsewhere with their funds.[870] The same might happen if the banker offered less competitive discretionary gifts. Nonetheless, the *discreziones* were attacked by several theologians such as St. Bernardine of Siena and St. Antoninus of Florence. The latter complained that:

> "The nobles, who do not wish to work, in case they lack money as they gradually consume, give it to a merchant or

a money-changer, principally intended to receive something annually at their [the depositee's] discretion, the capital, however, being kept safe. And although they call this a deposit, yet it is clearly usury."[871]

Montes Pietatis

There was another exception to the ban on usury by which more than the amount of the loan could be 'licitly' received, namely the *montes pietatis*. Based on the model of the *montes profane* (the system of public debt resorted to by many Italian States), the Franciscans established, first in Orvieto (in 1462) and later in many Italian cities, the *montes pietatis* with the purpose of collecting funds for the sake of providing credit facilities for the borrowers who may have a short-term need for money due to a temporary necessity.[i] These charitable financial institutions were similar in form to the modern co-operative credit banks. They had also similarities to pawnbrokers in that sometimes a pledge is required to be taken so as to cover the possibility of the loan not being repaid.

Yet, although the aim of the sponsors of the *montes* was exclusively philanthropic, they soon found themselves obliged to make charges to the borrowers in order to defray administrative expenses, such as rents and salary payments to employees. These administrative charges were defended by the Franciscans as being imperative for the continued existence of the *montes*.[872] Directly opposed to them were the Dominicans who rejected such charges on the grounds that they were no different from the prohibited 'interest charges' in light of the fact that both constitute payments

---

i The *montes* used to ask the borrower about the use of loaned funds and very often forced him to make an oath that the funds were to be used for paying necessities only. See, Brian McCall, 'Unprofitable Lending: Modern Credit Regulation and the Lost Theory of Usury' 30 Cardozo Law Review, 594

over and above the principal stipulated and agreed upon at the inception of the loan contract.⁸⁷³ However, the general position of the Church fell in favour of the Franciscans, since the *montes* were seen as a part of fulfilling the requirements of justice towards needy borrowers.[i] Pope Paul II (1417-1471) approved the *montes* on the ground that the charge was not profit, but only enough to accommodate the operational cost.[ii] The practice was also officially sanctioned by the 5th Lateran Council, convened in 1515, under the pontificate of Pope Leo X. In the proceedings of the Council, usury was declared, "when gain is sought to be acquired from the use of a thing, not fruitful in itself, without labour, expense, or risk on the part of the lender."⁸⁷⁴

Consequently, the *montes* spread throughout much of Europe, expanding its sphere of activity to encompass productive loans and even deposit banking.⁸⁷⁵ Many of which were run under the direct protection of the Popes themselves. The rates they charged varied from 6 to 15 per cent, but very often was below that offered by local pawnbrokers.⁸⁷⁶ The *montes* were the first institutions which lent openly at interest with the support of the Church itself. Perhaps, this is what Luther was referring to in his vigorous attack on the Holy See when he stated: "[such] transactions should be utterly condemned and prevented for the future, regardless of the opposition of the Pope and all his infamous laws, and though he might have erected his pious foundations on them."⁸⁷⁷ Nonetheless, it is worth remembering here that Luther himself, when he was offered 500 florins (in 1532) for the support of "poor youths prosecuting their studies in

---

i It was felt that, if the poor must borrow, it was better that they should borrow at a low rate of interest from philanthropic institutions than at an extortionate rate from usurers. See, ibid.

ii And, if in a particular year, a *montes pietatis* overestimated its costs and actually made a profit it was required to donate this money to another charity. McCall, 'Unprofitable Lending: Modern Credit Regulation and the Lost Theory of Usury', op. cit., 596

holy scriptures," he advised that the sum be lent out at interest, "because it is to be spent on such a good, useful and necessary work."[878] Similarly, Ebusuud Efendi, the Grand Mufti of the Ottoman Empire, authorised the act of interest-taking at the rate of 15 per cent by the Islamic pious foundations (*awqaf*) as a practical matter of necessity.

However, the papal justification of the *montes* appeared to open the door for private pawnbrokers to ply their trade in broad daylight. For if the *montes* could morally charge interest under the pretence of administrative costs, why should pawnbrokers not do likewise? Yet, the whole religious ban on usury became a dead letter in subsequent centuries owing not to this, but to the widespread theological approval of a relaxed variant of the *Lucrum Cessans* under which title payment beyond principal can be asked for from the outset of the loan contract, not as profit for lending money but, as a compensation for the 'lost' opportunity to make a profit elsewhere with the money loaned. In the presence of such entitlement there was obviously no need to employ any other complicated contrivances or colourful shifts.

Bay' al-'Inah

> "They treat Allah like a child. If they took *riba* openly, it would be less reprehensible." Abu Ayyub as-Sikhtiyani (685-748 CE)

Within the Muslim community, various usury-evading practices seem already to have been well-known going back as far as to the revelation of the Qur'an. They were referred to in a number of *ahadith* as *bay' al-'inah* (i.e. *'inah* sale transactions).[i]

---

i According to some jurists, the term *'inah* was derived from the root word of *'aun* which means assistance. It is called *bay' al-'inah* because the seller assists the buyer in obtaining his need. Other jurists were of the opinion that *'inah* was derived from the word *'ayn* which refers to cash. According

For example, the Companion Abdullah Ibn 'Umar ﷺ narrated that:

> "I heard the Messenger of Allah, ﷺ say: 'When you enter into *'inah* transactions, hold onto the tails of cattle, are content with farming, and you forsake *jihad* (struggle in the way of Allah), Allah will cause humiliation to prevail over you and will not withdraw it until you return to your religion.'"[879]

However, what *bay' al-'inah* is, and what the legal ruling may be regarding it, become matters of controversy between the *fuqaha* of the four schools of Islamic jurisprudence. A multitude of different forms of *bay' al-'inah* are presented in their literature. The common denominator amongst them is that they all include fictitious sale transactions employed in such a way as to camouflage an interest-bearing loan. We shall consider here three prime forms of these interest-masking sale transactions in the following order:

1) The dual *'inah* contract;
2) The tripartite *'inah* contract (*al-tawarruq*);
3) The Maliki form of *'inah* contract (*murabahah*)

These are of particular interest as the entire edifice of the modern Islamic banking system so-called, appears to have been founded upon them, as will be demonstrated below.

The Dual 'Inah Contract

The first and most notorious form of *bay' al-'inah* involves two persons and two transactions. It is commonly known therefore as the 'dual *'inah* contract'. It often works as follows: the lender sells an item to the borrower for a given price to be paid at a future agreed-upon date. The borrower then immediately sells the same

---

to this view, it was called *bay' al-'inah* since the main purpose of executing the contract is to obtain cash. See, Muhammad bin Muhammad Al-Hattab, *Mawahib al-Jalil fi Sharh Mukhtasar al-Khalil* (Beirut, Dar al-Fikr 1992), Vol. 4, p. 404.

item back to the lender for a lower price paid in cash. The net result of both transactions is that the borrower gains cash in hand together with a debt for a higher sum.[i]

Interestingly, this legal fiction is identical to what had been used by many medieval Christian money-lenders so as to circumvent the prohibition on usury, particularly the *retrovenditio*. It is possible that they may have borrowed it from their Muslim counterparts, as some have argued.[ii] It also seems to have found its way to Jewish usurers (known amongst them as the *mohatra* contract).[880] [iii] In fact, it is still very prevalent in the modern financial markets where it is used for stock lending between banks or brokers – referred to as "*repos*" (short for repurchase agreements).[881]

However, the vast majority of Muslim jurists, including the Hanafis, Hanbalis and Malikis are of the opinion that this form of *bayʿ al-ʿinah* is unlawful.[882] The Malikis, however, often subsumed it under the rubric of *buyuʿ al-ajal* (lit. credit sales) while providing different definitions for *bayʿ al-ʿinah*, as will be seen later in this section. The mainstay of the textual evidences adduced by the majority in support of their position, is that narrated by Aliya bint Ayfaʾ:

---

i   An example would be a lender selling goods for £110 payable in a year's time, and instantly repurchasing it for £100 in cash. Thus, the borrower has effectively borrowed £100 at a 10% interest rate.

ii A. Beattie, *False Economy: A Surprising Economic History of the World* (Penguin Adult 2010), p. 136. However, issuing a decree in 1679, the Holy Office of the Vatican concluded that the practice violates the biblical prohibition of usury.

iii The practice seems still to be gaining rabbinical approval today. Justice Cohen of the Israeli Supreme Court notes that, "A vendor may sell goods on credit at a price of 100 units payable at future date and immediately repurchase the goods at the price of 90 units payable cash down; each of the two contracts of sale would be valid." See, H. Moore, *The Future of Anthropological Knowledge* (Taylor & Francis 2003), p. 70

"I performed the pilgrimage with Umm Muhibbah and when we entered upon Aisha [883], Umm Muhibbah said to her: 'O, Mother of the believers, I used to own a slave girl and I sold her to Zaid ibn Arqam for 800 dirhams ... He then intended to sell her, so I purchased her from him for 600 dirhams cash.' She (Aisha) said: 'What an evil sale and purchase! Let Zaid ibn Arqam know that he has nullified his *jihad* with the Messenger of Allah unless he repents.'"[884]

What is important in respect of the sale mentioned in this hadith is that it appears to be fortuitous, in contrast to a pre-planned double-sale.[885] The slave girl was sold for 800 dirhams on credit. Later, the buyer, i.e. Zaid, decided to sell her. The original owner, i.e. Umm Muhibbah, offered to buy her back for 600 dirhams. The outcome of these transactions is that the article of sale had returned to Umm Muhibbah but she still had a debt of 200 dirhams. Therefore, Aisha considered this transaction usurious. This is further evidenced in the addendum to this hadith, which shows that Umm Muhibbah had asked whether she might retain her capital (i.e. the slave) and forego the extra 200 dirhams; Aisha replied by reciting the verse pertaining to the *riba* prohibition, that is *"If you repent you may retain your principal, suffering no loss and causing loss to none"* (Ch. 2, Verse: 279). Her citing this verse implies that Aisha considered the buy-back contract to be an infringement of the *riba* rules.

In the same vein, the Companion 'Abdullah ibn 'Abbas when asked about the legality of the act of a man who sold a dress made of silk to another for 100 dirhams on credit, and then repurchased it from him for 50 dirhams in cash, he responded that: "[this is selling] fewer dirhams for more dirhams (i.e. *riba*), with the dress in between."[886] In another narration, he added, "Verily, Allah is not deceivable. This [selling] is included amongst that which Allah and his Messenger have prohibited."[887] Unlike the previous hadith, the buy-back sale mentioned in this hadith appeared to be agreed upon from the outset of the transaction.[i]

Besides these *ahadith*, the Malikis and the Hanbalis also justified their prohibition of this form of *bay' al-'inah*, and the like, upon the principle of *sadd al-dhari'a* (lit. blocking the means). They maintained that although the buy-back contract might be in itself valid, it should be proscribed for it is commonly used as a means for receiving more than what had been paid, i.e. usury. A well-known Maliki jurist, Imam Ahmed al-Dardir, clarified as follows:

> "The outward appearance [of *buyu' al-ajal*] is lawful but because it results in what is prohibited it must be therefore prohibited, regardless of whether or not this result was the aim [of the two parties to the contract], pursuant to the principle of *sadd al-dhari'a* ... Thus, that which leads to *haram* is *haram* ... Accordingly, any sales frequently employed by the parties in order to achieve an outlawed end must be banned ... as is the case with selling a commodity for 10 on credit and then re-selling it for 5 in cash."[888][889]

The Shafi'is, on the other hand, do not subscribe to the principle of *sadd al-dhari'a*. Rather, the founder of the School, Imam Muhammad ibn Idris al-Shafi'i (767-820 CE), stated that:

> "The principle of my approach is that every transaction which is outwardly sound, I do not invalidate [either] due

---

i   In addition, the prominent scholar Ibn Taymiyyah, in his book: *Iqamat al-Dalil 'ala Ibtal al-Tahlil* (i.e. establishing the evidence for the invalidation of law-evading practices), asserted that: "... none of the Companions or the Followers allowed [*bay' al-'inah*]. On the contrary, the generality of the People of Madinah and the People of Kufa as well as many others prohibited it. This is a sufficient proof [for its prohibition]. Further, it should be considered as *ijma'* [on its prohibition]." Translated by the author of this thesis.

to suspicion or the customary practices of the two parties; [rather] I permit them [based upon] the soundness of their outward [form]. I [do, however] dislike (i.e. prohibit)[i] any intention which, if it were made apparent, would invalidate the sale."[890]

So, al-Shafi'i opines that the intention of the parties is immaterial in considering the validity of the buy-back sale contract. What is interesting in his statement, however, is the differentiation made between the judicial and religious realms. These realms are often referred to in the parlance of Islamic jurisprudence as *qada* and *diyana* respectively. Juridically, al-Shafi'i maintains that the intent of the parties is not to be pursued, nor their contracts to be annulled based upon suspicions or possible outcomes that it may or may not lead to. But, religiously, if their intent were indeed to circumvent the ban on *riba*, they would be committing a *haram* act, for which they would be held liable, but only in the afterlife in the court of God "Who alone knows the motives of men."[891] The only circumstance in which their fraudulent intentions may invalidate the buy-back sale contract is when they are made explicit in the contract itself.

The legal implications of this controversy are critical. For if the motives of the parties are external to the essentials of a valid sale contract, as held by the Shafi'is, the interest-masking sales contracts must be deemed operative, obligatory and enforceable under the Islamic legal system. But, if it is inherent to the validity of a sale

---

i   Please note that it was a custom amongst the early Muslim jurists to use the word 'dislike' instead of 'prohibit' lest the following Qur'anic verse be applied upon them: "*Do not say about what your lying tongues describe: 'This is halal and this is haram,' inventing lies against Allah. Those who invent lies against Allah are not successful – a brief enjoyment, then they will have a painful punishment.*" (ch. 16, verse: 116-7). In addition, as Imam al-Ghazali noted in his book: *al-Mustasfa fi 'Ilm al-Usul* (lit. The Clarified in Legal Theory): " … in many cases, al-Shafi'i may have said that: 'I dislike so and so,' while he meant that 'it is prohibited.'"

contract, as held by Malikis and Hanbalis, such transactions are not to be heard in Islamic courts. The kingdom of Saudi Arabia and Malaysia provide good examples here. Hanbali judges in the former often refuse any *'inah*-transaction cases, whereas their Shafi'i counterparts in the latter enforce them.[892]

Finally, in respect of the Hanafi position, although they share with al-Shafi'i his line of thinking, they prohibited the dual form of *bay' al-'inah* due to the aforementioned hadith of Aliya – a hadith which al-Shafi'i deemed to be *da'if* (weak).[893]

However, the dual form of *bay' al-'inah* has gained popularity mainly amongst the Malaysian and Indonesian Islamic banks. It has been widely used in creating large numbers of so-called Islamic financial products that simulated a similar end with their counterparts offered in conventional banks. Traditional financial facilities such as personal loans, overdrafts, credit cards and mortgages were restructured in such a way as to have them include a buy-back transaction and thus framing them as '*Shari'a*-compliant'.[894]

The Tripartite 'Inah Contract (al-Tawarruq)

The second commonly used form of *bay' al-'inah* is widely known as *tawarruq*.[895] The word literally means the act of seeking silver-based commodity money (*al-wariq*). Technically, it stands for an arrangement in which a person who in need of money (*mustawriq*) purchases a commodity at a deferred higher price with the purpose of selling it at market, to someone other than the original seller, at a lower price for ready cash. As this arrangement often involves three parties, i.e. the person who seeks the cash, the original seller of the commodity and the end buyer, it is also known as the 'tripartite *'inah* contract'.

An example of the classical *tawarruq* arrangement would be that: (A) being in need of £100 goes to the market and buys 10 kilos of wheat from (B) for £120 payable at a future agreed-upon date. (A) then offers the wheat for sale at a lower spot price, that is £100. The offer is accepted by (C), who pays the full amount in cash. Thus, (A) will leave the market with the sum needed (£100), along with a larger debt (£120) owed to (B).

It is said that such means of acquiring liquidity was resorted to by many of the Companions ﷺ who were short of money but at the same time did not want to engage in *riba*-based loan contracts.[896] The vast majority of the *fuqaha* of the four Schools of Law permitted this arrangement.[897][i] However, many of them stipulated that the original seller, i.e. (B) in the previous example, not be involved in any way, shape or form in the re-sale transaction concluded between the person who seeks cash (A) and the end buyer (C). This condition is evident in a number of their relevant *fatwas*. For Instance, the companion of Imam Malik, Ibn al-Qasim,[898] stated that:

> "I asked Malik (viz. Malik bin Anas (d. 795 CE), the founder of the Maliki School of Law) about a man selling a commodity for a hundred dinars till a fixed time. Once the transaction is completed between the two parties, the buyer says to the seller: 'Sell it on my behalf to any man for cash, for I am not proficient at trade'. Imam Malik said, 'There is no good in it,' and he forbade it."[899][900]

In the same vein, Imam al-Hasan al-Basri (d. 728), the renowned scholar, in response to a trader's query that, "I sell silk for a deferred

---

i Amongst those who prohibited this form of *tawarruq* were Ibn Taymiyyah and his disciple Ibn al-Qayyim. The latter said that:
"My sheikh (Ibn Taymiyyah) prohibited *tawarruq*, and people asked him again and again to allow it, but he still prohibited *tawarruq* [given that] the *'illah* (i.e. effective cause) of banning *riba* is achieved in *tawarruq*. [Furthermore] *tawarruq* is worse than *riba*, because *tawarruq* entails a higher cost and losses ... *Shari'a* does not forbid a lower harm (*riba*) and allow a higher harm (through *tawarruq*)." Ibn Qayyim al-Jawziyyah, *I'lam al-muwaqqi'in 'an Rabb al-'Alamin*, Vol. 3, p. 170, as translated in Aleshaikh, op. cit., p. 38-43

price, and when the buyer is female, she usually says: 'Sell it for me [in cash] as you know the market!' He replied, "Give the buyer the commodity and leave him. Do not sell it [for her], nor buy it [from her], only guide [her] to the market."[901]

Likewise, the prominent Hanafi jurist Muhammad bin al-Hasan al-Shaybani (d. 805 CE) stated, in his book *al-Mabsut*, "If he sells [a commodity] for [the benefit, or on behalf, of] a man, it is not appropriate for him to buy it for less than that, before payment is received, [neither] for himself [nor] for another."[902] To put it another way, from the perspective of Muhammad ibn al-Hasan, the seller must not re-purchase the commodity that he sold on credit for a lower cash price, before its payment is fully received, regardless of whether the purchase was for the benefit of the seller himself,[903] or for that of another person, as is the case with the *tawarruq* arrangement considered here. The same ruling is also found in another reliable book of the Hanafi School, namely the *Hashiyah* of Ibn 'Abidin. The author of the *Hashiyah* maintained, "if someone sells something [on credit] by himself or through his agent, or as an agent for someone else, he cannot buy it for less, for himself or for another."[904]

The reason for which these jurists, and others, prohibited the original seller from taking part in re-selling the commodity in question to a third party is apparently the recognition that the whole arrangement could be misused as an interest-masking contractual device. This is, indeed, precisely what Islamic Financial institutions (IFIs) are doing nowadays. The modus operandi of the *tawarruq* transaction as carried out by them works as follows: a customer approaches an IFI for an amount of money. The IFI purchases a given commodity for cash and sells it to the customer at a deferred higher price, which is usually to be paid in an agreed-upon number of instalments. The customer subsequently appoints the bank as an agent to sell the same commodity on the market to a third party for a cash price that is equal to what the bank had originally paid for it. Consequently, the bank sells the commodity on behalf of the customer and transfers the sum to him.

Because of the IFI's involvement in re-selling the commodity, this type of arrangement has become known as *al-tawarruq al-munazzam* (lit. organised *tawarruq*), as opposed to the *al-tawarruq al-fiqhi* (or classical *tawarruq*) mentioned above. It was introduced into the modern Islamic banking system in 2000 CE in the Kingdom of Saudi Arabia, first by the Saudi British Bank (HSBC), and later by al-Jazira Bank in 2002, before the practice was taken up by most of the IFIs in the Gulf region and throughout the Islamic world.[905] Notwithstanding, the International Islamic Fiqh Academy (OIC) in its 2009 resolution declared organised *tawarruq* impermissible (*haram*). Yet, it is still being implemented by many IFIs to this day.[906]

The Maliki Form of 'Inah Contract (Murabahah)

The two previous forms of *bay' al-'inah* are to be found in the Maliki legal sources under the title of *buyu' al-ajal* (i.e. the prohibited credit sales). Therein, afterward, the nature of *bay' al-'inah* is often examined. The relation between them, as explained by Khalil ibn Ishaq (d. 1365 CE) in his *Sharh*, is "the existence of the use of an artifice in each of them for the sake of paying less and taking more."[907]

However, in contrast with the other *madhhabs*, the Malikis define *bay' al-'inah* as "the sale by someone, from whom wares were ordered although they were not in his possession, after he purchases them, to the one who orders them."[908] Some of the Maliki *fuqaha* even recount the existence of 'the people of *'inah'* (*'ahl al-'inah*) who "set themselves up so that others may order wares from them, which they do not have. So [the people of *'inah*] go to the traders and buy [the wares] from them to sell [the wares] to those who had ordered them."[909]

The Maliki form of *bay' al-'inah* can be illustrated by the following example: (A) seeks a loan of 100 dirhams in order to purchase a silk dress from (B). Because of the *riba* prohibition, and instead of lending him the sum needed without interest, (C) offers to buy the dress from (B), and then re-sells it to (A) for 120 dirhams payable at a future agreed-upon date. Consequently, this would bring to (C) the same profit that he would have accrued had he lent (A) 100 dirhams at a 20% interest rate from the outset.

From the Malikis' perspective, therefore, such sale arrangements are to be identified as *bay' al-'inah*. However, they divide them into three types: permissible, disliked and forbidden. As noted by Ibn Rushd,:

> "That which is permissible is that a man passes a man who is one of the people of *'inah* and says to him, 'Do you have such-and-such wares that I can buy from you?' And he says to him, 'No,' but [later] tells him that he had bought the wares he asked about. So, he sells them for whatever [price], whether in cash or on credit."[910]

For instance, someone asks for a commodity from another, who does not find it available, and they separate without making any commitments. Then, the latter buys the sought-after commodity. Later, when he meets the would-be purchaser, he says 'I have obtained the commodity you asked me about, so you can buy it from me, if you wish.' In this case, it is permitted to sell it for whatever price agreed-upon whether in cash or on credit.

> "What is disliked is that he says to him, 'Buy such-and-such wares and I will buy them from you and give you a profit' without negotiating the profit."[911]

For instance, someone asks another to buy goods for him for such-and-such a price, on the understanding that he will give him a profit for them but without discussing the amount of such profit. This is considered to be *makruh* but not *haram*.

> "What is forbidden is that he tries to negotiate the profit, and says to him, 'Buy them for me for ten in cash and I will buy them from you for twelve on credit.' For that is *haram*; it is not *halal* and is not permissible, because he is a man who added extra for the loan."[912]

For instance, someone asks another to buy wares for him for ten dirhams in cash, on the understanding that he will buy them from him for fifteen on credit. Thus, the profit was agreed upon in advance. This is *haram* because it is tantamount to a usurious loan according to Ibn Rushd. In the same vein, Imam Ibn Juzayy al-Gharnati (d. 741 CE), in his *Qawanin*, added that:

> "'Buy it for ten and I shall give you fifteen for it later' ... this may be understood as *riba* since the method of the *madhhab* of Malik is to examine what leaves someone's hand and what it then receives, whilst the means, i.e. what is in between, is nullified — for it is as if this man gave someone ten dinars and took fifteen from him with delay."[913]

Another textual evidence used to support this prohibition is what Imam Malik has narrated in his *Muwatta'*, that the Companion 'Abdullah ibn 'Umar ﷺ disapproved of and forbade the scenario in which: "a man said to another, 'Buy this camel for me immediately so that I can buy it from you on credit.'"[914]

In spite of this, on the other hand, the position of Imam al-Shafi'i appears to permit this sale arrangement but with the precondition of the presentation of choice to the purchaser. In his *Kitab al-Umm*, al-Shafi'i explained that:

"When a man shows another some wares and says, 'Buy them and I will give you such-and-such a profit for them,' and then [the latter] buys them, the purchase is permissible [but only] when the one who had said 'I will give you a profit for them' has a choice such that if he wants he may buy them, or he may leave them. ... [otherwise,] if they sell it between them on the basis that they have bound themselves, then it is annulled because ... they bought and sold it before the purchaser took possession of it."[915]

Apparently, Imam al-Shafi'i is referring here to the famous hadith: "do not sell what you do not possess."[916] Indeed, this appears to be the case if the one who seeks a loan to buy a commodity and the lender concludes the sale contract for the commodity before it comes into his ownership. However, if that is not the case, it means the lender would bear the business risk that the would-be purchaser may change his mind, or ask for a better price, after the commodity in question has been bought. Not to mention the risk of loss if something untoward were to occur to the commodity whilst in the possession of the lender and before completion of the sale to the purchaser. Thus, by providing that the purchaser must retain the right of choice, the whole sale arrangement will by no means result in a risk free guaranteed rate of return for the lender. The same condition is also indicated by many Hanafis and Hanbalis.[917]

This state of affairs left the money-lenders with the problem of how to continue to secure the guarantee of a fixed return from such sale arrangements whilst meeting the legal requirement of not selling what is not in one's possession – a requirement that all Muslim jurists are agreed upon. Interestingly, IFIs with the help of their *Shari'a* boards have managed to achieve this in modern times by requiring the would-be purchaser to make a legally binding 'promise' (instead of concluding a prohibited future-sale contract) that he will buy the commodity in question once it is owned by them. Otherwise, if the promise is not fulfilled, he will be forced to pay all the relevant costs incurred.

This legal stratagem was first proposed by Dr. Sami Hamoud in the First Islamic Banking Conference held in Dubai in 1979 CE. After his proposal was assessed, the Islamic scholars participating in the conference issued a *fatwa* in its favour,stating that: "an Islamic finance institution may require its customer to sign a binding promise that he will purchase the finance property on credit (with an agreed-upon mark-up) once the bank buys it based on his order."[918] It is said that it was this *fatwa* that ushered in the birth of the contemporary Islamic banking industry.[919] The sale arrangement that involves such a promise has ever since become known as *murabahah* (lit. monetarisation).

The *fatwa* was able to derive an air of legitimacy in the context of the doctrinal dispute amongst the *fuqaha* of the four Schools of Law regarding whether or not the unilateral promise (*waʿd*) is juridically enforceable. Four relevant opinions stood out in this respect.[920] The first was the opinion of the majority of the *fuqaha*, including the Hanbalis, Shafiʿis, Zaharis, as well as some of the Malikis, that the fulfilment of a promise is non-obligatory from a legal perspective under all circumstances. The second was the opinion of the Hanafis who exclude only the occasion when the promise is contingent upon a condition, such as if (A) says to (B): 'Sell this dress to (C); if he does not pay you, I will.' Similarly, the third opinion, which is famous amongst the Malikis, excluded the case where the promise is attached to a cause and the promisee has acted upon that cause, such as if (A) says to (B): 'Demolish your home and I will lend you money to build a better one,' and then (A) does so. However, the fourth opinion, which is also featured in the Maliki *madhhab*, is that the fulfilment of a promise is legally obligatory in every case and thus enforceable in a court of law.

The very last opinion was the one cited as evidence in the aforementioned *fatwa*. Yet, there are two fatal flaws in this citation. The first is the fact that the subject of the previous differences of opinion between the *fuqaha* was the promise that involves a voluntary offer, not that made for the purpose of mutual exchange. This is clearly evident in the examples provided by the *fuqaha* themselves as well as in their definition of *wa'd* which is: "saying that something good will be brought about [by the promiser to the promisee] in the future."[921] Yet, the issuers of the *fatwa* seem to deliberately ignore this fact in order to give the impression that a number of the early respected classical *fuqaha* had actually permitted using legally binding *wa'd*, not only in the context of voluntary offers (*tabarru'at*) but also, in mutual exchange (*mu'awadat*), and thus such promises can be legitimately employed in a sale arrangement even though it results in the same thing as an interest-bearing loan contract. The second fatal flaw is the fact that such sale arrangements were identified by the Malikis as the prohibited *bay' al-'inah* regardless of whether or not they involve a promise. So, it is rather surprising to find an opinion in the Maliki *madhhab* being cited in order to justify the legality of making a binding promise in a sale arrangement that the *madhhab* already considers to be illegal *per se*.

This *fatwa* was enthusiastically received by the IFIs, nonetheless. Before long, it permeated the legal rulings of their *Shari'a* boards and proponents, including, but not limited to, Yusuf al-Qaradawi, Mohammed al-Mokhtar al-Salami, Mohammed Taqi Othmani, Abdullah a-Manee, Abdul Sattar Abu Ghudda, Ali al-Qurrah Daghi, and Hasan al-Shazli.[922] Reiterating its support of this *fatwa*, the Accounting and Auditing Organization for Islamic Financial Institutions (AAOIFI) laid down, in one of its so-called '*Shari'a* Standards' (which serve as a manual for Islamic bankers world-wide), that in a *murabahah* arrangement:

"The [Islamic financial] institution is entitled to receive compensation for any actual damage it has incurred as a result of the customer's breach of a binding promise. The compensation consists of the customer reimbursing the institution for any loss due to a difference between the price received by the institution in selling the asset to a third party and the original cost price paid by the institution to the supplier."[923]

By the inclusion of such a promise, the whole *murabahah* arrangement will, to all intents and purposes, become nothing but a profitable short-term risk-free investment that brings a fixed rate of return to the financier, or the IFIs. It almost goes without saying that this is the same end that interest-bearing loan contracts would result in. It cannot be surprising, therefore, to discover that the prevailing method of financing that has been used by the IFIs throughout recent decades is *murabahah*. It has been reported that it constitutes from 75 to 90 per cent of their assets.[924] This striking finding should raise a number of critical questions such as: How Islamic is Islamic banking today? Is its modus operandi interest free or interest masking? Does it really offer a viable alternative to banking capitalism or is it merely a variant of conventional banking? Further research is still needed in order to provide comprehensive answers to these final questions.

Conclusion

This thesis has shown that the scriptural teachings of Judaism, Christianity and Islam alike, disapprove of, in one form or another, the practice of lending money for profit. They are replete with passages containing either explicit prohibition of usury or unmistakeable evidence that the practice is scorned[925] and strongly condemned. While these passages remain intact, the theological interpretations of many of them have changed over time. The context, circumstances and nature of the interest prohibitions have long been a serious bone of contention, resulting in a wide range of assumptions and theories, some of which could be seen as an attempt to evade the literal sense of these passages. One reason for this tendency might lie in the very nature of the divine guidance, *per se*, which is held to be holy, just, good and valid for, and applicable to, every place and time. Indeed, this kind of dogma seems a likely candidate for inclusion as a central tenet of religious doctrine. Yet, when religious adherents endeavour to act in accordance with divine injunctions and rules in times and places other than those in which they were originally promulgated, certain dilemmas have arisen, the responses to which have varied.

At present, Christianity seems to separate the interest prohibitions from economics through the adoption of a theological interpretation that distinguishes 'interest' from 'usury'. The former is accepted, whilst the latter is not. The taking of interest therefore, is no longer a lively issue for most Christians today, although this was not the case for the greater part of their history.

Judaism, on the other hand, appears to interpret the biblical teachings on usury in a fashion that permits the taking of interest from gentiles, whilst prohibiting the same from fellow Jews. Yet, they developed several legal devices, most notably the *Heter Iska*, in order to evade the prohibition of taking interest even from fellow Jews. Muslims do not appear to have set a much better example.

Although Muslims claim to adhere to their anti-usury teachings, they have adopted and adapted many financial instruments that violate the spirit, whilst seemingly holding to the letter, of these teachings. In all three religions there are, however, pockets of society that have continued since the earliest times, to maintain the prohibition and act literally in accordance with their scriptural restrictions on the lending of money for profit. For them usury was, and still is, a mortal sin that corrupts both individuals and societies.

Bibliography

Abdul-Rahman MS, *Tafsir Ibn Kathir Juz': Al-Fatihah 1 to Al-Baqara 141 2nd Edition* (MSA Publication Limited 2009)

Abdullahi A, 'Religious minorities under Islamic law and the limits of cultural relativism' Human Rights Quarterly 1

Abulafia DA, *Christians and Jews: In the Twelfth Century Renaissance* (Taylor & Francis 1995)

Accounting and Institutions AOFIF, *Shari'a Standards: The Full Text of Shari'a Standards as at Shawwal 1428 AH-November 2007* (Accounting and Auditing Organization for Islamic Financial Institutions 2008)

Ackerman JM, 'Interest Rates and the Law: A History of Usury' Ariz St LJ 61

Adams T, *The Works of Thomas Adams: The Sum of His Sermons, Meditations, and Other Divine and Moral Discourses* (London 1629)

Ahmad MM, 'The notions of *dar al-harb* and *dar al-Islam* in Islamic jurisprudence with special reference to the Hanafi school' 47 Islamic Studies 5

Ahmed H and Aleshaikh NM, 'Debate on Tawarruq: Historical Discourse and Current Rulings' 28 Arab law quarterly 278

Ahmed SA, 'Global need for a new economic concept: Islamic economics' 1 International Journal of Islamic Financial Services 13

al-Ansari Z, *Asna al-Matalib fi Sharh Rawd al-Talib* (Al-Matba'ah al-Misriyyah 1357 AH)

al-Baladhuri Aa-AAIY, *Futuh al-buldan* (Dar wa Maktaba al-Hilal 1988)

al-Bukhari MII, *Translation of the Meanings of Sahih Al-Bukhari: Arabic-English*, Vol. 4 (Khan MM tr, Dar-us-Salam 1997)

al-Dasuqi MiAi', *Hashiyat al-Dasuqi* (Dar al-Fikr)

al-Din MYI, *Islamic Law: From Historical Foundations to Contemporary Practice* (Edinburgh University Press 2004)

al-Husayni Ma-DAa-Fa-SMM, *Taj al-'arus min jawahir al-qamus*, Vol. VIII (1st edn, al-Matba'ah al-Khayriyyah 1306 A.H.)

al-Jawhari ANIibH, *Taj al-lughah wa-sihah al-'arabiyyah*, Vol. II (Bulaq Press 1365 A.H.)

al-Kasani ABbMu, *Bada'i al-Sana'i fi Tartib al-Shara'i* (Dar al-Kutub al-Ilmiyah' 1986)

al-Kharshi Mi'A, *Sharh Mukhtasar Khalil* (Dar al-Fikr)

al-Khattab N, *Sunan An-Nasa'I: English Translation With Arabic Text*, Vol. 5 (Darussalam 2007)

al-Marghinani Ba-DAbAB, *Al-Hidayah fi Sharh Bidayat al-Mubtadi* (Dar Ihya' al-Turath al-'Arabi)

al-Masri RY, 'The Binding Unilateral Promise (*wa'd*) in Islamic Banking Operations: Is it Permissible for a Unilateral Promise (*wa'd*) to be Binding as an Alternative to a Proscribed Contract?' 15 Journal of King Abdulaziz University: Islamic Economics 29

al-Misiri Aa-FJa-DMbMa-i, *Lisan al-'Arab*, Vol. XII (Dar Sadir 1965)

al-Mutairi MZUoE, 'Necessity in Islamic law' (1997)

al-Nawawi YbS, *Rawdat al-Talibin*, Vol. X (Dar al-Nahdah al-Haditha 1966)

---, *Minhaj al-Talibin* (Maktabah al-Thaqafah 1992)

al-Omar F and others, 'Islamic banking: Theory, practice and challenges'

al-Qurtubi A-A, *Al-Jami 'li-Ahkam Al-Qur'an* (1987)

al-Razi F, *al-Tafsir al-Kabir* (Dar Ihya'al-Turat al-'Arabi 1990)

al-Sanhuri AA-RA, *Masadir Al-Haqq fil-Fiqh al-Islami*

al-Sarakhsi MIA, *al-Mabsut* (Dar al-Kutub al-'Ilmiya 1993)

al-Sawi AiM, *Bulghat al-Salik li-Aqrab al-Masalik ila Madhhab al-Imam Malik* (Dar al-Marif)

al-Sawi S, *A Polite Reconsideration of the Fatwa Permitting Interest-Based Mortgages for Buying Homes in Western Societies* (2001)

al-Shafi'i' MiI, *Kitab al-Umm* (Dar al-Maarifah 1990)

al-Shaybani Mia-H, *al-Makharij fi al-Hiyal* (1930)

al-Suwailem S, *Tawarruq Banking Products* (2009)

al-Tabari, *Tafsir al-tabari* (Dar al-Ma'arit 1972)

al-Tirmidhi AiMiI, *Jami al-Tirmidhi* (Darussalam 2007)

al-Zuhili SW, 'Islam and international law' 87 International Review of the Red Cross 269

al-Zuhayli W, *Financial Transaction in Islamic Jurisprudence* (Damascus-Syria: Dar al-Fikr al-Mouaser 2003)

al-Zuhaili W, *al-Fiqh al-islami wa-adillatuhu* (Dar al-Fikr 1997)

Aleshaikh N, 'Jurisprudence on Tawarruq: Contextual Evaluation on Basis of Customs, Circumstances, Time and Place' (Durham University 2011)

Alghanem AK, 'Tash ma Tash, Zayd 'akhu Obayd' (2011) <https://www.youtube.com/watch?v=9mSNRpzDm_g>

America RCo, *Tradition* (Human Sciences Press 1979)

Andreau J, *Banking and business in the Roman world* (Cambridge University Press 1999)

AostonGaor and Masters BA, *Encyclopedia of the Ottoman Empire* (Facts On File, Incorporated 2009)

Aquinas T, *Summa Theologica*

---, *Catena Aurea: St. Matthew* (John Henry Parker 1842)

Aronson R, *Jean-Paul Sartre, philosophy in the world* (NLB 1980)

Ashath ADSb, *English translation of Sunan Abu Dawud*, Vol. 4 (Al-Khattab N tr, Darussalam 2008)
Ashley WJ, *An Introduction to English Economic History and Theory: Part 1. the Middle Ages* (Adegi Graphics LLC 1906)
Ashley WJ, *An Introduction to English Economic History and Theory: The End of the Middle Ages* (1906)
———, *An Introduction to English Economic History and Theory: The Middle Ages* (1909)
Ashraf M, *The Muslim Conduct of State* (1945)
Averroës, *The Distinguished Jurist's Primer: A Translation of Bidayat Al-mujtahid* (Centre for Muslim Contribution to Civilisation 1996)
Bacon F, *Bacon's Essays* (Indo European Publishing 2010)
Badawi AZ, *The Theory of Prohibited Riba* (Centre for Islamic Law and Legal Heritage 2005)
Badawi AZ, *The Theory of Prohibited Riba* (Centre for Islamic Law and Legal Heritage 2005)
Badawi IZD, *Nazariyat al-riba al-muharram: fi al-shari'ah al-Islamiyah* (1964)
Baldwin JW, *Masters, princes and merchants : the social views of Peter the Chanter & his circle* (Princeton University Press 1970)
Baljon JMS, *The reforms and religious ideas of Sir Sayyid Ahmad Khan* (Sh. Muhammad Ashraf 1964)
Baron SW and Maimonides M, *Essays on Maimonides. An Octocentennial Volume. Edited by Salo Wittmayer Baron* (New York 1941)
Barzilai G, *Law and religion* (Ashgate 2007)
Basri E, *Ethics of business, finance, & charity according to Jewish law* (Haktav Institute 1987)
Beattie A, *False Economy: A Surprising Economic History of the World* (Penguin Adult 2010)
Bennison AK, *The Great Caliphs: The Golden Age of the 'Abbasid Empire* (Yale University Press 2009)
Bentham J, *Defense of Usury* (Payne and Foss 1816)
Bewley A and Bewley AA, *The Noble Qur'an: A New Rendering of Its Meaning in English* (Madinah Press 1999)
Blackstone W and others, *Commentaries on the Laws of England: In Four Books; with an Analysis of the Work* (Harper 1854)
Blitz RC and Long MF, 'The economics of usury regulation' The Journal of Political Economy 608
Bolingbroke HSJ, *The Work of Lord Bolingbroke: With a Life, Prepared Expressly for this Edition, Containing Additional Information Relative to His Personal and Public Character, Selected from the Best Authorities* (Carey and Hart 1841)
Bolles JA, *A Treatise on Usury and Usury Laws* (J. Munroe 1837)
Botticini M and Eckstein Z, *The Chosen Few: How Education Shaped Jewish History, 70-1492* (Princeton University Press 2012)

Bowring J and Office GBF, *Report on the commercial statistics of Syria* (Printed by W. Clowes for Her Majesty's Stationery Off. 1840)

Bowsher NN, 'Usury laws: harmful when effective' Federal Reserve Bank of St Louis Review

Brague R, *The Law of God: The Philosophical History of an Idea* (University of Chicago Press 2007)

Briggs M and Jordan P, *Economic History of England* (University Tutorial P. 1967)

Bromberg B, 'The origin of banking: religious finance in Babylonia' 2 The Journal of Economic History 77

Buchanan GW, 'Symbolic Money-changers in the Temple?' 37 New Testament Studies 280

Buell SW, 'Good Faith and Law Evasion' 58 UCLA L Rev 611

Bureau IER, *Thoughts on Islamic banking* (Islamic Economics Research Bureau 1982)

Çağatay Ne, '*Riba* and Interest Concept and Banking in the Ottoman Empire' Studia Islamica 53

Calvin J, *Calvin's Bible Commentaries: Harmony of the law, Part III* (Forgotten Books 1847)

———, *John Calvin's Commentaries On Ezekiel 13- 20 (Extended Annotated Edition)* (Jazzybee Verlag 2012)

Calvin J and Bindham CW, *Commentaries on the Four Last Books of Moses: Arranged in the Form of a Harmony* (Calvin Translation Society 1854)

Carroll J, *Jerusalem, Jerusalem: How the Ancient City Ignited Our Modern World* (Houghton Mifflin Harcourt 2011)

Chapra MU, *Towards a just monetary system : a discussion of money, banking, and monetary policy in the light of Islamic teachings* (Islamic Foundation 1985)

Chapra MU, 'The Nature of *Riba* in Islam' 8 Millah: Jurnal Studi Agama

Chapra U, 'Why Has Islam Prohibited Interest?: Rationale Behind the Prohibition of Interest' Review of Islamic Economics 5

Chazan R, 'The letter of R. Jacob ben Elijah to Friar Paul' 6 Jewish History 51

Christ K, *Christ* (University of California Press 1984)

Cleary P, *The Church and Usury : an Essay on Some Historical and Theological Aspects of Money-lending* (Christian Book Club of America 1972)

Cohen AA and Mendes-Flohr PR, *Contemporary Jewish religious thought: original essays on critical concepts, movements, and beliefs* (Scribner 1987)

Cohen B, *Law and Tradition in Judaism* (Jewish Theological Seminary of America 1959)

Coke E, *Institutes of the Laws of England* (Fletcher 1644)

Cornell T, *The Beginnings of Rome: Italy and Rome from the Bronze Age to the Punic Wars, C. 1000-263 BC* (Routledge 1995)

Corrie GE, *The History of the Reformation of the Church of England, chiefly as abriged from the larger history by Bishop Burnet and his son* (John Parker 1847)

Coulter FGL, *The Church and Usury: Error, Change or Development* (1999)

Crane TF, *The Exampla Or Illustrative Stories from the Sermones Vulgares of Jacques de Vitry* (Burt Franklin 1971)

Crim KR, *The Interpreter's Dictionary of the Bible: an illustrated encyclopedia. Supplementary volume* (Abingdon 1976)

Culpepper T, *A Discourse, Shewing the Many Advantages which Will Accrue to this Kingdom by the Abatement of Usury. Together with the Absolute Necessity of Reducing Interest of Money to the Lowest Rate it Bears in Other Countreys ... Humbly Presented to the High Court of Parliament, Etc* (London 1668)

Dabu IF, 'Tawarruq, Its Reality and Types' OIC Fiqh Academy 19th Session Online version available at http://www.iefpedia.com/english

Danby H, *The Mishnah* (Clarendon Press 1933)

Davies G and Bank JH, *A History of Money: From Ancient Times to the Present Day* (University of Wales Press 2002)

Davis E, *Challenging Colonialism: Bank Misr and Egyptian Industrialization, 1920-1941* (Princeton University Press 1983)

De Roover R, 'The scholastics, usury, and foreign exchange', 41 Business History Review 257

De Roover R, 'The scholastics, usury, and foreign exchange', 41 The Business History Review 257

De Roover RA, *Money, Banking and Credit in Mediaeval Bruges; Italian Merchant Bankers, Lombards and Money-Changers* (De Roover R and Mediaeval Academy of A eds, The Mediaeval Academy of America 1948)

De Roover RA, *The Rise and Decline of the Medici Bank: 1397-1494* (Beard Books Inc 1999)

De Soto JH, *Money, Bank Credit, and Economic Cycles* (Ludwig von Mises Institute 2009)

de Vaux R, *Ancient Israel: Its Life and Institutions* (McGraw-Hill 1965)

DeGeneres E, 'The Ellen DeGeneres Show' (2016)

Divine TF, *Interest: An Historical & Analytical Study in Economics & Modern Ethics* (Marquette University Press 1959)

Diwany TE, Ahmad T and Staff sECT, *Islamic Banking and Finance: What It Is and What It Could Be* (1st Ethical Charitable Trust 2010)

Doi ARI and Clarke A, *Shari'ah: Islamic law* (Ta-Ha 2008)

Driver GR and Miles SJC, *The Babylonian Laws*, Vol. 1 (Clarendon press 1952)

Easton SC, *A Brief History of the Western World* (Barnes & Noble 1962)

El Diwany T, *The Problem with Interest* (Kreatoc 2003)

El-Gamal MA, 'An economic explication of the prohibition of *gharar* in classical Islamic jurisprudence', 8 Islamic Economic Studies 29

El-Gamal MA, 'Interest and the paradox of contemporary Islamic law and finance', 27 Fordham Int'l LJ 108

---, *Islamic Finance: Law, Economics, and Practice* (Cambridge University Press 2006)

Bibliography

Elliott C, *Usury: A Scriptural, Ethical and Economic View* (Anti-Usury League 1902)

Epstein I, *The Babylonian Talmud* (Soncino Press 1935)

Ertl A, *The Political Economic Foundation of Democratic Capitalism: From Genesis to Maturation* (Universal Publishers 2007)

Fadel M, '*Riba*, Efficiency, and Prudential Regulation: Preliminary Thoughts' Wisconsin International Law Journal, Forthcoming 08

The Farewell Sermon of Prophet Muhammad, Vol. 11 (illustrated edn, Tughra Books 2004)

Farooq MO, 'The *Riba*-Interest Equivalence: Is there an *Ijma* (consensus)?' 4 Transnational Dispute Management

---, 'The *Riba*-Interest Equation and Islam: Re-examination of the Traditional Arguments' 6 Global Journal of Finance and Economics 99

Fassbender B and others, *The Oxford Handbook of the History of International Law* (OUP Oxford 2012)

Ferguson N, *The Ascent of Money: A Financial History of the World* (Penguin Pr 2008)

Flew A, 'The Profit Motive' 86 Ethics 312

First Vatican Council, https://www.ewtn.com/catholicism/library/first-vatican-council-1505 accessed 23/10/2023

Frank T, 'On Some Financial Legislation of the Sullan Period', 54 The American Journal of Philology 54

Franks CA, *He Became Poor: The Poverty of Christ and Aquinas's Economic Teachings* (William B. Eerdmans Publishing Company 2009)

Freeman MDA, *Lloyd's Introduction to Jurisprudence* (Sweet & Maxwell 2001)

Frierson JG, 'Changing Concepts on Usury: Ancient Times Through the Time of John Calvin' 7 American Business Law Journal 115

Gamoran H, 'Talmudic controls on the purchase of futures', 64 The Jewish Quarterly Review 48

---, 'Talmudic Usury Laws and Business Loans' 7 Journal for the Study of Judaism in the Persian, Hellenistic, and Roman Period 129

---, 'Mortgages in Geonic times in light of the law against usury' Hebrew Union College Annual 97

---, 'Investing for Profit: A Study of *Iska* up to the Time of Rabbi Abraham ben David of Posquieres' [Hebrew Union College – Jewish Institute of Religion] 70/71 Hebrew Union College Annual 153

---, 'How the Rabbis Interpreted Halakhah to Meet the Needs of the People: A Study of Mortgages During the Period of the Rishonim' [Hebrew Union College – Jewish Institute of Religion] 73 Hebrew Union College Annual 227

Gamoran H, *Jewish Law in Transition: How Economic Forces Overcame the Prohibition Against Lending on Interest* (Hebrew Union College Press 2008)

Ganzfried SbJ and others, *Kitzur Shulchan Aruch: the Code of Jewish law* (Mesorah Publications 2008)

George CH, 'English Calvinist Opinion on Usury, 1600-1640' Journal of the History of Ideas 455
Gerber H, 'Jews and Money-Lending in the Ottoman Empire' The Jewish Quarterly Review 100
Gerring J, 'Ideology: A definitional analysis' 50 Political Research Quarterly 957
Gibb HAR, *Whither Islam?: A Survey of Modern Movements in the Moslem World* (1973)
Gibbon E, *The History of the Decline and Fall of the Roman Empire* (Cosimo, Incorporated 2008)
Gilchrist J, *The Church and Economic Activity in the Middle Ages* (Macmillan 1969)
Goff JL, *The Usurer and Purgatory* (Yale University 1979)
———, *Your money or Your Life: Economy and Religion in the Middle Ages* (Zone Books 1990)
Goff JL and Cochrane LG, *Medieval Callings* (University of Chicago Press 1995)
Goldingay J, *Approaches to Old Testament Interpretation* (Clements Publishing 2002)
Goldsmith RW, *Premodern Financial Systemsa Historical Comparative Study* (Goldsmith RW ed, Cambridge University Press 1987)
Grisar H, *Luther* (K. Paul, Trench, Trubner & Co., Ltd., 1917)
Grisez GG, *The Way of the Lord Jesus* (Franciscan Herald Press Chicago 1983)
Guillaume A, *The Life of Muhammad: A Translation of Ishaq's Sirat Rasul Allah* (Oxford University Press 1955)
Habib I, 'Usury in medieval India' 6 Comparative Studies in Society and History 393
Halpin A, 'Ideology and law' 11 Journal of Political Ideologies 153
Hanbal Ai, *al-Musnad* (Matba'ah Mustafa Babi al-Halabi 1895)
Hardon J, *Catholic Dictionary: An Abridged and Updated Edition of Modern Catholic Dictionary* (Crown Publishing Group 2013)
Harkness G, *John Calvin: The Man and His Ethics* (Henry Holt and Company 1931)
Haskafi, *al-Durr al-Mukhtar fi Sharh Tanwir al-Absar* (Dar al-Kutub al-Ilmiyah, 2002)
Hassan K and Lewis M, *Handbook of Islamic Banking* (Edward Elgar 2007)
Hastings J, *Encyclopaedia of Religion and Ethics: Suffering – Zwingli* (Clark 1921)
Hawkes D, *The Culture of Usury in Renaissance England* (Palgrave Macmillan 2010)
Hayes C, *What's Divine about Divine Law?: Early Perspectives* (Princeton University Press 2015)
Helmholz RH, 'Usury and the medieval English church courts' 61 Speculum 364
Hisham Aa-MI and Ishaq MI, *The Life of Muhammad: A Translation of Ishaq's Sirat Rasul Allah* (Oxford University Press 1980)
Hobbes T, *Leviathan* (Digireads.com 2010)
Holdsworth WS, *A History of English Law*, Vol. 8 (2d edn, 1937)
Homer S and Sylla RE, *A History of Interest Rates* (Rutgers Univ Pr 1996)

Hoover CB, 'The sea loan in Genoa in the twelfth century' The Quarterly Journal of Economics 495

Howard AED, *Magna Carta: Text and Commentary* (University Press of Virginia 1998)

Hunt A, 'Ideology of Law: Advances and Problems in Recent Applications of the Concept of Ideology to the Analysis of Law, The' 19 Law & Soc'y Rev 11

———, *Explorations in law and society: Toward a constitutive theory of law*, Vol. 18 (Routledge New York 1993)

Ibn 'Abidin, *Radd al-Muhtar ala al-Durr al-Mukhtar* (Dar Ihya al-Turath al-'Arabi 1998)

Ibn Juzayy, *al-Qawanin al-Fiqhiyyah* (Dar al-Fikr 2007)

Ibn Nujaym, *al-Bahr al-raiq: sharh Kanz al-daqaiq* (Dar al-Kutub al-'Ilmiyya 1997)

Ibn Qayyim al-Jawziyyah, *The Hashiyah of Ibn Qayyim on the Sunan of Abu Dawud* (2 edn, Dar al-Kutub al-'Ilmiya 1415 AH)

Ibn Qayyim al-Jawziyyah, *I'lam al-muwaqqi'in 'an Rabb al-'Alamin* (Maktabat al-Kulliyat al-Azhariyah 1968)

Ibn Rushd, *Muqaddimat Ibn Rushd* (Dar al-Gharb al-Islami 1988)

Imber C, *Ebu's-Suùd: The Islamic Legal Tradition* (Edinburgh University Press 1997)

Iqbal M and Molyneux P, *Thirty Years of Islamic Banking: History, Performance and Prospects* (Palgrave Macmillan 2005)

Islahi AA, *Economic Thought of Ibn al-Qayyim (1292-1350 A.D.)* (International Centre for Research in Islamic Economics, King Abdulaziz University 1984)

———, 'An analytical study of al-Ghazali's thought on money and interest'

'Islamic institute blesses interest' (*BBC News*, 2002) <http://news.bbc.co.uk/1/hi/business/2488525.stm> accessed 30/01

Ismail MI, 'Legal stratagems (*hiyal*) and usury in Islamic commercial law' (Ph.D., University of Birmingham 2010)

Jackson SM and Loetscher LA, *The New Schaff-Herzog Encyclopedia of Religious Knowledge* (Baker Book House 1977)

Jacobs L, *Jewish Law* (Behrman House 1968)

———, *Theology in the Responsa* (Routledge and Kegan Paul 1975)

Jain LC, 'Indigenous banking in India'

Janin H and Kahlmeyer A, *Islamic Law: the Shari'a from Muhammad's Time to the Present* (McFarland & Co. 2007)

Jarhi MA and others, *Islamic Banking: Answers to Some Frequently Asked Questions* (Islamic Development Bank, Islamic Research and Training Institute 2001)

Jennings RC, 'Loans and Credit in Early 17th Century Ottoman Judicial Records: The *Shari'a* Court of Anatolian Kayseri' 16 Journal of the Economic and Social History of the Orient/Journal de l'histoire economique et sociale de l'Orient 168

Johnson P, *A History of the Jews* (Harper Perennial 1998)

Johnstone W, *Exodus* (Bloomsbury 1990)
Jones DW, *Reforming the Morality of Usury: A Study of Differences that Separated the Protestant Reformers* (University Press of America 2003)
---, *Reforming the Morality of Usury: A Study of Differences that Separated the Protestant Reformers* (University Press of America 2004)
Jones NL, *God and the Money-lenders: Usury and Law in Early Modern England* (Basil Blackwell Oxford,, United Kingdom 1989)
Josse JM, *Dinosaur Derivatives and Other Trades* (Wiley 2014)
Kaltner J, *Introducing the Qur'an: For Today's Reader* (Fortress Press)
Kamali MH, 'Law and society: The interplay of revelation and reason in the *Shari'a*' The Oxford History of Islam 107
Kamali MH, *Principles of Islamic Jurisprudence* (Islamic Texts Society 2003)
Kasani ABiM, *Bada'i al-sana'i fi tartib al-shara'i*, Vol. 5 (Dar al-Kutub al-Ilmiyah 1986)
Kay P, *Rome's Economic Revolution* (OUP Oxford 2014)
Kerridge E, *Usury, Interest, and the Reformation* (Ashgate 2002)
Khan F, 'How 'Islamic' is Islamic Banking?' 76 Journal of Economic Behavior & Organization 805
Kirschenbaum A, *Equity in Jewish Law: Beyond Equity: Halakhic Aspirationism in Jewish Civil Law* (KTAV Publishing House 1991)
Kisner MJ, *Spinoza on Human Freedom: Reason, Autonomy and the Good Life* (Cambridge University Press 2011)
Klein D, 'Islamic and Jewish Laws of Usury: A Bridge to Commercial Growth and Peace in the Middle East, The' 23 Denv J Int'l L & Pol'y 535
Kleinhenz C, *Medieval Italy: An Encyclopedia* (Taylor & Francis 2004)
Knight K and New Advent I, 'The Catholic Encyclopedia' (*New Advent*, 1995) <http://www.newadvent.org/cathen/> accessed 21/02/2016
Koyama M, *Evading the 'Taint of Usury': Complex Contracts and Segmented Capital Markets* (Department of Economics, University of Oxford 2008)
Koyama M, 'Evading the 'Taint of Usury': The usury prohibition as a barrier to entry' 47 Explorations in Economic History 420
Kramer SN, *The Sumerians: Their History, Culture, and Character* (University of Chicago Press 1963)
Kramnick I, *Bolingbroke and His Circle: The Politics of Nostalgia in the Age of Walpole* (Cornell University Press 1992)
Kuwait, *Al-Mawsu'at al-Fiqhiyyat [Encyclopedia of Islamic Jurisprudence]* (Dar al-Salasel 1998)
Kuznets, Simon Smith, transcribed by Lo, Stephanie, 'The Doctrine of Usury in the Middle Ages', https://studylib.net/doc/7641837/the-doctrine-of-usury-in-the-middle-ages accessed 6/11/2023
Langholm O, *Economics in the Medieval Schools: Wealth, Exchange, Value, Money, and usury according to the Paris theological tradition, 1200-1350* (EJ Brill Leiden/New York/Köln 1992)

Langholm OI, *Economics in the Medieval Schools: Wealth, Exchange, Value, Money, and Usury According to the Paris Theological Tradition, 1200-1350* (Brill 1992)

Lauterbach JZ and Stern D, *Mekhilta de-Rabbi Ishmael (JPS Classic Reissues)* (Jewish Publication Society 2010)

Leemans J, Matz BJ and Verstraeten J, *Reading Patristic Texts on Social Ethics: Issues and Challenges for the Twenty-First Century* (Catholic University of America Press 2011)

Leemans WF, *The Rate of Interest in Old-Babylonian Times* (Revue Internationale des Droites de l'Antiquité 1950)

Levy-Rubin M, *Non-Muslims in the Early Islamic Empire: From Surrender to Coexistence* (Cambridge University Press 2011)

Lewis B, *The Muslim Discovery of Europe* (W. W. Norton 2001)

Lewis MK, '5 Comparing Islamic and Christian attitudes to usury' Handbook of Islamic Banking 64

———, 'In what ways does Islamic banking differ from conventional finance' 4 Journal of Islamic Economics, Banking and Finance (JIEBF)

Lewittes M, *Jewish Law: an Introduction* (J. Aronson 1994)

Lichtheim G, 'The concept of ideology' 4 History and Theory 164

Locke J, *The Works of John Locke: Some considerations of the consequences of lowering the interest and raising the value of money (Letter to a member of Parliament, 1691)* (C. and J. Rivington 1824)

———, *An Essay Concerning Human Understanding* (T. Tegg and Son 1836)

Longman, Rees, Orme, Brown, Green & Longman, *A History of Rome* (1834)

Louis P, *Ancient Rome at Work: An Economic History of Rome From the Origins to the Empire* (Taylor & Francis 2013)

Lubetsky MH, 'Losing Interest: Financial Alchemy in Islamic, Talmudic, & Western Law' 19 Transnational Law & Contemporary Problems 231

MacDonald J, *A free nation deep in debt: the financial roots of democracy* (Princeton Univ Pr 2006)

Majah I, *Sunan Ibn Majah* (1952)

Mallat C and Ballantyne WM, *Islamic Law and Finance* (Graham & Trotman 1988)

Maloney RP, 'Usury in Greek, Roman and Rabbinic Thought' 27 Traditio 79

Maloney RP, 'The teaching of the fathers on Usury: an historical study on the development of Christian thinking' 27 Vigiliae Christianae 241

Marshall IH, *The Gospel of Luke: A Commentary on the Greek Text* (Eerdmans 1978)

Mastrofini M, *Discussion sur l'usure* (Guyot 1834)

Maudoodi SAA, *Interest and Modern Banking* (Adhunik Prokashani, Dhaka 1987)

Mayhew R and others, *Essays on Ayn Rand's Anthem* (Lexington Books 2005)

McCall B, 'Unprofitable Lending: Modern Credit Regulation and the Lost Theory of Usury' 30 Cardozo Law Review

McCall BM, *The Church and the Usurers: Unprofitable Lending for the Modern Economy* (Sapientia Press of Ave Maria University 2013)

McGovern JF, 'Rise of New Economic Attitudes in Canon and Civil Law, AD 1200-1550, The' 32 Jurist 39
McGrath AE, *Reformation Thought: An Introduction* (Wiley 2012)
McLaughlin TP, 'The Teaching of the Canonists of Usury' Mediaeval Studies 81
Meenai SA and Ansari JA, *Money and Banking in Pakistan* (Oxford University Press 2004)
Meislin BJ and Cohen ML, 'Backgrounds of the Biblical Law against Usury' 6 Comparative Studies in Society and History 250
Metcalf LS and others, *The Forum* (Forum Publishing Company 1918)
Millett P, *Lending and Borrowing in Ancient Athens* (Cambridge Univ Pr 2002)
Mills P, *Interest in Interest: The Old Testament Ban on Interest and Its Implications for Today* (1989)
Mills PS and Presley JR, *Islamic Finance: Theory and Practice* (Macmillan Houndmills 1999)
Mokyr J, *The Oxford Encyclopedia of Economic History* (Oxford University Press 2003)
Moore H, *The Future of Anthropological Knowledge* (Taylor & Francis 2003)
Muhammad M, Yaacob H and Hasan S, 'The Bindingness and Enforceability of a Unilateral Promise (*Waʻd*): an Analysis from Islamic Law and Legal Perspectives' Kuala Lumpur: International Shari'ah Research Academy for Islamic Finance (ISRA), Research paper
Munro JH, *Usury, Calvinism, and Credit in Protestant England: from the Sixteenth Century to the Industrial Revolution* (2011)
J. Murray, *Reasons Against the Repeal of the Usury Laws* (1825)
Muslim Ibn al-Haggag, *Sahih Muslim* (Thesaurus Islamicus Foundation 2000)
Nelson B, *The Idea of Usury: From Tribal Brotherhood to Universal Otherhood* (University of Chicago Press 1969)
Neufeld E, 'The prohibitions against loans at interest in ancient Hebrew laws' 26 Hebrew Union College Annual 355
Neusner J, *The Mishnah: A New Translation* (Yale University Press 1989)
–––, *The Economics of the Mishnah* (University of Chicago Press 1990)
Newman JH, *An Essay on the Development of Christian Doctrine* (J. Toovey 1846)
Nomani F, *The Interpretative Debate of the Classical Islamic Jurists on Riba (Usury)*
Noonan JT, *The Scholastic Analysis of Usury* (Harvard University Press 1957)
Noonan JT, 'Development in moral doctrine' 54 Theological Studies 662
North D, *Discourses upon Trade; Principally Directed to the Cases of the Interest, Coynage, Clipping, Increase of Money.* (1822)
North G, *Honest Money: The Biblical Blueprint for Money and Banking* (Dominion Press 1986)
Nursyamsiah T and Kayadibi S, 'Application of *Bayʻ al-ʻinah* in Islamic Banking and Finance: From the Viewpoint of Siyasah Shar 'iyyah'
Nyazee IAK, 'The concept of *riba* and Islamic banking' Online document

Bibliography

O'Brien BR, *God's Peace and King's Peace: The Laws of Edward the Confessor* (University of Pennsylvania Press 1999)

O'Brien G, *An Essay on Mediæval Economic Teaching* (A. M. Kelley 1967)

Oeltjen JC, 'Usury: Utilitarian or Useless' 3 Fla St UL Rev 167

Ord M, *An Essay on the Law of Usury* (W. Clarke and Sons 1809)

Oslington P, *The Oxford Handbook of Christianity and Economics* (OUP USA 2014)

Journal of the Institute of Bankers in Pakistan (1974)

Pamphlets on Money (University of California, Berkeley 1834)

Parkes JW, *The Jew in the Medieval Community: a Study of His Political and Economic Situation* (Hermon Press 1976)

Peterson CL, 'Truth, Understanding, and High-cost Consumer Credit: The Historical Context of The Truth in Lending Act' 55 Fla L Rev 807

Pirenne H and Glegg IE, *Economic and Social History of Medieval Europe* (Routledge 2005)

Plutarch's Lives, Vol. 2 of 2 (Forgotten Books)

Poitras G, *The Early History of Financial Economics* (Edward Elgar Publishing, Incorporated 2000)

Poliakov L, *Jewish Bankers and the Holy See from the Thirteenth to the Seventeenth Century* (Routledge & K. Paul 1977)

Poliakov L and Howard R, *The History of Anti-semitism: From the time of Christ to the court Jews* (University of Pennsylvania Press 2003)

Pope A and Cary J, *The Poetical Works of Alex. Pope* (Smith 1841)

Postan MM, *The Cambridge Economic History of Europe from the Decline of the Roman Empire: Volume 1, Agrarian Life of the Middle Ages* (Cambridge University Press 1966)

2 F and Powell JM, *The Liber Augustalis, Or Contitutions of Melfi Promulgated by the Emperor Frederick 2. for the Kingdom of Sicily in 1231* (Syracuse University Press 1971)

Psalidopoulos M, *The Canon in the History of Economics: Critical Essays* (Taylor & Francis 2002)

Qusi, '*Riba*, Islamic Law and Interest' (Temple University 1982)

Qutb S, Salahi A and Shamis AA, *In the Shade of the Qur'an* (World Assembly of Muslim Youth 1981)

R. H. Tawney and Eileen Power e, *Tudor Economic Documents: Being Select Documents Illustrating the Economic and Social History of Tudor England; in Three Volumes. Commerce, Finance and the Poor Law* (1924)

Rabinowitz JJ, 'Some Remarks on the Evasion of the Usury Laws in the Middle Ages' [Cambridge University Press] 37 The Harvard Theological Review 49

Radcliffe CJ, *The Law and Its Compass* (Faber 1961)

Rahman F, '*Riba* and interest' 3 Islamic Studies 1

Rahman F, *Islam* (University of Chicago Press 1979)

Ramadan T, *To Be a European Muslim* (Kube Publishing Ltd 2013)

Rayner JD, *Jewish Religious Law: A Progressive Perspective* (Berghahn Books 1998)
Rees A, *The Cyclopædia: Or, Universal Dictionary of Arts, Sciences, and Literature* (31, Longman, Hurst, Rees, Orme & Brown 1819)
Reisman Y, *The Laws of Ribbis: The Laws of Interest and Their Application to Everyday Life and Business* (Mesorah 1995)
Rida MR, *al-Manar* (Dar al-kitab al-jadid)
---, *al-Riba wa al-Mu'amalat fi al-Islam* (Cairo, Maktabat al-Qahira 1959)
Riemersma JC, 'Usury restrictions in a mercantile economy' 18 Canadian Journal of Economics and Political Science/Revue canadienne de economiques et science politique 17
Rist R, *Popes and Jews, 1095-1291* (OUP Oxford 2015)
Robinson I, *The Papal Reform of the Eleventh Century: Lives of Pope Leo IX and Pope Gregory VII* (Manchester University Press 2004)
Rodinson M, *Islam and Capitalism:* Transl. by Brian Pearce (University of Texas Press 1978)
Rose HS, *The Churches and Usury or, The Morality of Five Per Cent* (Clark 1900)
---, *The Churches and Usury or, The Morality of Five Per Cent* (F. Palmer 1910)
Rosenmeier J, *John Cotton on Usury* (JSTOR 1990)
Rosly SA, *Critical Issues on Islamic Banking and Financial Markets: Islamic Economics, Banking and Finance, Investments, Takaful and Financial Planning* (Dinamas Publishing 2005)
Rosly SA and Sanusi M, 'Some Issues of Bay' al-'Inah in Malaysian Islamic Financial Markets' 16 Arab law quarterly 263
Roy S, 'Historical Evolution of Interest and its Analysis in Economic Literature' SSRN eLibrary
Russell E, 'The societies of the Bardi and the Peruzzi and their dealings with Edward III', Finance and Trade Under Edward III 93
Ryan FW, *Usury and Usury Laws: A Juristic-economic Study of the Effects of State Statutory Maximums for Loan Charges Upon Lending Operations in the United States* (Houghton Mifflin 1924)
Ryan MJ, 'Law, legislation, and lending: An examination of the influence of the Crusades on the usury prohibition'
Saadallah R, 'Concept of time in Islamic economics', 2 Islamic Economic Studies 1415 AH
Saeed A, *Islamic Banking and Interest: a Study of the Prohibition of Riba and its Contemporary Interpretation* (Brill Academic Pub 1996)
Saggs HWF, *The Greatness that was Babylon: a Sketch of the Ancient Civilisation of the Tigris-Euphrates Valley* (Hawthorn Books 1962)
Saleh NA, *Unlawful Gain and Legitimate Profit in Islamic Law: Riba, Gharar, and Islamic Banking* (Cambridge University Press 1986)
Saleh NA and Ajaj A, *Unlawful Gain and Legitimate Profit in Islamic Law: Riba, Gharar, and Islamic Banking* (Graham & Trotman 1992)
Salleh, *Islam: Past, Present and Future* (Universiti Kebangsaan Malaysia 2004)

Samiullah M, 'Prohibition of *Riba* (Interest) & Insurance in the Light of Islam' 21 Islamic Studies 53

Schacht J, *An Introduction to Islamic Law* (Clarendon Press 1982)

Schramm B and Stjerna KI, *Martin Luther, the Bible, and the Jewish People: A Reader* (Fortress Press 2012)

Seligman ERA and Johnson AS, *Encyclopaedia of the Social Sciences*, Vol. 9 (The Macmillan company 1932)

Sen I, 'Money-Lenders in India' 11 J Soc Comp Legis ns 168

Shafer-Landau R, *Ethical Theory: An Anthology* (Wiley 2012)

Shaftesbury AACE and Klein LE, *Shaftesbury: Characteristics of Men, Manners, Opinions, Times* (Cambridge University Press 1999)

Shaharuddin A, 'The *Bay' al-'Inah* Controversy in Malaysian Islamic Banking 1' 26 Arab law quarterly 499

Shakespeare W, *The Merchant of Venice*, Vol. 7 (Lippincott 1916)

Sharma RS, 'Usury in Early Mediaeval India (AD 400–1200)' 8 Comparative Studies in Society and History 56

Shatzmiller J, *Shylock Reconsidered: Jews, Money-lending, and Medieval Society* (University of California Press 1990)

Siddiqi MZ and Murad AH, *Hadith Literature: Its Origin, Development and Special Features* (Islamic Texts Society 1993)

Siddiqui SH, *Islamic Banking: Genesis & Rationale, Evaluation & Review, Prospects & Challenges* (Royal Book Company 1994)

Skolnik F and Berenbaum M, *Encyclopaedia Judaica* (Keter Pub. House 1978)

Smith A, *The Wealth of Nations* (Digireads.com 2004)

Society TJP, *The Torah: The Five Books of Moses* (Jewish Publication Society 1999)

Soloveitchik JD, *Halakhic Man* (Jewish Publication Society of America 1983)

Stapleford JE, *Bulls, Bears & Golden Calves: Applying Christian Ethics in Economics* (InterVarsity Press 2002)

Statutes of the Realm, Vol. III (London 1963)

Statutes of the Realm, Vol. IV (London 1963)

Stein S, 'The laws on interest in the Old Testament', 4 The Journal of Theological Studies 161

Stein S, 'Interest taken by Jews from Gentiles', Journal of Semitic Studies 141

Steinsaltz A, *The Essential Talmud* (Basic Books 2006)

Stevens E and Rabbis, *Rabbinic Authority* (The Conference 1982)

Stevens ME, *Temples, Tithes, and Taxes: The Temple and the Economic Life of Ancient Israel* (Hendrickson Publishers 2006)

Stevenson J and Frend WHC, *A New Eusebius: Documents Illustrating the History of the Church to AD 337* (Baker Publishing Group 2013)

Ammannati F, *Religion and Religious Institutions in the European Economy, 1000-1800* (Firenze University Press 2012)

Swabey RH, *Usury and the Church of England* (1826 – 1878)

Sypnowich C, 'Law and ideology'

Taeusch CF, 'The Concept of "Usury" the History of an Idea' Journal of the History of Ideas 291

Tamari M, *With All Your Possessions: Jewish Ethics and Economic Life* (Free Press 1987)

Tawney R, *Historical Introduction to: Thomas Wilson, A Discourse Upon Usury By Way of Dialogue and Orations*

Tawney RH, *Religion and the Rise of Capitalism* (Transaction Publishers 1998)

Tawney RH and Gore C, *Religion and the Rise of Capitalism: An Historical Study* (Holland Memorial Lectures, 1922) (J. Murray 1964)

Thomas AS, 'Interest in Islamic economics understanding riba' (Routledge, 2006) <http://search.ebscohost.com/login.aspx?direct=true&scope=site&db=nlebk&db=nlabk&AN=106536>

Tigay JH and others, *Mishneh Todah: Studies in Deuteronomy and Its Cultural Environment in Honor of Jeffrey H. Tigay* (Eisenbrauns 2009)

Trachtenberg J, *The Devil and the Jews: The Medieval Conception of the Jew and Its Relation to Modern Anti-Semitism* (Varda Books 2001)

Usmani JMT, 'The Text of the Historic Judgment on *Riba*, 23 December 1999' 80 The Supreme Court of Pakistan

Valeri PM, 'The Rise of Usury in Early New England' Commonplace <https://commonplace.online/article/the-rise-of-usury-in-early-new-england/> accessed 6/11/2023

Van Baumer FL, *Main Currents of Western Thought: Readings in Western European Intellectual History from the Middle Ages to the Present* (Yale University Press 1978)

Van De Mieroop M, 'The invention of interest. Sumerian loans' in *The Origins of Value: The Financial Innovations that Created Modern Capital Markets* (Oxford University Press, Oxford) p 17

Visser WAM and Macintosh A, 'A short review of the historical critique of usury', 8 Accounting, Business & Financial History 175

Vogel FE and Hayes SL, *Islamic Law and Finance: Religion, Risk, and Return* (Brill 1998)

von Böhm-Bawerk E, *Capital and Interest: A Critical History of Economical Theory* (Macmillan and Co. 1890)

Waliyullah S, *Hujjatullah al-Balighah* (Lahore: Qawmi Kutub Khana, tr. Mawlana Abdul Rahim 1953)

Watson A, 'Comparative Law and Legal Change' 37 The Cambridge Law Journal 313

---, *Roman Law & Comparative Law* (University of Georgia Press 1991)

Watt L, *Usury in Catholic Theology* (Catholic Social Guild 1945)

Watt WM, *Islamic Fundamentalism and Modernity (RLE Politics of Islam)* (Routledge 1988)

Weber M and Kalberg S, *The Protestant Ethic and the Spirit of Capitalism* (Taylor & Francis 2013)

Wesley J and Emory J, *The Works of the Reverend John Wesley, A. M* (J. Emory and B. Waugh, for the Methodist Episcopal Church, J. Collard, printer 1831)

West HR, *An Introduction to Mill's Utilitarian Ethics* (Cambridge University Press 2004)

Wilson T, *A Discourse Upon Usury, With an Historical Introduction by R. H. Tawney* (G. Bell & Sons 1952)

Winthrop Papers (Boston 1931)

Wood D, *Medieval Economic Thought* (Cambridge University Press 2002)

Wright Q, 'International law and ideologies' 48 The American Journal of International Law 616

XIV PB, 'Vix Pervenit' (1745) <https://www.ewtn.com/catholicism/library/on-usury-3340> accessed 6/11/2023

Yaron R, *The Laws of Eshnunna* (Brill 1988)

Yate AA, *Ibn Rushd as Jurist* (University of Cambridge 1991)

(Ernst and Young (E&Y), 'World Islamic Banking Competitiveness Report 2016', <http://ceif.iba.edu.pk/pdf/EY-WorldIslamicBankingCompetitivenessReport2016.pdf> accessed 6/11/2023

Yusuf and eds K, *Fatawa al-Imam Muhammad Rashid Rida* (Dar al-kitab al-jadid 1970)

Zimmermann R, *The Law of Obligations: Roman Foundations of the Civilian Tradition* (Juta 1990)

Zipperstein E, *Business Ethics in Jewish Law* (Ktav Publishing House 1983)

Zucker LM, *S. Ambrosii De Tobia: a Commentary, With an Introduction and Translation* (The Catholic University of America 1933)

NOTES

INTRODUCTION

1. M.A. El-Gamal, 'Interest and the paradox of contemporary Islamic law and finance' 27 Fordham Int'l LJ 108, 131
2. M.K. Lewis, 'In what ways does Islamic banking differ from conventional finance' 4 Journal of Islamic Economics, Banking and Finance (JIEBF), op. cit. p. 18
3. M.O. Farooq, 'The *Riba*-Interest Equation and Islam: Reexamination of the Traditional Arguments' 6 Global Journal of Finance and Economics 99, 112
4. F. Khan, 'How 'Islamic' is Islamic Banking?' 76 Journal of Economic Behavior & Organization 805
5. T.E. Diwany, T. Ahmad and 1st Ethical Charitable Trust Staff, *Islamic Banking and Finance: What It Is and What It Could Be* (1st Ethical Charitable Trust 2010), p. 134
6. M.H. Lubetsky, 'Losing Interest: Financial Alchemy in Islamic, Talmudic, & Western Law' 19 Transnational Law & Contemporary Problems 231
7. J.M. Ackerman, 'Interest Rates and the Law: A History of Usury' Ariz St LJ 61, 72
8. M. Koyama, *Evading the 'Taint of Usury' Complex Contracts and Segmented Capital Markets* (Department of Economics, University of Oxford 2008), p. 19
9. R.A. De Roover, *The Rise and Decline of the Medici Bank: 1397-1494* (Beard Books Inc 1999), p. 13
10. A. Hunt, 'Ideology of Law: Advances and Problems in Recent Applications of the Concept of Ideology to the Analysis of Law, The' 19 Law & Soc'y Rev 11, 12; A. Halpin, 'Ideology and law' 11 Journal of Political Ideologies 153
11. C. Sypnowich, 'Law and ideology'
12. J. Gerring, 'Ideology: A definitional analysis' 50 Political Research Quarterly 957

13 G. Lichtheim, 'The concept of ideology' 4 History and Theory 164, 164-165
14 Sypnowich, op. cit.
15 Gerring, op. cit., p. 957
16 A. Hunt, *Explorations in law and society: Toward a constitutive theory of law*, Vol. 18 (Routledge New York 1993), p. 25
17 Q. Wright, 'International law and ideologies' 48 The American Journal of Inter-national Law 616, 616-617
18 M.D.A. Freeman, *Lloyd's Introduction to Jurisprudence* (Sweet & Maxwell 2001), p. 1-5, 1040
19 C.J. Radcliffe, *The Law and Its Compass* (Faber 1961), p. 92-93

Usury In Pre-Abrahamic Civilisations
20 Ezekiel, 18: 10-13
21 Dante, *The Inferno*, Canto XVII, 11.40-72 Ciardi Translation (1954)
22 N. Ferguson, *The Ascent of Money: A Financial History of the World* (Penguin Pr 2008), p. 34-37
23 W. Shakespeare, *The Merchant of Venice*, Vol. 7 (Lippincott 1916)
24 Qur'an 2:278
25 J.G. Frierson, 'Changing Concepts on Usury: Ancient Times Through the Time of John Calvin' 7 American Business Law Journal 115
26 Homer and Sylla, op. cit., p. 29
27 S.N. Kramer, *The Sumerians: Their History, Culture, and Character* (University of Chicago Press 1963)
28 M. Van De Mieroop, 'The invention of interest. Sumerian loans' Of Value The Financial Innovations that Created Modern Capital Markets (Oxford University Press, Oxford), p. 17-30
29 Ibid.
30 For several examples of such loans see Homer, op. cit., p. 177
31 Homer and Sylla, op. cit., p. 29
32 Ibid., p. 28
33 Kramer, op. cit., p. 78
34 C.L. Peterson, 'Truth, Understanding, and High-cost Consumer Credit: The Historical Context of The Truth in Lending Act' 55 Fla L Rev 807, 818
35 Kramer, op. cit., p. 165
36 R. *Yaaws of Eshnunna* (Brill 1988), p. 235
37 G.R. Driver and S.J.C. Miles, *The Babylonian Laws*, Vol. 1 (Clarendon press 1952), p. 11
38 Ibid., p. 39
39 B. Bromberg, 'The origin of banking: religious finance in Babylonia' 2 The Journal of Economic History 77

40 Ibid.
41 Ibid., 78-85
42 Ibid.
43 H.W.F. Saggs, *The Greatness That Was Babylon: a Sketch of the Ancient Civilisation of the Tigris-Euphrates Valley* (Hawthorn Books 1962), p. 290
44 See generally, IB Sen, 'Money-Lenders in India' 11 J Soc Comp Legis ns 168
45 R.S. Sharma, 'Usury in Early Medieval India (AD 400–1200)' 8 Comparative Studies in Society and History 56, 57; L.C. Jain, 'Indigenous banking in India'; W.A.M. Visser and A. Macintosh, 'A short review of the historical critique of usury' 8 Accounting, Business & Financial History 175
46 I. Habib, 'Usury in medieval India' 6 Comparative Studies in Society and History 393, 411; Visser and Macintosh, op. cit., p. 175
47 Sharma, op. cit., p. 75
48 Visser and Macintosh, op. cit., p. 175
49 Sharma, op. cit., p. 75
50 Ibid.
51 Ibid., p. 59-60
52 R.P. Maloney, 'Usury in Greek, Roman and Rabbinic Thought' 27 Traditio 79
53 Homer and Sylla, op. cit., p. 40
54 Ibid.
55 P. Millett, *Lending and Borrowing in Ancient Athens* (Cambridge Univ Pr 2002), p. 49; Ackerman, op. cit., p. 20
56 Ibid.
57 Millett, op. cit., p. 50
58 Ibid.
59 Maloney, op. cit., p. 79
60 Maloney, op. cit., p. 79
61 A. Flew, 'The Profit Motive' 86 Ethics 312
62 Aristotle, *Politics*, Book I, Chapter X. Plato, Laws, Book V. Quoted in Visser and Macintosh, op. cit., p. 175
63 Mansour M. *Al-Riba Fi Al-Shari'ah Al-Islamiyah Wa Al-Kanun* (Cairo, Dar Hira'1987), p. 7-8
64 Ackerman, op. cit., p. 69
65 Homer and Sylla, op. cit., p. 39-40
66 Ibid., p. 40
67 T. Cornell, *The Beginnings of Rome: Italy and Rome from the Bronze Age to the Punic Wars, C. 1000-263 BC* (Routledge 1995), p. 266; See also, J. MacDonald, *A Free Nation Deep in Debt: the Financial Roots of Democracy* (Princeton Univ Pr 2006), p. 26-27; Peterson, op. cit., p. 823

68 Cornell, op. cit., p. 266
69 Peterson, op. cit., p. 823
70 Cornell, op. cit., p. 266
71 The debt crisis that afflicted Rome was by no means rare. For examples, see J. Andreau, *Banking and Business in the Roman World* (Cambridge University Press 1999), p. 100-105
72 Ibid., p. 95-99
73 Ibid.
74 Andreau, op. cit., p. 132
75 T. Frank, 'On Some Financial Legislation of the Sullan Period' 54 The American Journal of Philology 54, p 54-55
76 Homer and Sylla, op. cit., p. 55-56
77 Quoted in J. Calvin, *Calvin's Bible Commentaries: Harmony of the Law, Part III* (Forgotten Books 1847), p. 136
78 *De Officiis*, 1, 42
79 Ibid., 2, 25
80 *Plutarch's Lives, Vol. 2 of 2* (Forgotten Books), p. 443
81 *De Beneficiis*, VII, 10
82 *Epistles*, LXXXI, 18
83 *De Officiis*, II, xxi
84 K. Christ, *Christ* (University of California Press 1984), p. 13
85 A similar view has been expressed in Diwany, Ahmad and Staff
86 See generally, G. Barzilai, *Law and religion* (Ashgate 2007)

Usury in Abrahamic Religions

87 *De Officiis*, 1, 42
88 Maloney, op. cit., p. 102
89 Ibid.
90 A.K. Bennison, *The Great Caliphs: The Golden Age of the 'Abbasid Empire* (Yale University Press 2009), p. 139
91 Islamic Economics Research Bureau, *Thoughts on Islamic banking* (Islamic Economics Research Bureau 1982), p. 187
92 Institute of Bankers in Pakistan, *Journal of the Institute of Bankers in Pakistan* (1974), p. 9
93 Joshua Trachtenberg, *The Devil and the Jews: The Medieval Conception of the Jew and Its Relation to Modern Anti-Semitism* (Varda Books 2001), p. 188; L. Poliakov, *Jewish Bankers and the Holy See from the Thirteenth to the Seventeenth Century* (Routledge & K. Paul 1977), p. 22-24
94 *Decretum Gratiani* is a collection of Canon law compiled and written in the 12th century.
95 St Ambrose states: *"where there is right of war, there also is the right of usury."* See, Poliakov, op. cit., p. 22-24; also D.A. Abulafia, *Christians and Jews: In the Twelfth Century Renaissance* (Taylor & Francis 1995), p. 61

96	Poliakov, op. cit., p. 22-24; M.J. Ryan, 'Law, legislation, and lending: An examination of the influence of the Crusades on the usury prohibition', 71
97	M. Botticini and Z. Eckstein, *The Chosen Few: How Education Shaped Jewish History, 70-1492* (Princeton University Press 2012), p. 212-222
98	Ibid.
99	F. Skolnik and M. Berenbaum, *Encyclopaedia Judaica* (Keter Pub. House 1978)
100	Botticini and Eckstein, op. cit., p. 217
101	Tamari, op. cit., p. 167
102	L. Poliakov and R. Howard, *The History of Anti-semitism: From the time of Christ to the court Jews* (University of Pennsylvania Press 2003), p. 76
103	Ibid., p. 164-167
104	B. Schramm and K.I. Stjerna, *Martin Luther, the Bible, and the Jewish People: A Reader* (Fortress Press 2012), p. 27
105	Ibid.
106	Lateran IV, Constitution 67, 1215, translated by J.T. Gilchrist in *Church and Economic Activity in the High Middle Ages*, 182-183
107	Botticini and Eckstein, op. cit., p 217
108	Gabor Agoston and B.A. Masters, *Encyclopedia of the Ottoman Empire* (Facts On File, Incorporated 2009), p. 75
109	*Dhimmis* have special legal status under the Islamic State. For further details See Abulafia, op. cit., p. 37-50
110	Ibid., p. 268; Raymond William Goldsmith, *Premodern Financial Systems: A Historical Comparative Study* (Raymond William Goldsmith ed, Cambridge University Press 1987), p. 88-89; Ronald C. Jennings, 'Loans and Credit in Early 17th Century Ottoman Judicial Records: The *Shari'a* Court of Anatolian Kayseri' 16 Journal of the Economic and Social History of the Orient / Journal de l'histoire economique et sociale de l'Orient 168, 184
111	J. Bowring and Great Britain. Foreign Office, *Report on the Commercial Statistics of Syria* (Printed by W. Clowes for Her Majesty's Stationery Off. 1840), p. 25
112	David ibn Abi Zimra, *Responsa* (Warsaw, 5642), question no. 890
113	For many examples, see H. Gerber, 'Jews and Money-Lending in the Ottoman Empire', The Jewish Quarterly Review 100, 104-8
114	Moses Israel, *Mas'at Mosheh*, II (Istanbul, 5497), question no. 74
115	Trachtenberg, op. cit., p. 188
116	R.H. Tawney, *Religion and the Rise of Capitalism* (Transaction Publishers 1998), p. 37
117	Tamari, op. cit., p. 165
118	M. Lewittes, *Jewish Law: an Introduction* (J. Aronson 1994) p 54-55; L. Jacobs, *Jewish Law* (Behrman House 1968), p. 1; A.A. Cohen and P.R.

Mendes-Flohr, *Contemporary Jewish Religious Thought: Original Essays on Critical Concepts, Movements, and Beliefs* (Scribner 1987), p. 309-310
119 The terms *Halacha* and *Aggadah* first appear in the Tannaitic literature (70-200 CE). See, J.D. Rayner, *Jewish Religious Law: A Progressive Perspective* (Berghahn Books 1998), p. 24-25
120 Ibid.
121 B. Cohen, *Law and Tradition in Judaism* (Jewish Theological Seminary of America 1959), p. 22-24
122 Lewittes, op. cit., p. 22
123 Ibid.
124 H. Danby, *The Mishnah* (Clarendon Press 1933), p. XVII; Lewittes, op. cit., p. 50-55
125 Ibid.
126 Ibid.
127 See, A. Steinsaltz, *The Essential Talmud* (Basic Books 2006)
128 L. Jacobs, *Theology in the Responsa* (Routledge and Kegan Paul 1975)
129 Ibid.
130 E. Stevens and Central Conference of American Rabbis, *Rabbinic Authority* (The Conference 1982), p. 33
131 J.D. Soloveitchik, *Halakhic Man* (Jewish Publication Society of America 1983), p. 13
132 C.F. Taeusch, 'The Concept of "Usury" the History of an Idea' Journal of the History of Ideas 291
133 *The Jewish Encyclopaedia*, Vol. xii, (Funk and Wagnells Co., New York and London, 1905), p. 388
134 Ex. 22:25; Deut. 23:19,20; Leviticus 25:36, 37
135 E. Zipperstein, *Business Ethics in Jewish Law* (Ktav Publishing House 1983), p. 40. This *responsum* is taken from Cohen, Abraham (ed.), *The Soncino Chumash*. (London: The Soncino Press, 1956), p. 485
136 I. Epstein, *The Babylonian Talmud* (Soncino Press 1935), p. 760
137 *Encyclopaedia Judaica*, op. cit., p. 28
138 J. Neusner, *The Mishnah: A New Translation* (Yale University Press 1989), p. 540-541
139 Encyclopaedia Judaica, op. cit., p. 28
140 T.J.P. Society, *The Torah: The Five Books of Moses* (Jewish Publication Society 1999), p. 366
141 Epstein, op. cit., p. 365-369
142 Ezek. 18:8, 13, 17; 22:12; Ps. 15:5 and Prov.28:8
143 R. de Vaux, *Ancient Israel: Its Life and Institutions* (McGraw-Hill 1965), p. 143-144
144 See K.R. Crim, *The Interpreter's Dictionary of the Bible: An Illustrated Encyclopedia*. Supplementary volume (Abingdon 1976), p. 534

145S. Stein, 'The laws on interest in the Old Testament' 4 The Journal of Theological Studies 161
146 B.J. Meislin and M.L. Cohen, 'Backgrounds of the Biblical Law against Usury' 6 Comparative Studies in Society and History 250, 259-260
147 Stein, op. cit., p. 164
148 Ibid.
149 H. Gamoran, *Jewish Law in Transition: How Economic Forces Overcame the Prohibition Against Lending on Interest* (Hebrew Union College Press 2008), p. 4-7; P. Johnson, *A History of the Jews* (Harper Perennial 1998), p. 173
150 W.F. Leemans, *The Rate of Interest in Old-Babylonian Times* (Revue Internationale des Droites de l'Antiquité 1950), p. 32-33
151 Johnson, op. cit., p. 173
152 B. Nelson, *The Idea of Usury: From Tribal Brotherhood to Universal Otherhood* (University of Chicago Press 1969); Stein, op. cit., p. 164; Gamoran, op. cit., p. 5-7
153 Meislin and Cohen, op. cit., p. 260
154 Tamari, op. cit., p. 62
155 Ibid.
156 Ibid.
157 Albrecht Alt, "The Origin of Israelite Law," in Essays on Old Testament History and Religion (Oxford, 1966), p. 81-132
158 W. Johnstone, *Exodus* (Bloomsbury 1990), p. 58
159 J.Z. Lauterbach and D. Stern, *Mekhilta de-Rabbi Ishmael (JPS Classic Reissues)* (Jewish Publication Society 2010), p. 351
160 Nelson, op. cit., p. 3
161 *The Babylonian Talmud. "Seder Nezikin II. Baba Mezia"*, as translated into English under the Editorship of Rabbi Dr. I. Epstein, (The Soncino Press, London, 1935). Folios 1- 24b by Salis Daiches and Folios 25a to the end by H.Freedman. BM 61b, pp. 365-369; BM 67a, pp. 391-393
162 Y. Reisman, *The Laws of Ribbis: The Laws of Interest and Their Application to Everyday Life and Business* (Mesorah 1995), p. 51
163 Rabbinical Council of America, *Tradition* (Human Sciences Press 1979), p. 357; J. Hastings, *Encyclopaedia of religion and ethics: Suffering – Zwingli* (Clark 1921) p. 556; Reisman, op. cit., p. 59-76
164 BM 5.2. Unless otherwise noted, all citations from the Talmud are from the Soncino version. But, for the text of the Mishnah for Baba Mezia, the translation is from Danby, op. cit., p. 355
165 BM 5.3
166 Siphre on Deuteronomy 263 (on 23.21), translated by Maloney, op. cit., p. 99. Henceforth, SD.
167 Reisman, op. cit., p. 68
168 The Babylonian Talmud, op. cit., *Baba Mezia*, 75b

169 Iggrot Moshe, Yoreh De' ah, part 1, sections 80.
170 Harav S.Z. Auerbach (Minchas Shelomo 27); Harav Y.S. Elyashiv (Mishnas Ribbis 4, note 21); Harav Y. Roth (Questions of Interest, pg. 61). See also Reisman, op. cit., p. 69
171 J. Neusner, *The Economics of the Mishnah* (University of Chicago Press 1990), p.93
172 The Babylonian Talmud, op. cit., *Sanhedrin*, 27a
173 Ibid., *Temurah*, 6b
174 Ibid., *Baba Mezia*, 71a
175 Siphra on Leviticus 25.38, translated by Maloney, op. cit., p. 105
176 The Babylonian Talmud, op. cit., *Kiddushin*, 20a
177 Ibid., *Sanhedrin*, 24b
178 The Babylonian Talmud, op. cit., *Baba Mezia*, 75b; *Mekhilta on Exodus* (Ex. 22.24) 3.149
179 The Babylonian Talmud, op. cit., *Baba Mezia*, 69b,70b,71a; Reisman, op. cit., p. 94-97
180 BM 5.6
181 SD 263 (on 23.21) and 113 (on 15.3). Also, Maimonides, see Hastings, op. cit., p. 557
182 J.T. Noonan, *The Scholastic Analysis of Usury* (Harvard University Press 1957), p. 19; D. Wood, *Medieval Economic Thought* (Cambridge University Press 2002), p. 161-167
183 R. De Roover, 'The scholastics, usury, and foreign exchange' 41 The Business History Review 257, 258; Divine, op. cit., p. 96
184 Wood, op. cit., p. 162-167
185 John T Noonan, 'Development in moral doctrine' 54 Theological Studies 662, 663
186 Germain Gabriel Grisez, *The way of the Lord Jesus* (Franciscan Herald Press Chicago 1983), Vol. 1, p. 894; John Henry Newman, *An essay on the development of Christian doctrine*, Vol. 1 (Toovey 1846), p. 28; John Paul II, *Veritatis Splendor*, p. 53
187 Father Gary L Coulter, *The Church and Usury: Error, Change or Development* (1999)
188 Ibid.
189 Tamari, op. cit., p. 163; see also, M.E. Stevens, *Temples, Tithes, And Taxes: The Temple And the Economic Life of Ancient Israel* (Hendrickson Publishers 2006), Ch. 6
190 Ibid.
191 Mathew 21:12
192 Ibid.
193 Baba Mestiza, Ch. 3
194 Stevens, *Temples, Tithes, And Taxes: The Temple And the Economic Life of Ancient Israel*, op. cit., Ch. 6

195 Saint Thomas (Aquinas), *Catena Aurea: St. Matthew* (John Henry Parker 1842), p. 712-713
196 Ibid., p. 712-713
197 J. Carroll, *Jerusalem, Jerusalem: How the Ancient City Ignited Our Modern World* (Houghton Mifflin Harcourt 2011), p. 91
198 George Wesley Buchanan, 'Symbolic Money-changers in the Temple?' 37 New Testament Studies 280
199 James A. Brundage, Bernard and the Jurists, in *The Cistercians and the Second Crusade*, ed. Michael Gervers (New York: Martin.s Press, 1992), p. 25
200 Matt. 25: 20
201 Matt. 25: 21
202 Matt. 25: 22
203 Matt. 25: 23
204 Matt. 25: 24-25
205 Matt. 25: 26-29
206 G. North, *Honest Money: The Biblical Blueprint for Money and Banking* (Dominion Press 1986), p. 71; J.E. Stapleford, *Bulls, Bears & Golden Calves: Applying Christian Ethics in Economics* (InterVarsity Press 2002), p. 108; Istituto internazionale di storia economica F. Datini. Settimana di studio and F. Ammannati, *Religion and Religious Institutions in the European Economy, 1000-1800* (Firenze University Press 2012), p. 157
207 C. Elliott, *Usury: A Scriptural, Ethical and Economic View* (Anti-Usury League 1902), p. 53
208 Ezek. 18:8, 15, 17;22:12; Ps. 15:5 and Prov, 28:8
209 D.W. Jones, *Reforming the Morality of Usury: A Study of Differences that Separated the Protestant Reformers* (University Press of America 2003), p. 25; Divine, op. cit., p. 25; P. Cleary, *The Church and Usury: an Essay on Some Historical and Theological Aspects of Money-lending* (Christian Book Club of America 1972), p. 32
210 Ibid.
211 M. Mastrofini, *Discussion Sur L'usure* (Guyot 1834), p. 47, quoted in and translated by Cleary, op. cit., p. 33-34
212 I.H. Marshall, *The Gospel of Luke: A Commentary on the Greek Text* (Eerdmans 1978) p. 273
213 Paul Mills, *Interest in Interest: The Old Testament Ban on Interest and its implications for today* (1989), p. 6
214 In addition to several other references, this section benefited largely from the work of Brenda Llewellyn Ihssen in Patristic text on social ethics, and used her translations for many of the Father's quotations mentioned here unless indicate otherwise. See, J. Leemans, B.J. Matz and J. Verstraeten, *Reading Patristic Texts on Social Ethics: Issues and Challenges for the Twenty-First Century* (Catholic University of America Press 2011)

215 In the forty-eighth thesis, entitled *Non Foenerandum*, Cyprian quotes Psalm 15,5, Ex. 18,7.8 and Dt. 23,20 to prove that usury is immoral. See, Cyprian, *De lapsis* 6 (PL 4,470-71).
216 Ibid.
217 Ibid.
218 Gregory of Nazianzus, *Oration* 16. As translated by Susan Holman, *The Hungry Are Dying: Beggars and Bishops in Roman Cappadocia* (Oxford: University Press, 2001), p. 183-192.
219 John Chrysostom, *Hom. in 1 Cor. 43*, PG 61.374.
220 Gregory of Nyssa, *Usura*. (PG 46:452; J 206)
221 John Chrysostom, *Hom. LVI in Mt.* (PG 58,556) As translated by Maloney, 'The teaching of the fathers on Usury: an historical study on the development of Christian thinking', op. cit., p. 257
222 Ambrose, *DT 88* (PL 14,792), p. 255
223 Basil, *Hom. in Ps.* (PG 29:264)
224 Gregory of Nyssa, *Ep ad Letoium* (PG 45,234). Translated by Maloney, 'The teaching of the fathers on Usury: an historical study on the development of Christian thinking', op. cit., p. 251
225 Augustine, *Ep. CLIV* (CLIII) 25 (PL 33,665) translated by ibid., p. 260
226 Ambrose, *In ps. 14*, v. 5, Migme, P.L., t. 9, col. 307 translated by Divine, op. cit., p. 30
227 Jerome, *In Ezechielem 18:15*, Migne, P.L., t. 25, cols. 176-7 translated by ibid., p. 31
228 Augustine, *Ennarationes in Ps. CXXVIII* (PL 37,1692) translated by Maloney, 'The teaching of the fathers on Usury: an historical study on the development of Christian thinking', op. cit., p. 260
229 *Horn. IV in Eccl.* (PG 44,673), *and Ep. ad Letoium* (PG 45,234), translated by ibid., p. 250
230 *Homilia II*2 (PG 29,272-73), translated by ibid., p. 248
231 Ambrose, *De Tobia*, 15.51 (PL 14.779); ed. L. Zucker, *Ambrosii, De Tobia*, 67
232 Ibid.
233 Clement of Alexandria, *Stromata*, PG 8.1024-25
234 Maloney, 'The teaching of the fathers on Usury: an historical study on the development of Christian thinking', op. cit.
235 *Adv. Marcionem* 4,17 (PL, 2,398-99) translated by ibid.
236 Ibid.
237 *Hom. II in Ps.14,* quoted in Divine, op. cit., p. 28-29
238 Gregory Nazienzen, *Or.* 16, PG 35.957
239 *Tractatus in Ps.* XIV 15 (PL 9,307), translated by Maloney, 'The teaching of the fathers on Usury: an historical study on the development of Christian thinking', op. cit., p. 246

240 Basil, *Hom. in Ps.* (PG 29.268)
241 *Contra Usurarios* (PG 46,446), translated by Maloney, 'The teaching of the fathers on Usury: an historical study on the development of Christian thinking', op. cit., p. 250
242 *Homilia IV* in Ecclesiasten (PG 44,671f.), quoted in ibid, p. 249
243 *Tractatus in Ps.* XIV, 30
244 Basil, *Homilia II* 3 (PG 29,273), Maloney, 'The teaching of the fathers on Usury: an historical study on the development of Christian thinking', op. cit., p. 255
245 As translated in M. Psalidopoulos, *The Canon in the History of Economics: Critical Essays* (Taylor & Francis 2002), p. 36
246 Ibid.
247 Psalidopoulos p, op. cit., p. 40
248 Basil, *Hom. in Ps.* (PG 29:273)
249 Basil's *Hex.* 7, (PG 29.147–64)
250 *Homily* 5, 5 quoted in Psalidopoulos, op. cit., p. 39
251 Ibid.
252 Mansi II. 9. Can. 20, as translated by Cleary, op. cit., p. 43
253 Translated in J. Stevenson and W.H.C. Frend, *A New Eusebius: Documents Illustrating the History of the Church to AD 337* (Baker Publishing Group 2013), p. 55
254 Cleary, op. cit., p. 44-45
255 Translated in Stevenson and Frend, op. cit., p. 55
256 Translated in Cleary, op. cit., p. 44
257 Noonan, *The Scholastic Analysis of Usury*, op. cit., p. 15
258 Also it was included in Gratian.
259 Mills, op. cit., p. 10
260 Noonan, *The Scholastic Analysis of Usury*, op. cit. p. 15
261 Ibid.
262 Simon Smith Kuznets transcribed by Stephanie Lo, 'The Doctrine of Usury in the Middle Ages' <https://studylib.net/doc/7641837/the-doctrine-of-usury-in-the-middle-ages> accessed 6/11/2023
263 I. Robinson, *The Papal Reform of the Eleventh Century: Lives of Pope Leo IX and Pope Gregory VII* (Manchester University Press 2004), p. 2
264 *Constitutum Constantini* c. 12, p. 83, quoted in ibid., p. 2
265 Mills, op. cit.
266 As found in the legislation of the Council of Vienne (A.D. 1312) translated by R.H. Tawney and C. Gore, *Religion and the Rise of Capitalism: An Historical Study (Holland Memorial Lectures, 1922)* (J. Murray 1964), p. 47
267 Ibid., p. 131-132
268 H. Pirenne and I.E. Glegg, *Economic and Social History of Medieval Europe* (Routledge 2005), p. 25

269 Ibid., also further discussion of this revival will be provided in the next chapter.
270 Translated by Divine, op. cit., p. 61
271 As found in the Canon 13th and 25th in the Second and Third Councils of the Lateran (1139, 1179) respectively. Ibid.
272 Ibid.
273 Brian M. McCall, *The Church and the Usurers: Unprofitable Lending for the Modern Economy* (Sapientia Press of Ave Maria University 2013)
274 In Islamic law, *commodatum* is recognised as *'ariya* (loan of use).
275 Divine, op. cit., p. 45-48; George O'Brien, *An Essay on Mediæval Economic Teaching* (A. M. Kelley 1967) 95-99; McCall, op. cit., p. 55-58, 63-67
276 Thomas Aquinas, *Summa Theologica* II-II, q. 78, a. 1, ad 6m, translated Fathers of the English Dominican Province (New York, Benziger Brothers 1947)
277 McCall, op. cit., p. 57
278 Aquinas, op. cit., q. 77, a. 1
279 O'Brien, op. cit., p. 97
280 Ibid.
281 *De malo*, q.13, art. 4, cited in Noonan, *The Scholastic Analysis of Usury*, op. cit., p. 53-54
282 C.A. Franks, *He Became Poor: The Poverty of Christ and Aquinas's Economic Teachings* (William B. Eerdmans Publishing Company 2009)
283 Aquinas, op. cit., q. 78, a. 1
284 Homer and Sylla, op. cit., p. 71
285 Quoted in Cleary, op. cit., p. 88
286 Cited in Noonan, *The Scholastic Analysis of Usury*, op. cit., p. 43-44
287 De Roover, 'The scholastics, usury, and foreign exchange', op. cit., p. 258
288 Ibid.
289 Noonan, *The Scholastic Analysis of Usury*, op. cit., p. 107-109
290 Quoted in Divine, op. cit., p. 52
291 O'Brien op. cit., p. 100; Noonan, *The Scholastic Analysis of Usury*, op. cit., p. 108
292 Noonan, *The Scholastic Analysis of Usury*, op. cit.
293 Ibid.
294 Divine, op. cit., p. 53
295 O'Brien, op. cit., p. 100
296 O'Brien, op. cit., p. 100
297 Divine, op. cit., p. 53
298 Noonan, *The Scholastic Analysis of Usury*, op. cit., p. 107-108
299 Aquinas, op. cit., II-II, q.78, a.2, ad.1
300 Noonan, *The Scholastic Analysis of Usury*, op. cit., p. 107-108

301 Aquinas, op. cit., II-II, q.78, a.2, ad 1m.
302 Ibid., II-II, q.62, a.4
303 O'Brien, op. cit., p. 102-104
304 Ibid; Divine, op. cit., p. 55
305 Quoted in O'Brien, op. cit., p. 104
306 Divine, op. cit., p. 55
307 De Roover, 'The scholastics, usury, and foreign exchange', op. cit., p. 262
308 Noonan, *The Scholastic Analysis of Usury*, op. cit., p. 112
309 William James Ashley, *An Introduction to English Economic History and Theory: The Middle Ages* (1909), v. 1, p. 102
310 Noonan, *The Scholastic Analysis of Usury*, op. cit., p. 119
311 In IV *libros sententarium*, IV:15:2, n.26. Quoted in ibid.
312 Mills, op. cit., p. 14
313 Ibid., p. 15
314 Divine, op. cit., p. 80-86
315 Noonan, *The Scholastic Analysis of Usury*, op. cit., p. 202-210
316 Ashley, *An Introduction to English Economic History and Theory: The End of the Middle Ages*, op. cit., p. 211-215
317 Noonan, *The Scholastic Analysis of Usury*, op. cit., p. 208-209
318 Ibid.; Ashley, *An Introduction to English Economic History and Theory: The End of the Middle Ages*, op. cit., p. 212
319 Ibid., p. 214
320 Ibid.
321 McCall, op. cit., 83; Noonan, *The Scholastic Analysis of Usury*, op. cit., p. 212-217
322 Ibid.
323 Noonan, *The Scholastic Analysis of Usury*, op. cit., p. 213-214
324 Ibid., p. 216
325 Luther's views on usury will be found in his *Sermon on usury of 1519; An den Christlichen Adel; Von Kauffshandlung and Wucher; the Sermon against usury od 1539; An die Pfarherrn wider den Wucher zu predigen;* and *Passim in the Tischreden* and in his letters. Unless otherwise noted, the passages cited here are found in Hartman Grisar, *Luther* (K. Paul, Trench, Trubner & Co., Ltd., 1917), translated by E.M. Lamound, op. cit.
326 Ibid., p. 88
327 Ibid.
328 Martin Luther, *Werke*, Erlangen de., XXIII, p. 319
329 E. Kerridge, *Usury, Interest, and the Reformation* (Ashgate 2002) p. 96: doc. no. 8: from Martin Luther, *Werke*, Erlangen de., XXIII, 283
330 S.M. Jackson and L.A. Loetscher, *The new Schaff-Herzog encyclopedia of religious knowledge* (Baker Book House 1977), p. 118

331 Grisar, op. cit., p. 89
332 Jackson and Loetscher, op. cit., p. 91
333 Translated in D.W. Jones, *Reforming the Morality of Usury: A Study of Differences that Separated the Protestant Reformers* (University Press of America 2004), p. 55
334 Grisar, op. cit., p. 93
335 Ibid.
336 Ibid., from *Sermon on Usury*, 1519
337 Ibid., p. 94
338 Ibid., p. 91, from *Werke*, Erlangen de., XXIII, 356
339 Ibid.
340 Ibid., LVI, 57
341 Ibid., XIII, 319
342 As quoted in Jones, *Reforming the Morality of Usury: A Study of Differences that Separated the Protestant Reformers*, op. cit., p. 57
343 Ibid.
344 Kerridge, op. cit., p. 106, doc. no. 13: from H. Zwingli, *Von göttlicher und meschlicher Gerechtigheit wie die zemmen und standind*: from *Huldrych Zwingli's Werke*, M. Schubert, J. Schulthess eds., I (Zurich 1828-42), pp. 438-439.
345 Ibid., p. 101 and 103: extracts from documents nos. 10 and 11, from P. Melanchthon, *Enrarratio Psalmi Dixit Dominus (Operum*, II, pp. 772-73 and *Definitiones Appellationum in Doctrina Ecclesiae Usitatarum*, in *Operu*, I, fo. 356.
346 Ibid.
347 As described by Divine, op. cit., p. 66
348 See for examples, M. Weber and S. Kalberg, *The Protestant Ethic and the Spirit of Capitalism* (Taylor & Francis 2013)
349 Cited in Georgia Harkness, *John Calvin: The Man and His Ethics* (Henry Holt and Company 1931), p. 206
350 Ibid.
351 Cited in Kerridge, op. cit., p. 45
352 Harkness, op. cit.
353 As collected in Kerridge op. cit., p. 94-95, doc. no. 7: from *Epistolae et Responsa* (Geneva, 1575); and *Sermon XXVIII*, in *Opera*, X, part 1; Munro op. cit., p. 26; R. Tawney, *Historical Introduction to: Thomas Wilson, A Discourse Upon Usury By Way of Dialogue and Orations* (New York, 1925), p. 118, citing the same sources.
354 Roger Fenton, *A Treatise of Usurie, Divided Into Three Books: the first defineth what is usurie, the second determinth that to be unlawful, the third removeth such motives as persuade men in this age that it may be lawfull* (London, 1612): electronic resource in the University of Toronto library. Cited in Tawney, *Historical Introduction to: Thomas Wilson, A Discourse Upon Usury By Way of Dialogue and Orations* op. cit., p. 118

355 *De usuris,* col. 247; Noonan, *The Scholastic Analysis of Usury,* op. cit., p. 366
356 Noonan, *The Scholastic Analysis of Usury,* op. cit., p. 366
357 *In Ezechielis,* 18:8, col. 431. Cited in ibid., p. 367
358 See, ibid., 370-373; Divine, op. cit., p. 89-91
359 Charles Du Moulin (Molinaeus), *Tractatus commerciorum,* n. 530. Cited in Noonan, *The Scholastic Analysis of Usury,* op. cit., p. 368
360 Divine, op. cit., p. 90
361 Noonan, *The Scholastic Analysis of Usury,* op. cit., p. 368; Divine, op. cit., p. 90
362 Noonan, *The Scholastic Analysis of Usury,* op. cit., p. 368
363 Ibid.
364 Ibid.
365 Ibid.
366 Generally see, Rev. Henry Swabey, *Usury and the Church of England* (1826 – 1878); G.E. Corrie, *The History of the Reformation of the Church of England, chiefly as abridged from the larger history by Bishop Burnet and his son* (John Parker 1847) and Charles H George, 'English Calvinist Opinion on Usury, 1600-1640' Journal of the History of Ideas 455; J. Rosenmeier, *John Cotton on Usury* (JSTOR 1990)
367 A. Rees, *The Cyclopædia: Or, Universal Dictionary of Arts, Sciences, and Literature* (31, Longman, Hurst, Rees, Orme & Brown 1819) sec. 31; G. Davies and Julian Hodge Bank, *A history of money: from ancient times to the present day* (University of Wales Press 2002), p. 218
368 Cap. 37 of *Leges Edwardi Confessoris,* an early twelfth-century English Collection of laws. See Aeg. Edw. Con. C. 3, as translated in B.R. O'Brien, *God's Peace and King's Peace: The Laws of Edward the Confessor* (University of Pennsylvania Press 1999), p. 201
369 Swabey, op. cit., p. 14
370 Ibid., p. 14-15
371 Prof. Mark Valeri, 'The Rise of Usury in Early New England' Commonplace <https://commonplace.online/article/the-rise-of-usury-in-early-new-england/> accessed 6/11/2023
372 See, M. Briggs and P. Jordan, *Economic History of England* (University Tutorial P. 1967), p. 102-113
373 Tawney, *Historical Introduction to: Thomas Wilson, A Discourse Upon Usury By Way of Dialogue and Orations* op. cit., p. 58
374 Briggs and Jordan, op. cit., p. 106
375 Ackerman, op. cit., p. 80
376 E. Coke, *Institutes of the Laws of England* (Fletcher 1644), p. 151-152
377 Thomas Wilson, *A discourse Upon Usury, with an historical introduction by R. H. Tawney* (G. Bell & Sons 1952), p. 230-233

378 eds. R. H. Tawney and Eileen Power, *Tudor Economic Documents: Being Select Documents Illustrating the Economic and Social History of Tudor England; in Three Volumes. Commerce, Finance and the Poor Law* (1924), p. 156-157
379 Wilson, op. cit., p. 276
380 Ibid.
381 Robert Bolton, *A Short and Private Discourse between Mr. Bolton and one M. S. Concerning Usury* (London, 1637), as quoted in George, op. cit., p. 463-468
382 Thomas Adams, *The Works of Thomas Adams: The Sum of His Sermons, Meditations, and Other Divine and Moral Discourses* (London 1629), p. 23
383 Ibid., p. 23
384 Ian Breward, ed., *The Works of William Perkins*, 3 vols. (Appleford, Eng., 1970), p. 94-95
385 Ibid., p. 63
386 D. North, *Discourses upon Trade; Principally Directed to the Cases of the Interest, Coynage, Clipping, Increase of Money. By Sir D. North* (1822), p. 4; J. Locke, *The Works of John Locke: Some considerations of the consequences of lowering the interest and raising the value of money (Letter to a member of Parliament, 1691)* (C. and J. Rivington 1824), p. 37
387 F. Bacon, *Bacon's Essays* (IndoEuropeanPublishing 2010), p. 69
388 T. Culpeper, *A Discourse, Shewing the Many Advantages which Will Accrue to this Kingdom by the Abatement of Usury. Together with the Absolute Necessity of Reducing Interest of Money to the Lowest Rate it Bears in Other Countreys ... Humbly Presented to the High Court of Parliament, Etc* (London 1668), p. 33-34
389 Quoted in George, op. cit., p. 473
390 *Winthrop Papers* (Boston 1931) II, p. 286, as quoted in Rosenmeier, op. cit., p. 555-556
391 R. H. Tawney and Eileen Power, op. cit., p. 142-143
392 Tawney, *Historical Introduction to: Thomas Wilson, A Discourse Upon Usury By Way of Dialogue and Orations* op. cit., p. 131
393 R. H. Tawney and Eileen Power, op. cit., p. 162; As also suggested by Rosenmeier, op. cit., p. 551
394 Ibid.
395 *Statutes of the Realm,* Vol. IV (London 1963), pt. 2, p. 1223-1224
396 Roger Fenton, *A Treatise of Usurie* (London, 1611), p. 2
397 Munro, op. cit., p. 267
398 12 Anne, c. 16
399 W. Blackstone and others, *Commentaries on the Laws of England: In Four Books; with an Analysis of the Work* (Harper 1854), p. 455

400 W. Blackstone and others, *Commentaries on the Laws of England: In Four Books; with an Analysis of the Work* (Harper 1854).
401 A. Ertl, *The Political Economic Foundation of Democratic Capitalism: From Genesis to Maturation* (Universal Publishers 2007), p. 194-195
402 Ibid.
403 Tawney and Gore, *Religion and the Rise of Capitalism: An Historical Study (Holland Memorial Lectures, 1922)*, op. cit., p. 153
404 For further details, see I. Kramnick, *Bolingbroke and His Circle: The Politics of Nostalgia in the Age of Walpole* (Cornell University Press 1992), p. 84-91
405 J. Locke, *An Essay Concerning Human Understanding* (T. Tegg and Son 1836), p. 8
406 Locke (*Essay on Human Understanding*) and Bolingbroke, op. cit.
407 T. Hobbes, *Leviathan* (Digireads.com 2010), p. 70
408 H.S.J. Bolingbroke, *The Work of Lord Bolingbroke: With a Life, Prepared Expressly for this Edition, Containing Additional Information Relative to His Personal and Public Character, Selected from the Best Authorities* (Carey and Hart 1841), p. 164; A.A.CE Shaftesbury and L.E. Klein, *Shaftesbury: Characteristics of Men, Manners, Opinions, Times* (Cambridge University Press 1999)
409 Bolingbroke, op. cit., p. 164
410 Ibid., p. 187
411 Kramnick, op. cit.
412 A. Pope and J. Cary, *The Poetical Works of Alex. Pope* (Smith 1841), p. 82
413 As quoted in Tawney and Gore, *Religion and the Rise of Capitalism: An Historical Study (Holland Memorial Lectures, 1922)*, op. cit., p. 162
414 Ibid., p. 163
415 For further details, see Shafer-Landau
416 A. Smith, *The Wealth of Nations* (Digireads.com 2004), p. 264
417 Smith, op. cit., p. 212
418 Ibid., p. 188-189
419 Ibid., p. 213
420 J. Bentham, *Defense of Usury* (Payne and Foss 1816)
421 Ibid., Lett. I, p. 14
422 Lett. IX, p. 91
423 Lett. I, p. 12
424 Bentham, Lett. I, p. 2
425 Ibid., Lett. X, p. 99
426 Ibid., Lett. I, p. 13
427 Ibid., Lett. III, p. 25-26
428 Ibid., Lett. XIII , p. 139-142
429 Ibid., p. 155

430 Ibid., Lett. VI, p. 45-49
431 Ibid., Lett. III, p. 32-37
432 Locke, *The Works of John Locke: Some considerations of the consequences of lowering the interest and raising the value of money (Letter to a member of Parliament, 1691)*, p. 7
433 Bentham, op. cit., Lett. III, p. 36
434 Ibid., p. 187-188
435 See, for example, *Reasons Against the Repeal of the Usury Laws* (J. Murray 1825)
436 F.W. Ryan, *Usury and Usury Laws: A Juristic-economic Study of the Effects of State Statutory Maximums for Loan Charges Upon Lending Operations in the United States* (Houghton Mifflin 1924), p. 57
437 Wilson, op. cit., p. 58
438 See Tawney (1925, 1571), Frierson (1969), Jones (1989), Kerridge (2002). In Art., Evading the 'Taint of Usury' The usury prohibition as a barrier to entry'
439 Mark Koyama, 'Evading the 'Taint of Usury': The usury prohibition as a barrier to entry' 47 Explorations in Economic History 420
440 As first termed by Ahmad. See, S.A. Ahmed, 'Global need for a new economic concept: Islamic economics' 1 International Journal of Islamic Financial Services 13, 14
441 M.A. Jarhi and others, *Islamic Banking: Answers to Some Frequently Asked Questions* (Islamic Development Bank, Islamic Research and Training Institute 2001)Islamic Research and Training Institute 2001 p. 11; S.H. Siddiqui, *Islamic Banking: Genesis & Rationale, Evaluation & Review, Prospects & Challenges* (Royal Book Company 1994), p. 15;M. Iqbal and P. Molyneux, *Thirty Years of Islamic Banking: History, Performance and Prospects* (Palgrave Macmillan 2005), p. 9
442 M.U. Chapra, 'The Nature of *Riba* in Islam' 8 Millah: Jurnal Studi Agama 1, 1-2
443 As quoted in M.U. Chapra, 'The Nature of *Riba* in Islam' 8 Millah: Jurnal Studi Agama
444 C. Imber, *Ebu's-su'ud: The Islamic Legal Tradition* (Edinburgh University Press 1997), p. 145
445 For several examples, see Neş'et Çağatay, '*Riba* and Interest Concept and Banking in the Ottoman Empire', Studia Islamica 53
446 J.M.S. Baljon, *The Reforms and Religious Ideas of Sir Sayyid Ahmad Khan* (Sh. Muhammad Ashraf 1964), p. 29
447 {Baljon, 1964 #254}Ibid.{Tawney, 1984 #49}{Baljon, 1964 #254} {Baljon, 1964 #254}{Baljon, 1964 #254}{Baljon, 1964 #254}
448 N.A. Saleh and A. Ajaj, *Unlawful Gain and Legitimate Profit in Islamic Law: Riba, Gharar, and Islamic Banking* (Graham & Trotman 1992), p. 28

449 A. Saeed, *Islamic Banking and Interest: A Study of the Prohibition of Riba and Its Contemporary Interpretation* (Brill Academic Pub 1996), p. 43
450 M. Rodinson, *Islam and Capitalism*, Transl. by Brian Pearce (University of Texas Press 1978), p. 168. However, some scholars argued that Muhammad 'Abduh did not issue such *fatwa*, nor did he approve simple interest. See for example, Ahmad Zaki Badawi, *The Theory of Prohibited Riba* (Centre for Islamic Law and Legal Heritage 2005)
451 E. Davis, *Challenging Colonialism: Bank Misr and Egyptian Industrialization, 1920-1941* (Princeton University Press 1983), p. 73
452 For a full list of references, see, M.O. Farooq, 'The *Riba*-Interest Equivalence: Is there an Ijma (consensus)?' 4 Transnational Dispute Management
453 'Islamic institute blesses interest' (*BBC News*, 2002) <http://news.bbc.co.uk/1/hi/business/2488525.stm> accessed 30/01
454 El-Gamal, op. cit., p. 3
455 Qur'an 27:192-195
456 Doi and Clarke, op. cit., p. 47
457 See, F. Rahman, *Islam* (University of Chicago Press 1979); M.H. Kamali, *Principles of Islamic Jurisprudence* (Islamic Texts Society 2003), p. 62
458 Qur'an 2:2; 31:3; 3:138
459 Kamali, 'Law and society: The interplay of revelation and reason in the Shari'a', op. cit., p. 120
460 Ibid.
461 Ibid.
462 Doi and Clarke, op. cit., p. 77
463 M.Z. Siddiqi and A.H. Murad, *Hadith Literature: Its Origin, Development and Special Features* (Islamic Texts Society 1993), p. 77-92
464 Ibid., p. 107
465 Source: Diwany, Ahmad and Staff, op. cit., p. 34
466 Siddiqi and Murad, op. cit., p. 73
467 M.Y.I. al-Din, *Islamic Law: From Historical Foundations to Contemporary Practice* (Edinburgh University Press 2004), ibid p. 35
468 Ibid.
469 Kamali, 'Law and society: The interplay of revelation and reason in the Shari'a', op. cit., p. 118, 120
470 Kamali, *Principles of Islamic Jurisprudence*, op. cit., p. 315
471 Ibid.
472 Ibid.
473 Kamali, *Principles of Islamic Jurisprudence*, op. cit., p. 155-156; Doi and Clarke, op. cit., p. 97-102
474 al-Din, op. cit., p. 51-52
475 Doi and Clarke, op. cit., p 117

476 For further details of these requirements see, al-Din, op. cit., p. 55; Doi and Clarke, op. cit., p. 112
477 Kamali, 'Law and society: The interplay of revelation and reason in the Shari'a', op. cit., p. 123
478 Ibid, p. 118
479 Ibid.
480 Abd al-Malik Ibn Hisham and Muhammad Ibn Ishaq, *The Life of Muhammad: A Translation of Ibn Ishaq's Sirat Rasul Allah* (Oxford University Press 1980), p. 72
481 al-Qushayri Muslim Ibn al-Haggag, *Sahih Muslim* (Thesaurus Islamicus Foundation 2000), Vol. 2, 676 (hadith no. 4148).
482 Ibid, Vol. 2, 676 (hadith no. 4149).
483 Ahmad ibn Hanbal, *al-Musnad* (Matba'ah Mustafa Babi al-Halabi 1895) *Bab al-Riba*, Vol. 2, p. 239; Ibn Majah, *Sunan Ibn Majah* (1952), Kitab al-Tijarah, Vol. 2, p. 764
484 Muhammad ibn Ahmad Ibn Rushd, *Muqaddimat Ibn Rushd* (Dar al-Gharb al-Islami 1988), Vol. 3, p. 215
485 Qur'an 5:3
486 *Sunan* al-Bayhaqi 3 :23
487 Farhad Nomani, *The Interpretative Debate of the Classical Islamic Jurists on Riba (Usury)*
488 W. Al Zuhayli, *Financial Transaction in Islamic Jurisprudence* (Damascus-Syria: Dar al-Fikr al-Mouaser 2003) p. 174; A.Z. Badawi, *The Theory of Prohibited Riba* (Centre for Islamic Law and Legal Heritage 2005); N.A. Saleh, *Unlawful Gain and Legitimate Profit in Islamic Law: Riba, Gharar, and Islamic Banking* (Cambridge University Press 1986), p. 15-16; Chapra, op. cit., 15-19.
489 Also known as *riba al-naqd* (the *riba* that occurs on the spot)
490 Al Zuhayli, op. cit., p. 174
491 Badawi, op. cit., p. 50
492 Al Zuhayli, op. cit. 10.3; for further details see, W. Zuhaili, *al-Fiqh al-islami wa-adillatuhu* (Dar al-Fikr 1997), Vol. 5, p. 3716-3719
493 Al Zuhayli, op. cit., p. 369; Imran Ahsan Khan Nyazee, 'The concept of *riba* and Islamic banking', online document; Farhad Nomani, *The Interpretative Debate of the Classical Islamic Jurists on Riba (Usury)* (2002)
494 A.A. Yate, *Ibn Rushd as Jurist* (University of Cambridge 1991) p. 53; Averroës, *The Distinguished Jurist's Primer: A Translation of Bidayat al-mujtahid* (Centre for Muslim Contribution to Civilisation 1996)
495 Averroës, *The Distinguished Jurist's Primer: A Translation of Bidayat al-mujtahid* (Centre for Muslim Contribution to Civilisation 1996), p. 215
496 Ibn Rushd, Vol. 3, p. 215

497 Nomani, *The Interpretative Debate of the Classical Islamic Jurists on Riba (Usury)*; for further details in this subject see the first chapter of Muhammed Imran Ismail, 'Legal stratagems (*hiyal*) and usury in Islamic commercial law' (Ph.D., University of Birmingham 2010)
498 For example, K. Hassan and M. Lewis, *Handbook of Islamic Banking* (Edward Elgar 2007); Tarek El Diwany, *The Problem with Interest* (Kreatoc 2003)
499 Such as, M. Umer Chapra, *Towards a Just Monetary System: A Discussion of Money, Banking, and Monetary Policy in the Light of Islamic Teachings* (Islamic Foundation 1985) and Abdulkader S. Thomas, 'Interest in Islamic economics understanding *riba*' (*Routledge*, 2006)
500 Muhammad ibn Abi Bakr Sa'd Taha Abd al-Rauf Ibn Qayyim al-Jawziyyah, *I'lam al-muwaqqi'in 'an Rabb al-'Alamin* (Maktabat al-Kulliyat al-Azhariyah 1968), Vol. 2, p. 99
501 Ibid; Abdul Azim Islahi, *Economic thought of Ibn al Qayyim (1292-1350 A.D.)* (International Centre for Research in Islamic Economics, King Abdulaziz University 1984), p. 8-10
502 Shah Waliyullah, *Hujjatullah al-Balighah* (Lahore: Qawmi Kutub Khana, tr. Mawlana Abdul Rahim 1953), Vol. 2 p. 474-475
503 Imber, op. cit., p. 115
504 Qur'an 2:173; 5:3; 6:145, 119; 16:115
505 See generally, Mansour Z. University of Edinburgh, Al-Mutairi, 'Necessity in Islamic law' (1997)
506 The verse 5:2 reads, "... help one another in acts of righteousness and piety, and do not help one another in sin and transgression ..."
507 Mohammad Fadel, '*Riba*, Efficiency, and Prudential Regulation: Preliminary Thoughts' Wisconsin International Law Journal, Forthcoming 08, 655, 680
508 Muhammad Rashid Rida, *al-Riba wa al-Mu'amalat fi al-Islam* (Cairo, Maktabat al-Qahira 1959); Salah al-din al-Munajjid & Yusuf and Khuri eds, *Fatawa al-Imam Muhammad Rashid Rida* (Dar al-kitab al-jadid 1970), p. 603-609
509 Ibid.
510 Muhammad Rashid Rida, *al-Manar* (Dar al-kitab al-jadid), p. 94
511 Yusuf and eds, op. cit., p. 608
512 Ibid.
513 Abd Al-Razzaq Ahmad Al-Sanhuri, *Masadir Al-Haqq fil-Fiqh al-Islami* (1967), p. 241-242
514 al-Badawi fully discussed and documented the views of Rashid Rida including opinions attributed to Muhammad 'Abdu in his famous Book I.Z.D. Badawi, *Nazariyat al-riba al-muharram: fi al-shari'ah al-Islamiyah* (1964)
515 A similar view expressed by Usmani, op. cit., p. 34

516 al-Tabari, op. cit., Vol. 4, part 6, 23-4
517 Qur'an 24:33
518 As quoted by Abd al-Mun'im Mahmud al Qusi, *'Riba,* Islamic Law and Interest' (Temple University 1982), p. 138-139
519 See, for instance, Muhammad Abu Zahra, *Buhith Fi al-Riba* (Kuwait 1970), p. 52
520 Dr. Jawed Ali; quoted by Usmani, op. cit., p. 34
521 Chapra, 'The Nature of *Riba* in Islam', op. cit.
522 Qur'an 2:278
523 Schacht, J., *'Riba'*, in Encyclopaedia of Islam, Leyden: E.J. Brill Ltd.; London: Lusac & Co., 1936, Old edition, Vol. 3, p. 1150
524 Nyazee, op. cit., p. 104
525 Ridha Saadallah, 'Concept of time in Islamic economics' 2 Islamic Economic Studies 1415 AH
526 Qur'an 2:275-279
527 Fakhruddin al-Razi, *al-Tafsir al-Kabir* (Dar Ihya' al-Turat al-'Arabi 1990), op. cit., Vol. 2, p. 355-356
528 Ibid.
529 Islahi, op. cit., p. 11
530 al-Ghazali, *Ihya*, Vol. 4, p. 92, as quoted in Abdul Azim Islahi, 'An analytical study of al-Ghazali's thought on money and interest', op. cit., p. 6
531 Ibn Taimiyyah, *Majmu al-Fatawa* (Matabiál-Riyad 1963), Vol. 29, p. 472
532 Chibli Mallat and William Morris Ballantyne, *Islamic Law and Finance* (Graham & Trotman 1988), p. 73, quoting al-Manar, May 24, 1906, p. 348
533 S.A. Meenai and J.A. Ansari, *Money and Banking in Pakistan* (Oxford University Press 2004), p. 215
534 U Chapra, 'Why Has Islam Prohibited Interest?: Rationale Behind the Prohibition of Interest' Review of Islamic Economics 5, 5
535 S.A.A. Maudoodi, *Interest and Modern Banking* (Adhunik Prokashani, Dhaka 1987)
536 See, for example, Fuad al-Omar and others, 'Islamic banking: Theory, practice and challenges'6; Paul S Mills and John R Presley, *Islamic finance: Theory and practice* (Macmillan Houndmills 1999), p. 9; Mahmoud A El-Gamal, 'An economic explication of the prohibition of *gharar* in classical Islamic jurisprudence' 8 Islamic Economic Studies 29
537 F.E. Vogel and S.L. Hayes, *Islamic Law and Finance: Religion, Risk, and Return* (Brill 1998), p. 77
538 Fadel, op. cit., p. 669; Some even argued that although the reason for the prohibition may not be fully comprehended by scholars today *"it is quite likely to become clear to us tomorrow."* See, Anwar Iqbal Qureshi,

Islam and the Theory of Interest: With a New Chapter on Interest Free Banking (Sh. Muhammad Ashraf 1974), p. 4

539 See above section: *Riba*: Interest, Usury or Both

Evading The Taint Of Usury

540 See above section: Usury in Ancient Rome
541 *A History of Rome* (Longman, Rees, Orme, Brown, Green & Longman 1834), p. 241-242
542 Ibid.
543 P. Kay, *Rome's Economic Revolution* (OUP Oxford 2014), p. 115
544 P. Louis, *Ancient Rome at Work: An Economic History of Rome from the Origins to the Empire* (Taylor & Francis 2013), p. 210
545 Kay, op. cit., p. 117-21; M. Ord, *An Essay on the Law of Usury* (W. Clarke and Sons 1809), p. 63-66
546 As quoted in *Pamphlets on Money* (University of California, Berkeley 1834), p. 18
547 Ibid.
548 For examples see, Oeltjen, op. cit.
549 J.L. Goff, *The Usurer and Purgatory* (Yale University 1979), p. 25
550 Noonan, *The Scholastic Analysis of Usury*; Ashley, *An Introduction to English Economic History and Theory: The End of the Middle Ages*, op. cit., p. 212
551 Book 44, Hadith 4460 as translated by Nasiruddin al-Khattab, *Sunan An-Nasa'I: English Translation With Arabic Text*, Vol. 5 (Darussalam 2007)
552 Similar hadiths have also been narrated by Abu Dawud and Ibn Majah in their *Sunan* as well as by Imam Ahmad in his *Musnad*. See Respectively, Book 22, Hadith 3325, Book 12, Hadith 2278 and Hadith no. 10190
553 Ibn Qayyim al-Jawziyyah, op. cit., p. 84
554 *Sunan* Abu Daud, Hadith No. 3455
555 A. Watson, 'Comparative Law and Legal Change' 37, The Cambridge Law Journal 313; Halpin, op. cit.
556 M.J. Kisner, *Spinoza on Human Freedom: Reason, Autonomy and the Good Life* (Cambridge University Press 2011), p. 115-116
557 R. Brague, *The Law of God: The Philosophical History of an Idea* (University of Chicago Press 2007) p. 18; See also, C. Hayes, *What's Divine about Divine Law?: Early Perspectives* (Princeton University Press 2015)
558 Works, XI, p. 248; cited in Nelson, op. cit., p. 78
559 Ibid., p. 78-79
560 Noonan, *The Scholastic Analysis of Usury*, op. cit., p. 364-367

561 Jones, *God and the Money-lenders: Usury and Law in Early Modern England*, op. cit., p. 19
562 J. Calvin, *John Calvin's Commentaries on Ezekiel 13-20* (Extended Annotated Edition) (Jazzybee Verlag 2012)
563 As cited in Nelson, op. cit., p. 40-41
564 Frierson, op. cit., p. 124
565 Ibid.
566 Homer and Sylla, op. cit., p. 322
567 Nelson, op. cit., p. 74
568 See, L. Watt, *Usury in Catholic Theology* (Catholic Social Guild 1945), p. 44
569 Divine, op. cit., p. 80-86
570 See above section: Extrinsic Titles
571 Divine, op. cit., p. 80-86
572 Ibid.
573 Ibid.
574 Ibid., p. 94-95
575 Divine, p. 102-3; also see, Watt, op. cit., p. 19-27
576 As indicated in Pope Benedict XIV, 'Vix Pervenit' (1745) 'Vix Pervenit' (1745) <https://www.ewtn.com/catholicism/library/on-usury-3340> accessed 6/11/2023
577 Ibid.
578 Ibid.
579 Matthew 5:42
580 For additional information, see Watt, op. cit., p. 40; Divine, op. cit., p. 80-86
581 As translated by Noonan, *The Scholastic Analysis of Usury*, op. cit., p. 391
582 Ibid., p. 115
583 Aquinas, II-II, q.78, a.2, ad 1m.
584 W.J. Ashley, *An Introduction to English Economic History and Theory: Part 1. the Middle Ages* (Adegi Graphics LLC 1906), p. 196
585 Ashley, *An Introduction to English Economic History and Theory: Part 1. the Middle Ages*, op. cit., p. 196.
586 De Roover, 'The scholastics, usury, and foreign exchange', op. cit., p. 257
587 Watt, op. cit., p. 42
588 Mills, *Interest in Interest: The Old Testament Ban on Interest and Its Implications for Today*, op. cit., p. 14
589 Watt, op. cit., p. 33-38
590 Ibid., op. cit., p. 45
591 For further information see, Coulter, op. cit.

592 Kevin Knight and Inc New Advent, 'The Catholic encyclopedia' (New Advent, 1995) <http://www.newadvent.org/cathen/> accessed 21/02/2016/2016
593 J. Hardon, *Catholic Dictionary: An Abridged and Updated Edition of Modern Catholic Dictionary* (Crown Publishing Group 2013), p. 226
594 Ibid p. 229; Knight and New Advent, op. cit.
595 cf. Second Vatican Council, 'Dogmatic Constitution on Divine Revelation,' Dei Verbum, (18 November 1965), 10.
596 Galatians 3:8
597 Abdul Khaleq Alghanem, 'Tash ma Tash, Zayd 'akhu Obayd' (2011) <https://www.youtube.com/watch?v=9mSNRpzDm_g>
598 See above section: *Riba* in the Fiqh literature.
599 As quoted in F.L. Van Baumer, *Main Currents of Western Thought: Readings in Western European Intellectual History from the Middle Ages to the Present* (Yale University Press 1978), p. 233
600 Ernst and Young (E&Y), 'World Islamic Banking Competitiveness Report 2016', <http://ceif.iba.edu.pk/pdf/EY-WorldIslamicBankingCompetitivenessReport2016.pdf> accessed 6/11/2023
601 See above section: The Concept of Usury in Jewish Law
602 More details about the *heter iska* will be included later in this chapter.
603 See, Tamari, op. cit., p. 185
604 Ellen DeGeneres, 'The Ellen DeGeneres Show' (2016)
605 R. Aronson, *Jean-Paul Sartre, Philosophy in the World* (NLB 1980), p. 185
606 See above in section: Jews and Usury
607 The Babylonian Talmud, op. cit., *Baba Mezia*, 69b,70b,71a; Reisman, op. cit., p. 94-7. For further details, see: J.H. Tigay and others, *Mishneh Todah: Studies in Deuteronomy and Its Cultural Environment in Honor of Jeffrey H. Tigay* (Eisenbrauns 2009); E. Neufeld, 'The prohibitions against loans at interest in ancient Hebrew laws' 26 Hebrew Union College Annual 355; S Stein, 'Interest taken by Jews from Gentiles' Journal of Semitic Studies 141
608 The Babylonian Talmud, op. cit., *Baba Mezia*, 5.6
609 *Mishneh Torah, Hilkhot Loveh u Malveh*, chapter 5, halakhah 1
610 Stein, 'The laws on interest in the Old Testament' p. 162
611 The Babylonian Talmud, op. cit., *Makkoth* 24a
612 Talmud Bavli, 70b-71a.
613 Cited in, Tamari, op. cit., p. 181
614 For a full list of references, see Stein, 'Interest taken by Jews from Gentiles', op. cit.
615 Robert Chazan, 'The letter of R. Jacob ben Elijah to friar paul' 6 Jewish History 51
616 See for example, Stein, 'Interest taken by Jews from Gentiles', op. cit.

617 Tamari, op. cit., p. 167; E. Basri, *Ethics of Business, Finance, & Charity According to Jewish law* (Haktav Institute 1987)
618 As quoted in A. Kirschenbaum, *Equity in Jewish Law: Beyond Equity: Halakhic Aspirationism in Jewish Civil Law* (KTAV Publishing House 1991), p. 33
619 As quoted in Tamari, op. cit., p. 182
620 *Encyclopaedia Judaica*, xii 244-256.
621 Weber and Kalberg, op. cit., p. 46
622 See for example, the statements mentioned above of Molinaeus, Salmasius, Wintrope and others.
623 Cited in Stein, 'Interest taken by Jews from Gentiles', op. cit., p. 143
624 Ibid., p. 181
625 Reisman, op. cit., p. 93
626 Tamari, op. cit., p. 182
627 Kirschenbaum, op. cit., p. 275-285
628 Ibid.
629 Please note that a similar opinion have been expressed in Tamari, op. cit., p. 165, as well as in Stein, 'Interest taken by Jews from Gentiles', op. cit., p. 142
630 See above in section: Jews and Usury
631 Goldsmith, op. cit., p. 88-89; Jennings, op. cit., p. 184
632 *Mishneh Torah, Hilkhot Avoda Zara*, chapter 1, *halakhot* 1-3
633 Nelson, op. cit., p. 3
634 L.M. Zucker, *S. Ambrosii De Tobia: a commentary, with an introduction and translation* (The Catholic University of America 1933), p. 49. The translation of passages from De Tobia are taken from this work.
635 Ambrose, *De bono morti*, as translated by studio and Ammannati, op. cit., p. 158
636 Zucker, op. cit., p. 82
637 Ibid., 11
638 Ibid., 35
639 Nelson, op. cit., p. 4
640 Zucker, op. cit., p. 67
641 Ibid., 67
642 Ibid.
643 Pirenne and Glegg, op. cit., p. 25
644 See above section: Jews & usury; Parkes, op. cit., p. 341-343
645 Poliakov, *Jewish Bankers and the Holy See from the Thirteenth to the Seventeenth Century*, op. cit., p. 22-4; Ryan, 'Law, legislation, and lending: An examination of the influence of the Crusades on the usury prohibition' p. 71; See also, J.W. Parkes, *The Jew in the Medieval Community: A Study of His Political and Economic Situation* (Hermon Press 1976), p. 297

646 See above section: Introduction to the medieval period
647 J. Shatzmiller, *Shylock Reconsidered: Jews, Money-lending, and Medieval Society* (University of California Press 1990), p. 46
648 Nelson, op. cit., p. 6, 15-16
649 Terence Patrick McLaughlin, 'The Teaching of the Canonists of Usury' Mediaeval Studies 81
650 Nelson, op. cit.
651 Ibid., op. cit., p. 16
652 Poliakov, *Jewish Bankers and the Holy See from the Thirteenth to the Seventeenth Century*, op. cit., p. 32
653 Ibid.; See also, R. Rist, *Popes and Jews, 1095-1291* (OUP Oxford 2015), p. 145
654 Lateran IV, Constitution 67, 1215, translated by J.T. Gilchrist in *Church and Economic Activity in the High Middle Ages*, op. cit., p. 182-183
655 As found in the Canon 13th and 25th in the Second and Third Councils of Lateran (1139, 1179) respectively. Translated by Divine, op. cit., p. 61
656 Nelson, op. cit., p. 10-11
657 Parkes, op. cit., p. 293, 347
658 Rist, op. cit., p. 144
659 Parkes, op. cit., p. 297
660 See, Stein, 'Interest taken by Jews from Gentiles', op. cit.
661 Parkes, op. cit., p. 293
662 F. 2 and J.M. Powell, *The Liber Augustalis, Or Contitutions of Melfi Promulgated by the Emperor Frederick 2. for the Kingdom of Sicily in 1231* (Syracuse University Press 1971), p. 12-13
663 See above section: The Fathers of the Church
664 Poliakov, *Jewish Bankers and the Holy See from the Thirteenth to the Seventeenth Century*, op. cit., p. 25
665 See above section: The Devil's Work; Parkes, op. cit., p. 283
666 Parkes, op. cit., p. 297
667 Abu Nasr Islma'il b. Hammad al-Jawhari, *Taj al-lughah wa-sihah al-'arabiyyah*, Vol. II (Bulaq Press 1365 A.H.), p. 287
668 Muhibb al-Din Abu al-Fayd al-Sayyid Muhammad Murtada al-Husayni, *Taj al-'arus min jawahir al-qamus*, Vol. VIII (1st edn, al-Matba'ah al-Khayriyyah 1306 A.H.), p. 301; Abu al-Fadl Jamal al-Din Muhammad b. Markram al-ifriqi al-Misiri, *Lisan al-'Arab*, Vol. XII (Dar Sadir 1965), p. 221
669 Ibid.
670 B. Fassbender and others, *The Oxford Handbook of the History of International Law* (OUP Oxford 2012), p. 396
671 M. Levy-Rubin, *Non-Muslims in the Early Islamic Empire: From Surrender to Coexistence* (Cambridge University Press 2011), p. 53-54

672   Ibid. For English translation of this covenant of protection, please see: W. Muir, *The Life of Mahomet and History of Islam, to the Era of the Hegira*: With Introductory Chapters on the Original Sources for the Biography of Mahomet, and on the Pre-Islamite History of Arabia (Smith, Elder 1858), p. 299-301
673   *The Farewell Sermon of Prophet Muhammad*, Vol. 11 (illustrated edn, Tughra Books 2004)
674   Abu Bakr ibn Mas'ud Kasani, *Bada'i al-sana'i fi tartib al-shara'i*, Vol. 5 (Dar al-Kutub al-Ilmiyah 1986), p. 193
675   *Sunan* Abi Dawud, Book 19, Hadith 3052. Graded by al-Albani as *Sahih* (authentic). See, Abu Dawud Sulaiman bin Ashath, *English Translation of Sunan Abu Dawud*, Vol. 4 (Nasiruddin Al-Khattab tr, Darussalam 2008)
676   *Sahih al-Bukhari,* Book 53, Hadith 3166. See, Muhammed Ibn Ismaiel Al-Bukhari, *Translation of the Meanings of Sahih al-Bukhari: Arabic-English*, Vol. 4 (Muhammad Muhsin Khan tr, Dar-us-Salam 1997)
677   Known as *ahkam ahl al-dhimmah* (lit. the rules of the people of *dhimmah*)
678   For a full list of references for each school, see: Ministry of Awqaf & Islamic Affairs in Kuwait, *al-Mawsu'at al-Fiqhiat [Encyclopedia of Islamic Jurisprudence]* (Dar al-Salasel 1998), Vol. 7, p. 131-2; Vol. 22, p. 74-5
679   Both the *dhimmi* and *musta'min* are sometimes referred to as *mu'ahad* (lit. contractee)
680   Kuwait, Vol. 7, p. 121
681   See, ibid, Vol. 20, 201-3; Muhammad Mushtaq Ahmad, 'The notions of *dar al-harb* and *dar al-Islam* in Islamic jurisprudence with special reference to the Hanafi school' 47 Islamic Studies 5; Sheikh Wahbeh Al-Zuhili, 'Islam and international law' 87 International Review of the Red Cross 269; Ahmad Sunawari Long; Jaffary Awang; Kamaruddin Salleh, *Islam: Past, Present and Future* (Universiti Kebangsaan Malaysia 2004)
682   al-Sarakhsi, op. cit., p. 114; Kuwait, Vol. 20, p. 202
683   Kuwait, op. cit.
684   Zakariyya al-Ansari, *Asna al-Matalib fi Sharh Rawd al-Talib* (Al-Matba'ah al-Misriyyah 1357 AH), Vol. 4, 204; Ahmad, op. cit.
685   B. Lewis, *The Muslim Discovery of Europe* (W. W. Norton 2001), 69-79; H.A.R. Gibb, *Whither Islam?: A Survey of Modern Movements in the Moslem World* (1973), p. 20; William Montgomery Watt, *Islamic Fundamentalism and Modernity (RLE Politics of Islam)* (Routledge 1988), p. 4
686   Lewis, *The Muslim Discovery of Europe*, op. cit.

687 Tariq Ramadan, *To Be a European Muslim* (Kube Publishing Ltd 2013), p. 23
688 Al-Zuhili, p. 278-279
689 Ahmad, op. cit., p. 6-12
690 Kuwait, op. cit., Vol. 20, p. 209-210
691 al-Sarakhsi, op. cit., Vol. 10, p. 62-63, See also, Kuwait, op. cit., Vol. 20, p. 209; Abu Bakr bin Mas'ud Al-Kasani, *Bada'i al-Sana'i fi Tartib al-Shara'i* (Dar al-Kutub al-Ilmiyah' 1986), op. cit., Vol..7, p. 131
692 al-Marghinani, op. cit., Vol..2, p. 396
693 See, also Kuwait, op. cit., Vol. 20, p. 209
694 Ahmad, op. cit., p. 36
695 Salleh, op. cit.. p. 2
696 Yahya b. Sharaf al-Nawawi, *Minhaj al-Talibin* (Maktabah al-Thaqafah 1992); See also, Yahya b. Sharaf al-Nawawi, *Rawdat al-Talibin*, Vol. X (Dar al-Nahdah al-Hadithah 1966), p. 208
697 For a full list of references for each school, see: Kuwait, op. cit., Vol. 20, p. 208
698 This part is drawn heavily on the translation provided for these evidences in Salah al-Sawi, *A Polite Reconsideration of the Fatwa Permitting Interest-Based Mortgages for Buying Homes in Western Societies* (2001)
699 Kuwait, op. cit., Vol. 20, p. 208
700 al-Sawi, op. cit., p. 17
701 Abu 'Isa Muhammad ibn 'Isa al-Tirmidhi, *Jami al-Tirmidhi* (Darussalam 2007), Book 1, Hadith 61
702 Qur'an 4:161
703 al-Sawi, op. cit., p. 17
704 Kuwait, op. cit., Vol. 20, p. 208; al-Sawi, op. cit., p. 77
705 Al-Kasani, op. cit., Vol..5, p. 192. As translated in al-Sawi, op. cit., p. 27-28
706 Al-Kasani, op. cit., Vol..5, p.192; al-Sarakhsi, op. cit., Vol. 10, p. 62-63
707 Muhammad ibn Ali Haskafi, *'al-Durr al-Mukhtar fi Sharh Tanwir al-Absar'* (Dar al-Kutub al-Ilmiyah', 2002) Vol. 1, p. 433
708 Muhammad ibn Muhammad Amin ibn 'Abidin, *Radd al-Muhtar ala al-Durr al-Mukhtar* (Dar Ihya al-Turath al-'Arabi 1998), Vol. 5, p. 186
709 This section draws heavily on the translation provided for these evidences in al-Sawi, op. cit.
710 Kuwait, op. cit., Vol. 20, p. 208
711 Book 36.27.35, *al-Muwatta of Imam Malik*, translated by Aisha Bewley, Diwan Press.
712 al-Sawi, op. cit. p. 21
713 al-Tirmidhi, Book 44, Hadith 3194
714 Ibid., Book 44, Hadith 3191

715 Kuwait, op. cit., Vol. 20, p. 208; al-Sarakhsi MIA, *al-Mabsut* (Dar al-Kutub al-'Ilmiya 1993), Vol. 14, p. 70
716 Qur'an 2: 197
717 al-Sawi, , op. cit., p. 18-19
718 Book 36, Number 35. As translated in, 'Translation of Malik's *Muwatta*', op. cit.
719 al-Tirmidhi, Book 44, Hadith 3194
720 al-Sawi, op. cit., p. 21-22
721 As translated in ibid.
722 A similar view has been expressed in ibid.
723 For further information, see ibid.
724 Al-Kasani, op. cit., Vol. 7, p. 132
725 J.A. Bolles, *A Treatise on Usury and Usury Laws* (J. Munroe 1837), p. 40
726 Y.D. 160:10
727 Respectively, *Rema* 160:14; *Shach* 160:37
728 *Shitah Mekubetzes* to *Kesuvos* 108a
729 Y.D. 160: 23
730 See, Reisman, op. cit., p. 72-74
731 *Rema* 160:09
732 Y.D. 160:11
733 *S.A. Harav* 9
734 Reisman, op. cit., p. 69
735 Samples of such forms can be found in Reisman, , op. cit., p. 419-424
736 Skolnik and Berenbaum, op. cit., Vol. 16, p. 30
737 BM 5:7
738 BM 5:2
739 BM 5:6; BM 5:14
740 Hillel Gamoran, 'Talmudic Usury Laws and Business Loans' 7 Journal for the Study of Judaism in the Persian, Hellenistic, and Roman Period 129
741 M.BM: 6:3-5
742 M.Bm: 8:8 and 8:2 and the Baraita in B.M. 69b.
743 T.BM 4:2
744 Neusner, *The Mishnah: A New Translation*, BM 5:2 BM 5:6; BM 5:14
745 See footnote 894 above.
746 See, Gamoran, *Jewish Law in Transition: How Economic Forces Overcame the Prohibition Against Lending on Interest.*
747 B. BM 72b
748 See footnote 894 above.
749 Y.D. 162:2
750 Hillel Gamoran, 'Talmudic controls on the purchase of futures', 64 The Jewish Quarterly Review 48

751 T. BM 6:11-12
752 *Sefer ha-yashar le-rabeinu tam, Helek ha-hidushim,* Simon Schlesinger, ed., #592. As quoted in Gamoran, *Jewish Law in Transition: How Economic Forces Overcame the Prohibition Against Lending on Interest,* 71
753 Hillel Gamoran, 'Mortgages in Geonic times in light of the law against usury' Hebrew Union College Annual 97, 99
754 For further information, see Hillel Gamoran, 'How the Rabbis Interpreted Halakhah to Meet the Needs of the People: A Study of Mortgages During the Period of the Rishonim' [Hebrew Union College – Jewish Institute of Religion] 73 Hebrew Union College Annual 227
755 T.B.M. 5:15; *Baraita* in Y.B.M. 5:7, 10c. Gamoran, 'Talmudic Usury Laws and Business Loans', op. cit., p. 140
756 BM 75a
757 Gamoran, 'Talmudic Usury Laws and Business Loans', op. cit.
758 Y.D. 160:16
759 BM 69
760 *Mordekhai,* BM 338
761 *Bris Yehudah* 31:n2. For examples, see: Jacob J. Rabinowitz, 'Some Remarks on the Evasion of the Usury Laws in the Middle Ages' [Cambridge University Press] 37 The Harvard Theological Review 49
762 Hillel Gamoran, 'Investing for Profit: A Study of Iska up to the Time of Rabbi Abraham ben David of Posquieres' [Hebrew Union College – Jewish Institute of Religion] 70/71 Hebrew Union College Annual 153
763 Reisman, op. cit., p. 378-391
764 Gamoran, 'Investing for Profit: A Study of Iska up to the Time of Rabbi Abraham ben David of Posquieres', p. 154
765 For a full list of references, see ibid.
766 M.BM 5:4
767 T. BM 4:11; B. BM 68a and 68b
768 B. BM 68b, 69a
769 See footnote 894 above.
770 Ibid.
771 *Shilukhim Veshutafin.* See, Gamoran, 'Investing for Profit: A Study of Iska up to the Time of Rabbi Abraham ben David of Posquieres', op. cit., p. 157
772 As quoted in ibid., p. 158
773 Ibid., p. 162-3
774 M.M. Postan, *The Cambridge Economic History of Europe from the Decline of the Roman Empire: Volume 1, Agrarian Life of the Middle Ages* (Cambridge University Press 1966), p. 44-46

775 *Teshuvot u-fesakim*, #140; *Temim de'im*, #60, as translated in Gamoran, 'Investing for Profit: A Study of Iska up to the Time of Rabbi Abraham ben David of Posquieres', op. cit., p. 162
776 Ibid.
777 R. Isreal Isselein, *Terumat ha-deshen*, #302, as translated in Gamoran, *Jewish Law in Transition: How Economic Forces Overcame the Prohibition Against Lending on Interest*, op. cit., p. 152-153
778 Ibid.
779 Ibid.
780 Ibid.
781 Ibid.
782 Ibid., p. 159-160
783 R. Solomon Canzfried, *Kisur shulhan arukh*, #66:3
784 As provided in *Sefer Bris Yehudah*
785 As described by R. Isserlien himself, see above section: Heter of Iska of Isserlien
786 Canon no. 25. Translated by Divine, op. cit., p. 61
787 Courson, *Summa* (lefevre, ed.), p. 41. Translated in John W. Baldwin, *Masters, Princes and Merchants: the Social Views of Peter the Chanter & His Circle* (Princeton University Press 1970), p. 298
788 Petrus Cantor, *Verbum Abbreviatum*, PL 205:157D, 158A. Translated in ibid.
789 Potthast, no. 3382. Translated in McLaughlin, op. cit.
790 For further information, see above section: Introduction to Medieval Period.
791 He depicted them as "*their coffers and leeches because all things they shall sucked up, they vomit into the fisc.*" Baldwin, p. 298
792 Ambrose, *De bono morti* translated by studio and Ammannati, op. cit., p. 158
793 As quoted in P. Oslington, *The Oxford Handbook of Christianity and Economics* (OUP USA 2014), p. 47
794 Ibid.
795 Ibid., p. 48
796 McLaughlin, op. cit., p. 98 -103; Noonan, *The Scholastic Analysis of Usury*, op. cit., p. 22-33, 39-40, 51-81; O.I. Langholm, *Economics in the Medieval Schools: Wealth, Exchange, Value, Money, and Usury According to the Paris Theological Tradition, 1200-1350* (Brill 1992), p. 37
797 Ibid.
798 Goff, p. 34. For the role of preachers in conduction the anti-usury campaign, see also Baldwin, p. 296-311; Langholm, p. 52, 88-97; John F McGovern, 'Rise of New Economic Attitudes in Canon and Civil Law, AD 1200-1550, The' 32 Jurist 39

799 Welter, ed., *Tabula exemplorum*, p. 8. As translated in J.L. Goff, *Your money or your life: economy and religion in the Middle Ages* (Zone Books 1990), p. 37-38

800 Similarly, St. Bernard of Clairvaux (d. 1153) declared Christian usurers worse than Jews calling them "baptized Jews."

801 Thomas of Chobham, *Summa confessorum*, p. 504. As translated in Goff, *Your Money or Your Life: Economy and Religion in the Middle Ages*, op. cit., p. 37-38

802 As translated in Goff, *The Usurer and Purgatory*, op. cit. p., 39

803 Peter the Chanter, *Summa*, par. 14, II, 35. As found in ibid., p. 3

804 Thomas of Chobham, *Summa confessorum*, p. 504. As translated in Goff, *Your Money or Your Life: Economy and Religion in the Middle Ages*, op. cit., p. 42

805 Baldwin, op. cit., p. 302

806 Welter, ed., *Tabula Wxemplorum*, p. 8. As translated in Goff, *Your Money or Your Life: Economy and Religion in the Middle Ages*, op. cit., p. 37-38

807 For further information, see J.L. Goff and L.G. Cochrane, *Medieval Callings* (University of Chicago Press 1995)

808 *Tabula Exemplorum*. As found in Goff, The Usurer and Purgatory, op. cit., p. 39

809 Ibid.

810 Ibid.

811 As said by Bernard of Siena. Quoted in Noonan, *The Scholastic Analysis of Usury*, op. cit. p., 77

812 Caesarius of Heisterbach, Dialogus miraculorum, ed. Joseph Strange (2 vols. Cologne 1851) 2.300 As translated in Goff, *The Usurer and Purgatory*, op. cit., p. 46-48

813 Canto XVII of Inferno, in Dante Alighieri, *The Divine Comedy*, translated Carlyle, Okey, Wicksteed, ed.C. H. Grandagent (New York, 1950), p. 93

814 For the canonist enforcement of usury, see McLaughlin, op. cit.

815 Can. 13, the Second Lateran Council, 1139 (pontificate of Innocent II)

816 Lateran, 1139, can. 13; Can. 25, the Third Lateran Council, 1179 (pontificate of Alexander III)

817 Lateran, 1139, can. 13; Lateran, 1179, can. 25; Can. 2, the Council of Lyons, 1274 (pontificate of Gregory X)

818 Interestingly enough, Robert of Courson, while he was a papal legate, is reported to have order the corpse of a recently entombed usurer to be removed from a churchyard. see, Baldwin, op. cit.

819 Lateran, 1179, can. 25; and other councils.

820 Can. 1, 5, the Council of Paris, 1212; Lyons, 1274, can. 2

821 Decretals of Gregory IX, 1230, v.19, can. 9

822 Paris, 1212, part V, can. 6; can. 25, the Council of Mainz, 1311
823 Lyons, 1274, can. 1,2; and many other local councils
824 Mainz, 1310, Id. 25
825 Paris, 1212, part V, can. 3, and other councils
826 Can. 29, the Council of Vienne, 1311; Clem. V, 5
827 As integrated into the *Corpus juris canonical: Clementine* V, 5 *(De usuris)* and *Sextus* V, 5 *(De usuris)*.
828 They will be punished as heretics according to Can. 29, the Council of Vienne, 1311
829 As integrated into the *Corpus juris canonical: Clementine* V, 5 *(De usuris)* and *Sextus* V, 5 *(De usuris)*
830 Richard H Helmholz, 'Usury and the medieval English church courts' 61 Speculum 364, 378; Jelle C Riemersma, 'Usury restrictions in a mercantile economy' 18 Canadian Journal of Economics and Political Science/Revue canadienne de economiques et science politique 17
831 See above section: The Church of England
832 The term was first used at the third Lateran Council in 1179
833 See above section: St. Ambrose's Justification of Usury as a Weapon
834 Odd Langholm, *Economics in the medieval schools: wealth, exchange, value, money, and usury according to the Paris theological tradition, 1200-1350* (EJ Brill Leiden/New York/Köln 1992)
835 For a full list of references, see McLaughlin, op. cit., p. 113-115
836 Baldwin, op. cit., p. 275
837 Noonan, *The Scholastic Analysis of Usury*, op. cit., p. 95-96
838 Baldwin, op. cit., p. 277
839 Noonan, *The Scholastic Analysis of Usury*, op. cit., p. 97
840 Ibid.
841 McLaughlin, op. cit., p. 97
842 Mills, *Interest in Interest: The Old Testament Ban on Interest and its implications for today*, op. cit.
843 McLaughlin, op. cit., p. 117-120
844 Baldwin, op. cit., 273-278
845 Noonan, *The Scholastic Analysis of Usury*, op. cit., p. 133-153
846 As quoted in Noonan, The Scholastic Analysis of Usury, op. cit., p. 135
847 As quoted in O'Brien, *An essay on mediæval economic teaching*, op. cit., p. 113
848 Ibid.
849 Noonan, *The Scholastic Analysis of Usury*, p. 133-153
850 For examples of sea loans contract, please see, Calvin B Hoover, 'The sea loan in Genoa in the twelfth century' The Quarterly Journal of Economics 495, p. 521-523
851 Noonan, *The Scholastic Analysis of Usury*, op. cit., p. 136-141
852 Ibid.

853 The triple contract was studied in great details above in section:
854 A series of examples taken from the account books of the bank was provided in De Roover, *The rise and decline of the Medici Bank: 1397-1494*, op. cit.
855 Noonan, *The Scholastic Analysis of Usury*, op. cit., p. 172
856 C. Kleinhenz, *Medieval Italy: An Encyclopedia* (Taylor & Francis 2004), p. 90
857 Jesús Huerta De Soto, *Money, bank credit, and economic cycles* (Ludwig von Mises Institute 2009), p. 64-67
858 Ibid.
859 Ibid.
860 Raymond Adrien De Roover, *Money, banking and credit in mediaeval Bruges;Italian merchant bankers, lombards and money-changers* (Raymond De Roover and America Mediaeval Academy of eds, The Mediaeval Academy of America 1948), p. 56-57
861 Ibid.
862 De Roover, 'The scholastics, usury, and foreign exchange', p. 267
863 Examples of which were given in De Roover, *Money, banking and credit in mediaeval Bruges; Italian merchant bankers, lombards and money-changers*, op. cit.
864 Ibid., p. 9; See also, Baldwin, op. cit., p. 291-295
865 As described by Raymond De Roover, 'The scholastics, usury, and foreign exchange' 41 Business History Review 257, op. cit.
866 McLaughlin, op. cit., p. 143
867 Barnard of Pavia, V:15:8; Baldwin, op. cit., p. 281
868 Noonan, *The Scholastic Analysis of Usury*, op. cit., p. 104-105
869 Ephraim Russell, 'The societies of the Bardi and the Peruzzi and their dealings with Edward III' Finance and Trade Under Edward III 93, 114-117
870 John Gilchrist, *The Church and economic activity in the Middle Ages* (Macmillan 1969)
871 As found in Wood, op. cit., p. 199
872 Divine, 58; O'Brien, *An essay on mediæval economic teaching*, op. cit., p. 106; Noonan, *The Scholastic Analysis of Usury*, op. cit., Ch. XV
873 O'Brien, *An essay on mediæval economic teaching*, op. cit., p. 106
874 O'Brien, *An essay on mediæval economic teaching*; Watt, *Usury in Catholic Theology*, op. cit., p. 6
875 Homer and Sylla, op. cit., p. 79
876 Noonan, *The Scholastic Analysis of Usury*, op. cit., Ch. Xd
877 Ibid., from *Sermon on usury*, 1519
878 As considered above in the section: The Reformers' Approach
879 *Sunan* Abu Daud, Hadith No. 3455

880 S.W. Baron and M. Maimonides, *Essays on Maimonides. An Octocentennial Volume. Edited by Salo Wittmayer Baron* (New York 1941), p. 214-215
881 J.M. Josse, *Dinosaur Derivatives And Other Trades* (Wiley 2014), p. 50
882 For a full list of references for each school, see: Kuwait, op. cit., Vol. 9, p. 96-97
883 Aisha bint Abu Bakr (613/614 – 678 CE) is one of prophet Muhammad's wives ﷺ.
884 Abu Bakr 'Abd al-Razzaq ibn Hammam al-San'ani, *al-Musannaf* (Johannesburg: al-Majlis al-'Ilmi, 1983), Vol. 8, 184-85 (hadith no. 14812, 14813). As translated in Muhammed Imran Ismail, 'Legal stratagems (*hiyal*) and usury in Islamic commercial law' (University of Birmingham 2010), p. 199-200
885 As noted by Ismail in ibid.
886 Muhammad ibn Abi Bakr Ibn Qayyim al-Jawziyyah, *The Hashiyah of Ibn Qayyim on Sunan of Abu Dawud* (2 edn, Dar al-Kutub al-'Ilmiya 1415 AH), Vol. 9, p. 241-242. Translated by the author of this thesis.
887 Ibid.
888 Ahmad bin Muhammad al-Sawi, *Hashiyat al-Sawi* (Dar al-Ma'arif), Vol. 3, p. 116. Translated by the author of this thesis.
889 Similar explanation was provided by the Hanbalis jurist Ibn Qayyim in: Ibn Qayyim al-Jawziyyah, *The Hashiyah of Ibn Qayyim on Sunan of Abu Dawud*, Vol. 9, p. 243-245.
890 Muhammad ibn Idris al-Shafi'i', *Kitab al-Umm* (Dar al-Maarifah 1990), Vol. 3, p. 90. As translated in, Muhammed Imran Ismail, 'Legal stratagems (*hiyal*) and usury in Islamic commercial law' (University of Birmingham 2010), p. 202
891 Ibid., Vol. 4, p. 114
892 Tita Nursyamsiah and Saim Kayadibi, 'Application of *Bay' al-'inah* in Islamic Banking and Finance: From the Viewpoint of *Siyasah Shar'iyyah*', op. cit., p. 123
893 al-Shafi'i', op. cit., Vol. 3, p. 7
894 For examples, see S.A. Rosly, *Critical Issues on Islamic Banking and Financial Markets: Islamic Economics, Banking and Finance, Investments, Takaful and Financial Planning* (Dinamas Publishing 2005), p. 87, 107; Saiful Azhar Rosly and Mahmood Sanusi, 'Some Issues of *Bay' al-'Inah* in Malaysian Islamic Financial Markets' 16 Arab law quarterly 263, 266-7; Amir Shaharuddin, 'The Bay' al-'Inah Controversy in Malaysian Islamic Banking 1' 26 Arab law quarterly 499, 506
895 For further information, see Nourah Aleshaikh, 'Jurisprudence on *Tawarruq*: Contextual Evaluation on Basis of Customs, Circumstances, Time and Place' (Durham University 2011)

896 Ibn al Hummam, *Fath al-Qadeer* (Beirut, Dar Ihya al-Turath al-'Arabi 1986), Vol. 7, p. 212
897 For a full list of references, see Kuwait, op. cit., Vol. 14, p. 147. See also, Aleshaikh, op. cit., p. 38-43
898 'Abd al-Rahman ibn al-Qasim al-'Utaqi (750 – 806), better known as Ibn al-Qasim, was one of Malik's main companions and had a tremendous influence in recording the positions of the school.
899 *Al-Mudawwanah*, 4:125. As translated in Sami al-Suwailem, *Tawarruq Banking Products* (2009), p. 30
900 Similar to this is Malik's statement in *al-Nawadir wa al-Ziyadat*: "And he should not sell it on behalf of the buyer who asks for that." As translated in ibid.
901 A. Ibn Abi Shayba, *Musannaf Ibn Abi Shayba* (Dar Al-Salafiah Bombay: undated), Vol. 5, p. 24. As translated in Habib Ahmed and Nourah Mohammad Aleshaikh, 'Debate on Tawarruq: Historical Discourse and Current Rulings' 28 Arab law quarterly 278, 786
902 As translated in ibid., p. 31
903 As is the case in the dual form of *bay' al-'inah* discussed above.
904 Ibn 'Abidin, Vol. 4, p. 114. As translated in Sami al-Suwailem, *Tawarruq Banking Products* (2009), op. cit., p. 32
905 Ibrahim Fadhil Dabu, 'Tawarruq, Its Reality and Types' OIC Fiqh Academy 19th Session Online version available at http://www.iefpedia.com/english, p. 5
906 Ibid.
907 Muhammad ibn 'Abd Allah al-Kharshi, *Sharh Mukhtasar Khalil* (Dar al-Fikr), Vol. 5, p. 105
908 Ahmad ibn Muhammad al-Sawi, *Bulghat al-Salik li-Aqrab al-Masalik ila Madhhab al-Imam Malik* (Dar al-Marif), Vol. 3, p. 129
909 Muhammad ibn Ahmad ibn 'Arafah al-Dasuqi, *Hashiyat al-Dasuqi* (Dar al-Fikr), Vol. 3, p. 88; al-Kharshi, op. cit., Vol. 5, p. 106
910 Ibn Rushd, op. cit., Vol. 22, p. 55
911 Ibid., Vol. 22, p. 56
912 Ibid.
913 Abu al-Qasim Muhammad Ibn Ahmad Ibn Juzay, *al-Qawanin al-Fiqhiyyah* (Dar al-Fikr 2007), Vol. 1, p. 171
914 *Al-Muwatta of Imam Malik*, Book 33.33.73, translated by Aisha Bewley, Diwan Press.
915 al-Shafi'i', op. cit., Vol. 3, p. 39
916 Narrated by at-Tirmidhi, 1232; al-Nasa'i, 4613; Abu Dawud, 3503, Ibn Majah, 2187, Ahmad, 14887.
917 See respectively, Muhammad ibn al-Hasan al-Shaybani, *al-Makharij fi al-Hiyal* (1930), op. cit., and Ibn Qayyim al-Jawziyyah, *I'lam al-muwaqqi'in 'an Rabb al-'Alamin*, op. cit.

Notes

918 As translated in M.A. El-Gamal, *Islamic Finance: Law, Economics, and Practice* (Cambridge University Press 2006), p. 33
919 Ibid.
920 For a full list of references, see Marjan Muhammad, Hakimah Yaacob and Shabana Hasan, 'The Bindingness and Enforceability of a Unilateral Promise (*Waʻd*): an Analysis from Islamic Law and Legal Perspectives' Kuala Lumpur: International Shari'ah Research Academy for Islamic Finance (ISRA), Research paper. Also, see, Kuwait, op. cit., Vol. 44, p. 72-78
921 Kuwait, op. cit., p. 72
922 Rafic Yunus al-Masri, 'The Binding Unilateral Promise (*waʻd*) in Islamic Banking Operations: Is it Permissible for a Unilateral Promise (*waʻd*) to be Binding as an Alternative to a Proscribed Contract?' 15 Journal of King Abdulaziz University: Islamic Economics 29, 30
923 AAOIFI: *Shariʻa* Standard No. 8, Accounting and Auditing Organization for Islamic Financial Institutions, *Shari's Standards: The Full Text of Shariʻa Standards as at Shawwal 1428 AH-November 2007* (Accounting and Auditing Organization for Islamic Financial Institutions 2008)
924 Saeed, op. cit., p. 78
925 http://www.thefreedictionary.com/scorned